The Shapes of Fancy

The Shapes of Fancy

Reading for Queer Desire
in Early Modern Literature

Christine Varnado

University of Minnesota Press
Minneapolis
London

This book is freely available in an open access edition thanks to TOME (Toward an Open Monograph Ecosystem)—a collaboration of the Association of American Universities, the Association of University Presses, and the Association of Research Libraries—and the generous support of the University at Buffalo Libraries. Learn more at the TOME website, available at: openmonographs.org.

A portion of chapter 1 was previously published as "Getting Used, and Liking It: Erotic Instrumentality in Philaster," *Renaissance Drama* 44, no. 1 (2016): 25–52; copyright 2016 by Northwestern University.

Published by the University of Minnesota Press
111 Third Avenue South, Suite 290
Minneapolis, MN 55401-2520
http://www.upress.umn.edu

Printed on acid-free paper

The University of Minnesota is an equal-opportunity educator and employer.

Library of Congress Cataloging-in-Publication Data
Names: Varnado, Christine, author.
Title: The shapes of fancy : reading for queer desire in early modern literature /
    Christine Varnado.
Description: Minneapolis : University of Minnesota Press, 2020. | Includes bibliographical
    references and index. |
Identifiers: LCCN 2019023522 (print) | ISBN 978-1-5179-0776-1 (hc) |
    ISBN 978-1-5179-0777-8 (pb)
Subjects: LCSH: Desire in literature. | Affect (Psychology) in literature. | Queer theory.
Classification: LCC PN56.D48 V36 2020 (print) | DDC 809/.93353—dc23
LC record available at https://lccn.loc.gov/2019023522

UMP KEP

For Ardis Marie

Contents

Introduction

Reading for Desire

In Ben Jonson's rambunctious 1614 city comedy, *Bartholomew Fair,* the gargantuan, infantile protagonist, a young aristocrat named Bartholomew Cokes, careens through the fair that shares his name on the day he is supposed to marry (spoiler alert: he never makes it to the altar), buying and eating everything in sight: gingerbread children, hobbyhorses, dolls, drums, gloves, and all manner of carnival commodities. He rhapsodizes on how he longs to listen to the siren song of the cutpurses who work the Fair, to feel their nimble fingers picking his pocket. At the climax of the play, he falls head over heels in love with the puppets in a puppet show, and invites the whole Fair back to his house for non-wedding revelry. How to fit this whirlwind of desire and consumption into the world of early modern sexuality? How to categorize the desire of a character who is a bottomless, promiscuous vortex of want—who wants everything except what he is supposed to want (marriage to a woman), and whose want is not the least bit satiated, no matter how much he consumes?

Bartholomew Fair's other plot involves a Puritan named Zeal-of-the-Land Busy, who debates at length whether it's okay to go to the Fair as long as you don't look around at the stalls, whether it's okay to look around as long as you don't like what you see, and whether it's okay to eat the Fair's signature dish of delectable roast pig as long as you don't look around for it, but only passively sniff it out, letting the pig find you. Zeal-of-the-Land Busy ends the play by getting into a fight with the troupe of puppets, which he loses. He gets flashed by a puppet-ghost proving it does not have any genitals, and he ends up in the stocks for his hostility toward the pleasures of the Fair. How should an analysis of the erotic economy of *Bartholomew Fair* account for these two characters, these two opposite poles of bottomless desire, one gluttonous and driven by an unquenchable appetite to consume and incorporate objects, and the other annihilating and consumed by an insatiable need to disavow and destroy them?

In another comedy from around the same time (c. 1610), this one a tragicomedy called *Philaster, or Love Lies a-Bleeding,* by masters of tragicomedy Samuel Beaumont and John Fletcher (who, not incidentally, lived together in a flat with "one bed," "one coat," and "one wench between them"),[1] a captive prince and a princess conduct their forbidden love affair by commissioning a beautiful servant boy to "bear their hidden love" back and forth—a boy who becomes an inseparable part of their relationship.[2] How to describe this boy's erotic function? Neither dominant nor submissive, he is instrumental to the ostensibly straight romance. In fact, he becomes the central affective stylist of their love, until his intimacy with the princess raises suspicions of impropriety. After a tearful reckoning in which they all threaten to stab themselves and beg to be stabbed by one another to prove their honesty, the beautiful boy confesses that he is actually a girl who disguised herself as a boy in order to be used in just this situation. In the play's resolution, all three of them continue to live together in a blissful domestic triad.

One way of asking the question this book seeks to answer is, what do we call these formations of desire, and others like them, in early modern drama and prose literature? They're something, to be sure—something outlandish, excessive, overwrought, peculiar, surprising, and in-between. But are they queer? In what sense could or should that word apply? What does it say about these and other shapes of fancy to call them queer, and what does it open up about the idea of queerness to use it or to appeal to it here? The word "queer" bespeaks an unexpected twist, turn, or crossing. As Eve Kosofsky Sedgwick explains in 1993, early in the life of queer theory, "The word 'queer' itself means *across*—it comes from the Indo-European root *-twerkw,* which also yields the German *quer* (transverse), Latin *torquere* (to twist), English *athwart.*"[3] "Queer" in this sense becomes an adverb rather than an adjective; a term that describes dramatic motion, rather than a category label.[4] From this (actually quite old) reframing of queerness, this book formulates a new way of reading for desire in literature. An adverbial queer analytic, as I develop and use it here, can illuminate the moments in texts where desire makes strange motions, takes strange shapes, or goes awry—and not even in the expected ways. It can account for turns of feeling that—although insistently, ineffably askew—may not result in anything as historically legible as same-sex sex acts or same-gender-desiring social identities. It can ultimately reveal that, at times, what is queer about the shape of desire or erotic energy in an early modern text is not a person, an act, or an identity, but rather the larger system or structure through which affects and relations circulate.

Stranger Shapes

The literature of Shakespeare and his contemporaries is dripping with eros; it is often called timeless, yet much scholarly energy has been spent describing its particular historical time. This book builds on a wealth of previous scholarship devoted to mapping the landscape of sex in early modern England through its literary canon. Much of that work is trained on important historical questions about who was doing what, when, and with whom, and how they thought about it.[5] Some of the desires archived in early modern literature are relatively more accepted relations—such as homosocial friendship, or eroticized relations of power and service—that made up the complex, contested regime of the early modern "normal," which was by no means what we would call exclusively "straight."[6] Other desires to be found there are more recognizably part of the history and prehistory of homosexuality: same-sex erotic acts (such as sodomy, a crime punishable by death) and deviant social types (like mannish women, effeminate tailors, and early dandies), which were specifically disciplined as sexually suspect.[7]

And then there are still other desires—desires that are neither of these two things. The modes of feeling and expression that are my subject here do not map easily onto this distinction between condoned and condemned. Nor do they fit into a definition of queerness that refers exclusively to same-sex contact; they do not really depend on the participants' matching genitals or matching genders. Instead, they are made queer by a twist to their shape—by their strange proliferations, their unaccountable excesses of intensity, their atypical and errant crossings. They wander into attachments to the wrong objects, too many objects, or none at all. These erotic dynamics have mostly escaped notice, both of early modern society's regimes for disciplining sexuality, and of modern scholars' methods for recognizing and naming queerness. They may attract quizzical interest, suspicion, or ridicule, or they may be part of the violent apparatus of power itself. But what interests me about them, and what induces me to rethink the notion of queerness around them, are their structural qualities of secrecy, impossibility, or excess—not how or whether they were disciplined, or whether they registered as nonnormative, or even sexual, in the period. In other words, certain "shapes of fancy" in literature are recognizable as queer because of *how,* and not *by whom,* they are expressed. My archive is a collection of dramatic figurations and structures, all of which fall athwart (to use Sedgwick's term), in different ways, of extant categorizations for desire.

The four affective modes unpacked in the following chapters are:

1. The desire to be made instrumental to others' erotic ends as an end in itself—that is, the pleasure of being used.
2. The bottomless, free-floating, promiscuous appetite that refuses to differentiate among objects at all, desiring everything in sight and never being satiated.
3. The paranoid suspicion that makes true what it suspects, knitting together the accused witch and the witchfinder in a violent collaborative dynamic of projection and desire.
4. The melancholic ideations that failed Protestant would-be colonizers express about the Native American people, places, and objects they encountered, then lost.

Each chapter of this book traces one of these modes of desiring through a different iconic early modern scene: being used in scenes of cross-dressed romance; bottomless desire in scenes of commodity consumption; projective paranoia in witch trial interrogations; and melancholic loss in Atlantic colonial encounters. These plots and settings (gender disguises, city markets and court patronage economies, witch trials, Atlantic voyages) have become canonized, in large part through the Renaissance scholarship of the twentieth century, as some of the definitive images and moments of the period. Critics working from materialist, religious, and historical paradigms have used them as sites for explaining contemporary ideologies of embodiment, gender, capitalism, demonism, nationhood, and racial difference. Each of these scenes is thus marked by a history of canonical critical readings that have both made them iconic and populated them with received meanings—which has kept us from attending to their more subtle, structural currents of desire. In the readings that follow, I expose the currents of eros running underneath these well-trod pathways through Renaissance literature by examining the structures, trajectories, and styles by which desire is produced and transmitted.

These "shapes of fancy" include some impulses that signal what Carla Freccero calls a "certain unsettling in relation to heteronormativity," a disturbance or departure from some normative trajectory of desire.[8] But they also include urges and attachments that circumvent or refuse received notions of erotic investment altogether. In redefining queerness as an affective mode, I am departing from the governing questions asked under the historicist paradigm—"How did people think about this in the period?" and "What acts and/or persons were specifically suspected and condemned as queer?"[9]—to ask instead, "What queer desires potentially go unnoticed by that approach?" By accounting for these more diffuse modalities of feeling, I want to reach toward the goal proposed by Eve Sedgwick of articulating "some ways of understanding human desire that might be quite to the side of prohibition and repression."[10] And, thinking along the same lines as Adam Philips, I am interested in the "unforbidden pleasures" that have always filled out the tapestry of human life, but that we have not had the language to articulate under interpretive systems focused on prohibition—a bias shared by Western religious and legal codes and by certain received readings of Foucault and of psychoanalysis.[11] I trace these four affective modes through early modern drama and prose in order to ask other questions—questions about what it means to read literature, such as:

1. What counts as desire, and how is desire constituted in text and performance? What are the features of a text that can have, speak, or be animated by desire?

Psychoanalytically informed literary criticism has long moved past imputing a coherent subjectivity to authors or analyzing characters as though they were imaginary people. Desire can reside in every formal nook and cranny of a play or narrative—in a stage sequence, a scene change, a turn of phrase, an interjection, an offhand descriptive term, a stage direction, an aside, an image, a silence.[12] Here I argue that something very much like Peter Brooks's notion of "narrative desire" operates in drama and nonfictional prose as well as in fiction: desire as a motor driving the action, shaping the contours of what the work shows and when, which the reader or spectator then apprehends and uses to make meaning from the text or performance.[13]

2. On what grounds can readers and spectators recognize erotic feeling or erotic energy in a text?

The immaterial, ineffable, often perverse phenomena this book attends to are inherently problematic to historicize. They often have a vexed, unclear relationship to ideology. They raise the question of how we as readers can recognize something we are able to call erotic, and what we define the erotic against. When we recognize desire in texts from distant times, places, and cultures, what acts of readerly identification are involved in that recognition, and to what consequence?[14] What readers experience as the trace of desire in a literary text is often called "affect": embodied states of feeling, figured in language. The "turn to affect," starting from Gilles Deleuze and Félix Guattari's reading of Spinoza's *Ethics* in *A Thousand Plateaus* and continued in the work of thinkers like Brian Massumi and Teresa Brennan, has marshaled the idea of affect for literary criticism as a concept that permits feeling and its expression—involuntary as well as willed, collective as well as individual—to be an object of analysis, without the assumptions of interiority or the self-contained Cartesian body that attend the concept of emotion.[15] Sparked by Sedgwick's engagement with the affect theory of Silvan Tomkins, queer theorists in particular—among them Heather Love, Lauren Berlant, and Ann Cvetkovich—have articulated a language of affect that knits together mood, relationality, embodiment, and nonverbal and linguistic expression.[16] In other words, affects are legible. Their textual residues, their aesthetic and libidinal effects, constitute a body of significations—content that can be read. My approach to desire is founded in affect theory's claims that states of feeling are communicable and transmissible, both in life and through art; that they can be archived; and that they can have surprising historical persistence.

There is a wealth of scholarship on the history of feeling in the early modern period, and on representations and theories of emotion, humoral theory, and the passions, chiefly exemplified by the work of Gail Kern Paster.[17] The object of that work's analysis—the figurative manifestations of bodily affect in literature as well as the tacit, fantasmatic systems, economies, and theories that can be extrapolated from such traces—is closely related to mine. In fact, early modern discourses of affect seem to cry out for a queer analysis. The literature is replete with languages of dangerous excess, threatening copiousness, embarrassment, intemperance, degeneration, permeability, and involuntary compulsion. By rethinking queerness as a collection of affective stances in this book, I perform a queer reading of the language of early modern affect. I take a rich, complicated vocabulary for constructing embodied feeling in the past, and connect it to a history of desire that is now called sexuality, a history that includes the present.[18]

3. What is the precise relation between desire and queerness? What, if anything, does queerness necessarily have to do with sex, or with identity?

Out of Alan Bray's foundational work on homosexuality in Renaissance England and the wealth of scholarship that followed it, mostly on the social and political meanings of sodomy between men, the premise that sexuality was conceptualized in the period as a matter of "acts, *not* identities" came to define the field, both for those who agreed and those who questioned it.[19] In this book, I depart from the terms of this long-standing debate. Indeed, as Valerie Traub crucially reminds us, Bray did not remain within the acts-or-identities paradigm either, turning to the dynamics of affect and love animating same-gender social bonds in his later book, *The Friend.*[20] I contend that queerness can instead be a quality of affect staged in a text. However, it would be a lie to say that I am uninterested in acts.[21] These texts are made of acts. In their dramatic liveliness, they stage vivid representations of characters acting in and on their worlds: speaking, emoting, consuming, destroying, making, losing, and indeed romancing and having various forms of sex. My readings are intimately concerned with parsing the various figured acts that plays and pamphlets stage, half-stage, indirectly describe, allude to, wink at, or refuse to stage. Crucially, I treat genital, nongenital, and perhaps-genital acts together as equally salient transmissions of desire. What is decentered in my analysis are the historical questions of what evidence these acts might furnish about contemporary sexual practices, and whether and which of these acts are linked to operative social categories. This book explores how jettisoning those agendas, and approaching figurations of eros instead from a posture of unknowingness and openness to affect, can open up new nuances of meaning for the present as well as the past—revealing both to be replete with what Sedgwick calls "unexpectedly plural, varied, and contradictory" understandings of desire, with effects that resonate beyond the confines of any discrete historical moment.[22] What emerges from this shift is a reconception of what we regard as the literary trace of queerness, and a new theory of how desires—especially weirdly, unconventionally nonnormative ones—are held and communicated in texts.

While *The Shapes of Fancy* expands the utility of the word "queer" beyond individual persons, acts, or historical models, the connection between queerness and desire is one that I emphatically do not jettison. To me, queerness is inalienably a phenomenon occurring *in the realm of desire.* But that realm is more capacious than we have thought, exceeding not only genital eroticism but also sometimes the boundaries of the human. The notion that desire can circulate at larger scales than that of the discrete human subject is both very old and very new. In fact, as the turn toward other-than-human models of agency and vitality in the recent theoretical conversation known as posthumanist thought has shown, the history of collective and transmaterialist ideas of affect and animacy (in the sense of that word provocatively offered by Mel Y. Chen, "a quality of agency, awareness, mobility, or liveness") is much longer and more global than the relative temporal and cultural blip—constructed and promulgated by early modern Europeans and now largely belied by recent knowledge produced in biology, ecology, and physics—that centered the individual human.[23] Though recent work in feminist and queer theory shares these ontological concerns regarding the nature of life and matter,[24] scholars have not yet fully pondered the implications of the posthumanist turn for rewriting the history of sexuality, or for rethinking the models of desire operative in early modern literature. I argue here that desire is not always oriented toward or confined to natural human bodies. Rather, it is often staged through prosthetic material objects—clothing and accessories, animals, body parts, instruments, ornaments—that carry erotic charges, altering the shape of desire in the scene.[25] Material things transmit affect, mediate relations, engender connections, and indicate or hold investment. At times they seem to possess agency or animation in their own right. Thus, in a systemic model of queerness, human and non-human materials participate in the same affective networks, congealing feeling and transmitting desire—both within the worlds created in texts, and through time, to us. Queerness, in this larger dramatic and structural sense, is that which crosses, that which sits *athwart,* that which thwarts and torques existing categorizations. Queerness uses the materials to hand in surprising and inventive ways to transmit desire (not always successfully); it flouts expected timelines and trajectories of proper development; it spins into backward motion, or stands stubbornly still; it upends expected orders of similitude and difference; it generates weirdness and excess, wallows in the degraded, and emphasizes its own artifice.

If queer is these specific, new, oblique things, it is decidedly not, then, "anything" or "everything."

For one thing, queerness has a history, and it is the history of activism, art, and knowledge production around same-sex eroticism. To use the term "queer" to describe these additional vagaries of desire beyond object choice is to place them, very deliberately, within the historical penumbra of dissident desiring, next to the stories and fates of subjects past and present who have suffered much more explicitly from the violence of heteronormativity. This is an essentially beholden, indebted intellectual move. It would be impossible to recognize the feelings, affective stances, and relationalities described in this book *as queer* without the epistemological frameworks of queer scholarship and activism that have taught me to query the political and aesthetic meanings of desire itself.[26] Moreover, each of the qualities I explore in the following chapters is rooted in that history. Every one of this book's guiding affects— being used; having more than one partner; bottomless appetite; roving, promiscuous receptivity; refusing marriage; being paranoid and/or being persecuted; secret projective sexual suspicion; longing for impossible metamorphosis and lost, unspeakable love objects—has been used to characterize same-sex desire and same-sex desiring people, or has been a fruitful, communally cultivated value of queer cultures and cultural productions, or both.

For another thing, my definitional extension of "queer" to the level of representational systems is not a limitless expansion. It is a frame shift that opens up new realms of specific content, which can then be described and elaborated. This imperative—to create new groupings and orders of description in which the elements reveal new attributes and relationships as a result of the new organizing framework—draws not only on Deleuze and Guattari's notion of deterritorialization and reterritorialization in rhizomatic thought,[27] but also on Sedgwick's insistence on the proliferating specificity of difference in the realm of desire in her introduction to *Epistemology of the Closet*. Sedgwick's Axiom 1, "People are different from each other," blossoms into a list of some of the axes of desire, besides gender of object choice, along which people can cleave apart and together, the most salient of which to me here may be, "To some people, the nimbus of 'the sexual' seems scarcely to extend beyond the boundaries of discrete genital acts; to others, it enfolds them loosely or floats virtually free of them."[28] Sedgwick's reading practice is decidedly not about exploding erotic binaries into the infinite free play of multiplicity. "To the contrary," she writes, "a deconstructive understanding of these binarisms makes it possible to identify them as sites that are *particularly* densely charged with lasting potentials for powerful manipulation—through precisely the mechanisms of self-contradictory definition, or more succinctly, the double bind."[29] Maggie Nelson describes Sedgwick's emphasis on specificity in *The Argonauts*. Sedgwick's thought, she writes, is relentlessly trained on "talking and writing about that which is more than one, and more than two, but less than infinity."[30] More than one, more than two, but less than infinity: this range contains many configurations that we don't have ready language to talk about, once we've noticed that the familiar binary logics of sexual sameness versus difference, historical repression versus license, or lover and love object don't begin to cover the complex and contradictory reality of desire. Nelson goes on to insist: "This finitude is important. It makes possible the great mantra, the great invitation, of Sedgwick's work, which is to "pluralize and specify. [. . .] This is an activity that demands an attentiveness—a relentlessness, even—whose very rigor tips it into ardor."[31]

This book illuminates some of the things that, in Sedgwick's words, "we know and need to know about ourselves and each other with which we have, as far as I can see, so far created for ourselves almost no theoretical room to deal."[32] "A tiny number of inconceivably coarse axes of categorization have been painstakingly inscribed," she argues, "in current critical and political thought: gender, race, class, nationality, sexual orientation are pretty much the available distinctions."[33] But we know, from the textual complexity of lived experience, that "even people who share all or most of our own positionings along these crude axes may still be different enough from us, and from each other, to seem like all but different species."[34] What we do with those "rich, unsystematic resources" of knowledge—especially oppressed people, especially through "the precious, devalued arts of gossip"—Sedgwick calls "*nonce* taxonomy," "the making and unmaking and remaking and redissolution of hundreds of old and new categorical imaginings concerning all the kinds it may take to make up a world."[35] Inspired by Sedgwick, I want to think outside of the indispensable, yet still coarse, identity markers that have been so definitive in politically engaged criticism—the markers of bodily sex and social gender; the markers of historical oppression—to document some of the "reservoir of unrationalized nonce-taxonomic energies" that I see swirling and circulating through early modern literature.[36] This new map of affective modes produces a new kind of desire, one that looks different from the desire explicated in more historicist studies. Desire in this book is diffuse and distributed throughout scenes, not confined to binary subject/object relations. Though it is predicated on an interplay between identification and otherness, it is not defined by sexual sameness or sexual difference in the realms of anatomy or gender. And though it is discursively constituted, it constantly escapes categorization. All of this yields a more expansive—and accurate—picture of the world, in that it serves to get some of the stances and impulses we have not yet had words to describe named and included on the vast, submerged continent of queerness, alongside the various more familiar forms of homoeroticism and homosociality.

4. How does the mind work? How stable or accessible
is the human psyche in history?

This is perhaps the most daunting of the *other* questions I explore in what follows. One of the most compelling vocabularies, to me, for making and pondering interpretive frameworks is that of psychoanalysis, because it takes eros to be an originary and inherent quality of language as well as a primary vector of access to texts. Each of the qualitatively queer structures of desire I unpack in the following chapters is subtended by a different psychoanalytic concept traced through a different textual archive: fetishistic instrumentalization, polymorphous perversity, paranoia, melancholia. These terms provide a vocabulary for linking the literary figurations of the past to structures of desire that are part of the discourse of sexuality today. One of my aims is to expand the utility of psychoanalytic terms for early modern literary studies beyond a concern with excavating the complex history of the subject, or interiority, or the unconscious.[37] I also deliberately want to refuse the anxiety of anachronism over using concepts that postdate early modern literature to read it—an anxiety seldom applied to historical materialist concepts with the same scrutiny as it is to psychic or erotic ones.[38]

My definition of desire is a psychoanalytic one: a craving or affinity that is infused with both the pleasure of investment (however ideational) and the pain of irremediable lack. Desire is a feeling—in all of the complex embodied and linguistic ways that that is signified in texts—that can be occulted as well as explicit. It can attach to collectivities or to formal features as easily as to human subjects or objects. Desire can be negative as well as positive; it can include heightened states of aversion, agitation, and rage. In including non-alloerotic (non-partner-directed) states and objectless desires within the scope of my readings, I am considering the field of the erotic as potentially extending far beyond genitality to include the whole range of possible libidinal investments. I am drawn to this appealingly weak definition of the sexual, which sees eros as a constitutive force infusing all of life, and refuses any final demarcation between erotic and nonerotic forms of desire.[39] As Elizabeth Freeman argues, the historical, performative, and erotic methodologies ("sex as technique, rather than topic") enabled by this psychoanalytic model can yield "such an expansive sense of what sex is that it obliterates any distinction between the sexual and the nonsexual." She goes on to ask, "Wasn't my being queer, in the first instance, about finding sex where it was not supposed to be, failing to find it where it was, finding that sex was not, after all, what I thought it was?"[40]

Historically (dating back to Freud), the tradition of psychoanalytic criticism about early modern literature has mostly centered on the Oedipal family romance, on drama (specifically tragedy), and on Shakespeare.[41] *The Shapes of Fancy* breaks out of that mold, offering a more diffuse and distributed psychoanalytic account of how desire is staged, one in which eros is a structuring condition of texts, not something that inheres in imagined interiorities or anxieties of sexual difference. To reduce psychoanalytic concerns to the normative telos of the Oedipal plot obscures a deep and pervasive affinity for perverse erotic impulses throughout Freud's theory. Jonathan Dollimore argues that polymorphous perversity is the originary human state for Freud, and that it continually subverts the violent, fragile process of forming a "normal," alloerotic, heterosexual, subjectivity: "Freud is unrelenting in finding perversion, especially homosexuality, in those places where it is conventionally thought to be most absent, and where identity is dependent upon that supposed absence."[42] Despite how Freud is sometimes used as an avatar of a "modern" heteronormative understanding of sexuality, a closer look reveals that there is no seamless, unitary modern model to appeal to; indeed, the same could be said of the narrative proffered in Foucault's *History of Sexuality, Part 1*. Even at the supposed Victorian ur-moment of modernity, eroticism is not confined to the genitals, to the individuated subject, or to any one way of interfacing between bodies and the world. It has never been totalizingly contained by the discursive apparatus of any time.

In pursuit of a more supple psychoanalytic theory, I gravitate toward the work of critics who deemphasize the Oedipal narrative, decenter sexual difference, and seek to complicate ("pluralize, and specify") the unified drive theory plots of orthodox Freudianism, namely those inspired by the theories of Melanie Klein and Donald W. Winnicott.[43] The contribution of the British object relations school that most informs my approach here is their emphasis on the flexibility of desire in moving between danger and safety, sociable and antisocial impulses, forbidden and unforbidden pleasures. Rather than collapsing desire into a streamlined narrative, Klein in particular acknowledges currents of multiplicity and internal conflict (as Sedgwick describes it, "the invitingly chunky affordances" of her concepts) that Freud smooths out in his endeavor to construct strong theories of development and drive.[44] Greater interpretive nuance is possible for a theory describing affective life, Sedgwick asserts, because it is "qualitative," and thus allows for ambivalent, shifting *readings* of the world. It allows for how we are "equipped from birth to apprehend a qualitative essence in different kinds of life experiences."[45] This, along with what Sedgwick calls the "almost literal-minded animism" of Klein's psychic object world, make it particularly well suited to a book focused on reading, and on reading early modern texts in particular.[46] The plays and pamphlets I read here, like "human mental life" in Klein's model, are populated not with abstractions or repressions "but with things, things with physical properties, including people and hacked-off bits of people."[47] It is these psychic, figural, bodily, and made things that make up the material substrate in which I ground my close readings of affective stances, stylistic tropes, and registers of expression.

This book is in one sense an experiment in adapting and using a set of theoretical tools honed on and in a series of later historical moments (sometimes lumped together as "modern"), stretching over multiple, overlayered, thick pasts and into the present, to draw out unarticulated erotic content in Renaissance archives. It carries the questions asked and the insights enabled by psychoanalytic theory (and the strain of queer literary theory that draws on it, exemplified in the work of Sedgwick and Heather Love), from its origins in the Victorian-to-modernist time frame, further back through time to early modern archives. This move layers in other temporal dimensions, in a field of sexuality studies that has mostly been concerned with the axis of oscillation between an historical "then" and a readerly "now," when in fact we also have much to learn from attending to the vast sea of representations in between those two moments. All of this is premised on my contention that what a specific historical and cultural moment knows about itself (even if we, from our distant vantage point, could tell) does not delimit all that can be said about the desires operating in its literature. I am informed here by Wai Chee Dimock's theory of resonance, which sees texts' meanings as "traveling frequencies" resonating through time, altered by their contacts in each idiosyncratic instance of reception, "causing unexpected vibrations in unexpected places."[48] Time in this model is not a neat contextual container but a "destabilizing force," "deadening some words and quickening others," allowing texts to acquire "a semantic life that is an effect of the present, rather than of the age when the text was produced."[49]

I am reading, and reading for, desires that are not fully described by any sexual or social terms in their own moment. The following chapters thread between the dual imperatives of theoretical expansion and textual rootedness, temporal unmooring and thick historicizing. At times I analyze conventional erotic or sexual tropes, but then my readings go on to blur distinctions between historically sexual and nonsexual, marked and unmarked impulses. By describing the ways in which affective structures can cross definitional regimes and types of evidence, this reading practice makes itself portable to other periods, other genres, other archives. The texts discussed here are a set of supersaturated case studies. Not by any means the only places these affective dynamics appear, they are illustrative in their very particularity. They are examples to think with. I intend for them to open up other vectors of reading for desire; to enable readers to notice these, and variants of these, modes of feeling in other texts (from this and other historical moments); and to invite readers to use these methods to develop and test new "*nonce* taxonomies."[50]

I navigate a subtle and historiographically delicate interplay here between considerations of production-side textual phenomena and reception-side interpretive phenomena. This is not a new history of sexuality, in which I discover new early modern ideologies about desire; nor am I simply "reading queerness into" early modern texts. Both of these are valuable projects to which other scholars are dedicated, but I am engaged in another, third endeavor. What this book uncovers, through an affectively attuned and temporally mobile queer reading practice, is a layer of erotic resonances that exist in a meso-level space in between the best-guess reconstructions of historical inquiry (what happened, and how people thought about it) and the motivated ideations of presentist interpretation (what we read into texts). While I do not make claims about how early modern subjects thought or behaved, the affective and erotic content I address in these texts is *really there.* It's really there in the figural sense, in the way that literary reading makes visible—a way of seeing, which, I contend, is as valid as materialist historical research. While language and aesthetic production (and erotic desire, which manifests in and through them) take wildly different forms in every time and place, they exist. They are legible. Desire, like language and culture, is at once radically various and contingent, and centrally constitutive of the human.[51] Psychoanalytic theory has given us the interpretive tools to flesh out the dream worlds of literary texts. And reader-response theory has given us the tools to understand how texts continue to dream in the world through us—to describe how their affective imaginaries can exceed the explicit ideological parameters of their own times and places. The readings in the following chapters draw out hauntings from undecided futures, which are visible only retrospectively, through the thick web of discourses, desires, and interpretive traditions that have come after.[52] One might call this presentist, but not if presentist means a projection of the present onto the past. By presentist, I mean nothing more than an accurate sense of how multiple—and how very much *not* guaranteed to lead to any one or another future outcome—any present really is. History, after all, includes now.

In short, this book is about much more than these four select "shapes of fancy" and how they revise a working definition of queerness for current early modern literary studies and queer theory—although it does do that. It demonstrates how eros in any text is both situated, grounded in the historical conditions of its production and reception—circulating among bodies and material objects—and yet always and everywhere, escaping them. It asks how textual figurations of strong feeling—like bottomless hunger, thwarted longing, or being used to others' ends—can reach across centuries to titillate and disturb in unexpected ways. It interrogates how such transtemporal hailings alter existing schemas of sexuality, periodization, historical change, and historical time. These fundamental theoretical questions are applicable far beyond my archive of early modern texts. They go to questions of what reading is, how readers make meaning, and how reading works across time.

Antipodean Fancies

I want to pursue the idea that queerness can inhere in dramatic systems through a case study in excess, a play from late in the life of the commercial London theater before it was shut down by Puritan authorities: Richard Brome's 1638 comedy *The Antipodes*. This play is structured by several kinds of inversion and deviance. Its queerness, however, permeates its entire dramatic economy, far in excess of any particular homoerotic dynamic. At the center of the play is a melancholic young husband, ironically named Peregrine, who so gorges himself on reading travel narratives that he is unable to consummate his marriage with his wife of three years.

> In tender years he always loved to read,
> Reports of travel and of voyages.
> And when young boys like him would tire themselves
> With sports and pastimes and restore their spirits
> Again by meat and sleep, he would whole days
> And nights (sometimes by stealth) be on such books
> As might convey his fancy round the world. (1.1.131–37)[53]

Right away, we can see Peregrine as a kind of queer figure in that he refuses an insertive, heterosexual role. His case involves nothing so straightforward as a homoerotic love object, though. Instead, Peregrine is consumed by a surfeit of reading, born out of an overwhelming, crippling desire to be elsewhere, to escape his life by displacing himself:

> His mind was all on fire to be abroad;
> Nothing but travel still was all his aim.
> There was no voyage or foreign expedition
> Be said to be in hand, but he made suit
> To be made one in it. (1.1.139–43)

In his father's narrative, Peregrine's abnormal predilection dates back to early childhood, then fans into full flame when he's a young man. But an itinerant voyager was not what Peregrine's parents wanted him to be when he grew up:

> His mother and
> Myself opposed him still in all and, strongly
> Against his will, still held him in and won
> Him into marriage, hoping that would call
> In his extravagant thoughts. But all prevail'd not,
> Nor stay'd him—though at home—from travelling
> So far beyond himself that now, too late,
> I wish he had gone abroad to meet his fate. (1.1.143–50)

In an old and durable story, Peregrine's parents' best efforts to normalize his desire have utterly backfired. Their prohibition on traveling abroad, the involuntary marriage they force him into in order to "call in his extravagant thoughts"—none of it has worked. Now he is so consumed with the desire to read that the reading, and the desire for more reading, consumes his life, distracting him from all normal duties, including (especially) his conjugal ones.

Here, then, is the first methodological point I will use *The Antipodes* to think through. What are the stakes of calling Peregrine's obsession queer, of connecting this dramatization of deviant desire from 1638 to the larger history of something called sexuality? I make these claims by means of what Wai Chee Dimock calls a diachronic historicism, in which texts' changing, traveling resonances move across long temporal spans, picking up losses and distortions, sounding different vibrations in new contexts, and developing significant dialogues with resonances from other times.[54] Here I connect this comedy's representation of excessive reading to a genealogy of queer resonances echoing *forward* in time from 1638. If, for example, we are able to see the queerness of Peregrine's passive resistance, it is thanks to the negative turn in psychoanalytically inflected queer theory, formulated by Leo Bersani and promulgated by Lee Edelman and others, which posits that queerness can inhere in antirelational, antisocial, unproductive, and self- and other-destructive affects.[55] This theory, forged in the crucible of the AIDS epidemic, rejects a definition of queerness as strictly a positive social fact (an act, a relationship, a group identity). Rather, it insists on the queer political and affective content of antisocial refusal (like Peregrine's), annihilation, and loss. It acknowledges extreme negative affects as just as intense, and just as constitutive of queerness, as any positive passion, resisting the affective imperatives of political agency and identitarian pride. Queer theorists of bad feeling—including Ann Cvetkovich, Jack Halberstam, Lauren Berlant, and Heather Love—have extended the notion of queerness beyond a requirement of direct, purposeful transgression against normativity, elaborating the queer potentials of depression, failure, stasis, and loss as forms of passive resistance, or merely queer existence.[56] With the insight that of course queerness is, and has been, sometimes not agentive, constructive, or even voluntary, this work has further plumbed the queer resonances of things not done: of stagnation, error, passivity, and blockage like the one that afflicts Peregrine.

To name Peregrine's impasse as a species of queerness is to see its libidinal and cultural content as part of the history of dissident desiring that gave us the term "queer" in the first place. Peregrine's obsession with reading travelogues calls forth a history of desire that is seen as a problem: a history of outsize predilections that embarrass everyone but the desirer; a history of pleasures stigmatized as frivolous and freeloading; and a history of disappointed parental expectations. Moreover, Peregrine's fantasy is trained on a desperate desire for escape from life as it is, to an exotic elsewhere—any elsewhere. Feeling along with José Esteban Muñoz that "the here and now is a prison house," Peregrine seems almost to be following Muñoz's queer utopian injunction "to think and feel *a then and there.*"[57] His desperation for escape is both the cause and the effect of his not exactly consensual marriage to a woman. His inability to accomplish the act of marital consummation—the symptom that finally spurs his parents to bring him in for a course of early modern "conversion therapy"—is a particularly evocative form of passive refusal to comply with compulsory heterosexuality. In other words, Peregrine's bizarre fixation is only legible as a mode of erotic relation to the world in light of a history of queer affects and politics stretching over the ensuing centuries between that moment and the present.

Reading texts that are the products of a four-hundred-years-bygone popular culture requires retheorizing how affect, identification, and difference work across historical distance. One of my objectives here is to turn the conversation about early modern sexuality away from the intensely productive recent critical debates about the writing of history, toward pondering the reading of literature instead. Literary theory strives to account for how desire—and not just individual desire—structures narrative; to account for the multilayered complexes of production-side and reception-side desires that generate texts; and to account for how readers make meaning from language, both within the psyche and communally. In the interest of developing new literary methods for perceiving affective linkages between our time and others, this book argues for the critical utility—

and theoretical productivity—of an identificatory mode of reading. By identificatory, I do not mean identitarian (shaped by a prior identity). I mean what Carolyn Dinshaw calls "a queer historical impulse, an impulse toward making connections across time between, on the one hand, lives, texts, and other cultural phenomena left out of sexual categories back then, and, on the other, those left out of current sexual categories now."[58] Dinshaw's queer, historically desiring, yet uncategorized reader is the active maker of affective relations with the past— fictive, fashioned, *made* relations in which "discourses, people, places, and things, *in their very indeterminateness*" are put into contact, made to touch.[59] But readerly identification can also feel less voluntary, like the shock of being identified, being hailed, by something in a text. I am thinking here of the queer hailing that Sedgwick calls camp-recognition, which asks, "what if the right audience for this were exactly me?," and which wonders if there might be others out there who "can see it from the same 'perverse' angle." Sedgwick's camp subject acknowledges that these perceptions derive from fantasy—although fantasies, including the fantasy that "whoever made this was gay too," are "not infrequently true."[60]

I want to use Dinshaw's and Sedgwick's models of identification to construct a new queer theory of reading. It must be grounded in reader-response theory, particularly the idea that there is no reading without reading *for* something, even if that something is not explicitly present to consciousness. This is because the phenomenon we call reading is an "interaction," as Wolfgang Iser describes it, between a desiring, imagining reader and a text. The text structures and provokes the reader's ideations through its constitutive blanks, silences, and negations every bit as much as through its content.[61] Reading is thus the reader's act of assembling meaning, through a dynamic process akin to a performance's realization of a script, from the repertoire provided by the formal features of the text. There is nothing innocent or objective about the reader, however. In Roland Barthes's phrasing, "this 'I' which approaches the text is itself already a plurality of other texts, of codes which are infinite, or more precisely, lost (whose origin is lost)."[62] The process of intertextuality, as Barthes describes it here, applies not only to the body of conventions, citations, and codes (what Kristeva calls a "mosaic of quotations") that go into a text's production, but also to the complex of available codes and other texts—from multiple historical moments—that the reader brings to the interaction.[63] As readers, we are intertextual clouds of citations. When the texts being read are four hundred years old, the available structures and codes (what Barthes calls the "already read") in the interaction must consist—must even mostly consist—of citations and codes from the time after, the time in between the text's production and its being read.[64] Intertexuality thus works retrospectively. What is "already read" in a present reader's interaction with an early modern text has not, from the point of view of the text's history, yet been written. This is one of the ways in which reading does strange things to time. We are reading *The Antipodes* from the future, with an intertextual lens (inextricable from our very eyes and minds) of material that Richard Brome and his players dreamed not of.

That the deviant desire dramatized onstage in *The Antipodes* is an obsession with reading is a stroke of metaresonance that Barthes would have loved. Peregrine's problem evokes the history of reading as a queer form of escape—imaginative escape for the materially and socially immobilized, particularly as used by protoqueer young people. This queer history, not coincidentally, forms part of the basis for Sedgwick's defense of readerly identification in her theory of reparative reading—the child or adolescent "reading for important news about herself, without knowing what form that news will take."[65] Reparative reading emerges out of Sedgwick's imperative—which I share—to ask what else is happening in a text, what else is it doing, that goes unnoticed by a "paranoid reading" practice of anticipating and exposing the historical power dynamics congealed there. Sedgwick locates that something else in the reader, with a call to openly own and reclaim reparative motives of love and pleasure with respect to one's objects of study. "The desire of a reparative impulse," as she puts it, "is additive and accretive. [. . .] it wants to assemble and confer plenitude on an object [such as a text or textual object or author-object] that will then have resources to offer an inchoate self."[66] The meanings readers may make out of the urgency of their own need are thus as unpredictable as the objects of culture, high and low, to which they will attach.

The content of Peregrine's reading desire is a hodgepodge of strange beasts from the widely circulated cheap printed pamphlets recounting foreign and wondrous phenomena. He is characterized as pregnant with these marvels, as needing a "man-midwife" to "deliver him of a huge tympany of news—of monsters,/Pygmies and giants, apes and crocodiles, men upon women/And women upon men, the strangest doings" (1.1.177–81). One source of these images is the long cultural afterlife of *The Travels of Sir John Mandeville*, a fanciful travel tale from the fourteenth century that combines material from a number of preexisting narratives of travel to the East with vernacularized versions of wondrous late ancient and classical legends (such as the kingdom of Prester John, pygmies, giants, and anthropophagi). This plot point is a satirical commentary on print culture. As innovative historicist work has demonstrated, the reading and enjoyment of cheap print pamphlets was an intensely popular and communal activity in the period, involving shared oral recitation and performance of printed texts, as well as public debate over its content.[67] One historical sense in which Peregrine's desire for reading may be called queer, then, is that it is suspiciously private. He spends "whole days/ And nights (sometimes by stealth)" alone in his room, even hiding the extent of his consumption—an autoerotic, antisocial relation to what could be a social act. The play consistently points up the thematic connection between reading and sex, as well as the connection between the desire for reading and the desire for travel stirred by the burgeoning long-distance trade industry, both of which depend on incitement of a desire to be elsewhere. How easily, especially when attempts are made to thwart and deny them, these desires can grow in the wrong direction, out of control, feeding on themselves until they reach an intensity that obstructs normative social and sexual life. Moreover, Peregrine's reading frenzy is queer in its structure as well as in its social effects. Like Bartholomew Cokes and Zeal-of-the-Land Busy, whom I mentioned in the opening paragraphs—and also, famously, like Duke Orsino in Shakespeare's *Twelfth Night*, with his ruminations on whether "music be the food of love"—Peregrine's desire is directed not toward any object that could actually fulfill it, but toward desire itself.[68] A bottomless desire for reading is a desire for one's senses and imagination to continually be stimulated by new images, which breed new desires.

Though plays watched by audiences in the London commercial theater and prose narratives circulated in cheap print pamphlets are of course two very different kinds of texts, I bring them together here in order to make visible their commonalities as forms of popular media trading in desire.[69] Both plays and prose narratives dramatize desire within a finite frame of temporal, spatial, and material constraints. Both kinds of media incite and channel the imaginative appetites of their respective audiences. Prose tracts stage the operations of desire through bodies and things via a combination of written description and visual representation (woodcuts and engravings). The text also functions as a thing, bodying forth events for a reader who was not present, inviting its audience—its readers—to imagine a scene transpiring in the mind's eye. In the theater, many of the same material things that attract meaning in printed pamphlets and tracts are also physically present on the stage, in their doubled roles as stage properties. The theatrical prop becomes a player, giving a material body to the thing it represents, engendering affective connection in the fleeting space and time of the theater.

An intertextual model of reading makes Brome's analogy between reading and theater explicit. A text is the set of instructions that guides a reading, just as a script guides a dramatic performance. As I read Iser's theorization, each act of reading is a performance in that it is an idiosyncratic, participatory, made realization, a "reconstitution" of that script.[70] Shoshana Felman also describes the theatrical quality of reading, which, she says, begins not with the text but with the text's effect on the reader: "The very act of telling, of narration, proceeds then from the potentially infinite repercussion of an *effect of reading.*" This performative action is in turn embodied in the text's telling of its story: "Narrative as such turns out to be the trace of the action of a reading; it is, in fact, *reading as action.*"[71] How much more true this is for theater, when the storytellers, whose performances furnish the frame for the audience's experience, are not narratorial voices inside the text but subjective, embodied readers of the text. Actors read their parts, and companies of actors and directors playing multiple, shifting roles collectively read playwrights' plays.[72] A performance of a play is, in a technical sense, reading. The meaning of a theatrical performance, in the view of Keir Elam, is produced out of an "interaction" that is essentially intertextual in nature. What Elam calls the theatrical "frame," the event in which an audience member participates, is, in both its production and its reception, made up of and decoded by other texts.[73] Theater is apprehended through a communal process of reception conditioned by the spectator's "horizon of expectations" (an idea from Hans Jauss's aesthetics of reception), made up of every kind of preexisting knowledge and influence.[74] "Every spectator's interpretation of the text is in effect a new construction of it according to the cultural and ideological disposition of the subject," Elam concludes. "It is the spectator who must make sense of the performance for himself."[75] But performance is also embodied. Printed dramatic texts are memorial traces (sometimes many years after) of a communal, bodily transmission of affect experienced within the ritualized, aesthetic constraints of medium, genre, time, and space. What would it look like to seriously ponder the implications of these theoretical claims—which, it must be noted, locate the production of meaning in the *historically specific and contingent* phenomena of the texts and codes available to each reader or spectator in each interaction—for the study of premodern sexuality? The following chapters represent one attempt to find out: to rehabilitate old theoretical tools and develop new ones in order to think more deeply about what it means to read literature, about what reading is, and what it can do.

In a Queer Time and Place

The cure in *The Antipodes* runs queerer than the disease. To cure him, Peregrine's father calls in a madcap doctor, who prescribes not bodily physic but "medicine of the mind, which he infuses/So skillfully, yet by familiar ways,/That it begets both wonder and delight" in onlookers (1.1.24–26). The "medicine of the mind" he prescribes for Peregrine is a fantastical cure by drama, a play within a play put on by a troupe of players in a huge London house under the patronage of a "fantastic lord" who dresses like a bizarre pauper. The play they stage is a risky, carnivalesque dramatization of faux travel to the Antipodes, an upside-down land on the other side of the world, where everything is the opposite of how it is in England. This psychotherapy-by-drama plot is at once a topical commentary on the pleasures and dangers of the theater and a meditation (which can travel beyond its topical moment) on the nature of desiring. Desire, in the economy of this play, is not removed by disciplining the desirer or by supplying the desirer with an appropriate satiating object. No, wayward or excessive desire is addressed by transgressing further and more explicitly. Desire is solved by being further inflamed—by theater, which, like reading, is an art form predicated on the stoking and inviting of new desires and identifications in its viewers.

Peregrine's crippling longing to be elsewhere is dealt with by going all in—by giving him a sleeping draught and taking him elsewhere to show him a theatrical "anti-London" of class, gender, and customary backwardness. The play's pervasive pro-transgression, pro-excess, pro-fiction, pro-displacement model of desire cured by more desire gives it an overarching queer dramatic structure, within which a riot of other forms of stylistic and relational queerness is staged. One of the ways in which a cure by drama works on Peregrine— or on any of us, for that matter—is by bending time, creating the finite, enchanted, defamiliarized time apart of performance. The displacement Peregrine experiences is, he thinks, spatial, to the furthest possible land from England on the globe—though in fact it is chemical, psychic, affective, and theatrical: he hasn't gone anywhere. It is also, crucially, temporal. Peregrine is transported into the space of the show in a pharmaceutical time warp brought about by Hughball's sleeping draught. He is told he has slept for eight months, the duration of the entire voyage to the Antipodes. So in addition to the lie about where he is, Peregrine does not know *when* he is. What's more, the fantastical images from Mandeville that fill his head, that condition what he expects to see, are from a three-hundred-year-old book. Peregrine's standpoint is a rich metaphor for our situation as readers of early modern literature. We may think we know when, not to mention where, we are, but we may well be wrong. And our sense of distance or difference from our objects of study has far-reaching effects on our readings of the desires we encounter there.

Using spatial defamiliarization to comment on temporal defamiliarization is appropriate to the methodological conversation I'm intervening in here, for the original emphasis on historical alterity, the otherness of the past, in New Historicist criticism emerges from the influence of anthropology, particularly Clifford Geertz, on the early work of Stephen Greenblatt.[76] Historicism's decades of predominance in early modern studies engendered an enduring critical stance that "the past is a foreign country," which must be approached ethnographically, disavowing all assumptions of comparability between past and present forms. The history of this mapping-on of space to time is a circular one, however. As Johannes Fabian points out, the construction of spatial alterity itself in the ethnographic paradigm is deeply reliant on narratives construing the other-space, the object-space, as temporally before the space of the looker, and expected to become more like it in a possible future.[77] The anthropological location of the other in space that attracted Greenblatt is thus predicated on a distancing temporal fiction, and on a colonial fantasy of the other's progress toward a foreknown present.

That Peregrine's displacement in *The Antipodes* is explicitly fictional particularly foregrounds the interplay of alterity and identification, difference and likeness, in reading and spectatorship. This is of course the same oscillation that shapes our critical stance toward early modern texts, both in terms of content, in asking what factors of anatomy, gender, or status constitute a like *(homo)* or unlike *(hetero)* coupling in a given context, and in terms of method, in questioning what proportions of identification and difference structure our relations to sexualities—and texts—from the past, and why.[78] In this respect, *The Antipodes* can even be read as a fable dramatizing the terms of the debate within early modern sexuality studies over the differing agendas and methodologies of historicism and queer theory— and over the larger critical values and imperatives they enable and hinder.[79] This book, while squarely a part of that conversation, sits athwart the opposition between history and theory that has structured recent critical exchanges. It is not my aim to invent-discover (to use Bruno Latour's term) a new taxonomy of early modern eroticisms, or of buried sexual types.[80] Instead, this book teases out the ways in which the temporal moments embodied in textual artifacts are made porous, lingering, sticky, jarring, and otherwise heterogeneous by the operations of affect and desire in reading. In both form and content, I read *The Antipodes* as a dramatization of what is called queer temporality—the idea that historical time and historical change are not a linear, one-way progression.[81] Reading texts this way means remaining alert to the ways in which the past is still, uncannily, with us in the present.[82] This is what Shakespeare means when he has Hamlet say "The time is out of joint," as he is trying to make sense of the ethical and affective memorial demands made on him by the return of a specter from the past (1.5.189).[83] Jacques Derrida spins this line into a theory of the disjointure always present within historical time: "'The time is out of joint': time is *dislocated*, disarticulated, dislodged, time is run down, on the run and run down, *deranged*, both out of order and mad. Time is off its hinges, time is off-course, beside itself, disadjusted. Says Hamlet."[84] The point I take from Derrida's meditation on the out-of-jointness of any one time to itself is that the phantasms of desire that erupt in culture, which seem to come from the past or the future, are radically epistemologically and ontologically undecidable in their meanings. Or, to put it another way, as Hamlet has just said of the specter addressing him with its own unresolved desires, "There are more things in heaven and earth" than are dreamt of in any one, cohesive early modern philosophy (1.5.168). To take Derrida's out-of-joint model as an historiographic stance toward early modern literature means that reading can work both ways through time. Not only can Shakespeare be used to understand later chapters in European history, but the retrospective hauntings of later moments can be used to read Shakespeare.

I use this idea to mine the queer potential of past aesthetic forms. Instead of locating queerness in a supposedly "modern" future, I look backward instead, to passé, "over," or dated styles of thinking and being for what they reveal of the complicated currents of sexuality in time. In their pioneering studies of queer temporality and queer history, Jack Halberstam and Heather Love argue that certain "backward" queer styles of being (the gender inversion of butch and drag aesthetics, for instance; refusals of the respectability and assimilation offered by modern, liberal gay rights; recalcitrant shame; and resolutely isolated or unaffiliated queer life) have the power to thwart the expected trajectories of maturation, development, and progress imposed by heteronormativity and neoliberal capitalism on both individual and cultural scales.[85] I find in their call to attend to affects (and critical stances) supposedly consigned to the past—to ask what and who gets plowed under in a modernizing, supersession narrative of the history of sexuality—a crucial intervention for how to think about eros in early modern texts. I read the strange backwardnesses of desire in Renaissance texts as forms of queerness that are absolutely not "over," that are still around, haunting and complicating the present.

When I mention at parties that I am writing a book about queer desires that have no clear or necessary relationship to consummation, and that do not correspond to coherent, politically legible sexual identities, I am sometimes met with the assumption that such disjointed urges belong only to the distant past of early modern England—that by and large we live today in a state of basic coherence between desire, act, and social identity, in the bright modern light of gay pride. This is far from the truth. In fact, this narrative reflects only a quite recent and limited perspective of white-normative, bourgeois, metropolitan, gender-conforming, secular, liberal-individualist, post-Stonewall, settler colonial and Western European gay and lesbian subjecthood. Anyone aware of the experiences of older (or underage), rural or small town, Southern, nonwhite, trans/genderqueer/gender-nonconforming, poor and working-class, intergenerationally and communally obligated, religious, non-Western, or other so-called closeted queer subjects—that is, the majority of queers who live and have lived in the world—will recognize that there is still an urgent need to attend to and excavate the affects of unlegitimated, undocumented, even unarticulated or unexpressed queer desires, because such longings and such lives do not belong to the past. They are still very much here, now; they are as much a part of the present as the readier images of self-realization. As Sedgwick contends in *Epistemology of the Closet*'s axiom 5, "The historical search for a Great Paradigm Shift may obscure the present conditions of sexual identity," the underlying structural problem with the dominant historical accounts of homosexuality (Michel Foucault's, David Halperin's) is that they are premised on a "unidirectional narrative of supersession," in which one distinct past model of same-sex relations and gender identity is eclipsed by another—and the superseded model then drops out of the frame. That is not how reality works, today or ever; as my fellow Mississippian William Faulkner puts it, "The past is never dead. It's not even past."[86] I want to attend instead to what Sedgwick calls the "relations enabled by the unrationalized coexistence of different models during the times they do co-exist."[87]

This is what I take from Latour's assertion that "we have never been modern": that the modernizing narrative of ascendant individuation, secularization, rights, and notions of identity has never been the whole, or even an accurate, story; that the messy interdependences supposedly superseded in modernity's work of individuating purification have instead never gone anywhere.[88] I want to read with an awareness of what Elizabeth Freeman calls "temporal drag," the visceral pull of the past on the present,[89] and an alertness to what Jonathan Goldberg calls the "non-self-identity of any historical moment" to itself.[90] I think it is important to note where fantasies of historical difference are fantasies of progress—not that difference (and change) do not exist. They do, but their status ought to be questioned, not assumed. The idea of modernity can only be constituted by its others, by what is abjected as nonmodern. The quest to isolate difference and change in the past risks making the huge and erroneous assumption that there exists a coherent "homosexuality as we *conceive* of it today," which can be contrasted to that past.[91] The present is then reified as foreknown, inevitable, homogenized, and renaturalized by having its history told in this linear fashion—when in reality history is an unruly, rushing river, its every moment full of continually becoming forms whose mutations are not determined in advance.

Early modern England, with its ultracanonical literary tradition organized around the mythologized figure of Shakespeare, is a particularly susceptible and thus important site for dismantling the fixation on the absence or presence of sexual identity. It has functioned in the cultural imaginary as a locus of obsession with the "before" of "homosexuality as we conceive of it today"—a moment just before, when a commercial theater of men and boys and its supposedly sexually fluid star playwright could be thrillingly construed as *other* than gay, yet, at the same time, a teleological before, defined in terms of the heteronormative/homophobic regime that it confirms, in its very beforeness, as incipient, fully formed, just around the bend of history. The culture war version of this has taken the form of a fixation on whether Shakespeare and company "were gay" or "had no access to that concept"—neither of which would begin to encompass reality, even if we could access it (we can't).[92] Even as this book steps aside from what Dimock calls synchronic historicism, the effort to pin down what specific terms and discourses of sexuality were available "in the same slice of time," I want to draw attention to the ideological work done by centering the question for so long[93]—most urgently to the risks of assuming that only those desires officially named and registered in contemporary social discourses existed or mattered. Instead, I see the textual shapes of erotic desire, then and now, as Dimock sees texts themselves: "emerging phenomena, activated and to some extent constituted by the passage of time." "The 'object' of literary studies," she continues, "is thus an object with an unstable ontology, since a text can resonate only insofar as it is touched by the effects of its travels."[94] Desire then becomes the kind of complex, networked, active object, crossing between archival registers and orders of knowledge and disciplinary tools, that concerns Bruno Latour: "these strange situations that the intellectual culture in which we live does not know how to categorize."[95]

For who, in any time, has ever lived in a state of perfect coherence between the totality of their invisible desires, the sum of their bodily acts, and their definitive social identity? I would not suppose this to be true of anyone, no matter how flawlessly, obediently heteronormative—or how liberated, enlightened, and gay—in all appearances. This is not how desire works, and not (I feel safe in assuming) how it has ever worked. In departing from archivally legible acts and identities for more nebulous traces of feeling, I link the uncategorized impulses and longings in early modern literature to those still experienced in the present, by acknowledging that not all erotic feelings contain the desire to act; not all desires to act result in acts; not all acts carried out are seen or recorded, in any archive; and not all archived acts are set down or read in the expected ways, then or now.[96] To ask it another way: Are you perfectly sure that when whoever has survived to do historical research on this planet in five hundred years (admittedly a best-case scenario in light of looming environmental catastrophe, but supposing someone does) tries to reconstruct early twenty-first-century sexualities, they will be able to read the totality of *your* desires in the archive?

"The Fancies Were Begot"

Meanwhile, *The Antipodes* posits its own theory of how desire is generated, which is worthy of detailed attention, as it provides a beautiful example of how close reading can complicate models of historical change. At the beginning of act 2, the madcap doctor and the odd lord plot together over the performance: "Your fancy and my cure shall be cried up/Miraculous. Oh, you're the lord of fancy," gushes the doctor, to which Letoy demurs, "I'm not ambitious of that title, sir." His reasoning is that "fancy"—a term with complex early modern meanings having to do with the ability to envision and materialize one's desire or artistic creation, which I unpack in more etymological detail in chapter 2—is more powerful and pervasive than any one artist of it (2.1.5–7). Letoy describes "fancy" as a force that is simultaneously ancient and sempiternal, and endlessly novel and self-renewing: "Ages before the fancies were begot,/And shall beget still new to the world's end" (2.1.8–9). The way this couplet situates fancy in historical time encapsulates one of the arguments of this book: no one is lord of fancy, as its "begetting" is shared across time, between us and those who lived and fancied "ages before." The vagaries of desire that can be imagined (or staged) now have most probably been "begot," "ages before," whether they were recorded or remembered. But at the same time, this is not to say that the shape of desire is at all static or fixed throughout time. Instead, it "shall beget still new to the world's end." This model of fancy's begetting does not hew to a unidirectional line of progress or development. It is constantly generating new forms of itself from itself, multiplying through history in unpredictable ways. Its ongoing new begetting is not figured in terms of sexual generation, but instead as an asexually propagating organism that grows and reproduces collectively, as desires are spread communally through the *longue durée* of culture.

Letoy's notion of fancy describes how desire paradoxically

abides by both constancy and change, and how constant self-refreshing generativity can be itself a kind of constancy—if we assume that fancy in every age is just as actively begetting "still new" forms of itself, as it was in the beginning, is now, and ever shall be. This must change how we read. We are not, then, looking at a literary text as a record of the ideologies of desire available to be thought and expressed at a moment in time. Every text (drama, nonfiction prose, poetic, etc.) is instead a moving target, its idiosyncratic set of imaginative representations archiving a teeming assemblage of cultural desires: residual and emergent and otherwise/unspecified shapes of fancy (the otherwise/unspecified category being what chiefly interests me here)—which is itself in motion through time, and undergoing constant alteration as soon as it exists in the world through being produced, viewed, and read.

Moreover, the constant, unpredictable generation of new forms of fancy, persisting from "ages before," can serve as the common ground for a paradoxical form of readerly identification: the certainty that we do not "Know What That Means" (in Eve Sedgwick's words) with respect to the ideological and erotic content of specific literary forms.[97] Letoy's model of how the theater generates audience desire puts the lie to the idea that there is one single early modern audience reception of this, or any other, play. Though others have parsed the topical political valences of Brome's satire,[98] more recent work on the diversity of early modern audiences and the social effects of theater has advanced the position that even in ideological terms—not to mention aesthetic ones—there was no single agenda guiding how spectators or readers would have responded to its incitements, nor one public consensus about what they meant.[99] It is frequently acknowledged that the fictional travel in *The Antipodes* does not comment or conjecture on life in any real place on the globe. Only incidentally a satire of London custom, it is for the most part a dramatic exercise in inversion and identification, giving the play of comparison and difference free rein for the delectation—and sexual aid—of one participant/reader. But there is nothing "mere" about the "pleasure and amelioration" it affords Peregrine; he enters it and is altered by it.[100] To me, this is one of the most important things that happens in theater, and in reading, regardless of the text's date of production.

It engenders a fictive, feverish displacement that is at once deranging and curative, giving rise to identifications that cannot be predicted in advance.

The Antipodes partakes in queer formal experimentation in the explicitness with which it draws attention to its own artificiality, highlighting its hybrid and citational structure. Letoy tells his favorite actor to give his "incorrigible" desire for verbal improvisation free rein: "Take license to yourself to add unto/Your parts your own free fancy" (2.1.93–94). This pleasure-generating performance practice is construed as archaic and dated—part of the rougher, merrier past of the theater, as it was done "in the days of [the great Elizabethan-era fools] Tarleton and Kemp" (2.1.101). Brome is playing with historical time and style here. A self-consciously literary protégé and imitator of Jonson, he is known for this kind of fanciful treatment of contemporary concerns. Brome's plays are not realist; they take place in a world of escalating, outrageous fiction that heralds the novel. So this innovative, therapeutic theatrical experiment—the first appearance on the English stage of any kind of psychiatry or mental therapy—in this late, decadent Caroline play, is mining the anachronistic, defamiliarizing potential of supposedly superseded dramatic forms. Letoy's play also experiments with the thrill of immersive, participatory theater, centuries before *Sleep No More* (a 2011 site-specific adaptation of *Macbeth* staged throughout a fictional 1930s Scottish hotel), drawing on the archaic history of ambulatory, site-based performance dating back to the medieval town cycle plays. Peregrine and his wife, as well as Blaze (the owner of the house) and Blaze's wife, shall be "not alone/Spectators, but, as we will carry it, actors/To fill your comic scenes with double mirth" (2.1.41–43). The "odd lord" leads them, in masks, to a margin of the stage where they can comment on the action and even join in. These formal properties add up to a demonstration of the queer potential of past aesthetic forms. As Valerie Rohy, who thinks about many of these same questions in later literary canons, puts it: "As queer theory has turned back to the question of temporality, it has discovered in itself the ageless anachronism whose other name is literariness."[101] I intend the moments of anachronism I have entertained here, both external to the text and within it, as reading exercises that raise real methodological questions. How does the act of reading work, in the disjointed time of lived experience? In what sense is reading inescapably historical? In what sense can reading be seen as constitutively queer? And how do these theoretical claims fit together and alter each other?

The World Turned Upside Down

Cast in a seductively liminal role where he is both the audience for the play and a leading character, Peregrine gives himself over to the altered state of theater. Letoy's players enact a world where all power dynamics are reversed, and transgressions forbidden in England are not only licensed but required. Women rule over their husbands; they order the reluctant men to have sex with and impregnate other women. Servants in "the Antipodes" rule over their meekly submissive masters. The law declines to lock anyone up—except when a maid sexually harasses a gentleman who rejects her advances, then lies to the constable about it, she is believed and he is taken away. A "man-scold" is mocked and ducked for talking back to his wife. Poets are richly remunerated for their poems, and aging parents are sent off to school. Topically, the inset metadrama stages a substantive debate about sexual norms and mores, presenting a set of real alternatives to the existing sexual order of married, heteronormative monogamy. Critics have frequently pointed out that in order to protect himself, Brome skirts around making any critique of the political order—his anti-London is not a republic, or anything other than a municipal government within a monarchy, like actual London. And Peregrine is reminded that "the Antipodes" is the opposite of England "only in custom." But the critique of custom it stages is very much a political one, even a politically queer one. It asks the onstage spectators and the audience to imagine a world in which married spouses do not have exclusive sexual rights over one another's bodies, and a world in which groups of people of various ages and social statuses are knitted together in complex domestic arrangements that intermingle new biological, social, and economic relations of kinship (where servants command their masters to have children with other servants and masters, and wives maintain a claim to the children their husbands sire with other women). This world of inversion does not include any explicitly same-sex pairings, but it is queer in that it challenges the larger structure of naturalized, hierarchized sexual difference, the patriarchal social order thought to inevitably arise from it, and the moralizing assumptions that keep it in place. Peregrine takes the point exactly when, watching it all unfold, he asks, "Can men and women be so contrary/In all that we hold proper to each sex?" (4.1.160–61). Suddenly, what is "proper to each sex" is a matter of what "we hold" it to be. Why should all power and property attach to men rather than women? Why should a person's only chance at having a child depend on the fertility of their sole legal spouse? Indeed, what the play within the play is doing looks a lot like queer theory: dramatizing and thinking through how sexual life could be ordered otherwise, and in the process inviting its spectators (both inside and outside of the text) to insert themselves and their desires into its thought experiment wherever they feel moved to do so.

The play within the play oscillates wildly between success and crisis, as its dramatic frame only incompletely contains Peregrine. On a mad run, he breaks into the tiring-house where the players store their costumes and props, and, believing himself to be in an exotic enchanted castle, takes a sword from the wall and ransacks the storage gallery of fantastical beasts of wood and fabric. To hear the hysterical leading player tell it, he "kills monster after monster, takes the puppets/Prisoner, knocks down the Cyclops, tumbles all/ Our jiggumbobs and trinkets to the wall" (3.1.306–8). He cuts the hanging devils' masks and painted skin coats all to pieces in a fury; then, "with a reverent hand," he takes the stage crown and royal robes out of a prop closet, and "crowns himself King of the Antipodes, and believes/He has justly gain'd the kingdom by his conquest" (3.1.314–17). This unexpected swerve into a fantasy of kingship is first incorporated into the play by Byplay's improvisational skill, and eventually breaks the frame altogether.[102]

At the climax of the play within the play, Peregrine cements his "kingship" by going to bed with the "daughter" of the last king— played by his actual wife, Martha, brought into the action in order to get the sex, and the possible child, she craves. The consummation takes place in a mock exotic wedding tableau that is at once a send-up of the fantasy of colonial rulership through the traffic in women, and a sex role-playing game that functions—barely—to compensate for Peregrine's uncooperative desire. Peregrine is told that the state over which he newly rules presents to him "the daughter/The only child and heir apparent of/Our late deposed and deceased sovereign,/Who with his dying breath bequeath'd her to you" (4.1.441–44). Even in this utterly artificial mock royal wedding, a totally implausible narrative of legitimacy is still supplied to the delusional conqueror—and though the story does not square at all with his supposed seizure of the kingdom by puppet slaughter, he does not question it. Nor does he question, or react, to the sudden news that his wife is dead—or to the claim that "her fleeting spirit/Is flown into and animates this princess" (4.1.448–49). The closer he gets to heterosexual congress, the further away Peregrine seems to drift, dissociating "back again to Mandeville madness" (4.1.466) and musing that he has read of a far-off people "where on the wedding night the husband hires/Another man to couple with his bride/To clear the dangerous passage of a maidenhead" (4.1.463–65)—after all, "she may be of that serpentine generation/That stings of-times to death, as Mandeville writes" (4.1.467–68). Out of time and out of excuses, he is told, "For the safety of your kingdom you must do it" (4.1.474), then escorted out.

It Takes a Crowd

Meanwhile, in the interstitial spaces of the drama's unfolding, offstage, in the margins of the play within a play—margins as ample and affording of various dalliances as the many rooms of the house—the sexual initiation of Peregrine's wife, Martha, has already taken place without him. She has been aided to joy—and stoked into a state of further desire—by the lady of the house, a knowing married woman named Barbara. Valerie Traub uses this lesbian sexual initiation to elaborate on the dynamics of ignorance, knowledge, and power around procreative sex and female touch.[103] But in addition to introducing female/female erotic pedagogy into the play, the sexual assistance plot contributes to the play's overarching queer dramatic economy: a world in which a surfeit of desire is addressed by venturing into still more forms of desire, and supposedly dyadic and marital sex acts actually end up being anything but. In a major subplot running through the play, Peregrine and his wife are not the only patients with a sex problem targeted by the theatrical cure. Peregrine's father, the one who hired the "Doctor," is also being driven mad—but with anxiety that his much younger second wife, Diana, will give her favors to other men. The Doctor has a performance-based cure for Old Joyless too: he stokes his jealousy to a fever pitch by having Letoy attempt to seduce Diana in front of him. Letoy leads them through a sadistic mind game, tormenting him and tempting her, then threatening her when she rejects him—until he reveals that Diana is his long-lost daughter, abandoned when he suspected his wife of infidelity, and the whole performance of seduction was a test of her virtue. This plot stages another therapy by surfeit, this one a form of extreme desensitization by exposure to what one fears most. What makes it queer is that the cure is to be found in giving up on policing purity and embracing the defilement one fears. Barbara's husband, the owner of the house, is also a satisfied former patient, immune to jealousy ever since "he knew the worst/He could by his wife" (5.2.253–54)—which includes, it is strongly implied, a former and perhaps ongoing affair with the Doctor. The husbands cured in this way discover that, once free to give up the paranoid position of terrible, anticipatory alertness to the dangers posed by their wives' sexuality, they can access a depressive position and live on, repairing and enjoying their marriages in this fallen state.[104] As a bonus, the seduction is revealed at the last minute to have—ostensibly—been a ruse, the wife pure after all. Even though this may not be true, from the husbands' perspective it does not matter; the change is wrought in them when they see themselves cuckolded and are liberated from the anxiety of enforcing monogamy.

Thus, in the resolution of *The Antipodes,* the potentially reproductive heterosexual consummation that is supposed to furnish the normativizing ends of the play and the play within a play actually (like Peregrine) fulfills its function in a hilariously roundabout, hyperbolically multiplied and mediated fashion. First, it is not a dyadic sex act. The stage is crowded with bodies whose movements and speech and exertions are all required as part of a massive communal effort to get a single sex organ in (or near!) another sex organ. The crowded quality of the sex does not by itself depart from a contemporary sexual norm. Rather, heterosexuality called for a good deal of publicity and communal interest in sex and reproduction in early modern England, including gossip, surveillance, and festivity around the consummation of marriages.[105] In a way, sex is most crowded at its most socially normative: in ordinary, non-Antipodean, straight wedding ceremonies, which are also communal acts of theater coordinated to facilitate the completion of heterosexual sex. But Traub observes that through its intensively sexualized performances and metaperformances of voyeurism, *The Antipodes* comes particularly "close to making sex public."[106] Theatrical artifice works on Peregrine's desire by pointing up and making bizarrely, hyperbolically explicit the ritual functions that are implicit in the wedding ceremony (the creation of a bounded, ritual time and space, special dress, narrative trappings giving the illusion that the groom has won the bride through conquest). What queers this act of communally effectuated sex is the sheer excess of its metatheatrical ruse, and the antisocial refusal it aims to cure.

The spectacle has to compensate for fact that the marital sex act has not happened at the right dramatic moment; it is three years overdue. Just as Peregrine's reading habit failed to conform to the normative balance of public and ideational pleasures, in marriage he has failed to link the public rite to the expected genital activity. The cure by drama must layer illusions of time travel and spatial displacement on top of this delay. It only works if it can stimulate and sustain the fantasy that the sex is not what it is—that Peregrine is not where he is or when he is, and that his wife is not who she is. All of this ludic artifice adds up to a climax that dramatically denaturalizes the male penetrative act at the center of patriarchy, making it a joke. This sex is *theatrically* queer. It is brought about not by masculine action but by time-bending drug trips, elaborate deceptions, and art that points up its own artifice. It depends on fantastic noblemen who flout sumptuary customs and own troupes of players for their own pleasure; secret sexual instruction and group sex in spare rooms; self-referential love letters to the theater; overstuffed wardrobe closets and overblown verbal styles; and—creepily, presciently—sneaky uses of emergent discourses of the mind to make a space for desires that would have no way to find expression otherwise. (There is

another available reading of *The Antipodes* as an early psychothera-
peutic narrative that would point up other ambivalences in the text,
such as working-through versus conversion and aversion models, and
the open question of therapy's normativizing agenda.) The play's cure
by drama can be seen as a collective act of professional (indentured?)
therapeutic sex work through role-playing; and the Doctor's services
a perverse form of sadomasochistic sex therapy, offering not a cuck-
olding fantasy but the real thing.

Furthermore, even in the actual bedchamber, there is evidence
that the couple is not alone. Barbara is there. Indeed, she confirms
that she thinks penetration was accomplished, "not fathom-deep, I
think, but to the scantling/Of a child-getting, I dare well imagine"
(5.1.28–29). It is fair to wonder how close an onlooker would have to
be to know this; it invites us to imagine that Barbara is a participant
in the consummation itself, effecting it and making it a threesome.
This instrumental relational mode will be examined in much greater
detail in chapter 1. However, Doctor Hughball is there too, super-
vising the conjugal relations—making it easy to expand the possible
triad by imagining that the two facilitators accompanied, or perhaps
demonstrated for, the married couple. The father's sickness and his
cure are also simultaneous with Peregrine's therapeutic sojourn; their
wives are even the same age. Though they have different manifest
content, Peregrine's neurosis around reading and sex shares a structure with his father's paranoid jealousy: travel literature and cuck-
olding anxiety, respectively, expand into fixations that consume all
available space. This can, notably, be read as an early representation
of a psychodynamic, rather than humoral or spiritual, transmission of
mental patterns between parents and children.

Ironically, after using his travel obsession to avoid sex, Peregrine ends up traveling—after a fashion—to have sex, in a dysfunctional inversion of the exotic travel trope. The sexual conquest that is
supposed to have been his domestic patriarchal right (and obligation)
can only take place in an imaginary space: a multiply delusional
state of chemical alteration, pretended displacement, theatrical illusion, fake conquest, and mock marriage, all in order to sexually possess his own wife. In sum, the climactic sex in *The Antipodes* may be
the queerest act of heterosexual intercourse in early modern drama.

Even as the play moves toward its end, consummation is not brought about by making people want the right things, or by disciplining them out of their odd desires. The ineradicable queerness of how desire works is allowed to stand, and is integral to the resolution.

The Shape of Things to Come

The four chapters that follow each draw on dramatic features found in *The Antipodes* to interrogate the categories of "queer" and "erotic" as they come unmoored from individual human subjects. The first chapter, "Getting Used, and Liking It," takes up the desire to be made instrumental to others' erotic ends in two comedies where a supposedly heterosexual couple cannot do it alone. They use an ambiguously gendered third party as an erotic go-between, effecting dynamics that turn out not to be "straight," or even dyadic, at all. In Beaumont and Fletcher's tragicomedy *Philaster, or Love Lies a-Bleeding*, the passionately instrumentalized, secretly cross-dressed servant boy, called Bellario, is used as a communications device to transmit desire between the hero, Philaster, and the princess, Arethusa. The chapter juxtaposes Bellario's submissive ecstasy at being used against the transgressive erotic prowess of Mary Frith, the real-life masculine woman known as Moll Cutpurse, embodied onstage in Thomas Middleton and Thomas Dekker's *The Roaring Girl* (1611). These queer go-betweens get used, with their willing and enthusiastic participation, as technologies of affective and erotic transmission, effectively becoming prosthetic sexual instruments with an attraction and agency of their own, all the more potent for their virtuosity as both tools and objects. This chapter also touches on the queer excesses that result when a ruse is concocted to cure desire by surfeit—in this case a wayward son's announcement of the notorious genderqueer cutpurse, the Roaring Girl, as his intended bride.[107] Moll Cutpurse accomplishes the heterosexual couple's union—with the son's actual fiancée dressed in menswear from Moll's tailor—largely through the phobic disturbances that her gender and sexuality incite in the forbidding father of the groom.

Being made instrumental is a queer relational mode that expands our understanding of early modern erotic dynamics beyond more commonly understood notions of service or triangulation. Instrumentality subverts the binary distinctions between agency and passivity, man and woman, servant and master, lover and beloved, natural and artificial; it ultimately calls into question the definition of sex as an act that involves only two people, or only human bodies. Considering three-way, instrumentalizing erotic bonds as forms of queer relationality opens up the possibility of noticing other erotic groupings in literature, including group erotic configurations that include some instances of heteroeroticism as part of a larger queer erotic structure, and collectivities composed of a mix of taboo and uncensured eroticisms (e.g., the vectors of queer identification and desire among ex-suitors, siblings, and new spouses that is preserved as a four-way love relationship at the end of *Twelfth Night*). All of this yields a picture of early modern eros that allows us to consider female, male, cross-gendered, and more complexly gendered desires as part of the same erotic system.

Peregrine's bottomless appetite for reading finds structural echoes in chapter 2, "Everything That Moves," in which promiscuous desires or fancies, although they may be marked with sexual and gendered meanings, nonetheless spread out to infuse the entire structure of the comedies in which they operate. This chapter takes up the insatiable, all-consuming desire for too many objects at once, embodied by the ravenous man-child Bartholomew Cokes and the equally ravenous, self-disavowing Puritan Zeal-of-the-Land Busy who rampage through Ben Jonson's *Bartholomew Fair* (1614); and by the perpetually dissatisfied Duke Orsino, whose desire is the central problem in William Shakespeare's *Twelfth Night* (1601). It examines how the indiscriminate appetites of capricious fancy and voracious hunger give rise to queer economies of generation in both the material and aesthetic realms. Bartholomew Cokes's abortive wedding day rampage through the Fair, destroying what he cannot buy or incorporate within himself, is read as a kind of antireproductive, uncontained queer hunger that can be considered through Freud's notion of non–heterosexually differentiated polymorphous perversity, or even Leo Bersani's defiantly antisocial queer appetites.[108] The insatiable model of desire in this chapter is predicated on lack: it grows by feeding on itself, proceeding out of lack and back into lack again. I juxtapose Cokes with *Twelfth Night*'s Orsino, both of whom are bottomless vortices of want. If they attain something they seek, then they instantly desire something else; they do not know what they want, and they want everything—except marriage with an appropriate woman. Rather than commodities in the market, the goods Orsino desires are courtly service and masculine friendship, but the libidinal orientation figured in his speeches is a similarly proliferative lack. His endlessly impressionable romantic "fancy" operates according to an asexual mechanism of fantastical generativity that produces only more and more mercurial desires.

My reading of *Twelfth Night* brings to light an historical connection between the psychic and material/aesthetic realms of desire. I trace how the language of "fancy," which in the 1500s means the ability to conjure imaginary forms—particularly artistic objects—in the mind's eye, shifts in meaning over the next three centuries to a term that denigrates aesthetic and ornamental desires as unproductive, effeminate, and sexually suspect. I trace the afterlife of early modern fancy not to solve for the origins of its pejorative connotations, but in the belief that words are thick with constantly changing resonances (in Dimock's sense, traveling frequencies), which lexicographers only incompletely and belatedly record, and that looking at the circulations of affect around a word can make visible surprising convergences and valences of meaning unrecoverable by empirical means.[109] In tracing out the erotic mechanisms of which Orsino and Bartholomew Cokes are early avatars, I uncover an emergent economy for the production and reproduction of desire in which prodigious consumption functions as capitalism's monstrous, queer double of sexual reproduction.

With the third and fourth chapters, this book takes a dark turn. The systems of communal pleasure produced in the commercial theater give way to two historical affective systems founded in projection and violence: witch hunts and colonialism. Chapter 3, "It Takes One to Know One," unpacks the erotic structure of the early modern witch hunt through two key examples of sensationalistic popular literature from the witch trials that roiled Scotland and England from the 1590s through the 1620s. The final chapter, "Lost Worlds, Lost Selves," takes up documents of failed Protestant colonial ventures in the Atlantic: Jean de Léry's sojourn to the doomed French colony in Brazil, and Thomas Herriot's and John White's willfully projective reports and images from the already lost English venture at Roanoke. The desires explored in *The Shapes of Fancy* thus progress from more positive affects—from the mutually gratifying stance of getting used; through the roving, insatiable energies of fancy and the double-edged ambivalence of free-floating lack—to the negative affects of paranoia and melancholia. These last two chapters turn away from straightfor-wardly erotic or relational desires organized around gratification (the go-between's satisfaction in a specific way of being used; the vora-cious desirers who want to consume everything and nothing). Rather, they address the erotic dynamics animating entire discursive systems of knowledge production (about witches, and about Native American people) in scenes of profound historical violence against gendered and raced bodies.

This turn to violence is politically unfamiliar and uncomfort-able. Since its reclamation as an activist rallying cry circa 1990, "queer" has often been defined by its liberatory political force. Its earliest theoretical explications detail its potential to expand the ambit of what sexual politics can disrupt and change about the world: heteronormativity, wider realms of cultural production, subcultural survival, canon formation, pedagogy, political dissent, work, nation-alism, the family, the ideology of everyday life.[110] "Queer" has had such a productive and varied life as a term of opposition to structures of power that it has, in many contexts, been difficult or impossible to notice moments in texts where it does something besides contesting norms—moments where a turn of desire that can be called queer affect or queer eros is implicated with, even constitutive of, the ap-paratus of historical power and violence.[111] It has happened, though, and it keeps happening. It happened in the nineteenth century, in the homoerotic and colonialist discourses through which European men enjoyed and consumed the bodies of young brown men and boys.[112] It happens today, in popular culture's love and theft of styles, traditions, dance moves, gestures, and linguistic forms from Black and Latinx queer and trans street and nightlife subcultures.[113] It is perpetually visible in the telltale mix of paranoid homoerotic investment, dis-avowal, and projective rage that is the calling card of the secretly gay-desiring homophobe, an affective genealogy that includes the persecutory master-at-arms John Claggart in Melville's *Billy Budd* (1924); the belligerent Roy Cohn, lawyer to Joseph McCarthy and Donald Trump; and too many antigay clergymen and politicians to name.[114] And, as I argue in the second half of this book, we can see it happening in early modern texts. As the critical purchase and political stakes of queer and other antihomophobic rubrics are being debated in new ways (for example, Jasbir Puar's intervention naming deployments of queer rights and queer liberation in the service of imperialist politics as "homonationalism"), it is vital to attend to the sexist, racist, and colonialist shapes taken by queer erotic energies through history, confronting head-on the complicated intertwinings of power, violence, and desire.[115]

In probing the queer dynamics of early modern historical violence, the second half of *The Shapes of Fancy* departs from England and moves into the transnational context, in which fears of difference and the threat of foreignness are primary drivers of twisted erotic affect. It introduces two genres of writing, witch pamphlets and colonial voyage narratives, that brought new forms of desire into England from elsewhere, as alluring and threatening objects for English readers' and audiences' delectation. Chapter 3, "It Takes One to Know One," turns to Scotland, recounting the production of the witch as an "internal other" in *Newes from Scotland* (1591), a popular pamphlet from the Edinburgh witch panic of 1590, which took place under the rule (and with the invested participation) of James VI (later James I). The chapter goes on to examine a later English witch, Elizabeth Sawyer, whose story is dramatized in John Ford, Thomas Dekker, and William Rowley's true-life domestic tragedy *The Witch of Edmonton* (1621). In *Newes from Scotland*'s account of the presumptive witches' detection, torture, and fantastic confessions (including a Sabbath meeting with the devil, storm-raising necromancy, and plots against the king's life), and in *The Witch of Edmonton*'s dramatization of the framing process leading up to Sawyer's trial and execution, I describe how the affective machinery of paranoid suspicion produces a witch as a kind of queer figure, defined by the deviant, blasphemous, seductive, and rebellious desires projected onto her, who must be abjected from the community in death. The witch hunt scene is, like the theatrical cure in *The Antipodes,* a dramatic technology for the correction of desire—not only the desires of the wayward and/or unlucky subjects taken up in its machinery, but the social desires of a whole community. It is also a purpose-driven dramatic system that collectively stokes specific fantasies in order to produce a certain kind of subject (in *The Antipodes,* a heterosexually functional husband; here, a witch). The dramatic drive of the witch hunt is to create something—a witch—out of the whole cloth of communal conflict and ideation. That the thing it seeks to produce never existed is no obstacle. One of the chief lessons of this book is that desire can produce anything.

This chapter goes on to link the projective dynamics of witch production to a larger history of sexual secrets and sexual persecution. The question of why and how the witch hunt is so effective in producing witchcraft confessions and the names of more implicated witches is directly, topically connected to the history of queerphobic paranoia, most memorably in the twentieth-century witch hunts for communists—and crucially, inextricably, for homosexuals—staged in the House Un-American Activities Committee and the Senate hearings of Joseph McCarthy. The paranoid suspicion that powers the witch trials is not so much a queer desire as a queer-producing and queer-persecuting mechanism of power. My argument here draws on the work of Eve Kosofsky Sedgwick, in dialogue with the object-relations psychoanalytic theory of Melanie Klein, to define paranoia as a projective form of interpretation based in negative affect, which attributes the secret malice it fears in itself to others, and thus often discursively brings about the very thing it suspects. I use Klein's notion of part-objects to describe how the paranoid desire of the witch panic is routed through the everyday things—ropes, razors, hairs, musical instruments, cats, dogs, straw, scraps of soiled linen—that function as uncannily effective tools, both of witchcraft and of witch finding, materializing the persecutory anxieties of others and projecting them onto the body of the accused. What Sedgwick calls "paranoid reading" also shapes *The Witch of Edmonton*'s second plot, a violent, seemingly unrelated tale of bigamy that runs parallel to the witch plot. The bigamy plot also produces a kind of queer figure—

a bigamist rather than a witch—by dramatizing the construction and collusive maintenance of a secret, deviant erotic identity. Reading the bigamy plot alongside the witchcraft plot vividly illuminates that the basis of the witch hunt's paranoid erotics is secret sexual deviance— specifically the communal investment in using suspicions of witchcraft to occlude, then rectify, all of the other deviant desires (including, in this chapter: bigamy, master/servant rape, inheritance fraud, fornication, murder, treason, heresy, bestiality, and sodomitical group sex with the devil) whose allure must be kept at bay.

The fourth chapter, "Lost Worlds, Lost Selves," moves into the Atlantic world, taking up the melancholic tone of belatedness and thwarted desire that suffuses two accounts of failed New World colonial ventures: Jean de Léry's account of the short-lived French Huguenot colony in Brazil, *Histoire d'un voyage* (1578); and Thomas Harriot and John White's reports from the failed English colony at Roanoke, *A Briefe and True Report of the New Found Land of Virginia* (1590). I argue that in these texts' representations of Native American people and things, we can detect a distinctly queer and melancholic form of colonial desire, which bodies forth fantastical ideations of nonlinear, nonbiological models of relationality across time. I read Jean de Léry's affectively overwrought narrative, saturated with homoerotic and cross-cultural longing, in which he (favorably) compares the bodies, customs, and ceremonies of the Tupinamba Indian men—his obsession—to those of the French, as voicing a queer colonial melancholia predicated on excessive identification and loss. In Léry's *Histoire,* as in Harriot and White's accounts, ethnographic technologies of description are deployed in the service of a futile, impossible affective end: to keep, hold onto, memorialize, create for public consumption, and even become something once present that is now lost (and that was never there in the exact, projectively fantastical form in which the European interlopers imagine it): the Tupinamba and Algonkian societies the voyagers have irreversibly, genocidally altered with their presence, however brief and foreclosed. What these documents narrate is the loss of a fantasy akin to Peregrine's: the longing to be elsewhere, to live otherwise; the fantasy of another self, as imagined through the eyes of a lost, unpossessed other. They register the would-be colonizer's longing for an impossible transformation into something he could never become in order to have something he could never have.

Like paranoia, melancholia is an erotic stance with a particularly vexed relation to the truth, reality, or presence of the love object. That is, both are investments in objects that were never really there exactly as imagined. The collective social apparatus of the witch hunt needs the witch to exist in the same way as the failed colonizer needs his perfect foil, the lost American other, to continue to be accessible to him. The impossibility of both these desires provides the narrative fuel for their respective genres of print literature. My reading of colonial desire in this chapter draws on Frantz Fanon's and Homi Bhabha's analyses of colonialism's fraught psychic conflicts between identification and difference, self and other, affecting the colonizer as well as the colonized.[116] My readings of Léry, Harriot, and White uncover strange resonances of affiliation and eruptions of longing, like Peregrine's, for things to be otherwise—for another role to play, another possible outcome, another time and place in which the narrators could inhabit other relational modes, whose impossibility cannot even be mourned. These Protestant texts from early moments of failed and abandoned colonial ambition ultimately make visible how melancholia, the persistence of identification with the unmournable other in memory, is constitutive of the construction of whiteness and heterosexuality, just as it infuses the construction of gender. Far from being righted and resocialized, as Peregrine is, the voyage writers in this chapter face the absence of anything like resolution. Instead, their accounts spin colonial longing into impossible imagined futures whose echoes continue to haunt the racial politics of the present. I conclude by drawing an analogy between the affective load borne by colonial voyagers' invested, melancholic ethnography—epitomized in the surreal queer genealogy that John White constructs through the ornate portraits of ancient Picts in his coda to the Virginia text—and the equally fantastical, identificatory investments we bear as modern critics to early modern texts. In the conclusion, "The Persistence of Fancy," I ponder the queer political potential of readerly love under current austerity conditions in American higher education.

This is a book about interpretation—what we see, what has

gone unseen, and how both are conditioned by a host of subjective desires, investments, and historical positionalities. It is a book about how to go about looking for important things that are hard to see, and an intervention into some of the methodological, disciplinary, and political norms that have made certain things harder to see and name, and others easier. It uses queer theory and early modern literature to perform some of the functions of queer theory (generating new, transportable paradigms with which to think) and some of the functions of literary criticism (close readings that bring out new resonances in old texts). Its argumentative mode is speculative and experimental; its sustaining fantasy is of a community of readers who will learn different things from reading it than I have learned writing it. And its act of faith is that reading for desire can further complicate what we think we know about historical difference, sex, feeling, and time, bodying forth new, politically vital demands and affinities between readers and the objects of our critical investment and love.

1

Getting Used, and Liking It

Erotic Instrumentality and the Go-Between

Oh my god, she used me. I was used . . . I was *used! Cool!*
—*American Pie* (1999)

In two very different cross-dressing comedies from the first decade of
the seventeenth century—Thomas Middleton and Thomas Dekker's
rollicking city comedy *The Roaring Girl* (1611), and Francis Beaumont and John Fletcher's wrenching, hilarious tragicomedy *Philaster,
or Love Lies a-Bleeding* (c. 1610), the couple at the center of the
romance plot cannot do it alone. Two lovers need, commission, and
use an ambiguously gendered third party to negotiate the social, affective, and sexual demands of their prohibited love match. In both
plays, the messenger who serves as a conduit for their love is an androgynous figure whose gender presentation is at odds in some way
with their bodily sex. In *The Roaring Girl,* a young aristocrat, whose
love match with a girl of modest means is forbidden by his father,
brings in his friend, the notorious real-life cross-dresser and cutpurse Mary Frith, aka Moll Cutpurse, or the Roaring Girl, as a sham
fiancée to show his father now much worse it could be. In *Philaster,* Princess Arethusa and the beloved Prince Philaster love each
other, but Arethusa's tyrannical father has usurped Philaster's throne
and promised her in marriage to a boorish foreign prince, forcing
the lovers to conduct their secret love under the watchful eyes of
the court. The messenger who serves as a conduit for their love is
an ambiguously gendered, beautiful servant boy who is secretly a

girl, Bellario (belatedly renamed Euphrasia). Both of these queerly gendered characters are positioned, with their enthusiastic consent, as go-betweens. They act as instruments to facilitate the couple's sexual union while also becoming an integral part of it, transforming the ostensibly heterosexual marriages (the supposed ends of comedy) in both plays into three-way intimate relationships routed through a queer third party. This chapter elucidates the particular pleasures of getting used in this way, and liking it. By analyzing how the cross-dressed go-between transmits and generates affect, knowledge, and desire—and how it definitively alters the erotic configurations in which it participates—I demonstrate that being made instrumental can be regarded as a queer mode of relation, one that can expand our thinking about early modern sexuality and its representations in literature.[1]

My call to attend to the affective nuances of relational dynamics in drama is particularly important at the current moment in sexual politics, when same-sex desires are becoming increasingly normativized even as gender identity is becoming widely understood in more of its complexity. What, exactly, does it mean to say that a bond between a man, a woman, and a boy—or between a man, a woman, and a roaring girl—is queer? Is queerness strictly a matter of the genders—or number—of the partners involved, or can it inhere in more stylistic or structural features? Both Bellario in *Philaster* and Moll in *The Roaring Girl* confound the polar, gendered power dynamics that are usually assumed to structure both same- and opposite-sex encounters in the period: user/used, subject/object, agent/recipient, active/passive, master/servant, giver/taker, and dominant/submissive. Both figures' queer appeal inheres in their androgyny—Bellario's eerie beauty, Moll's prodigious gender hybridity—and in their virtuosic linguistic performance. Their eloquent affective output extends their respective plays' erotic economies—and offers readers and audiences a way to apprehend them—beyond the logics of anatomical sex and gender identity by which homo- and heteroerotic bonds alike have usually been categorized.

By articulating how instrumentality works as a mode of erotic relation in these two plays, which are not usually compared, I advance a set of techniques for recognizing it when it appears elsewhere, across other texts and genres. Reading these two characters through an erotics of getting used makes visible the dramatic moments in these plays and others, such as John Lyly's *Gallathea* (1592), Shakespeare's *Troilus and Cressida* (1602), and Richard Brome's *The Antipodes* (1638, discussed in the introduction), where erotic dynamics pull away from social categories; where heteroerotic and queer desires come into unexpected contact; and where desire operates athwart of gender in ways that disturb previous critical assumptions about what sex and love look like, and what constitutes queerness in early modern literature. Whereas *Philaster* turns out to be a play about innocence misread, *The Roaring Girl* is a play about the uses of sexual dissidence when it is hyperbolically legible and public. But both hinge, as *Troilus and Cressida* and *Gallathea* also hinge, and as *The Antipodes* playfully problematizes, on fathers' attempts to dictate children's sexual interactions, and on the erotic possibilities circulating around and outside of social norms. These disparate instantiations of the instrumental relational mode demonstrate its variety and flexibility; the central role of patriarchal prohibition in creating the conditions that bring it about; and the varying kinds of risk, violence, and paranoid suspicion that can attend it.

"A Pretty, Sad-Talking Boy"

Beaumont and Fletcher make the erotics of being instrumentalized the hinge of the play's dilated love triangle plot. The collaborating authors' own storied, queer friendship serves as an interesting comparison to these dynamics in the play. The two men famously "lived together on the Banke side, not far from the Play-house, both batchelors," and "lay together," in a relation of social and romantic intimacy described as "a wonderfull consimility of phansey . . . which caused the dearnesse of friendship between them."[2] Their domestic and affective bond (as described thirdhand, by outside onlookers—a perspective that will also prove salient to *Philaster*'s plot) is not only dyadic; their intimacy also appears to be furthered and facilitated by a third (they "had one wench in the house between them, which they did so admire") and by clothing ("the same cloathes and cloake, &c., betweene them").[3]

My reading of *Philaster* starts from the contention that the queerness of such relations can exceed the binary gender designations of the participants—that Beaumont and Fletcher's arrangement is queer for additional reasons besides that both are men, and that Philaster and Arethusa's bond, triangulated through Bellario, is queer in some of the same ways. Relatively little scholarship exists on *Philaster*, especially compared to the wealth of criticism on more widely read cross-dressing comedies such as Shakespeare's *Twelfth Night* (1602) or, for that matter, *The Roaring Girl*; but the work that does exist focuses mostly on political and ideological questions of transgression rather than on desire.[4] I read *Philaster* here as a play about the transmission and legibility of eros and affect—about the pleasures and difficulties of communicating one's true heart to another, and the dangers of being misread by others, both inside and outside the relationship.

Early on in the play, Arethusa asks her exiled lover how they will communicate, how they can "devise/To hold intelligence" between them.[5] Philaster suggests, as a solution, the use of his secret servant boy as a message bearer:

> I have a boy,
> Sent by the gods, I hope, to this intent,
> Not yet seen in the court. (1.2.111–13)

Thus the inaugural conditions of the plot dictate that the two lovers' exchange of "intelligence" cannot occur directly or naturally. They must "devise" to use Bellario as a mediating technology for "holding" and conducting affection between them. But unbeknownst to Philaster, or to any of the other characters in the play, and presumably to the audience as well, Philaster's boy was originally a girl named Euphrasia, who earlier disguised herself as a boy in hopes of being taken up as Philaster's servant. In being so used, this secretly cross-dressed servant boy, Bellario, becomes erotically instrumental, the play's central object and carrier of desire.

This boy, whom Philaster has kept hidden from the court,

seems not quite natural or human, unmarked by any social context except for his unabashed devotion to Philaster and desire to be used to his ends. Philaster explains that while out hunting, he found this "pretty, sad-talking boy" (2.3.7) weeping by a fountain. He is accessorized with an elaborately braided flower garland, which he gazes at, weeps over, and fondles in a semiprivate ritual as he tells his story to Philaster (who reminisces about this meeting to the princess):

> A garland lay him by, made by himself,
> Of many several flowers bred in the vale,
> Stuck in that mystic order that the rareness
> Delighted me. But ever when he turned
> His tender eyes upon 'em, he would weep
> As if he meant to make 'em grow again. (1.2.117–22)

Bellario's garland is more than a piece of handiwork. It has a "mystic order"; its "rare" form represents specific content. The garland materializes affect by encoding it in an abstract symbolic language, which the boy interprets to Philaster and Philaster interprets in turn to Arethusa:

> Then took he up his garland, and did show
> What every flower, as country people hold,
> Did signify, and how all, ordered thus,
> Expressed his grief, and to my thoughts did read
> The prettiest lecture of his country art
> That could be wished, so that, methought, I could
> Have studied it. (1.2.130–36)

The boy's signal feature, besides his beauty and his blankness, is his "art": his uncanny ability to translate affective states like grief and love into systems of signification, to create and interpret meaning through aesthetic form. The flower garland's intricate design, or "order," which implicates it in a folk tradition of artistic and social symbols, makes it an index through which the boy can "read" his interior grief, love, and pleasure—through which he can, vitally, bring feelings into speech. The garland and the speech together constitute an act of aesthetic production, which adheres to a set of formal conventions in order to communicate interior content.

From Philaster's secondhand recounting, Bellario's speech echoes Ophelia's famous flower speech in *Hamlet*, in which Ophelia articulates specific affects to specific flowers ("There's rosemary: that's for remembrance. Pray,/love, remember. And there is pansies: that's for thoughts," etc.).[6] Bellario's speech, however, is far from mad; it is the epitome of premeditated "order," its signifiers scintillatingly effectual in bringing about its speaker's desired affective ends. In fact, Bellario's garland is a key to reading this play as a meditation on being made instrumental. The garland enacts the function that the boy will fulfill for Philaster and Arethusa. Bellario takes it up as he himself will be "taken up," a moment that will be remembered again at the end of the play when he, now transformed into she, reminisces about her desire to become an instrument and her use of artifice to actualize it. Like the character called Bellario, the garland is a purpose-made invention that materializes desire in highly stylized form, making it legible—and generating mutual, complementary emotions and desires in others. The boy's performance here, a seductive act of art and criticism ("the prettiest lecture . . . that could be wished"), incites intense pleasure in Philaster, engendering a dynamic of shared, mirror-image affects in master and boy:

> I gladly entertained him,
> Who was glad to follow, and have got
> The trustiest, lovingest, and the gentlest boy
> That ever master kept. Him will I send
> To wait on you, and bear our hidden love. (1.2.136–40)

The complementary pleasures of their respective roles—the distinct senses in which they are glad to "entertain" and to be entertained; the bond that makes this "gentlest boy" the logical vessel to "bear" Philaster's "hidden love"—seem to grow out of mutual pleasure and curiosity, with Philaster as audience/pupil and Bellario as artist/teacher of the feelings written in the flower garland. This affective exchange is generated in and mediated through both the garland and the boy's acts of creation, interpretation, and expression with it, metonymically illustrating how the boy will be used by the couple. He is not merely a messenger bearing erotic content; he is also a generator of that content, desired as the messenger and the message in one. His function will be to "bear" their love, which carries a triple meaning: to carry, as a messenger bears a message; to gestate and give birth, as a mother bears a child; and to accommodate receptively, as a passive sexual partner—or any recipient of an action—bears being acted upon. The overlapping processes of transmitting, making, and receiving desire are folded here into a single instrument: the body of the boy.

In an important sense, the boy becomes, like his flower garland, a thing used in the service of Philaster's pleasure. Being made instrumental in this way does not, however, suggest a lack of investment in how he gets used. It is significant to Bellario's role as the erotic catalyst of the play that before we see him onstage, we hear his desire, ventriloquized by his closest intimate: his disquisition on his feelings, and his gladness "to follow."[7] Thanks to the boy's virtuosic talents of signification, Philaster's reading of him is perfect; in being taken up into Philaster's service the boy is attaining what makes him "glad": "to follow" and to "bear" a "hidden love." This is far from an inert or subordinated position. The word "instrumental" describes a thing used to effect a desired end,[8] a thing fashioned or made to fit a specific purpose (a meaning it shares with "performance"),[9] and a necessary, integral component without which the whole desired end could not come about.[10] Bellario's instrumentality weaves together all three of these coexisting definitions.

The instrumentalized go-between is marked by an ambiguous or undecided sex. Bellario functions onstage as a boy right up until the moment at the end of the play when he dramatically regenders himself and becomes Euphrasia, a transformation that furnishes the play's last-minute swerve from incipient tragedy to comedy. He is instead she, and therefore cannot have committed the crime of which she stands accused with Arethusa, since penetration (the only act the play's disciplinary apparatus can imagine as sexual) is taken to require the presence of an anatomical male. The girl Euphrasia's cross-dressing—in fact, his passing and functioning as a boy—becomes the crucial fact that, in hindsight, alters the sexual economy of the play. Yet I want to insist on the productivity of reading Bellario/Euphrasia's gender and erotic functioning as the play presents him/her—as a boy, but as a boy whose gender will be, or has retroactively been, supercharged by the revelation of cross-dressing that will come at the end. In fact, as Jeffrey Masten has pointed out, the text's construction of Bellario is gender ambiguous at the outset, in that various printed editions of the play present the character in a variety of "hybrid" or "dissonant" ways via character listings and speech prefixes.[11] Thus the possible knowledge of Bellario's female sex may exist, for audiences (and, as Masten describes, in even more detailed ambiguity for readers), in constant tension with his dramatic presentation as a boy. Once the play had begun its life in performance (1610) and then in print (1620), the audience's knowingness or unknowingness of the character's so-called "true" sex would have become an unknown dimension of its reception. As a titillating secret about the play, the gender twist might have circulated in the form of hints or spoilers, or it might even be insinuated in tacit associations with Ophelia in the flower speech. In light of the way gender is made and unmade at the center of the plot, reading Bellario's regendering back through the play gives every scene in which he appears the potential for a skewed, doubled libidinal significance: the one the play stages, with Bellario as a servant boy, and the one that an audience or reader may or may not know in advance, with Bellario as a cross-dressed girl. This retrospective reading practice serves to highlight the doubled quality of gender itself, by pointing up the extreme deferral and curious inconsequence of the gender reveal, and the lingering queerness of the resolution.

More permanently gender ambiguous than the girls who temporarily disguise themselves as boys in comedies where cross-dressing is a plot device, most famously William Shakespeare's *As You Like It* (1599) and *Twelfth Night* (1602), Bellario—and in a different respect, as I will argue, Moll Frith in *The Roaring Girl*—is a character whose masculine yet androgynous gender performance does not line up exactly with his ostensibly female bodily sex. Unlike heroines such as Rosalind or Viola, who don men's clothing onstage as a disguise that is part of the dramatic action, Bellario/Euphrasia is dressed as a boy for the entire play, including the final scene (where the play ends minutes after the gender revelation). More than merely cross-dressed, he is a passing masculine androgyne with an affective orientation toward both the man and the woman in the couple. Bellario confesses to being a woman not even to save his own life, but only when continuing to pass as male is about to cost Philaster's and Arethusa's lives—when, under suspicion of having had sex with the princess, Bellario is sentenced to be tortured by Philaster, who must repeatedly be restrained from stabbing himself rather than carry out the sentence. Bellario only outs himself to prevent his master's suicide and his mistress's condemnation—and then only in a secret revelation to his amazed father, Dion. When Dion brings Bellario back to the group and reveals "it is a woman," the character who is now Euphrasia explains that her transformation into Bellario was undertaken for the furtherance of her own ends, to effect maximum intimacy with Philaster given the handicap of her low birth. The character voices a passion so immanently overcoming that it led her to shed one identity and take on a new one:

> My blood flew out and back again as fast
> As I had puffed it forth and sucked it in
> Like breath. (5.5.158–60)

Yet the ends of this desire are neither consummation—"You left a kiss/Upon these lips then which I mean to keep/From you forever" (5.5.163–65)—nor marriage—"Never, sir, will I/Marry. It is a thing within my vow" (5.5.186–87). The play makes a curious distinction between love and lust here, naming this passion "love,/Yet far from lust," because its aims are decidedly outside of the heterosexual dyad. Even at the end of the play, Bellario still does not desire marriage. His aim is not sexual union but proximity and service: "For could I but have lived/In presence of you I had had my end" (5.5.168–70).

"This Boy . . . Would Outdo Story"

The mutuality of pleasure, generated over a three-way connection, differentiates the erotics of being used from other instances of erotic triangulation in early modern drama. For instance, in the case of

Twelfth Night, perhaps the iconic example of a cross-dressed boy deputized as a go-between in a heterosexual courtship, the desires circulating among Orsino, Viola, and Olivia are not the queer triadic instrumentality I describe here. In *Twelfth Night*'s go-between scenes, the parties' desires are in conflict, at odds, concealed from each other, and obstructed by each other's utterances. Viola's cross-dressed flirtations with her master and his unwilling target, Olivia, are not structured by a three-way passion. Viola declares that her singular object choice is Orsino in an aside to the audience even as she agrees to serve as his romantic go-between: "Yet a barful strife!/ Whoe'er I woo, myself would be his wife" (1.4.41–42). This aside foretells the resolution of the plot even as it anticipates the roundabout "strife" of its comic dilation. The various longings of all three are decidedly not being mutually gratified by and through Viola's instrumentalization as Orsino's surrogate suitor. Unlike Arethusa, Olivia does not love the prince who sends her this boy. Instead, she is intent on prying the boy apart from his master, recasting Cesario not as a messenger but as a sexual subject in his own right, and reorienting his desire toward her. *Twelfth Night*'s group erotic dynamic is structured instead by the mechanism of perpetually unsatisfied, polymorphously confused desire, exemplified in Orsino's renunciation of women and marriage, which will be the focus of the next chapter.

What sets *Philaster*'s erotic configuration apart from disguise and triangulation plots like *Twelfth Night,* then, is the complete convergence between the desires of the instrumentalized boy and the desires he is being used to facilitate. Philaster fashions Bellario as the link that can "hold intelligence" (1.2.109) between himself and Arethusa. But as a self-fashioned, embodied communication technology, the desires Bellario so volubly transmits are also immanently his own. Being used *is* Bellario's decidedly not secret inward desire, his queer relational mode, which, as the action of the play unfolds, is all too easily interpreted as something far less queer, and far more dangerous.

Bellario's doubled capacity to be at once a desiring subject and a cipher for others' desires makes him the perfect erotic instrument, central to both the couple's "hidden love" and the play's erotic economy. In his transactions with the prince and princess, he is thoroughly acted upon and used. In his words, he is "nothing," a surrendered subject whose entire substance and meaning derives from Philaster: "Sir, you did take me up/When I was nothing, and only yet am something/By being yours" (2.1.5–7). Yet to say that he is given over to Philaster's desires is not—and this is the crux of instrumentality—to evacuate the character of erotic activity or agency. Bellario's service role is a creation of his desire. The scene in which Philaster sets up the go-between relationship tells the story of how the character's first object choice toward Philaster is transmuted into a three-way relation of being used. At first Bellario is inconsolable at being sent away to conduct Philaster's "hidden love." He pleads to be used more strictly in order to stay:

> What master holds so strict a hand
> Over his boy that he will part with him
> Without one warning? Let me be corrected
> To break my stubbornness—if it be so—
> Rather than turn me off, and I shall mend. (2.1.35–39)

Philaster's commissioning of Bellario as his and Arethusa's instrument complicates what had looked like a homosocial/homoerotic master/servant bond between a prince and his boy, extending the queer investment flowing both ways between them into a new and triadic shape:

> Thy love doth plead so prettily to stay
> That, trust me, I could weep to part with thee.
> Alas, I do not turn thee off. Thou knowest
> It is my business that doth call thee hence,
> And when thou art with her thou dwellest with me.
> (2.1.40–44)

Philaster answers Bellario's plea with his own admission of desire for the boy; moreover, he appeals to Bellario's desire for him, articulating the mutual payoff of Bellario's instrumentality—and the mutual pain of extending their intimacy. Philaster reassures him that this does not diminish their bond: "I do not turn thee off" implies that Bellario remains activated for Philaster as well. Note that Philaster says "when thou art with her thou dwellest with me," and not "when thou art with her I am with her." That is, he does not make his boy his agent or surrogate, emptying out Bellario's subjectivity in order to act by proxy upon Arethusa. Rather, Philaster posits his instrument, Bellario, as being in the same intersubjective relation to both Arethusa and himself. Their love seems to have a transitive property, according to which Arethusa will love Bellario in Philaster's place.

Deputized to communicate two parties' love to one another, the instrumental third instead communicates and receives his own love with both of them. He becomes the medium, the vital substance in which the couple's romantic connection lives, through his ability to engage in relations across gender difference and outside of social convention. Philaster's exquisitely overwrought commissioning of Bellario to serve as his erotic instrument is pointedly not a bond of homosocial "service," a relation predicated on power play with the differentiated roles of master and boy.[12] Instead, Bellario's paradoxically active, doubled function demonstrates that instrumentality is structurally queer, beyond the polar positions of dominance and submission. More than a mere intermediary, Bellario becomes the affective stylist of the relationship between Philaster and Arethusa, the generator of its tenor and its content. When Arethusa asks him if his master loves her, he responds with an elaborate recital of love's *affects*:

> If it be love
> To forget all respect to his own friends
> With thinking of your face; if it be love
> To sit cross-armed and think away the day,
> Mingled with starts, crying your name as loud
> As loud as men i' the streets do "Fire!";
> If it be love to weep himself away
> When he but hears of any lady dead
> Or killed, because it might have been your chance;
> [. . .]
> Then, madam, I dare swear he loves you. (2.3.48–60)

This picture of Philaster's supposed distraction, obsession, and compulsion appears, like the flower garland, to be Bellario's invention. The play represents Philaster's lovelorn affect only through Bellario's speech, which is structured like a flower garland in its iterated, ornamented series of conditionals. The speech is purpose-made to please Arethusa. She in turn enjoys its "cunning" for its own sake without worrying about its truth value: "Thou knowest a lie/That bears this sound is welcomer to me/Than any truth that says he loves me not" (2.3.61–64). But at the same time it is also saturated with the truth of Bellario's identification with, and lovesickness for, Philaster.

This speech traces a fine line between a dead serious rehearsal of the conventional affects of Petrarchan love and a subtle send-up of the extremity of those affects, combining earnestness and exaggeration in a highly aestheticized, melodramatic register. In other words, its style of wooing displays many of the hallmarks of what will come to be called camp style, a queer aesthetic that theatrically fuses elements of "the exaggerated, the fantastic, the passionate, and the naïve."[13] Bellario's hyperbolic Petrarchan images casting romantic love as self-annihilating pain and/or sympathy ("to weep himself away/When he but hears of any lady dead/Or killed, because it might have been your chance") hearken back to the death-bound language in which Arethusa and Philaster first declare their love, and to the recent Elizabethan past, exemplifying "the passionate, often hilarious antiquarianism" of camp.[14] Bellario's tone here corresponds to what Susan Sontag calls the "epicene style"—that is, high artifice. In Sontag's words, from her canonical 1964 essay "Notes on Camp," it is a style that shows, and effects, "the convertibility of 'man' and 'woman,' 'person' and 'thing.'"[15] There is substantial overlap here between the overwrought emotional rhetoric that is a generic feature of tragicomedy and Bellario's camp style. In fact, the way in which Beaumont and Fletcher's trademark excessive, self-referential tragicomic language functions in this play, as the signature affective dynamic of the three-way relationship at its center, opens up a new potential line of argument for the queerness of tragicomedy as a genre. Several of the hallmarks of tragicomedy described by Eugene M. Waith—not only the "distillation of emotion" and "sensationalism" that I note here, but also the centrality of "artifice" and the history of the genre's

degradation as "decadent," "trivial," and reactionary "debauchery"—
are immediately recognizable and resonant through queer history.[16]

Camp, according to Sontag, is also inherently citational:
"Camp sees everything in quotation marks."[17] We see this citation-
ality in Bellario's recital of a string of affects conventionally said to
indicate love, each set apart by the distancing "if it be love." Camp
citation, however, exceeds quotation to add its own gloss of extrav-
agance. Philaster remarks that Bellario's peculiar affective intensity
reads as even stranger than the familiar discourse, of which Philaster
has read, of boys' homoerotic devotion to their masters:

> The love of boys unto their lords is strange.
> I have read wonders of it, yet this boy
> For my sake—if a man may judge by looks
> And speech—would outdo story. (2.1.57–60)

Bellario's performances (and fabrications) of affection linguistically
"outdo" and overreach the preexisting conventional discourses of
love that they cite. But it is also the animated, instrumental way in
which Bellario effects connection between Arethusa, Philaster, and
himself that exceeds "story." He communicates a passion for being
instrumentalized that exceeds even the normal "strange" love of
other boys' submission to their masters. In its distinctiveness from
more storied contemporary forms of same-sex eros like service, Bellario's instrumentality is nonnormative in *how* it departs from affective and relational norms. The supererogatory excess of affect with
which Bellario outdoes story is a queer quality: not structured by a
received sexual role, it inheres instead in the fluid, multidirectional
currents of affective energy that structure this three-way relation.

"Hew Me Asunder"

This queer utopian triad goes all wrong when its embodied system
of affective communication breaks down. Bellario's preternatural
beauty is the object of court gossip, his "angel-like" looks compared to Hylas and Adonis and his extravagant clothing speculated
upon: "'Tis a sweet boy; how brave she keeps him!" (2.4.18–26).[18]

To women and men alike, his submissive and demure affect, and his intimate presence in the bedchamber where Arethusa clothes him in finery, are legible as an erotic bond. Rumors are spread, and given credence, that Arethusa is a "lascivious lady/That lives in lust with a smooth boy" (3.1.10–11), a "whore" (3.1.63). The implication of this libel is that Arethusa's indecent doings are clearly knowable and readable as a result of the unmistakable, universally irresistible significance of a handsome, "smooth" young boy. The question at issue is Arethusa's virginity and thus her value: under suspicion of having been deflowered, she is ordered to banish Bellario. This touches off a chain of misapprehensions. Philaster confronts Bellario in an interrogation laden with double meanings because the audience knows, while Bellario does not, that Philaster believes he has been betrayed: "O, Bellario,/Now I perceive she loves me. She does show it/In loving thee, my boy. She has made thee brave!" (3.1.156–58). The problem here, which Beaumont and Fletcher gleefully exploit for tragicomic pathos, is that the relationship between Bellario and Arethusa can be read in two ways: that they are sleeping together and thus betraying Philaster; or that he is serving as a romantic instrument, a go-between, and thus remaining faithful to them both. But those two possibilities look very much alike because both depend on the existence of an erotic charge between the princess and the "brave" young boy. The second, queer possibility slips too easily underneath the dominant, suspicious interpretation, the only one legible to the conventional and lasciviously minded courtiers.

Philaster attempts to prize knowledge of erotic acts from Bellario to guess at the nature of their bond: "Tell me, my boy, how doth the princess use thee?/For I shall guess her love to me by that" (3.1.168–69). He asks about each of her endearing touches: "What kind of language does she feed thee with?" (3.1.177); "And she strokes thy head?" (3.1.190); "And she does clap thy cheeks?" (3.1.191). But then he asks, "And she does kiss thee, boy? Ha?" with kissing marked as a border between acceptable and unacceptable contact for the go-between (3.1.192). When Bellario denies that Arethusa kisses him, Philaster, in a haze, appeals to a logic of surrogacy to trick a disclosure out of him, saying that *he* ordered Arethusa, if she loved him, to give herself to Bellario:

Why, then she does not love me. Come, she does;
I bade her do it; I charged her by all charms
Of love between us, by the hope of peace
We should enjoy, to yield to thee all delights
Naked, as to her lord; I took her oath
Thou shouldst enjoy her. Tell me, gentle boy,
Is she not parallelless? (3.1.195–201)

If these were the terms of the arrangement—which they are not—it would be the kind of triangulation described by Sedgwick, where a central homosocial and homoerotic bond is enacted through affective exchange with (and of) a woman.[19] Anxiety about this competing, rivalrous relational mode comes through in Philaster's question, "Is she not parallelless?" "Parallelless" is a word that boasts three pairs of parallel letters, two phallic and one curlicue. It means without an equal or counterpart, and it describes the precarious state in which all three lovers find themselves. The three-way bond is allergic to pairs and parallels; they threaten to throw it off balance, though it is paradoxically made up of three of them. If Arethusa is "not parallelless"—if she has had a "parallel" partner in bed—then she and Bellario are parallel traitors, Bellario and Philaster are parallel traffickers in women, and Arethusa is parallel to every common whore. The line between what Philaster wants and what he fears (or perhaps fantasizes) is razor thin; the dynamic of erotic instrumentality is too indeterminate, too subtle, too queer to be stable in its signifiers.[20] Indeed, the play's crisis of communication dramatizes just how tenuous the boundary is between queer instrumentality and many far less delicate forms of heterosexual (and homosocial) tragedy predicated on triangulation.

Arethusa and Bellario struggle, over the next three acts, to communicate some truth that Philaster will believe, flooding him with fabulously gruesome, hyperbolic fantasies of piercing, rending, opening, and sectioning their bodies, as though to reveal their desire there. "Hew me asunder, and whilst I can think/I'll love those pieces you have cut away/Better than those that grow, and kiss those limbs/Because you made 'em so" (3.1.245–48), cries Bellario when Philaster draws his sword (but cannot kill him). Arethusa wishes she could

"Make my breast/Transparent as pure crystal, that the world,/Jealous of me, may see the foulest thought/My heart holds" (3.2.130–33).[21] The play's obsession with the illegibility of interior feelings builds to a crisis around the opacity of both bodies and language, and their insufficiency to signify intimate bonds of love, loyalty, and desire.[22] The queer pathos of this miscommunication is that in a sense, Philaster is reading Bellario and Arethusa correctly: they do love each other. But not even a barrage of tour de force Beaumont and Fletcher tragicomic affect aimed at Philaster can get through to him that their intimacy centrally includes him. In the harsh collision of their alternative sign system with the codes of normative masculinity and patriarchy, he has forgotten how to read them, forgotten the beautiful, queer sign system into which he was initiated when he first saw Bellario weaving feelings into flowers (or flowers into feelings) by the fountain.

With the network of intimacy routed through Bellario broken, the three are powerless to transmit their love and pain to one another. When they all encounter one another wandering in the woods, each of them begs to be stabbed by the others in a desperate attempt to signify something of their old intimacy with one another, even if through annihilation. Philaster asks them both to stab him; Bellario refuses—the first time he seriously resists obedience. Philaster then stabs Arethusa, at her request; but before she can reciprocate, he is attacked by an intruding avatar of heteronormative masculinity, a "Cuntrie Gentellman" (who stabs Philaster, then tries to kiss the bleeding Arethusa). The wounded Philaster comes across Bellario asleep in the woods, and stabs him. Waking, ecstatic, to being stabbed—"Oh, death I hope is come! Blessed be that hand;/It meant me well. Again, for pity's sake!" (4.6.26–27)—Bellario takes the blame for stabbing Arethusa, offering his life in place of Philaster's. Finally convinced of Bellario's purely instrumental love, Philaster creeps out from under the bush where he's hiding and embraces him, forming the homoerotic "love lies a-bleeding" tableau of the play's subtitle.

After they survive their wounds, imprisonment, being sentenced to death (twice), an abortive wedding masque, and a political coup, the three lovers are nearly undone again at the end of the play by the persistent rumor of heterosexual sex between Arethusa and Bellario. Bellario is condemned to be tortured—and Philaster is condemned to do the torturing—to clear Arethusa's name; it is only Philaster's effort to stab himself instead that finally induces Bellario to confess to being Euphrasia. Bellario's sudden regendering puts the sexual accusations to rest, preventing tragedy; however, it also casts the protracted cycle of doubts, rejections, and stabbings in a new (exasperating, ridiculous) light. Philaster condemns it as "a fault" that Bellario declined to "discover" "what we now know" (5.5.146–50) when they were first accused. But it is more interesting to think of the play's entire overwrought tragicomic dilation as predicated on (indeed only possible because of) the fiction of Bellario's gender—and to think that from the perspective of the integral, instrumental third, it is a fiction worth maintaining *almost* to the death.

The only other example in early modern drama of such complete gender surprise, in which the audience is shocked by the gender unmasking of a character not previously suggested to be crossdressed, is Ben Jonson's *Epicoene, or The Silent Woman* (1609). In that play, the genders of the ruse are reversed. The silent woman of the title, who has been married to the old man Morose, is revealed in the last scene to be a beardless boy, and an instrumentalized boy at that—although not in the same willing, participatory sense in which Bellario is instrumentalized. The boy, a gentleman's son, has been wholly owned and co-opted, groomed from childhood by a city wit to masquerade as a woman and marry a miser, as a plot to thwart the miser's plan to disinherit his nephew. The character of Epicoene has none of the beautiful Bellario's allure: she masks as a performatively stupid, shrewish, antierotic figure. Epicoene's gender reveal also has the opposite effect to Bellario's on the plot's resolution: instead of resolving sexual anxiety, her unveiling as a boy plunges several men who claim to have slept with her into sodomitical suspicion, and mocks the gender performances of every caricatured social type satirized in the play's sweaty, annoying city milieu. In both plays, the last-minute surprise gender change invites a doubled reading practice, where the audience's memory of the play they have just seen is rewritten at the climactic instant. But the resignification performed by Bellario's gender unmasking in *Philaster* is not about derision or gender satire, as in *Epicoene*. Rather, it is about desire,

and the audience is implicated in the queer frisson that retrospectively makes visible moments of sexual ambiguity and multivalent,
contradictory pleasure.[23] Putatively opposite-sex pairs are revealed
to have been secretly same-sex pairs and vice versa, raising the titillating questions of what the characters sexually implicated with the
cross-dressed figure knew, and when and how they knew it.[24] The
two versions of the plot, one featuring Bellario as a boy and the other
featuring Bellario as a girl in disguise, are brought into being and
coexist in a dialectical relation, with neither eclipsing the other and
with the constant oscillation between them generating a particularly
queer comedic energy.

Even after the gender reveal—in which, it is important to keep
noting, nothing is revealed to the audience except a name and a
backstory—Bellario as a boy remains operative in the text. Bellario
(revealed as Euphrasia) explains that his male persona was assumed
with the transformative seriousness and permanency of a religious
vocation:

> . . . understanding well
> That when I made discovery of my sex
> I could not stay with you, I made a vow,
> By all the most religious things a maid
> Could call together, never to be known
> Whilst there was hope to hide me from men's eyes
> For other than I seemed, that I might ever
> Abide with you. Then I sat by the fount
> Where first you took me up. (5.5.175–83)

The garments that made it possible for Bellario "never to be known . . .
For other than I seemed" are the sole means of access to the instrumental role he craves. Bellario is not, in the end "really a woman"
but rather a purpose-built, artificial creation, fashioned to facilitate
the fulfillment of a nascent desire: to be near Philaster, and to serve
him. Then, when the boy is commissioned as the instrumental bearer
of Philaster's love to Arethusa, that persona becomes a vehicle to
effect the transmission of others' desire. Yet at the same time it is
important not to overenunciate the difference the revelation of gender

disguise makes: in his ardent functioning as an instrumental erotic technology, Bellario is Euphrasia and Euphrasia is Bellario. Bellario is a body, a mask, a shell, an exoskeleton, a persona; but Bellario is not a ruse. It is Euphrasia's desire that drives him, and it is Bellario's masculine-appearing body through which that desire is enacted. Understanding erotic instrumentality as the structuring dynamic for this character makes visible a Bellario whose dramatic functioning is not most saliently conditioned by a provisional, sartorial gender performance (in contrast to the canonical criticism's emphasis on boy actors playing women), but by a mode of relation conjured holistically by and with his functional, artificial, instrumental body.

"In Counterfeit Passion"

I want to set Bellario's submissive erotic instrumentality against the swashbuckling, agentive instrumentality of Mary Frith, also known as Moll Cutpurse, in *The Roaring Girl*, a play with which *Philaster* might seem to have little in common. Moll, the Roaring Girl of the title, is, to a much more flamboyant degree than Bellario, a gender-queer character. If *Philaster* dramatizes a queer instrumentality founded in malleability, pathos, and surrender, then *The Roaring Girl* depicts a powerful go-between who actively shapes and dominates the relationships she facilitates. The premise of Middleton and Dekker's madly successful city comedy features a gentleman's son, Sebastian, in a dilemma more typically associated with early modern daughters: his father, Sir Alex, has forbidden him from marrying his chosen love, Mary Fitz-Allard, deeming her dowry insufficient and promising disinheritance if he weds her. Sebastian proposes, as a solution, a performance of gender and sexual monstrosity so scandalous that it will change his father's mind: he will to pretend to marry Moll Cutpurse, his friend and compatriot in debauched London city life, as a grotesque and unacceptable decoy fiancée. From Sebastian's first use of her name, Moll functions as an instrumental third whose sexual meanings can shift as needed according to context.

While the intermediary in *Philaster* fulfills his function through his innocent appearance, his class status (and his cross-dressing) submerged until the end, the plot of *The Roaring Girl* explicitly traffics in the violation of taboo. Whereas Bellario's performances of affect are the private currency of Philaster and Arethusa's "hidden love," the instrumentality plot of *The Roaring Girl* depends on the public quality of Moll's queerness. Sebastian's ruse leverages her strangeness and notoriety:

> There's a wench
> Called Moll, mad Moll, or merry Moll, a creature
> So strange in quality, a whole city takes
> Note of her name and person.[25]

Moll is to function instrumentally to the couple by means of the deviant sexual associations attached to her. As Sebastian explains to his disallowed fiancée:

> All that affection
> I owe to thee, on her in counterfeit passion
> I spend to mad my father: he believes
> I doat upon this roaring girl, and grieves
> As it becomes a father for a son
> That could be so bewitched. (1.1.100–105)

Sebastian counts on the assumption that Moll embodies a sexual transgression so enormous that Sebastian's class transgression in marrying Mary will look mild by comparison, and his father will consent to the original match.

Moll's masculine attire is the material substance of her monstrosity, and a central object, in its own right, of her own and others' investment and fixation. Though she appears mostly in men's clothing, in some scenes she wears women's garments on one part of her body and men's clothes on the rest—for example "a frieze jerkin" (a man's short coat) "and a black saveguard" (a woman's riding skirt) (2.1.161). As with Bellario/Euphrasia, Moll's menswear is not a temporary device. Instead, it is the clothing of the character, a structuring precondition to her functioning as a sexual go-between who facilitates—and queers—the heterosexual pairing at the center of the play. Our understanding of both these comedies' gender dynamics has been shaped by the enduring tradition of materialist and feminist dramatic criticism focused on boy actors in women's parts, and on the self-referential theatricality with which that practice infuses the comic resolution of cross-dressing plays—especially in the critically mystified moment of revelation, where the boy actor playing the heroine removes her masculine disguise to reveal his imaginary female identity.[26] But the queer go-betweens I am pondering here—a boy who is not known to be female until the very end of the play, and who never appears in women's clothing; and a cutpurse whose permanent masculine dress is in no sense a disguise—require a different kind of attention to the imaginary efficacies of the boy actor's body, and to the prosthetic gendered garments and accessories that surround it.

Both characters' staged embodiments attest to how men's garments, like the women's clothing worn by boy actors, can constitute an artificial sex. But then, as Will Fisher has taught us to see in his study of accessories and body parts, all gender—especially, though not exclusively, in early modern England—can be seen as prosthetically "materialized," assembled from both corporeal and man-made elements into hybrid forms that communicate a complex range of social meanings.[27] With their full inhabitation of masculine garments and accessories, Bellario and Moll both call into question the constitution of gender to an even further degree than other cross-dressed characters of early modern literature, casting doubt on the ontology of sex itself. I strongly agree with Simone Chess that it would be inaccurate to say that Moll Cutpurse—or, I would add, Bellario/Euphrasia—is a woman in the same sense as Shakespeare's Rosalind and Viola may be.[28] In fact, in both cases, Moll's and Bellario's genital anatomies are unknown, or at least open to debate, from both the text's and audience's perspectives.[29] The phraseology of "cross-dressing," then, is not right here. As Sawyer K. Kemp argues in a groundbreaking retheorization of the relation between embodiment and sartorial performance in Shakespeare, gender is much more than clothing; it is affective and material, a social experience.[30] Thus, for both Bellario and Moll, their constitutive, full-time practice of masculine presentation installs them, in different ways, as a different order of body, one that confounds binary sex or gender: a body of trans experience. In this respect, they resonate more productively across time with a spectrum of queer masculinities—with genderqueer butches, transgender men and others on the transmasculine continuum, queer "bois," and full-time drag kings—than with the feminine heroines who have been the focus of so much early modern cross-dressing criticism. Bellario in particular is an ambiguous fit with respect to the butch/femme dynamic that Valerie Traub traces in *The Renaissance of Lesbianism in Early Modern England.* It is the femme, she argues, "defined primarily as *lack,* the blank space made intelligible only by the implied presence of the tribade or the butch," who "has operated, both historically and in contemporary culture, as an erotic cipher."[31] Yet Bellario serves as an erotic cipher by means of a sartorially masculine presentation, which Traub observes "has more in common with current discourses of transgender and intersexuality than with butch affect and style."[32] Nor do I see Bellario as fitting into the mold of the chaste femme, whose historically silenced desire Traub seeks to uncover. I want instead to make legible Bellario's strange potency as a staged cipher that splits and exceeds these historical categories altogether.

The erotic configurations I point out in *The Roaring Girl* and *Philaster* are instances of queer relationality that are not accounted for by either heteronormative or homoerotic models of the dyad. What is queer about them is not (just) the genders or the presumptive genital combinations of the participants, but rather the specific kinds of eros at play: the mediated, surrogated, even performative, stylized, and artificed pleasures generated by the instrumentalized third. Making such affective resonances visible across time, and mining their significance, requires what Jack Halberstam calls a "perverse presentism": a methodology that acknowledges the relevance of "what we do not know in the present to what we cannot know about the past."[33] This means that I am not searching texts from the past for examples of sexual categories that exist today, as if accounts of past sexualities could confirm either the arbitrariness or the inevitability of current sexual regimes (what Sedgwick calls the fallacy of a coherent "sexuality as we *conceive* of it today").[34] Along with Sedgwick, I do not want to pretend that the definition of queerness is stable from my own critical perspective in the present. My interest is in elucidating what new literary reading practices, drawing on a thick history of all that has transpired between then and now, can add to texts from the past—not in defining all that eroticism means, or doesn't mean, in an early modern text at the moment of its production. My approach, informed by Traub's call "to keep open the question of the relationship of present identities to past cultural formations," requires embracing, rather than shrinking from, the resonances between the forms of queerness at issue in early modern plays and other moments of erotic polysemy, crisis, artifice, and undecidability, both from that time and from others.[35]

With that said, one of the singular features that sets *The Roaring Girl* apart from other early modern plays is that it has at its center an actual person who was unapologetically queer and absolutely, historically real. Of all the queer feelings and affective modes this book explores, those on display in *The Roaring Girl* are most manifestly connected to nonnormative genders and sexual subcultures to come. Its protagonist, an openly masculine woman who wears mostly men's clothes, has recently attracted renewed critical attention in the burgeoning field of early modern trans studies, as a figure who demands and incites an expanded historical theorization of gendered embodiment and transformation.[36] A notorious thief, entertainer, and scandalous City character, Moll Frith was at the peak of her celebrity when this play was produced, a living person who moved in the familiar spheres of the Bankside theater industry and the City underworld. In fact, as the epilogue of the play advertises, "The Roaring Girl herself" is at times physically present in the Fortune theater during the play's run there. On at least one occasion she appeared on the stage (in men's apparel, of course) and sang a song, accompanying herself on a viol; she may have made other cameo appearances or ad-libbed comic turns as herself in this play.[37] Thus Moll is recognizable outside of the world of the play as a queer subject—though her very real, historical nonnormativity is only one of the ways in which she resonates through queer history. In the spirit of Carolyn Dinshaw's contention that "queer histories are made of affective relations," and that the work of premodern sexuality studies is "to make such histories manifest by juxtaposition, by making entities past and present touch," I suggest looking forward from the figures of Moll Cutpurse and Bellario to future reverberations of erotic instrumentality that might be brought to bear to analyze them both.[38] A differently historicized reading of these plays can then reveal a new, nondyadic deep structure of desire and power centered on the agentive instrumentality of the genderqueer third.

As a supposedly female-bodied person who wears men's clothing in daily life, Moll Frith exemplifies the contemporary London type called the "man–woman" or "masculine–feminine," a target of widely circulated polemic, including the 1620 pamphlet, *Hic Mulier. Or, The Man-Woman,* which offers "a Medicine to cure the Coltish Disease of the Staggers in the Masculine–Feminines of our Times."[39] A wealth of canonical scholarship has used Moll and her celebrity turn onstage to examine the political, social, and sexual meanings of the early modern cross-dressing hysteria/vogue.[40] Thus before Moll appears onstage her contours are already drawn by an existing paranoid discourse; her deferred entrance and the extensively dilated buildup of dialogue anticipating her appearance mirrors the rapidly proliferating body of anti-cross-dressing discourse. In one of Moll's first appearances in the play, she moves through the shops, outfitting herself with masculine accessories and flirting with the shop wives, with a swaggering bravado that defies description as "the Coltish Disease of the Staggers" lamented in the pamphlet. London city shops are a central site for the construction of gender and social meaning; James Bromley reads the shops as the locus of a specifically queer materiality, where gallants fashion a sartorial masculinity based in surface and style—a rebuke and an alternative to the patriarchal obsession with false seeming.[41] Even within this extravagant space, the shopgoers speculate on Moll's physical and social excess:

GOSHAWK: 'Tis the maddest fantasticall'st girl:—I never knew so much flesh and so much nimbleness put together.
LAXTON: She slips from one company to another, like a fat eel between a Dutchman's fingers.—*[Aside]* I'll watch my time for her. (2.1.189–92)

Moll's unusual bodily sex and sexual role are openly debated, even among citizens who know her on a familiar basis. In fact, the play repeatedly raises, without resolving, the question of Moll's genital anatomy. Moll Frith is a signal example of the intervention Colby Gordon makes into theorizing early modern embodiment: that the genital configurations of particular bodies, fictional figures and historical people alike, are fundamentally unknowable. Offering a needed corrective to the normative critical bias that assumes all bodies to "really" possess a "natural" underlying fleshly materiality (always assumed to be a typical genital anatomy of one or the other binary sex), Gordon historicizes the ideologies of technology and artifice that constitute the morphology of all created bodies. If not only all gender, but all *bodies* are prosthetic, then there is no natural, unadulterated "body beneath" to be counterposed against gender "performance."[42]

Moll's body and bearing make her vulnerable to sexual speculation about just this matter, instigated by the lecherous gallant Laxton:

> MISTRESS GALLIPOT: Some will not stick to say she's a man
> And some both man and woman.
> LAXTON: That were excellent, she might first cuckold the
> husband and then make him do as much for the wife.
> (2.1.194–97)

The question of public interest, it seems, is what Moll's ambiguous sex or sexuality might allow her to do in carnal contact. Though he gravely mistakes her for a sexually receptive woman and a prostitute, Laxton does hit upon a truth: at the root of Moll's prodigious potency and inexhaustible desirability is her bisexual potential as a facilitator of sex with both male and female bodies. When Laxton propositions her, Moll wounds him in a sword fight and takes his purse. It's a moment of triumph in the play, but the violence is real (and threatens in *Philaster* too). The openly artificial and erotically efficacious queer bodily styles of "Masculine–Feminines" like Moll—and many other subcultures of female masculinity that have existed in other times—exert a deranging force on patriarchal sexism, even as they are persecuted within it.[43] One truth that a lens of erotic instrumentality makes visible is that objectification and agency, vulnerability and power can coexist; they are not mutually exclusive binaries. In light of this, I want to shift from seeing the masculine–feminine as strictly an object—of gazes, of polemic, of conflicting desires in the period, and of critics' objectifying interests and analyses—to ask instead what the masculine–feminine body *does,* how it acts on and within erotic economies.[44] Seeing Moll's transgressive sex and gender as erotically instrumental allows us to reframe so-called cross-dressing in terms of the dresser's effects on dramatic dynamics and affective exchanges. What connections does the masculine–feminine "third" produce, onstage and off? How does she alter the structure of a play?

The triad formed by Moll, Sebastian, and Mary is the obvious erotic center of the play: Moll is enlisted to legitimate Sebastian's marriage to Mary. But Moll does not appear onstage in her instrumental capacity with Sebastian and Mary until well into the second half of the play, in act 4. Far more stage time is devoted to another triad in which Moll alters and queers the affective investments at stake between two other characters: Sebastian and his father, Sir Alex Wengrave. In many ways the father/son pairing is the dominant relationship of the plot (it is, for one thing, the bond on whose restoration the comic resolution depends); moreover, the affects incited in the father—merely through the discourse of notoriety that surrounds her, before she appears onstage—reveal the constellation of queer investments that Moll brings about and makes visible.

Sebastian's plot works spectacularly; his performance of "counterfeit passion" sparks a frenzy of not at all counterfeit passion from Sir Alex. So intense is his incoherent derangement that it must be displaced onto a fictional stranger, a "passionate old man" tormented by his son's desire for a monstrous creature, "woman more than man,/ Man more than woman":

The sun gives her two shadows to one shape:
Nay more, let this strange thing walk, stand or sit,
No blazing star draws more eyes after it.
Sir Davy: A monster, 'tis some monster.
Sir Alex: She's a varlet. (1.2.130–35)

Like the queer charade to which he proves so susceptible, Sir Alex uses substitution to stoke his aristocratic friends' revulsion at a double-sexed yet supposedly female body. This monologue uses stock tropes of gender aberration ("a thing/One knows not how to name: her birth began/Ere she was all made," 1.2.128–30), with an emphasis on the "creature's" qualities of attraction and celebrity ("no blazing star draws more eyes after it"). What I find interesting, however, is the elaborate displaced affliction: the son's object choice exerts a self-alienating, self-annihilating, "fantastical" effect on the father's body and mind, which he displaces onto a fictive "aged man" he meets (1.2.64). His prodigal son's waywardness, Sir Alex says, sends the old man into "fits": "you might see his gall/Flow even in's eyes: then grew he fantastical [. . .] and talked oddly" (1.2.88–93). The old man laments his son's rebellion as direct violence to the core of a father's being, a wedge that "doth cleave/My very heart-root" (1.2.104–5), and "a whirlwind/Shaking the firm foundation" of his existence (1.2.115–16).

This self-martyring paternal reaction indexes the dangers and consequences for the parent/child bond in the aftermath of a coming-out moment: a revelation of a sexually deviant object choice. Read as the crazed lamentations of a homophobic parent, this language resonates within the context outlined by Sedgwick for the dramatic effects of sexual disclosures on the patriarchal figures who receive them. Sedgwick describes how the eruption of queerness within the bonds of the family threatens the recipient as well as the subject of the news: "In fantasy, though not in fantasy only, against the fear of being killed or wished dead by (say) one's parents in such a revelation there is apt to recoil the often more intensely imagined possibility of its killing *them*."[45] Sir Alex voices a performatively literal fantasy of himself in the grave much like the one Sedgwick describes:

> Oh thou cruel boy,
> Thou wouldst with lust an old man's life destroy;
> Because thou see'st I'm half-way in my grave,
> Thou shovel'st dust upon me: would thou might'st have
> Thy wish, most wicked, most unnaturall! (1.2.157–61)

This is the weaponization of nonnormative sexual desire as retaliation against the patriarchal social structure, by a son who has already been threatened with an extreme form of harm—disinheritance—as a consequence of his actual choice of a mate. Moll's instrumental function here catapults a parent/child conflict from the social and economic realm (well trodden in early modern drama) into what, even in a 1611 city comedy, can be called the realm of sexuality, where children's rebellious erotic choices have affective and social consequences that cut both ways, against the parent as well as against the child. Though Sebastian's object choice is not exactly same sex, he occupies an analogous position to Sedgwick's "gay subject": one who has lost authority over his own social definition through his problematic choice of partner.[46]

Outing Sebastian to his appalled friends, Sir Alex appeals to the "questions of authority and evidence," which Sedgwick notes are often first to arise when queerness appears ("How do you know you're really gay? [. . .] Hadn't you better talk to a therapist and find out?").[47] He calls Sebastian ill and delusional—"Th'art sick at heart, yet feel'st it not" (1.2.149)—for persisting in a desire figured as a disease no one should want to have. He asks, "What gentleman but thou, knowing his disease/Mortal, would shun the cure?' (1.2.149–51). Sir Alex objects that it's illegal: "What, sayst thou marriage? In what place, the sessions house? And who shall give the bride, prithee? An indictment?' (2.2.131–33). He asks Sebastian, "Why, wouldst thou fain marry to be pointed at?" (2.2.135). These mocking threats, like the father's self-murdering histrionics, read as eerily modern. Sir Alex keeps appealing to questions of evidence to assuage his hysteria: he is assured that "it was never known/Two men were married and conjoined in one" (5.2.104–5). Any alleged marriage to Moll must be the same curious mix of null and abomination as a marriage between two men, of "no such matter" and "never known."

After sending an angry mob after Sebastian, Sir Alex reveals in an unheard aside his resolve to murder the object of his son's affection: "*[Aside]* Her blood shall quench it then" (1.2.177). The potential for violence occasioned by a deviant object choice—to the child, to the parent, back to the child, and (as can also happen in cases of gay coming out) to the child's love object—arises, according to Sedgwick, "partly from the fact that the erotic identity of the person who receives the disclosure [Sir Alex] is apt also to be implicated in, hence perturbed by, it," with the ultimate disturbance being the unspoken, ghosting suggestion that something like the son's queer predilection might be present in the father.[48] In fact, if Sebastian's performative faux engagement to a notorious "masculine–feminine" cutpurse functions dramatically, in its scandal and enormity, like a gay engagement, it does precisely what Sedgwick says a child's coming out does, and implicates the father in a homophobic/homoerotic dynamic. Sir Alex lies to the assembled gentlemen that he has "upon my knees wooed this fond boy/To take that virtuous maiden [Mary Fitz-Allard]" (1.2.164–65). Sir Alex places himself in the posture of a romantic supplicant when in fact he has forcibly insinuated himself into his son's sexual trajectory, and the reproductive continuation of their patrilineal bond through Mary Fitz-Allard is the very route he has foreclosed. Alone onstage, Sir Alex vows revenge on his son in a chilling incestuous, homoerotic twist on the Petrarchan figure of love as an amorous hunt:

I'll be most near thee when I'm least in sight.
Wild buck, I'll hunt thee breathless, thou shalt run on,
But I will turn thee when I'm not thought upon.
(1.2.183–85)

By occasioning violent, even eroticized displays of identification and domination between father and son, Moll makes visible the energy of the Oedipal plot, which links the unruly appetites of sons for the wrong conjugal objects with the deaths of fathers and the problem of succession, and highlights a father's life-or-death interest, under patrilineage, in the appropriateness of his son's sexual desire.

This is the first and perhaps most crucial relationship that Moll queers in the play, on which her subsequent participation in Sebastian and Mary's coupling depends. Like Bellario, she functions as a cipher for mediating affective content between father and son—content that would not exist without her. She is the object, agent, and occasion—the instrument—of those affects, through the dialogue's figuration of her queer body and sexual notoriety. Queerness's tendency to alter other relations in an orbit of proximity to itself derives, as Sedgwick observes, from how it makes visible the contingent, relational condition of all desire, "because erotic identity, of all things, is never to be circumscribed simply as itself, can never not be relational, is never to be perceived or known by anyone outside of a structure of transference and countertransference."[49] This idea—that the erotic is not a hermetically contained, organic, interior truth bearing only on conjugal relations between individuals, but rather a magnetic force that exists in and through all relationalities—is particularly visible in early modern drama, where discourses of love, identification, and affiliation often spread out to implicate the whole set of staged relations in the play. This is one of the ways early modern texts can rebut a narrow, modern definition of eroticism as strictly associated with individuals or with genitality ("modern" in the delusional, myopic sense that Latour says "we have never been," as this is not at all the model of eros advanced in the thought of Freud). The kind of queerness Moll generates is relational in Sedgwick's sense: it is visible in the "counterfeit passions" she attracts and the nonsexual bonds of kinship and service she alters, showing them to be equal in weight—and even dramatically prior—to the ostensibly central marriage plot. One of the things the instrumentalized go-between vividly shows is that eroticism itself is a collective phenomenon, a force that connects people and things in interimplicated webs of power, desire, and violence.

"Both with Standing Collars"

Like Bellario, Moll's erotic charge inheres in the clothing and objects that construct her remarkable body. When she finally enters the stage ("*Enter Moll, in a frieze jerkin and a black safeguard,*" 2.1.161) in a soldier's short coat and a woman's riding petticoat, Moll appears as a man from the waist up and a woman from the waist down—the "half man/half woman" Sir Alex deplores and the *Hic Mulier* pamphlet condemns. Her (men's) tailor chases her down in the street to discuss the measurements for her new breeches:

TAILOR: It shall stand round and full, I warrant you.

MOLL: Pray make 'em easy enough.

TAILOR: I know my fault now: t'other was somewhat stiff between the legs, I'll make these open enough, I warrant you. (2.2.86–89)

This performative back-and-forth about the breeches' style and fit ("And make sure you leave enough room in the crotch!" "Oh yes, I didn't leave nearly enough room in the crotch last time! I'll leave more!") makes the tailor legible as a prurient City type with a long accumulated tradition of sexual suspicion—notably bisexual suspicion, of both lechery with women and effeminacy and homosexual contact with men—as a result of the physical intimacy, undress, and small, sharp phallic instruments involved in their trade.[50] Here he is established as a co-constructor of Moll's prosthetic phallic body. As James Bromley argues, the play posits a queer, nondualist ontology of the relationship between material things and human bodies, in which "the construction and aestheticization of ostentatious selfhood" takes place through accessorizing and ornamentation, portending Oscar Wilde's aesthetic philosophy of surface in early modern material culture.[51] Moll's transactions with her tailor are literally dramatically instrumental: this street scene brings Sir Alex in sight, for the first time, of the object of his obsession. Lurking onstage to spy on Moll's swaggering exchanges, he well understands the parts being gestured at in the tailor's dialogue: "Hoyda, breeches? What will he marry a monster with two trinkets? What age is this? If the wife go in breeches, the man must wear long coats like a fool!" (2.2.76–78). Now the "monster" of Sir Alex's phobic ideation has "two trinkets," a reference to the legs or points of her breeches, which is immediately readable as a fantasy of two testicles. His lament, "I have brought my son up to marry a Dutch slop and a French doublet, a codpiece-daughter!" (2.2.90–91), repeats this doubling of foreign men's phallic garments, and adds atop it Moll's male-and-female status as a "codpiece-daughter."

Acting the part—to gall his father—of an infatuated apologist for the freedom to love whom he will, Sebastian proposes to Moll in the middle of the street. Moll picks up on the language of excessive, repeated doubling, turning it into a queer refusal of marriage and a statement of sexual ambidexterity:

> I have no humor to marry, I love to lie o'both sides o'th'bed
> myself, and again o'th'other side; a wife you know ought
> to be obedient, but I fear me I am too headstrong to obey,
> therefore I'll ne'er go about it. I love you so well, sir, for
> your good will I'd be loath you should repent your bargain
> after, and therefore we'll ne'er come together at first. I
> have the head now of myself, and am man enough for a
> woman; marriage is but a chopping and changing, where a
> maiden loses one head and has a worse i'th'place.
> (2.2.36–45)

Like Moll's overlapping, layered-on assemblage of garments, this is not a straightforward image of bisexuality or hermaphroditism. "I love to lie o'both sides o'th'bed myself; and again o'th'other side" asserts a third position, in excess of the usual two. Not only, Moll brags, can she move between the man's and the woman's part in bed, but she can also perform something more: an encore entailing some novel third sexual role. She can be "more than one, and more than two, but less than infinity."[52]

Laying "o'both sides o'th'bed" is an additive, sex-positive corollary to Philaster's paranoid, negative interrogation of Bellario's sexual implication with Arethusa: "Is she not parallelless?" Both turns of phrase seem to describe a sexual reality outside the mathematical constraints of the dyad. Using at least a triple negative, Philaster sets up an impossible bind in which Arethusa cannot be verified "parallelless" without having been "paralleled" (in bed) by Bellario or himself. No one can be redeemed unless all three are simultaneously together, making each "parallelless." Moll's third side of the bed literally, grammatically posits an outside to the sexual binary (hetero or otherwise)—what is the "other side" to "both sides"? She constructs herself as both sexually self-sufficient and versatile: man enough for herself; man enough to satisfy and master women sexually; and man enough that any man she would take as a partner would become the woman and she the man—all three.

As is true of the body brought into being as Bellario in *Philaster*, Moll augments and adds to heterosexual pairings. She takes and transmits, amplifies, and obtains gratification from erotic positions squeezed in between, added on beside, and slipped underneath heteronormative structures. "'Twixt lovers' hearts, she's a fit instrument," Sebastian exults, "And has the art to help them to their own" (2.2.197–98). Moll is a "fit instrument" in the precise way Sebastian asserts because of her supererogatory erotic versatility—her prowess at lying three different ways on a two-sided bed. Like Bellario's "country art" of encoding and expressing feelings, Moll's art is the art of relationality, deployed to her own and others' erotic ends. Sir Alex's evil henchman, Trapdoor, inflames his homophobic/homoerotic passions with graphic representations of what Moll's cross-gendered dress can do in sexual encounters:

> TRAPDOOR: She comes in a shirt of male.
> SIR ALEX: How, shirt of mail?
> TRAPDOOR: Yes sir, or a male shirt, that's to say in man's apparel.
> SIR ALEX: To my son?
> TRAPDOOR: Close to your son: your son and her moon
> will be in conjunction, if all almanacs lie not: her black
> saveguard is turned into a deep slop, the holes of her
> upper body to button-holes, her waistcoat to a doublet, her
> placket to the ancient seat of a codpiece, and you shall
> take 'em both with standing collars. (3.3.19–28)

Trapdoor paints a body not merely disguised but deformed by men's clothing. Her "black saveguard" will turn into an exposed "deep slop" (a grotesque allusion to exposed female genitals as well as to Moll's extravagant Dutch breeches). Her bodice will be full of "button-holes," and the placket on her skirt (a slang term for the vagina)[53] will conversely transform into "the ancient seat of a codpiece." Not only will this body be sexually conjoined with Sebastian's, but it will also morph from a female body into something else: a monstrous, hermaphroditic body. The disorienting slippage between anatomical and artificial objects in Trapdoor's rant blurs which pieces are body parts and which are garments, evoking a body whose substance exceeds natural or human materiality.

The unanswerable question raised by the entire play—the question of what Moll's codpiece covers up—cannot be unasked; Trapdoor's rant conjuring the "ancient seat of a codpiece" over the thing itself makes us think it. The pair of "standing collars" Trapdoor evokes, the coup de grâce in his nightmare portrait to Sir Alex of Moll having sex with his son, fetishistically evokes the absent presence of Moll's penis. The fantasy that so maddens Sir Alex is of a double penetration, a double penis, or two penises in homosexual contact. Sebastian's and Moll's matching ruffs of starched cloth—"standing" because they are held erect from the inside by wire frames—are twin erect phalli. Trapdoor suggests that Moll's and Sebastian's bodies will take the same phallic shape, and that the sexual contact between them will be anal ("your son and her moon will be in conjunction"). This confluence of sexual similarity and sodomitical intercourse derives from the coexistence, in Moll, of a sexually functional prosthetic masculinity—her "standing collar"—with a carnal body that is even more suspect for being sexually unspecified—her "moon," the "ancient seat of a codpiece." Moll's sartorial body may be doubly gendered or undecidable, but it is decidedly phallic. In the homophobic/homoerotic fantasy/nightmare conjured to torment Sir Alex, their sexual congress will render Sebastian's body like Moll's: two bodies of the same polluted yet sexually potent, abject yet masculine substance—in other words, two gay bodies.

In the secret assignation where Moll brings Sebastian and Mary together, she performs what Sebastian calls the "kind office" of facilitating—and participating—in their erotic congress:

Enter Sebastian, with Mary Fitz-Allard like a page, and Moll [in man's clothes].

SEBASTIAN: Thou hast done me a kind office, without touch
Either of sin or shame; our loves are honest.
MOLL: I'd scorn to make such shift to bring you together
else. (4.1.39–41)

Presenting cross-dressed Mary to Sebastian, Moll asks, "My tailor fitted her, how like you his work?" (4.1.69). It is apparent that, in the sartorial and sexual senses, Moll has "turned" or "pimped" Mary out.[54] "Turned out" means both "stylishly dressed" and "sexually initiated," especially where a loss of innocence is involved; the idea of Moll as a bawd or pander ghosts this scene. But Mary's page outfit, like Moll's masculine dress, changes the balance of power. It is not just a disguise; it is the structuring condition of Mary's participation in the erotic encounter. It is produced out of—and in turn productive of—a tridirectional, queer circuit of libidinal energy linking Mary, Sebastian, and Moll. Like "pretty" Bellario's "glad to follow" enthusiasm for being used, Mary's masculine clothing confounds any zero-sum opposition between objectification and erotic agency; it highlights the complicated relations of mutual pleasure involved. This is the climactic moment of Moll's mediating function where, I have argued elsewhere, it is possible to imagine, without any great strain to dramatic convention, that there is cross-dressed, genderqueer, three-way sex.[55] Here, however, I want to draw attention to the queer relational mode being staged. Moll continues to effect Sebastian and Mary's contact, commenting on the homoerotics of their onstage kiss:

> MOLL: How strange this shows, one man to kiss another.
> SEBASTIAN: I'd kiss such men to choose, Moll,
> Methinks a woman's lip tastes well in a doublet.
> (4.1.45–47)

Moll effects a three-way circuit in which she is an instrumental component, not only facilitating the scene but shaping it into a queer—as well as a fully sexual—union.

The stage has been set for understanding this triadic encounter as a moment of queer relationality by my reading, in the introduction, of Richard Brome's *The Antipodes*. Like both *Philaster* and *The Roaring Girl*, *The Antipodes* confutes the assumption that sex is a dyadic phenomenon, conjuring offstage scenes of explicit erotic instrumentality. Peregrine's wife, Martha, deranged with sexual frustration resulting from his mania for reading travel narratives, implores the herald-painter's wife, Barbara, one of the co-orchestrators of the fantasy travel cure for Peregrine's wanderlust, for hands-on instruction:

> . . . he does not
> Lie with me and use me as he should, I fear;
> Nor do I know how to teach him. Will you tell me?
> I'll lie with you and practise, if you please.
> Pray take me for a night or two, or take
> My husband and instruct him—but one night.
> (1.1.261–66)

The instruction Martha asks for—and receives—is transitive, even fungible, equally applicable to women and to men. Barbara's sexual facilitation is more direct and literal than either Bellario's or Moll's. The experienced married woman takes on the absurdly virginal married woman as a sexual protégée: "Come, I'll take charge and care of you—[. . .] And wage my skill against my doctor's art/Sooner to ease you of these dangerous fits/Than he will rectify your husband's wits" (1.1.274–77). Barbara's queer erotic "skill" is used here in one or more lesbian encounters, in the service of effecting activity and desire where there was none before. In *The Antipodes,* heterosexual marriage suffers a blockage that only queer instrumentality can remedy. Barbara reports at the end, perhaps from firsthand experience, that the couple are heartily cured: "Up? Up and ready to lie down again;/There is no ho with them!" (5.2.261–62). Like Moll, Barbara disavows any identity as a bawd or procurer, insisting on the social normativity of her erotic service: "I trust she is no bawd that sees and helps,/If need require, an ignorant lawful pair/To do their best" (5.1.44–46). This is ironic because although Barbara is neither androgynous nor outside of the social gender binary, she is an uneasy fit with any notion of so-called normative sexuality. The play gradually reveals a sexual backstory for the character that puts the lie to dyadic, married monogamy: the Doctor who concocts Peregrine's fantasy cure also cures husbands of their jealousy by surfeit, accomplished by (at least feigning) sex with their wives. Barbara hints that the Doctor may have fathered her children and that they remain lovers. They may both be present, and even participate, at the consummation of Peregrine and Martha's marriage. She tells her blithely unjealous husband that "nor the doctor/Nor I came in a bed tonight. I mean/Within a bed" (5.1.98–100). These hints of deviance condition Barbara's queer instrumental function; her participation reshapes marital sex into something less dyadic, and less, not more, heteronormative than it was before.

The grouping of Mary, Sebastian, and Moll—three costumed bodies kissing in the chamber, with the father fuming in hiding behind them—is a particularly literal staging of Sedgwick's notion of a "never not relational" erotics, a tableau that makes the ineffable phenomenon of relationality visible onstage.[56] The erotics of instrumentality work every which way in the father's chamber scene; every link in the triad is fully queered through the dynamics of being used. Mary is simultaneously, enthusiastically regendered, objectified, and instrumentalized; she takes on some of the qualities of a queer instrument in being "turned out" by Moll. The pleasurable traffic in Mary connects Moll and Sebastian in quasi-homosocial masculine friendship. Moll is the occasion of Sebastian's Oedipal glee at engaging in queer erotic acts in his father's chamber. Sebastian, in turn, is the mediating term for a female homosocial bond between the pair of cross-dressed Marys. Everyone in turn gets used, and likes it. But even this three-part network is not a closed system; it is inescapably linked to the patriarchal bonds that press upon it. The lovers are not unseen in the chamber. Sir Alex is lying in wait for them, becoming progressively more agitated as the erotic energy mounts. One of the payoffs of attending so closely to the homophobic contours of Sir Alex's obsession with Moll in earlier scenes is that it allows us to notice how eroticized the father's frenzy is here, at the scene of queer three-way consummation. Moll borrows his viol—takes it off the wall at Sebastian's invitation—to play and sing a song that functions as a dramatic substitution for a barely invisible three-person sex act. In Moll's practice of borrowing men's instruments at their behest, it is not only she who performs as a willing instrument, on command. The men are also willingly instrumentalized, used for their viols, out of their queer cravings for Moll to temporarily appropriate and wield their instruments.

As with Bellario's flower garland, Moll's borrowed viol makes her body into an instrument, a partially artificial technology of intimacy—technically, a cyborg—that exceeds the human subject, problematizing taxonomies of natural order.[57] The technology that is Moll engenders an erotic network with multiple nodes: the three participants; the material things they use; and the others (onstage and in the audience) who interpret the triad through their own anxieties and lusts. Moll's instrumental efficacy here is akin to that of a sex toy or dildo. She transmits sexual pleasure between Sebastian and Mary (and also generates it with each of them separately), but remains detached. As Traub observes, the dildo "pries female erotic pleasure apart" from the penis, from the "apparatus of reproduction (and the body of man) that confers upon women's desire its social legitimacy."[58] Moll disconnects erotic pleasure not only from the male penis but also from the sexual dyad. Like a dildo, Moll also disconnects erotic pleasure and performance from the so-called natural human body, full stop. Her multiple, phallic garments and accessories (rendered in detail in the play's title page illustration)—her sword, her pipe, her hat, her ruff, the viol she wields—add up to a prodigious, prosthetic body of sex and style that defies categorization. Like Bellario, Moll's body is a thing used within the play—by herself, Sebastian, Sir Alex, Trapdoor, and Mary—toward their differing ends. It is also a thing used *by* the play, as its locus of aesthetic and dramatic energy.

"I'd a Forefinger In't"

In both *Philaster* and *The Roaring Girl,* the erotic instrument has moments of functioning as a perfect generator and communicator of pleasure and desire. Embodying this role permanently, however, is impossible. Both Moll and Bellario/Euphrasia slip in and out of their mediating positions. Though *Philaster* is the tragicomedy, *The Roaring Girl* swerves in the direction of tragedy as well. Sir Alex commissions Trapdoor to "ensnare her very life," plotting with him to rape and/or murder Moll (or, failing that, to frame her in a crime and "find law to hang her up") (1.2.232–34). As he lays out luxury goods in his chamber in hopes that she will steal them, Sir Alex's triple fixation on

The Roaring Girle.

OR
Moll Cut-Purse.

As it hath lately beene Acted on the Fortune-stage by
the Prince his Players.

Written by *T. Middleton* and *T. Dekkar.*

My case is alter'd, I must worke for my liuing.

Printed at *London* for *Thomas Archer*, and are to be sold at his
shop in Popes head-pallace, neere the Royall.
Exchange. 1611.

Figure 1. Frontispiece to *The Roaring Girle, or Moll-Cut-Purse,* by Thomas Middleton
and Thomas Dekker, featuring the notorious Moll in her full complement of prosthetic
garments and bodily accessories, 1611. Woodcut. Private collection/Bridgeman Image.

his family jewels, Moll's fantasy phallus, and Moll's death reinforces how much like a crush homophobic hate can look.

The play's strange resolution averts the tragedy through a performance—almost a dumbshow or masque—that puts a stylized twist on the stock comic gender-reveal moment. Moll is presented, "*masked, in Sebastian's hand*" (5.2.129), almost as a puppet in a show, playing not herself but a nameless "fair bride," whom Sir Alex instantly accepts because she appears properly gendered. Her costume must be assumed to consist of a mask or heavy veil and women's clothes. In other words, she appears in drag (for her). Much of the criticism on *The Roaring Girl* tends to glance off the resolution or to read it as depressing evidence of the play's "rehabilitation" of proper patriarchal gender roles; it can feel like a compulsory normalization even though it is a ruse.[59] In this mute moment, Moll would seem to be what I am adamant that the instrumental go-between is not—an invisible, inconsequential prop for patriarchal marriage and inheritance. However, remembering Moll's function as something like a dildo—a purpose-made, artificial object—reveals a more interesting underlying dynamic, in which Moll's queerness is sustained in the resolution. As the masked bride, she (it?) functions as something closer to a fetish (or puppet) of patriarchal marriage, an artificial materialization that stands in for an unreal fantasy. It is not really even a rehabilitation of compulsory gender performance so much as the most cursory pantomime of femininity (faceless, motionless, silent). The joke inheres in how readily the decoy bride is—again—believed to be the real thing. Like a prosthetic phallus, the figure fulfills its purpose solely through where it is located and what it appears to be doing. The prodigal son makes certain that his father pardons him before his consort is unmasked to reveal—Moll, the Roaring Girl. When, just in time, Mary is escorted in, this time in women's clothing and surrounded by the trappings of patriarchal community (two lords, citizens, and their wives), Moll tells Sir Alex, "I'd a forefinger in't" (5.2.170). Taking credit for both the prank and the happy ending, Moll archly reminds Sir Alex of her sexual stake in both his son and in Mary.

Even with Moll in drag in a dress, the play's comic resolution directly contravenes the conventional ending of the cross-dressing play, where the heroine's "real" femininity is climactically revealed. If anyone is revealed as a "real" woman, it is the boy actor playing Mary Fitz-Allard, who emerges out of her class and gender cross-dressing into her status as a gentlewoman. There is no such insistence on femininity, or marriage, or heterosexuality for Moll, just a reassertion of her instrumental centrality. By removing her transgressive body from the bride position and substituting Mary's, she effects both Sebastian's union with Mary and his reconciliation with his father. Sir Alex announces that his land will be merged—in another three-way bond—with Sir Guy Fitz-Allard's title and Mary's virtue. Rather than rings, keys are exchanged, in a climactic reinheritance ceremony that brings into speech some of the incestuous father/son erotic language that had been ghosting Sir Alex's disgust: Sebastian gets the keys to his father's "best joys," "fertile lands and a fair fruitful bride" (5.2.202–4). As in many comedies, there is no heterosexual marriage onstage in the resolution; this pseudowedding between father and son is the stand-in.

Yet it is significant that at the close of the play, Moll remains defiantly alone. She ridicules Sir Alex for his assumption that she would ever marry a man: "He was in fear his son would marry me,/ But never dreamt that I would ne'er agree" (5.2.213–14). She says she will marry when she sees "honesty and truth unslandered,/ Woman manned but never pandered"—in effect, at doomsday (5.2.219–220). I would venture that Moll comes closer than any other figure in early modern drama to being a queer character. Her uses of masculine tools and accessories as instruments of butch self-styling and erotic prowess with women, combined with her self-aware rejection of patriarchal marriage, render her sexually marked for her refusal of a heteronormative fate. Moreover, she is a subject who is recognized as queer for these reasons, as part of a regime of recognition that extends into the present. I place the character of Moll Cutpurse near the nebulous beginnings of a multinodal genealogy of sexually dissident ways of being that stretches from the histories of style, seduction, and survival lived by working-class butch women and other participants in female masculinity; through the aesthetically and culturally generative street-based queer urban subcultures on both sides of the Atlantic—from early modern London's shops and promenades, to the Harlem Renaissance, to the drag ball scene—with their signature mix of aristocracy and demimonde, celebrity and criminality, high and low style; to late twentieth and early twenty-first century scenes of patriarchs reacting to declarations of gay identity and same-sex marriage, some of which echo with painful precision those staged in 1611. Like an historical instrument of some eerily durable, magnetized substance, Moll alters erotic networks both within and outside of the play, drawing other subjects into her queer orbit while she herself remains uncaptured by heteronormativity.

"Come, Live with Me"

A contrasting story of gender transformation and queer marriage, recorded in Montaigne's travel journal (1581), serves as a tragic mirror to the tragicomic plots of *Philaster* and *The Roaring Girl*. Montaigne's tale from Vitry-le-François of a girl, originally called Mary, who, like Bellario/Euphrasia, put on men's clothes and left her village to live as a man, is, as *Philaster* threatens to become, a tragedy of interpretation. Due in part to its prominent role in historicist scholarship on the period, this story is not only instructive about the life-and-death stakes of Bellario's erotic instrumentality in *Philaster*, or the social meanings of Sebastian and Moll's queer sham marriage. It also offers a site for examining the readings and misreadings (both in the period and subsequently) of female-bodied figures in masculine clothing: their bodies, their erotic capabilities, and the circuits of pleasure and relation they effect. Montaigne writes that passing through the town, he heard the story of a weaver, "a well-favoured young man, and on friendly terms with everyone,"[60] who married a woman (after a brief engagement to another woman), and lived with her for four or five months, "to her contentment, as they say."[61] But when this young man was recognized by someone from his old village, his bodily sex was brought before the court and he was condemned to hang—not for falsifying identity or for committing same-sex marriage, but for "illicit inventions to supplement the defect of her sex."[62] The young man is said to protest that he prefers to be hanged rather than "to be returned to a girl's estate."[63] But in his trial and death—as in Montaigne's narrative, which regenders him as female—he is forcibly returned to a girl's estate, his gender realigned with her sex in an act of state violence.

This anecdote has generated widespread critical discussion attempting to parse its significance for early modern ideas of bodily sex and social gender. Stephen Greenblatt famously uses it, in his reading of *Twelfth Night,* as evidence for the persistence of the Galenic or "one-sex" model of sexual difference, where the vagina is homologous to the penis, only turned in on itself, in the period's sexual imaginary.[64] As Thomas Laqueur has influentially put it, before the Enlightenment, "*sex,* or the body, must be understood as the epiphenomenon, while *gender,* what we would take to be a cultural category, was primary or 'real,'" and "it was precisely when talk seemed to be most directly about the biology of two sexes that it was most embedded in the politics of gender, in culture."[65] This is the established historicist use of Montaigne, in which this story reveals an ideology that is illuminating in the difference of its codes from those operating today. In this reading, made canonical in arguments by Greenblatt and Traub, because the sodomy laws of Renaissance France defined sodomy for women as using an artificial instrument to penetrate another woman, and because the sentence handed down in this case was death, we can thus understand the protagonist as a person executed for using a dildo on a woman while being female bodied.[66] This version of the story, in which the crime is counterfeiting the physical apparatus of manhood in sexual relations with a woman, is certainly available behind Montaigne's stylish storytelling, but this influential interpretation does not follow necessarily or transparently from Montaigne's text. Instead, I submit that reading a death sentence for penetrative sodomy into this anecdote is a motivated act of reading like any other (and, as Traub points out, the same reading committed by the court who condemns him).[67]

Looking at this story in light of *Philaster*'s erotically instrumental go-between and *The Roaring Girl*'s simultaneously historical and invented masculine heroine raises other possibilities—possibilities that have been foreclosed by a too-faithful adherence to a New Historicist paradigm where contextual discoveries are regarded as solving for the contemporary meanings of a text. Reading *pendue des inventions illicites à suppléer au defaut de son sexe* ("hanged for illicit inventions to supply the defect of her sex") as exclusively about sodomy laws governing the illegal use of penetrative "devices" (Greenblatt's word, which does not appear in Montaigne) narrows down the proliferation of "illicit inventions"—sartorial, material, rhetorical, aesthetic, and erotic—at play in this story to a single, presumed invention, Greenblatt's imagined phallic "device."[68] But the young weaver is himself, like Bellario and Moll Cutpurse, an "invention"; his clothing, his weaver's trade and the textiles he creates, his new name, his citizenship, his friendships, his courtships, his marriage, and the sex he has with his wife are all "illicit" —and virtuosic— inventions. What he has attempted to *supply* for himself with these inventions (a sense of *suppléer* that Greenblatt passes over in favor of "supplement") is not only the strictly anatomical *defaut* (translated by Greenblatt as "defect") of his ostensible genital lack, but the flawed, faulty, *default* conditions of the world into which he was born as a girl—conditions that required him, like Euphrasia and like Mary Frith, to invent a new self and use it in new ways in order to function as he desired.

Thinking about all of the other kinds of "illicit inventions" that can supplement the often insufficient, default conditions of bodily sex also opens up the usefulness of this anecdote for reading *Philaster,* a play in which the passing, female-bodied boy and his pleasing rhetorical inventions generate affective and erotic frictions that exceed the problem of sex. The two stories share the same premise: a passing young masculine-presenting subject who began life as a girl now lives in intimate relation to another woman. Yet in Beaumont and Fletcher's plot, Bellario's voluntary revelation that he is female-bodied is the fortunate stroke that narrowly averts his torture and execution, whereas in Vitry-le-François it seals the young weaver's fate. The tragic end of the Montaigne story ghosts *Philaster*'s last-minute happy ending, signaling the problems and risks of interpretation that attend the genderqueer erotic instrument. In *The Roaring Girl,* the social threat posed by Moll's masculinity is homoerotic/homosocial. She is the target of violence for suspected sexual relations with Sebastian, never with Mary (despite her quite open boasts regarding women's sexuality). In *Philaster,* however, despite all the mutual erotic energy that animates Bellario's relations with

Philaster and with Arethusa alike, the social threat posed by Bellario falls entirely on Arethusa. In contrast to the story of the young weaver, *Philaster* does not end in tragedy because Bellario's "inventions" for and within the erotic triad are harder to pin down. Bellario's erotic "invention"—including his invention of himself, and the sartorial and rhetorical artifice involved in his performance—takes place in the service of being made instrumental, in three-way relation rather than a dyadic marriage bond, and thus exceeds legal categories of sex crime and marital status. His instrumentality is a form of affective and relational "invention" that troubles the category of what counts as sexual activity—or a sexual relationship, full stop. Both *Philaster*'s and *The Roaring Girl*'s flirtations with tragedy and scandal, then, are problems with the signification and interpretation of erotic desire, of lovers whose intimacy is both all too visible and totally misunderstood.

In one sense, the revelation of Bellario/Euphrasia's female sex is a reinscription of a natural sex and gender binary that arguably contains some of the erotic transgression of the instrumentality plot. In a literal dramatic sense, looming tragedy is turned into comedy by removing an imaginary, illicit penis from the sexual equation. But that reading does not adequately express the lingering queerness of *Philaster*'s ending. Despite its recuperation of the supposed truth of bodily sex, the comic resolution preserves the queer intimacy of the three-person relationship, which, crucially, does not depend on binary sex in any way. Bellario/Euphrasia refuses to be safely slotted into a socially acceptable marriage, emphasizing that his desired outcome was precisely "never to be known" as female bodied (5.5.179). "Never, sir, will I/Marry," he says. "It is a thing within my vow" (5.5.186–87). He also abjures any preference between the members of the couple; being revealed as a girl does not render his desire heterosexual or dyadic. He asks only to be permitted to be with, and to serve, Philaster and Arethusa equally:

> But if I may have leave to serve the princess,
> To see the virtues of her lord and her,
> I shall have hope to live. (5.5.188–90)

The hope of the character who remains dressed as Bellario is to continue to please, to continue to "see the virtues" and engender the pleasures of both partners.

The inclusive domesticity of this resolution is a stark contrast from the putatively heterosexual pairing off at the ends of other cross-dressing comedies such as *Twelfth Night*. It is also markedly different from Moll's defiant, unincorporated queer solitude at the end of *The Roaring Girl*. With the substitution of a woman rather than a man as a third party in Philaster and Arethusa's household, all anxieties about sexual impurity ironically evaporate. Other critics' readings of *Philaster* have pointed out how this resolution shuts down the subversive possibility, flirted with throughout the play, of sex between man and boy, which it does.[69] However, though certain suspicions of dyadic contact are put to rest, these are only the limited sexual possibilities envisioned by the patriarchal gaze of the court onlookers, to whose satisfaction the social order is restored. All other, stranger erotic shadings and insinuations are sustained. In fact, the resolution's wry turn away from the misogynistic suspicion of the plot's crisis leaves space for the rehabilitation of some of those lost, misdirected, and bleeding signifiers through which the three parties tried to communicate their love when Bellario was a boy.

The erotic instrumentality that Bellario embodies is, in the end, expansively social and communal. Just as Bellario/Euphrasia refuses to choose between her lord and her lady, Arethusa also abjures all jealousy and suspicion of Bellario/Euphrasia, in a speech addressed triangularly to both man and boy:

> I, Philaster,
> Cannot be jealous, though you had a lady
> Dressed like a page to serve you, nor will I
> Suspect her living here.—Come live with me,
> Live free as I do. She that loves my lord,
> Cursed be the wife that hates her. (5.5.193–95)

Bellario/Euphrasia remains with Philaster and Arethusa in their home; the change in her supposed, or surface, sex hardly seems to matter to Arethusa or to Philaster, who declares that he "must call thee still" Bellario (5.5.145). While other early modern comedies efface the possibility of female-female carnal contact outside of the carnivalesque time of cross-dressing (as in *Twelfth Night* and *As You Like It*), here, in a play where the cross-dressing isn't exactly cross, and never ends, the potential for (in some sense) female/female eroticism is less than half effaced.[70] Arethusa alludes to Bellario/Euphrasia's love for Philaster (and also blurs the boundaries of identification and desire for him with her initial "I, Philaster"), but then extends a passionate invitation to Bellario to "Come live with me," the two of them living "free" in communion with the same lord. Their bonds of love are inextricable from one another. Arethusa's love for Bellario depends on Bellario's love for Philaster to enable it, and Arethusa's love for Philaster depends on Bellario's love and service to Philaster to deliver and effectuate it. What is not salient to the triad here is the fact that Bellario has been revealed as a woman. The person known as Bellario will continue to function in his instrumental role of mutual service and affection.

What is even queerer about *Philaster*'s resolution is how thoroughly the third is integrated into a permanent three-partner relationship, at least in the second quarto (in the first quarto, Bellario/ Euphrasia is married off to a nobleman at the last moment).[71] Far from being a device that fulfills its function while remaining detached and unaltered, Bellario/Euphrasia is so thoroughly instrumental that he becomes a vital part of the erotic configuration; like a metamorphic Galathea of dildoes, he is an artificial invention, which, transformed by queer polyamorous love, miraculously becomes the very flesh of the relationship. The boy's whole body is an instrument, being used as a surrogated sexual organ to the pleasure of all parties. Echoing both a common Shakespearean trope and a classical encomium in praise of generation, Philaster alludes to the poignancy of the beautiful, androgynous young man's failure to sexually reproduce: "I grieve such virtue should be laid in earth/Without an heir" (5.5.196–97). But in the version of the final scene where Bellario never marries, his uncannily efficacious "virtue" and allure is folded into Philaster and Arethusa's bond instead, where it enjoys a queer form of ethical and relational generativity. The triad's affective plenitude allows them to be generous in pardoning the court gossip who attempted to undo them with sexual slanders. In the king's final speech, it may well be all three of their hands that are joined in one, in hopes of a world where multiple "plenteous branches spring/Wherever there is sun" (5.5.214–15).

Instrumentality is not a coherent social phenomenon, but an affective mode that appears largely to have flown under the discursive radar in the period. As a mode of group intimacy, its form exceeds the very idea of individual subjectivity, resonating more with artificial and technological forms of being. Erotic instruments function in their intimate networks as tools; they multiply and transmit desire, and in being used, they also generate desire themselves. They relay erotic energy, convert it into new forms, and send it in different directions, among subjects of various genders, along trajectories of feeling that exceed gender transgression or gender discipline. The resulting triads and other networks highlight the insufficiency of a subject-based model of sexuality to describe all the dimensions intimacy can take. Crucially, the notion of erotic instrumentality that I have developed here can itself be used; like Bellario, being used to others' ends is its aim. It invites readers to pursue it in other texts, to spawn new metaphors for how desire works in multinodal networks, and to ask new questions about what those configurations can do, dramatically and socially. Following it through these two comedies yields some cumulative effects: a logic of instrumentality draws attention to groupings and collectivities that include some heteronormative social positions (like betrothal or marriage), acknowledging that these do not preclude participation in queerness. This insight allows us to reverse the usual framework for sexuality studies, which usually asks how nonnormative queer bonds fit within heteropatriarchal systems, and ask instead how heteroerotic bonds, like the one between Sebastian and Mary in *The Roaring Girl*, function as part of larger queer affective structures. Reading for an erotics of instrumentality also allows us to notice qualitatively queer valences of desire between characters who are in some sense of different sexes—as between Arethusa and Bellario, or Moll Frith and Sebastian. It also allows the female/female desires in these plays—a full-time transvestite turning out her protégée at her men's tailor, and a passing servant boy's performative declarations of love for his mistress—to be considered as part of the same affective systems as the masculine homoerotic and homosocial desires, like the love at first sight between a weeping shepherd boy and a handsome prince. In other words, by de-emphasizing sexual difference, a notion of being used puts female, male, trans, and genderqueer desires on the same map. And it contests female queer invisibility by naming queer impulses that escape censure—like the resolution of *Philaster*—as both erotic and queer, keeping them from being sanitized, erased, compartmentalized, or folded into something else, like friendship.

Erotic instrumentality is an insistently material relational mode, but *not* one predicated on the natural body as the ultimate determinant of affiliations or roles. Objects like Bellario's garland and Moll's viol carry queer desire through these plays, among heterosexual pairings and gay pairings and queer triads. Attending to the erotic activities of these things problematizes the location of sexuality within the boundaries of the natural body: erotic energy lodges in prostheses and mediating technologies, figuring them, rather than human genitalia, as the salient organs of sexuality, and calling into question whether relationality and desire are necessarily moored to the human organism at all. Thus the instrumental body is qualitatively different from the social body implicated in most studies of past sexual acts and identities, and it offers a different way to think the relation between early modern embodied subjects and material objects. The body being used is neither. It becomes a differently organized, mechanical body that makes use of prosthetic objects, and becomes prosthetic in itself. We see this in the metonymic resonance between Bellario and his communications device: the newly fashioned, newly deracinated, newly male Bellario, sitting by the fountain and crying with his flower garland, an artfully made object that upon interpretation encodes a story of inordinate feeling—but not one so fixed that those who see the beautiful cipher won't read their own feelings into it. In being used and liking it, the go-between materializes queer feelings that extend the notion of sexuality itself. In its ability to decouple intimacy from a prescribed sex, gender role, or number of partners, it bears, like "hidden love," the potential to redefine where—and what—we do and don't perceive desire to be.

2

Everything That Moves

Promiscuous Fancy and Carnival Longing

> I want it all or nothing at all.
> —Miisa, "All or Nothing" (1994), *But I'm a*
> *Cheerleader* film soundtrack (1999)

Whereas the erotic go-between described in the previous chapter exceeds the sexual dyad, transforming it into a tightly bound network of use, love, and service, the fancies that populate what follows here are more free-floating, their aims more desultory. I turn now to the vagaries of bottomless desire: insatiable and indiscriminate appetites for too many objects at once. Unanchored and diffuse, this form of desire does not resolve in any specific erotic ends; instead, it is a boundless lack that is not satisfied, and that knows not what, if anything, would give satisfaction.

This mode of promiscuous fancy shapes the affects of wanting and consuming in two very different comedies: the stylized, mercurial, courtly world of shifting shapes and symbols in William Shakespeare's *Twelfth Night* (1601); and the earthy, sensual world of market pleasures and desiring mobs in Ben Jonson's *Bartholomew Fair* (1614). This juxtaposition may seem strange; but both plays are structured by an underlying erotic economy in which excessively proliferating desire feeds on itself, generating more lack, more longing, and more unfulfilled hunger. Both plays' protagonists—the perpetually dissatisfied Duke Orsino in *Twelfth Night* and the voracious, insatiable Bartholomew Cokes in *Bartholomew Fair*—are bottomless vortices of lack. The moment they attain anything they desire, their interest instantly detaches from it and redirects to something else. Though satisfied by nothing, they persist in desiring everything— everything, that is, except for what each claims, in their respective comic plots, to want: marriage to a woman. Insatiable desire governs other plots in these two plays as well: it is evident in *Twelfth Night* in Malvolio's deluded wish for cross-gartered stockings as an instrument of erotic gratification; and in the range of problematic appetites staged among Jonson's fairgoers vis-à-vis the products and pleasures of the Fair—particularly Bartholomew Cokes's negative foil, the abstemious Puritan Zeal-of-the-Land Busy, whose eroticized disavowal and annihilation of the Fair is no less a form of bottomless hunger than Cokes's.

"The Food of Love"

Twelfth Night (subtitled *What You Will*) both begins and ends by obliquely referring to the strange shapes and capacities of Orsino's desire. It begins with a soliloquy on the prodigious swiftness with which he loses interest, again and again:

> If music be the food of love, play on.
> Give me excess of it that, surfeiting,
> The appetite may sicken and so die.
> That strain again—it had a dying fall;
> Oh, it came o'er my ear like the sweet sound
> That breathes upon a bank of violets
> Stealing and giving odor. Enough, no more!
> 'Tis not so sweet now as it was before.[1]

Desire is figured here as an absurdly accelerated cycle of excess, surfeit, and aversion: *if* music is the "food" of love, it is not the victual that satiates appetite but rather the fuel that inflames it. By inflaming his appetite, Orsino hopes to kill it, to move through a sickening point to aversion, a state without the hunger of desire. The sensuous pleasure of the music he solicits—labor performed onstage, by musicians of his household, who work for him—is abruptly reversed when it begins "stealing and giving odor," making desire distasteful. These opening lines betray the chronically unfixed, even non-alloerotic (non-partner-oriented) quality of Orsino's desire. The conceit of the comedic plot is that he desires Olivia; but the erotic cathexis figured in this opening speech has nothing to do with her, or with any beloved at all.

This is only the first of many moments in *Twelfth Night* where erotic desire appears to autoerotically—or autophagically—feed on itself, rather than proceeding forward and outward toward fulfillment in external objects. Orsino's desire has been understood as confused and un-self-aware in other criticism on *Twelfth Night*. René Girard makes many of the same observations in *A Theatre of Envy*: that the play's heterosexual pairings are conflicted and at odds, fraught with humiliation and ulterior motives; and that Orsino's renunciatory love-sickness signals some pathological appetite ("since all objects that can be possessed prove valueless, I will renounce them once and for all in favor of *those objects that cannot be possessed*").[2] Girard couches his reading in languages of intemperance, secret gluttony, sinful nature, secret guilt, sophistry and self-abuse, anxious misogyny, and performative renunciation—that is, he describes Orsino in every way as a queer figure, without using the word. A closer look, at this solilo-quy and at *Twelfth Night* next to *Bartholomew Fair*, offers up myriad reasons to use the word, ways to understand these affects as the hall-marks of a queer mode of expression, a queer erotic bent:

> O spirit of love, how quick and fresh art thou,
> That, notwithstanding thy capacity
> Receiveth as the sea, naught enters there
> Of what validity and pitch so'er,
> But falls into abatement and low price
> Even in a minute. So full of shapes is fancy
> That it alone is high fantastical. (1.1.9–15)

The "spirit of love" Orsino hails is not bound toward any ultimate climax; rather, it is ceaselessly motile in producing and reproducing *itself*. Its "quickness" and "freshness" give it a prodigious "capacity" for new objects of desire. It takes them in as indiscriminately as the sea—and negates their value and specificity just as quickly, moving on "even in a minute" to receive the next object, in an endless succession of canceled loves. What strikes me as queer about the structure of this desire—besides how falling out of love appears to be its repetition compulsion—is how it behaves like an impressively capacious, promiscuously receptive organ. Its receptivity is not entirely passive either: it undoes the world's allocation of more "validity and pitch" to some objects than others. In its prodigious receptivity, all things—and people—end up at the same "low price" once love is done with them. But at the passage's ending, notice that the love objects that fall in and out of favor so fast do not disappear completely. Rather, they pile on one another in what Orsino calls the "fancy," packing it "full of shapes." These lines figure fancy—the capacity for desiring—in spatial, even bodily, terms: as a densely populated internal reservoir of past, present, and future love objects coexisting in a jumble that defies any heteronormative model of supersession or progress: out of love, but still part of the "high fantastical." It is this mechanism for the production and reproduction of desire, through surfeit and lack, that is my object of analysis in this chapter.

Such a capacious fancy might almost contain the volume of existing scholarship addressing desire, particularly same-sex desire, in *Twelfth Night* (while *Bartholomew Fair* lies at the opposite pole, with little critical attention to its erotic structure). But I propose here, in full knowledge and enjoyment of its additive, even superfluous, quality, *another* queer reading of *Twelfth Night*: one that locates the play's queerness in its articulation of an unmoored, unsatisfiable appetite that feeds on its own lack. Other readings have offered varying verdicts on the reinscription of normative gender and heterosexuality in the play's resolution.[3] Or they have focused on specific relational bonds, like the homosocial friendship between Sebastian and Antonio, or the homoerotic flirtation between Olivia and Cesario/Viola.[4] Currents of queer attraction run every which way throughout the cast of characters: Orsino to himself; Orsino to Cesario/Viola; Olivia to Cesario/Viola; Malvolio to Olivia; Olivia to her dead brother; Viola to Sebastian; Sebastian to Viola; and Antonio to Sebastian. In my view, however, the queerness of *Twelfth Night* permeates beyond its cross-dressing intrigues or even its same-sex interactions, to a more pervasive structural queerness at the level of the play's underlying symbolic and erotic economy—the mechanism by which desires, and their objects, are generated.[5] In what follows, I argue that "fancy" in the play amounts to a polymorphously queer model of erotic generativity. I understand the mode of desiring proffered through Orsino in connection with contemporary notions of fancy, a shifting conception of imagination that functions as a queer, asexual double of heterosexual reproduction, generating not offspring but fantastical, artificial, and aesthetic objects of desire. I connect this model to an emergent hierarchy of value that construes the desire for fancy things as a marker of sexually suspect and unproductive masculinity. In this reading, what is queer about Orsino is not the gendering of the intimacy he shares with his manservant Viola/Cesario, but his account of how desiring happens and how it feels—an account that, by virtue of its protagonistic centrality, stands as the play's model of eros itself.

"So Full of Shapes"

As the title of this book suggests, the idea of fancy serves as a link between the play of queer affect in literary forms and the history of "sexuality" as it is commonly understood. The desires on display in this chapter have aesthetic, economic, and sexual consequences— namely, the gradual shift in meaning of the term "fancy" over the ensuing three centuries, to characterize a taste for pleasurable and beautiful things as a degraded, promiscuous, queer desire for improper, unproductive love objects. Fancy pertains to the negative of sexual reproduction: to material products—from high art to a monstrous baby—fashioned by appetites distinctly other than those resolving in so-called natural or legitimate procreative sex. Over the sixteenth and early seventeenth centuries, "fancy" develops from an older definition synonymous with "fantasy" or "phantasy" into a complex explanatory ideology for how images formed in the mind are bodied forth in material forms.[6] The term originally describes "the process, and the faculty, of forming mental representations of things not present to the senses." It is, in this early use, "chiefly applied to the so-called creative or productive imagination, which frames images of objects, events, or conditions that have not occurred in actual experience."[7] Yet around the same time, an erotic definition develops in which "fancy" can mean desire itself, "amorous inclination, love,"[8] or, when used as a verb, the cathexis linking desire to the conjured object of libidinal fantasy: "to be or fall in love with."[9] This is the definition we all know. But from its inception, erotic fancy has not been a necessarily pleasant state.

Elsewhere in Shakespeare, negative uses of "fancy" refer to the pain of unsatisfied desire, glancing at the queer economy of "fancy" outlined here. In *A Midsummer Night's Dream* in 1590, "fancy-sick" describes love's physical toll on an enamored Helena—her blood, the vital material of nutrition and generation, is wasting away from her: "All fancy-sick she is and pale of cheer/With sighs of love that costs the fresh blood dear" (3.2.96–97). In this case, "fancy" connotes a love that physically consumes itself, expending its potential for self-perpetuation in pathological desire. Helena is harshly disciplined for her unnatural, enchanted cathexis onto Demetrius. Her sickness prefigures the sickness of pregnancy, which "costs the fresh blood dear" (3.2.97) in gestation and birth. This is fancy functioning as a trace of reproduction; its figurations mimetically inscribe an asexual semblance of sexual generativity onto an unnaturally desiring, nonreproductive body. Though Helena's fancy is turned violently inward, rather than free-floating in a sea of shapes, it is no less capricious than Orsino's desire. In both instances, "fancy" is a negatively charged synonym for love, connoting aspects of desire that occur outside of alloerotic or reproductive couplings. Because this reading of the word has the potential to reveal the vexed, fickle, and unsatisfying dynamics underlying most (if not all) desire, it would be easy to simply take the discourse of fancy in *Twelfth Night* as giving voice to an early modern register of tormented, illicit love that goes under the name of Petrarchanism. "Fancy's" emergent seventeenth-century connotation of imaginative facility with aesthetic and poetic production places the term close at hand for English translations of Italian verse and English Petrarchan poetry; translations of Petrarch's sonnets used "fancy" for so many terms that it came to signify everything and nothing.[10] Indeed, the proximity of the erotic and poetic vocabularies puts *Twelfth Night*'s language of fancy at risk of being read instrumentally, as a kind of missing link in a grand

Petrarchan narrative of desire. Melissa Sanchez has illuminated the inherent perversity—even the inherent queerness—of Petrarchan language, pointing out how its erotic power dynamics of abjection and masochism constitute early modern England's rhetorics of both love and politics.[11] What I see in the erotic economy of *Twelfth Night*, though, is not quite the same as the Petrarchan sort of perversity. Orsino's speech does not voice Petrarchanism's fixated, avowedly sadomasochistic orientation toward a singular beloved, despite its strangely truncated Petrarchan language figuring love as appetite; its perversity is of a more free-floating, structural kind. The play gives its desiring characters some of the same objects figured by Petrarchan love (hunger and food, music, and sweet scent in Orsino's first speech; elsewhere, plays on painting, the *blazon*, and Virgilian allusions). But this language contains a comment about itself and the desire it represents. It is an already anachronistic reference, for an audience in 1602, to a literary tradition that is marked as quaint and artificial, a register that signifies not only linguistic art in talking about erotic desire but also its inverse: the constitution of desire through the artifice of language. Fancy thus not only conjures a trace of reproduction, but reverses it, taking up the bodily consequences of sexual desire and implicating them with the production of art.

By attending to the denaturalizing effects of Petrarchan language in *Twelfth Night*, we can relearn some basic lessons of psychoanalytic literary criticism: that desire is always produced and mediated by language, taking shape within the structures of language that give it its vocabulary for narrating itself; and that desire's constitution through language endows it with more, not less, disruptive, queering potential. Fancy in the first scene of *Twelfth Night* posits at the outset that none of the loves represented in the play are anything that could be called natural. On the contrary, its image of love does not appear to be object oriented at all. "If music be the food of love," then the putative beloved is, necessarily, not. Orsino does not want her to materialize; this form of longing does not end in the disillusionment of comparing embodied presence to idealized absence, or even in the inevitable repulsion that is delayed by, and follows from, sexual consummation. The only desire voiced in a sustained way here is the craving for his appetite to self-annihilate without satisfaction.

At the same time as "fancy" acquires its valences of love and eros, it begins to differentiate from "imagination," into a definition emphasizing aesthetic prowess—"aptitude for the invention of illustrative or decorative imagery"—that is, the ability to fashion images for purposes of pleasure.[12] The word's simultaneous connotations of spectral illusion,[13] hallucinatory delusion,[14] original invention,[15] and artistic improvisation[16] are all subtly contiguous with these mental processes. When considered under this cluster of emergent meanings, the closing lines of Orsino's speech carry a new implication: that fancy can make and desire any object it wants. In fact, the soliloquy appears in this light to be far more an autoerotic valorization of Orsino's own capacity for imaginative fantasy than to have anything to do with Olivia, or any other extant love object. If fancy is the faculty of forming mental images "of things not present to the senses," then it must include the ability to imagine an erotic object that *could exist, but doesn't* (yet).[17] In this sense, fancy is an eroticism founded in absence, which feeds on desire. It can take the impression of a lack and reproduce it as a fantasy, shaped by the mind's own, not necessarily virtuous predilections. The range of possible fantasy objects, then, is by no means limited to real, natural, heteroerotic, or socially acceptable object choices.

Alongside its self-negating, abortive attitude toward external love objects, the fancy Orsino describes possesses hints of a queer generativity as well; if it can be "full of shapes," it may be imagined not only as a receptive orifice but a generative matrix, a psychic womb that conceives and makes mental forms inside itself. Early modern figurations of fancy are used to account for all kinds of generative processes that exhibit some uncanny spark: poetry, art, science—and human reproduction, when it goes awry. Even an artificial object, such as a picture of a "blacke-a-more," had the potential to become unnaturally naturalized in the body of a child by the telekinetic force of a woman's transgressive imagination or fancy.[18] The well-known early modern theory of the "mother's fancy" is not only about racial anxiety and the disobedient female imagination; when subjected to a queer analysis, it also introduces imagination into the mechanism of reproduction. It allows fantasy and fiction to become part of how sex, birth, and descent work. It also notes the unpredictable physicality with which unruly erotic drives can work on the body, and the power of uncontained imagination to bear disruptive, surprising shapes into the world. By engaging it here, want to move fancy away from a primary association with female sexuality gone wrong and to draw out the other, promiscuous forms of generativity embedded in its mechanism. In fact, the transgressive mother's fancy is perhaps the one kind of wayward desire that does not seriously threaten in *Twelfth Night* or *Bartholomew Fair*. Decoupled from heterosexual reproduction, fancy does more varied and interesting work in these two plays as a shaping force that shadows or queers generation, emphasizing its artifice, and diverting erotic energy away from attainment, to longing and lack.

The erotic sense of fancy carries over into a whole range of colloquial meanings indicating loose or uncontained sexualities: someone who is "fancy-free" or "fancy-loose" is untethered by heterosexual marriage. In *A Midsummer Night's Dream,* the term illustrates a well-known image of queer virginity in a passage about a vestal votaress immune to Cupid's hailing arrows of love: "And the imperial votress passèd on/In maiden meditation, fancy-free" (2.1.163–64).[19] This vestal virgin's queer imperviousness, however, is shadowed, immediately preceded in the scene, by Tatiana's evocation in memory of her pregnant friend the Indian votaress, whose body swells with imaginative pleasures that are not contained by heterosexual models of reproduction. In her artful imitation of ships at sail in the harbor, it is she who seems to "grow big-bellied with the wanton wind" (2.1.129). As Alicia Andrzejewski explicates, the Indian votaress's pregnancy is neither produced by, nor productive of, heterosexual erotic desires or social bonds; instead it generates a queer kinship between women that reaches beyond death.[20] The pair of votaresses here are both implicated in a model of desire figured as fancy, through which we are reminded that heterosexual generation is not the only kind—and that desire may not resolve in, or even be necessary for, generation at all.

Orsino's fancy is figured as replete with forms; its fullness of shapes resonates strongly with Freud's term for the wide-ranging capacities of infantile desire, polymorphous perversity.[21] "Polymorphous" literally means many shapes—"full of shapes." In asserting that human desire is primally, originally "polymorphously perverse,"

Freud contends that sexual norms—including, crucially, the taboos "against members of one's own sex" and against "the transferring of the part played by the genitals to other organs and areas of the body"—must be taught and enforced by disciplining children into (hetero)normative human sexual subjects.[22] Thus the heterosexual telos of the marriage plot depends on more originary auto- and homoerotic energies to make even its performance possible. Imagining desire in *Twelfth Night* as polymorphously perverse—that is, as encyclopedically flexible, infantile, and unable to differentiate among proper and improper objects—reveals an erotics of nonfulfillment cycling through the play, only incompletely resutured to heterosexual objects even in the comic resolution. I would name what Orsino describes as "fancy" in *Twelfth Night* as an affective mode of polymorphous perversity. The opening speech does away with any language of a developmental trajectory or timeline for love; it also confounds clear-cut distinctions between natural and unnatural processes of desiring. It traces the expected sequence of object oriented desire in the negative, as an absent presence full of artifice and caprice—not to say deviance—and shadows nonreproductive homo- and autoerotic interactions with hints of generation.

Though the last phrase of Orsino's opening speech might appear to be a tautology (if "fancy" corresponds to "fantastical"), I think it is instead a suggestive pun that plays with the multiple valences of the term "fancy" to gesture toward the queer stakes of the desire it is figuring. In my reading, the phrase, "so full of shapes is fancy/That it alone is high fantastical" links the "high fantastical" virtuosity of the fancy in generating novel images to the indiscriminate erotic "appetite" that causes the fancy to be "so full of shapes." There is a suggestion here that art and poetry, the material forms by which creativity enters the world, are attributable in some sense to the promiscuous, unappeasable force called fancy. Unsatisfied, wandering lust, proliferating in a crowded pile of fantasmatic "shapes" filling one's "fancy," may be where aesthetic production comes from. Of course, the figuration of desire in the rest of the play expands far beyond this single speech. But the groundwork is laid for the play's subsequent explorations of loss, obstruction, and doubt: sexual difference will be erased, confused, or insignificant; available love objects will be substituted for inaccessible ones; prosthetic garments will become the objects of disproportionate investment, speculation, and thwarted hope; and desire will fail to follow any of the predictable paths.

Fancy reveals that heterosexual reproductivity is not a prior or inevitable condition; rather, it is inescapably supplanted by, and utterly dependent on, auto- and homoerotic energies to animate it and make it possible. For the doubly twinned foursome of Olivia, Viola, Sebastian, and Orsino, fancy works tacitly as well as explicitly to demonstrate that the primary bonds of love and desire in the play are not the superficially normalized matches eventually instated at the resolution, but the web of homoerotic and incestuous affinities that precede them.[23] These bonds are based on the likeness that Aubrey, looking back nostalgically at Beaumont and Fletcher's symbiotic collaboration, called "a wonderfull consimility of phansey."[24] When Sebastian appears in Illyria and sees Olivia, his ultimate heterosexual object choice, for the first time, he implores "fancy" to keep his sister Viola's image before his eyes instead—"Let fancy still my sense in Lethe steep./If it be thus to dream, still let me sleep" (4.1.57–58)—because he believes he is seeing Viola in a dream. Viola cries out to her own fancy after she unknowingly impersonates Sebastian and fights with Antonio, who loves Sebastian and cannot understand why Viola does not know him. Viola begs to be "taken" for one so close to her that he is almost indistinguishable from herself: "Prove true, imagination, oh, prove true,/That I, dear brother, be now ta'en for you" (3.4.342–43).

Act 1, scene 2 juxtaposes the images of Olivia and Viola mourning their brothers, whose shapes in these two sisters' fancies do more than just take precedence over possible romantic couplings; they turn the women from heteroerotic attractions. Orsino's man, Valentine, describes Olivia's practice of memory:

> But, like a cloistress, she will veilèd walk
> And water once a day her chamber round
> With eye-offending brine. All this to season
> A brother's dead love, which she would keep fresh
> And lasting in her sad remembrance. (1.1.27–31)

This language leaves an open question as to whether Olivia's mourning is more akin to summoning a spirit by means of the fantastical arts, cultivating a plant, or pickling a vegetable. Though her brother has passed into the realm of fantastical shapes, Olivia wants to preserve him in her fancy, where she can continue to interact with him, with the "brine" of her tears. The language of pickling here ("brine," "season," "keep fresh") gives the process a salient materiality, by which the dead brother's fancy image in Olivia's memory (that is, in her imagination) must be manufactured and preserved with the brine of her tears. Olivia's fancy also forecloses her participation in heterosexual reproduction; her eroticism is directed toward a dead man. In refusing a heterosexual love object, she has, in Freud's language of narcissism, "substituted for real objects imaginary ones from [her] memory."[25] She has withdrawn from people and things in the external world and replaced them in her fantasy life. Moreover, the dead brother's impression alters Olivia's performance of sexual identity, to that of a celibate nun who has spectacularly "abjured the sight/And company of men" (1.2.39–40).

Viola's desire for her absent brother is also stoked by an image that her fancy constructs from language, a narrative she receives from the Captain. The Captain describes in florid detail how Sebastian, in the shipwreck, bound himself to a floating mast and rode the waves:

> I saw your brother,
> Most provident in peril, bind himself
> (Courage and hope both teaching him the practice)
> To a strong mast that lived upon the sea.
> Where, like Arion on the dolphin's back,
> I saw him hold acquaintance with the waves,
> So long as I could see. (1.2.11–17)

Viola's imagination shapes these words into a verbal effigy in the form of her brother's body. She pays the Captain for his words: "For saying so, there's gold" (1.2.17). The purchase of this verbal conjuration marks the breakdown between nature and artifice: if the story of Sebastian on the mast were a purely fictional tale, made in the crucible of the Captain's imagination, it would still have an affective and market value to Viola, whose fancy manufactures it into a valuable substitute love object. What fancy is doing here resonates with Derrida's critique of the "natural" through the idea of the "dangerous supplement," in his reading of Jean-Jacques Rousseau. As in Derrida, absence is functioning for Olivia and Viola as the primary condition for desire. The (absent) brothers are conjured with words, ritual, tears—all supplements that are actually the point, the enactment of the desire itself. This echoes Derrida's reversal of Rousseau, in which he recasts the absence-based "supplements" (masturbation and writing) as primary attractions and defenses, rather than secondary to the pleasures of presence (partner sex and speech): "The supplement has not only the power of *procuring* an absent presence through its image; procuring it for us through the proxy [procuration] of the sign, it holds it at a distance and masters it."[26] The mental images conjured by fancy in *Twelfth Night* are this kind of active, procuring supplement: mediating, autoerotic, queer objects of desire in their own right. Tracing the persistence of fancy reveals the truth of Derrida's point that when we interact with another, present body, we, like Olivia and Viola, are always already interacting with the image of the absent body—and our construction of said image—in our fancy. The Captain's narrative actually has something to offer Viola that Sebastian in the flesh would not; it is pure form, absent of subjectivity. It can be used to Viola's fancy.

If fancy induces Viola to autoerotic substitution, it spurs Olivia's desire to swerve and attach to "Cesario," Viola's purpose-made masculine persona. The homoerotic tension between the two women has been influentially glossed, by Traub and others, as lesbian desire.[27] About this relationship, which hardly appears to need queering, I would point out that, like the polymorphously perverse Orsino, Olivia can also conjure (auto)erotic objects through the power of her fancy. We know that her fancy hosts the form of an ideal Cesario/Viola; we do not know whether that ideal form is anatomically male. It is an open question whether Olivia starts to suspect that Viola is a woman in their exchange in act 3, scene 1:

VIOLA: Then you think right. I am not what I am.
OLIVIA: I would you were as I would have you be. (132–33)

If Olivia does start to suspect, it is not at all clear whether perhaps Viola as a female *is* "as [Olivia] would have [her] be."[28] To be specific, we are not at all sure whether or not the ideal Cesario/Viola in Olivia's fancy possesses that "little thing" that "would make" the Viola "tell them how much [she] lack[s] of a man"—that is, a penis (3.4.271–72). If no, Olivia's attraction is homoerotic. If yes, then Olivia's desire "swerves" toward the heteroerotic,[29] but there is nothing "natural" about the body onto which it cathects. Olivia's fancy-image of Cesario/Viola is then supplemented by the presence of a prosthetic phallus, added not by nature but by the artifice of imagination—a fancied apparitional counterpart to the young transmasculine weaver from Vitry-le-François, discussed in chapter 1, whose sartorial and sexual "inventions" were discovered and punished in Montaigne.[30] Either possibility decouples natural from heteroerotic, and unnatural from homoerotic, desire. With or without the "little thing," Cesario/Viola's imagined body cannot fit into any category of the natural or heteronormative; Olivia's construction is inevitably the product (and object) of a queered desire.

I am trying to highlight that Olivia is doing to Cesario/Viola what the audience is also doing to the boy actor playing Viola: speculating about what he looks like under his clothes. The audience enjoys the erotic frisson of imagining a prosthetic female body that we know is not physically there between the boy actor's body and Cesario's clothes (which are really Sebastian's clothes).[31] The actor playing Cesario/Viola is tasked with communicating a gorgeously awkward, ambiguous negotiation between performing a girl and performing a girl in disguise as a boy. Yet though the cross-dressed boy-heroine received a great deal of critical and theatrical attention in the late twentieth century, audiences of our current historical moment have been given a chance to wonder in a newly defamiliarized way about Olivia's imagination and desire. The early twenty-first century has seen a spate of highly acclaimed productions of *Twelfth Night* with casts made up entirely of male-bodied actors, notably including Declan Donnellan's long-lived Cheek By Jowl production (which has had its most recent life as a Russian-language production dating from 2003), and the celebrated Shakespeare's Globe productions of 2002 and 2013 starring Mark Rylance as Olivia. These productions tend to center Olivia as the avatar of gender art and gender fancy in the play, pointing up the contrast between male actor playing "real" woman (Olivia) and male actor playing woman playing boy (Cesario/ Viola). Critical responses to these performances often emphasize the character's femininity and the success of the male actor in seamlessly embodying an ideal image of feminine beauty (Ben Brantley on Rylance's Olivia: "reserved but emotionally ripe," "woven out of starlight," "seemed to float across the stage").[32] However, even in productions where a male-bodied Olivia is staged as the consummate woman, the dramatic indeterminacy around the shape of her desire remains. Feminine gender does not entail any necessary directionality of desire, any more than it requires a female body. We still cannot know her fancy.

"It Should Be One of My Complexion"

In stark contrast to Orsino's love rhapsody with himself, Malvolio's spectacular amorous failure, and the failure of his yellow cross-gartered stockings to fulfill their hoped-for erotic function, exemplify a manifestation of fancy that seems at first glance to be object oriented, or even heterosexual. However, the affair of the stockings ultimately ends up contributing to the overarching structure of polymorphously perverse desire in the play. Pondering a prank letter which implants in his fancy a delusion that Olivia is in love with him, Malvolio muses, "'Tis but fortune; all is fortune. Maria once told me she did affect me, and I have heard herself come thus near, that, should she fancy, it should be one of my complexion" (2.5.20–23). Malvolio's infatuation with Olivia may be the most straightforwardly heteroerotic cathexis in the play, and even it can only be articulated in negative terms. It is founded on a lie and can only be phrased as a not very near, hypothetical, future subjunctive affection. Any possibility of dyadic erotic congress in this play—heteroerotic or homoerotic, cross-dressed or merely ridiculously costumed—can only be spoken as disavowal, hearsay, and equivocation.[33] Malvolio's dancing, indirect expressions of investment in Olivia come to a bad end. The play subtly disallows goal-oriented, possessive erotic agendas; all proactive efforts to attain a partner are met with some form of humiliation (see Olivia's gifts and entreaties to Cesario/Viola)—but none more than Malvolio's.

What does become a perverse erotic object are the yellow cross-gartered stockings, which he fancies might offer him access to Olivia's fancy. In a cruel etymological irony, the ornaments hanging from stockings, "the ornamental tags, appended to the ribbons by which the hose were secured to the doublet," are called "fancy."[34] Falsely thinking it is at Olivia's behest, he pays specific, ritualistic attention to making a cross with the stockings' fancy as he dresses. It doesn't work; the stockings fail to engender, in Olivia, who "detests" the fashion (2.5.175), any specific sensation of lack for Malvolio. They are so unpleasant to wear that Malvolio's only pleasure in them is in the masochistic pain of wearing them for her pleasure: "This does make some obstruction in the blood, this cross-gartering. But what of that? If it please the eye of one, it is with me as the very true sonnet is: 'Please one, and please all'" (3.4.19–22). Unlike the erotic objects in Orsino's polymorphous sea, Malvolio's low social pitch remains constant. His attempt to use a prosthetic adornment to raise it backfires, plummeting both him and his fancy stockings "into abatement and low price,/Even in a minute" (1.1.13–14).

Widening the frame to consider the afterlife of this word makes visible the ramifications of fancy in the material, commercial, and aesthetic realms—and, sooner than one might think, in the history of sexuality. Following Eve Sedgwick's suggestion that nonce taxonomies can hone and transmit "skills for making, testing, and using unrationalized and provisional hypotheses," I posit a "nonce etymology" of fancy: an unfalsifiable queer genealogy of the concept's associations with artistic production, commodity desire, and various forms of gender and sexual transgression through the centuries between *Twelfth Night* and today.[35] I do this not to retroactively relabel fancy as a form of queerness in the period, but to point out how the mechanisms of fancy allow queerness to enter the imaginative world of a play. The richly proliferating definitions of imaginative fancy at the beginning of the seventeenth century congeal over the next three centuries into a long list of connotations pointing away from heteronormativity and a patriarchal social order. Fancy as desire becomes an adverbial that can work *on* someone (fancy-baffled, fancy-caught,

EVERYTHING THAT MOVES

fancy-framed, fancy-struck) in the early to mid-seventeenth century, giving it a slightly more threatening erotic efficacy.[36] By the early to mid-nineteenth century, the early definition of "amorous inclination" becomes an adjective (used in compounds like "fancy-man"), which derives its literal meaning from love ("a person who is fancied"),[37] but which is actually used to mean "a kept mistress" ("fancy-girl" or "fancy-piece"), one who lives outside the bonds of patriarchal domesticity, improperly diverting and consuming resources from heterosexuality.[38] "Fancy-man," however, refers by 1811 to "a man kept by a lady for secret services," or (though the *Oxford English Dictionary* presents these as though they are the same thing) "a man who lives upon the earnings of a prostitute."[39] What starts out as an economic slur and a sex-work pejorative then narrows, by the twentieth century, to index effeminate or homosexual masculinity: the word passes through "fancy Dan," "a dandy, a showy buy ineffective worker or sportsman," and thus into the lineage of "dandyism," a key subcultural term in the eighteenth and nineteenth centuries' incipient discourses of homosexuality.[40]

But this process is part of a larger reordering of meaning around the word "fancy" taking place in areas that "intersect with, touch, or list in the direction of sex" to varying degrees.[41] The assorted dirty uses of "fancy" cluster around early fragmentary and informal suspicions about nonnormative erotic inclinations, what the people who have them are like, and what they do in the world. By tracing the word across its sexual, nonsexual, and quasi-sexual meanings, the outlines emerge of a qualitative queerness: it refers to desires that are excessive in a free-floating and superfluous way. Along with its older connotations of illusion and delusion, the word describes caprice and irrational or fantastical whims as far back as the mid-sixteenth, and into the late fifteenth, centuries.[42] In the mid-eighteenth century, it begins to describe objects of intricate or ornamental appearance; "fancy" as the skill of the mental imagination comes to refer instead to the variation in an original design.[43] Then, later in the eighteenth century, it becomes a common adjective delineating a category of things that are fancy—which of course includes many of the decorative objects associated with women's economic consumption (baskets, cakes, trimmings, dresses, needlework).[44] It is this category that appears to draw together the earlier connotations of resource-consuming sexuality ("fancy-woman," "fancy-man") with a new denigration of ornamental goods as frivolous, excessive, and non-useful. In this descriptor (the one still in use today), we can see the same dual suspicions of insatiable consumption and capricious desire that I unpack in *Twelfth Night* and *Bartholomew Fair*, combined with overlayered anxieties about people who have too much sex, do too little work, or do work that is too ornamental—by which many women and men are cast under suspicion of being either prostitutes or freeloaders by virtue of their tastes and pastimes. I would even take this nonce etymology one step further and ask what later queer terms or affiliations can be linked back with their possible connections to "fancy." For example, in an "obsolete" meaning from 1712 with intriguing never-to-be-recovered associations, "fancy" is defined as "an alleged name for the pansy."[45] "The fancy" also serves as a somewhat cryptic in-group shorthand for the collectivity of devotees ("fanciers") of some subcultural pursuit, especially boxing,[46] and a term for the breeding of animals or plants with specific aesthetic features, especially varied colors, for ornamental purposes.[47] These are all gay resonances; "fancy" as the art of breeding is quite literally the queer, aestheticizing, artificial double of natural sexual reproduction. Situating Malvolio's thwarted love plot within the space marked out by these associations—where erotic imagination and social categories collide, and where manufacture and style operate on sexual desire—drives home how "fancy" queers heterosexuality by decoratively breeding, embroidering, or painting it into something else.

One place where the "history that will be"[48] is written around and about men's erotic uses of stockings is in Freudian discourses of fetishism. Clearly Malvolio's stockings have something in common with Freud's notion of the fetish: an intimate garment that becomes an erotic repository in its own right, even as it signals the denial of heterosexual sex.[49] For as much as the psychic motions of the imaginative fancy described in these early philosophical definitions are echoed in Freud's model of the ego's libidinal cathexis, the risks of fancy and fetish are slightly different. A thing of consuming fancy does not become the ultimate object, the idol, of a fixed desire as a fetish object does. In fancying, the thing of fancy instead carries the shaping impressions of all the fantasies that produced it. The risk that fancy and the fetish share, however, which is consonant with early capitalist anxieties about consumer desire, is that material things, and not human love objects, are driving the process. As Malvolio's failed fetishistic fancy cuts him off from any ability to effect a causal relationship between word and action, Orsino's desire reverses and redirects itself, floating, disconnected from the heteronormative hierarchy of object choices. The fancier surrenders to being shaped by these made things (which can be thing-embodied people—in *Twelfth Night*, the creation called Cesario—and inanimate materials—in *Bartholomew Fair*, roast pig, gingerbread children, puppets, and dolls). The incipient global circuits of commodity desire and consumption operating in the period have a host of material effects on ideologies of gender, religion, colonialism, and race.[50] The next section of this chapter will unpack how some of these circuits map specifically onto desire, figuring consuming fancy as at once promiscuous and abject—the affectively overwrought longing for, and excessive consumption of, the wrong things.

"Pray Thee Long"

The capacious, capricious appetite that goes by the name of fancy in *Twelfth Night* appears in a different form in Jonson's teeming, odiferous London setting. Desire in *Bartholomew Fair* is a promiscuous force that can, and does, animate many different body parts and objects apart from and other than the genitals. The play dramatizes the carnivalesque urban space of the notorious two-week market festival beginning on St. Bartholomew's Day (August 24) in the Smithfield environs of the Priory Church of St. Bartholomew the Great, an annual tradition of almost five hundred years' standing in 1614, when the play was staged. Like most city comedies, the play is centrally concerned with the circulations of sex: where desire goes awry, what it threatens, and how it is (and isn't) recontained. The structure of the play, with its peripatetic shifts from stall to stall and subplot to subplot inside the Fair, enacts a sprawling, disjointed array of dramatic investments. However, *Bartholomew Fair* is not an eclectic accretion of brief unrelated incidents. Instead, its scenes of desiring are knitted together by an underlying through line of promiscuous fancy, transmuted into a frenetic carnival longing that circulates everywhere and is never sated.

The overlapping comic plots of the play all insistently foreground marriage, sex, and reproduction: married couples, pregnancy cravings, competing suitors, the threat of prostitution, and, most absurdly, the gargantuan, infantile protagonist, Bartholomew Cokes, who is contracted to marry a young gentlewoman on the very day of the Fair (though he never makes it). But for me, the central joke of the play is that the libidinal energies of its interlocking comic plots take every conceivable twist and turn other than their ostensible aims of heterosexual congress or marriage. Not only do this play's permutations of desire refuse and decenter the heterosexual dyad to an even greater degree than most city comedies; the characters' appetites are not even reliably fixed on single objects, resulting in a pervasive economy of roving, insatiable carnival longing. Existing scholarship on *Bartholomew Fair* has largely unpacked the ideological and historical valences of specific content, such as Jonson's satirical godly Puritan, Zeal-of-the-Land Busy. Because of its voluminous and seemingly chaotic scope, critics have not been inclined to synthesize an account of how erotic desire works in the play as a whole. Indeed, without this holistic structural reframing, making visible the polymorphously perverse and unsated mechanism of desire that I find governs the Fair, most critics do not seem to have seen anything specifically queer about the play.[51]

Bartholomew Fair is fundamentally a play about wanting. The Fair is a space where desires of all valences are excited, the fairgoers enticed from every direction and by every kind of object. They seek and find the pleasures of roast pig, beer, toys and trinkets, pastries, musical ballads, purses, and puppet shows. However, these moments of consumption do not provide ends or resolution for the roaming, autoerotically fueled want that ranges through the play, taking on a dramatic life of its own. In scene 6 of act 1, for example, the Littlewit family is preparing to go to the Fair. John Littlewit, a proctor, has the license for Bartholomew Cokes's abortive marriage, but he also has his own "affair i' the Fair," "a puppet-play of mine own making," which he is producing in collaboration with Lantern Leatherhead, the hobbyhorse maker.[52] With him travel his wife, Win; her passionate and loopy mother, Dame Purecraft; and one of the mother's two suitors, the hot Puritan named Zeal-of-the-Land Busy. The Littlewit husband and wife long to go to the Fair, he to preside over his puppet play and she to watch it, but Win's mother will not consent to such a "profane motion" (1.5.132). To get them to the Fair, John Littlewit proposes "a device, a dainty one."[53] He instructs his wife to *long*:

> Win, long to eat of a pig, sweet Win, in the Fair; do you
> see? in the heart of the Fair. . . . Your mother will do
> anything, Win, to satisfy your longing, you know; pray
> thee long, presently, and be sick on the sudden, good Win.
> (1.5.135–40)

The reason her performative longing can have such an effect is that Win Littlewit is pregnant—or at least possibly pregnant. In criticism and stagings of the play, Win is commonly assumed to be far enough along in her pregnancy that her condition is publicly apparent. However, there is nothing in the text to contravene the reading that her pregnancy is still in the early stages of invisibility, or even potentiality. Win's "longing" sounds a more fantastical note if she is not visibly pregnant. As a young married woman who has not yet borne children, Win's reproductive status is an object of sustained projection, desire, and anxiety from her mother and relatives.[54] If she is regarded as only "a little bit pregnant," or even "prepregnant," in a state of pregnancy watch, then her cravings—like a sudden, all-consuming "longing" to eat of a pig in the Fair—are social signs telegraphing the possibility of a bodily state that, in an age before pregnancy tests, remains for quite some time more of a fictive, social wish than a palpable fact. That Win's is the inaugural longing in a play laden with longings typifies the queer admixture of real and imaginary, natural and deviant urges involved in the production and reproduction—fantasmatic and material—of desires and their objects in this play.

"What Do You Lack?"

The play cuts rapidly back and forth between the dithering Little-wit party and the accidental title character, Bartholomew Cokes. The reluctant groom is nineteen years old, a giant, spoiled man-child of unbridled and obscene appetites. Bartholomew Cokes's defining orientation is toward indiscriminately consuming as much of every pleasure and commodity as possible, though he is never satiated. In his first appearance, he pleads wheedlingly to his man, Wasp (whom he calls by the overly familiar pet name Numps), to be allowed to see his own marriage license—"Is this the license, Numps? For love's sake, let me see't. I never saw a license" (1.5.29–30). His infantile position of unrestrained indulgence, from his first appearance, completely overshadows the plot point of his supposed impending marriage to Mistress Grace Wellborn (who is none too pleased about it) scheduled for later the same day. The Fair is the first, last, and central end for Cokes, far surpassing his wedding: "I am resolute Bartholomew, in this; I'll make no suit on't to you; 'twas all the end of my journey, indeed, to show Mistress Grace my Fair" (1.5.52–57). Cokes's relation to the Fair is one of autoerotic identification and in-corporation. He calls it "my Fair, because of Bartholomew; you know my name is Bartholomew, and Bartholomew Fair" (1.5.58–59). Wasp describes his charge as embodying the Fair's superfluous trinkets and objects within himself:

> Would the Fair and all the drums and rattles in't were i'
> your belly for me; they are already i' your brain. He that
> had the means to travel your head, now, should meet finer
> sights than any are i' the Fair, and make a finer voyage
> on't to see it all hung with cockleshells, pebbles, fine
> wheat-straws, and here and there a chicken's feather and a
> cobweb. (1.5.81–86)

These fancy objects are generated in Cokes's fancy: the inner space of his psyche is "all hung with" the excess, worthless materials—shells, pebbles, straw, feathers, cobwebs—that make up the festival landscape. Bartholomew Cokes is a walking empty Fair, a Fair-space that, like a hungry gorge, attempts to suck all of the commodities of the Fair into himself. Wasp complains:

> If he go to the Fair, he will buy of everything to a baby
> there; and household-stuff for that too. If a leg or an arm
> on him did not grow on, he would lose it i' the press. Pray
> heaven I bring him off with one stone! And then he is such
> a ravener after fruit! You will not believe what a coil I had
> t'other day to compound a business between a Catherine-
> pear woman and him about snatching! 'Tis intolerable,
> gentlemen. (1.5.100–107)

Cokes's body is figured as dis-assemblable and exchangeable with the Fair. Though he can be counted on to leave the Fair with a prodigious haul of goods, he would lose his legs or arms (or potentially a more crucial body part, the ambiguous "stone" of Wasp's lament) if they were not attached. Cokes's ravenousness knows no limits. By act 3, he is driving Wasp ahead of him through the Fair, laden with goods but at every instant hailed into fancying more by the vendors' crying:

> LEATHERHEAD: What do you lack, gentlemen? Fine purses,
> pouches, pin-cases, pipes? What is't you lack? A pair
> o'smiths to wake you i' the morning? Or a fine whistling
> bird?
> COKES: Numps, here be finer things than any we ha'
> bought, by odds! And more delicate horses, a great deal!
> (3.4.15–19)

The hobbyhorse maker's cry—the incantatory question cried by all the Fair's vendors, "What do you lack?"—encapsulates the mechanism of desire at work in *Bartholomew Fair*. The marketgoers' fancy, which proceeds from the incitement of lack, feeds on that lack to generate new lacks and more desires for an endless cascade of new objects, so that eventually the consumer is consumed with a surfeit of want and longing. This cycle has often been articulated in Marxist or materialist terms, as the way in which capitalism manufactures commodity desires in order to consume its own surplus and fuel its expansion. As many other early modern plays, including Marlowe's *The Jew of Malta* (1592), Chapman, Jonson, and Marston's *Eastward Ho!* (1605), and Jonson's *The Alchemist* (1610)—as well as Marx's *Capital* (1867)—make clear, uncanny generativity and suspect desires are integral to the idea of capitalist accumulation at its inception.

In particular, *The Alchemist,* another Jonson comedy that problematizes the wanting and getting of material goods, is animated by a force that is related to, but not exactly synonymous with, promiscuous fancy: the generative logic of alchemy, thematized in the play as a vehicle—in both the literal and metaphorical senses—for the desire to acquire wealth without labor. *The Alchemist* shares *Bartholomew Fair*'s concern with the transactions of desire through physical substances (and *Twelfth Night*'s concern with the workings of material objects on desire). Whereas the economies of *Twelfth Night* and *Bartholomew Fair* are powered by sensory and aesthetic appetites, the cheat of alchemy seeks an outside or exception to the natural laws governing materiality and then shades into a flirtation with magical overreaching or necromancy. For the con artists Subtle, Face, and Doll, alchemy is a show, a performative supplement to their swindling. It is a means of getting goods without labor by playing on their parade of customers' desires. *The Alchemist*'s chiefest desiring consumer, Sir Epicure Mammon, can be read alongside Bartholomew Cokes and Orsino, for what he wants is the object that offers a bottomless sea of other objects of desire: the philosophers' stone, which can transmute worthless substances into gold. Mammon voices the tensions between the ancient fantasies around alchemy and the new role of the consumer in a capitalist economy in his rhapsodies of future economic conquest, not through ingenuity or virtue, or by making anything, but through sheer purchasing power:

SURLY: And do you think to have the stone with this?
MAMMON: No, I do think t' have all this with the stone.
SURLY: Why, I have heard he must be homo frugi,

A pious, holy, and religious man,
One free from mortal sin, a very virgin.
MAMMON: That makes it, sir; he is so: but I buy it;
My venture brings it me. (2.2.95–101)

This capitalist consumer and self-styled "venturer" expresses a bottomless notion of his own desert. To have every possible object of
desire, tangible and intangible, he need only have a near-infinite
amount of money. By Mammon's logic, money is desert: to be able
to buy something is to desire it, and to desire it is to deserve it. This
kind of tautological justification echoes the one heard in our current moment of postmodern finance capital, in the argument that the
agents of financial institutions, whose venturing caused the cata-
strophic destruction of wealth in the global financial crisis of 2008,
deserve astronomical salaries and bonus payments (underwritten by
the public in the form of state bailouts) in reward for their pursuit
of the unfettered generation of money. But there is also a Trumpian
nihilism to Mammon's position. The money is but the necessary condition for the over-the-top fantasy of promiscuous domination he narrates, which includes hiring the most "sublimed pure" wives of the
most upstanding citizens to be his whores, the "purest and gravest
divines" to be his flatterers, and the lustiest ladies' men to be his
eunuchs, "to fan me with ten estrich tails/A-piece, made in a plume
to gather wind" (2.2.55–70). The more he can consume, destroy, and
debase by his expenditure, the more it proves his power.

The lust for the philosophers' stone is a flexible, mercenary
version of desire that feeds on itself, not fixed on any specific object,
or even limited to a finite number of objects. In Jonson's extended
political metaphor, alchemy—and capitalism—desire to transform
what has been a scarce resource used in goal-directed transactions—
gold—into a magically self-propagating currency that can fulfill an
endless series of wants, including (as we shall also see in *Bartholomew
Fair*) the antisocial desire to consume and destroy other people. *The
Alchemist*'s model of insatiate desire is mediated through money—
gold, currency, property, investment shares. However, reading it
here, alongside these other scenes of desiring, allows us to notice

how the erotic structure of capitalism is connected to polymorphous fancy, alchemy, magic, fetishism, eating, swindling, and sexual perversion, as overarching mechanisms of bottomless desire.

This kind of erotic analysis of Jonson's city comedies has the potential to expand the scope of what a materialist critical lens can do. By transporting the substances and forces that are commonly the objects of materialist analysis into the realm of desire, it troubles a strict distinction between material and affective or erotic economies. Following on Deleuze and Guattari's concept of "desiring-production," which conceives of both desires and their objects as machines within a larger complex of machines generating social affects and relations, I read the market processes staged in *Bartholomew Fair* as a model dramatizing the production and reproduction of desire itself.[55] As Wasp, exasperated, reminds Bartholomew Cokes, all of his desiring is productive of nothing but more desiring. There is no proper, socially reproductive place in Cokes's aristocratic household for all of these objects to go: "Why the measles should you stand here with your train, cheaping of dogs, birds, and babies? You ha' no children to bestow 'em on, ha' you?" (3.4.25–27). Whereas Win Littlewit's potential reproductivity could serve as a semirespectable pretext for her longing to eat Bartholomew pig, Bartholomew Cokes's appetite for the fancy goods of the Fair makes him a defective and unaccountable sort of man. Wasp likens him to a colonialist trope attributing a form of fancy desire to Native Americans: "a kind o' civil savages that will part with their children for rattles, pipes, and knives. You were best buy a hatchet or two, and truck with 'em" (3.4.30–32). What Cokes buys instead is a prodigious load of trinkets to add to the bundle Wasp already carries, which must already be huge and sprawling enough to be played for laughs. Cokes's satisfaction at any of these purchases, however, is negligible; each one recedes instantly into craving for the next object to catch his fancy. He remarks, without a hint of self-awareness, "I do want such a number o' things" (3.4.81–82).

Like Orsino's ceaselessly ebbing, abating fancy in *Twelfth Night*, Bartholomew Cokes's desire echoes a Freudian notion of polymorphous perversity, in which libidinal energies are not focused on an external love object, or even on a genital drive. Instead, like Orsino's fancy, Cokes's longing is directed everywhere except toward a socially appropriate heterosexual marriage, and it is newly redirected by each new object that enters his sphere of vision. Though Cokes's insatiable, polymorphously perverse brand of object-relations is predicated on the utter opposite of refusal, it is still, like Orsino's fancy, a form of negative desire—desire based on lack—because it is never abated or lessened by any object he obtains. Lack is everywhere in it, the undiminished by-product of each act of consumption.

If promiscuous fancy is a mechanism of desire driven by lack, it manifests particularly acutely in the plots of *Bartholomew Fair* where lacking becomes an object of desire in its own right. These scenes are powered by eroticized investments in not seeing, not consuming, not enjoying things. This form of negative anti-fancy based in refusal is centrally staged through Zeal-of-the-Land Busy, the Puritan suitor, who has been understood as a caricature of the passionate asceticism found in certain forms of social-control Protestantism.[56] Busy's investment in pleasures *not* consumed provides the affective inverse to Cokes's gargantuan hunger. Zeal-of-the-Land Busy marches his party into the Bartholomew Fair in act 3, calling out to the others to "walk on in the middle way, fore-right; turn neither to the right hand nor to the left. Let not your eyes be drawn aside with vanity, nor your ear with noises" (3.2.27–29). Win's artificed longing for roast pig at the Fair has been transmitted, as a palpable, salivating hunger, to everyone else, in a contagion of appetite that overpowers religious prohibition. But this craving is sustained by the negative energies mixed in with it: Busy and Dame Purecraft's masochistic pleasure in condemnation, their pleasure in yielding to the lure of the roast pig and their disavowal of that pleasure, their denunciations of the Fair, and their denials that pleasure is their motive at all.

The toymaker and puppeteer, Leatherhead, attempts to hail Win into looking—and by looking into wanting:

What do you lack? What do you buy, pretty mistress? A fine hobby-horse, to make your son a tilter? A drum to make him a soldier? A fiddle, to make him a reveller? What is't you lack? Little dogs for your daughters! Or babies, male, or female?

The objects on offer here make visible how fancy based on "lack" functions as a ghost or shade of sexual reproduction. Win's potential, incipient reproductivity is the public subject for the vendor's spiel, as it was for her campaign to go to the Fair in the first place. However, neither the reproductive kind of desire—the kind that would put one in the family way—nor the natural human baby that it would generate is on offer at the Fair. Instead, the "babies, male, or female" conjured as objects of desire here are fictive and imaginary—the baby dolls that Leatherhead suggests Win lacks, but also the son or daughter whose ghostly potentiality makes it a particularly defined lack. In the economy of the Fair, these artificial ornaments and knickknacks—toys, simulacra, miniatures, musical instruments, imitation weapons, small pets, and uncanny artificial babies—are the material things through which consumers' longings are stoked and solicited. Like the erotically instrumental go-betweens discussed in the previous chapter, they are the generators, transmitters, and objects of desire.

The toys' fetishistic allure is precisely why such fine distinctions must be policed between acceptable and unacceptable gazes and affects toward them. Busy characterizes these suspiciously icon-like items as diabolical for the way in which they work on fairgoers' desires:

> The wares are the wares of devils. And the whole Fair is
> the shop of Satan! They are hooks, and baits, very baits,
> that are hung out on every side, to catch you, and to hold
> you as it were, by the gills; and by the nostrils, as the
> fisher doth: therefore, you must not look, nor turn toward
> them. (3.2.35–43)

The "hobby-horses and trinkets" are both the "baits" that solicit the senses and the "hooks" that "catch" and "hold" the fairgoer in a seductive cycle of lacking, longing, and wanting. His anxiety makes reference not only to the contemporary Puritan idea that Satan offers bait to appeal to sinners' existing weaknesses (in Thomas Adams's famous formulation, "Satan like the Fisher baits his hooke according to the appetite of the fish"[57]), but also to contemporary understandings of the role of the mental fancy in erotic love, in which desire is thought to enter the body chiefly through the eyes. The peril of fascination, theorized in the Neoplatonist writings of Marsilio Ficino, is conceived as a pathological state of bodily depletion caused by gazing on the love object, in which the lover is infected by rays emanating from the object that have their own materiality, entering through the eyes and penetrating into the organs of the body.[58]

To look at the fancy things of the Fair is a dangerous desire, but—and this is crucial to understanding the queer valence of Busy's Puritan disavowal—if one looks, it had better not be indifferent or unmoved looking. "Aye child," Dame Purecraft interjects to Win, "so you hate 'em, as our brother Zeal does, you may look on 'em" (3.6.58–61). Under Dame Purecraft and Busy's rules, fervently prurient, passionate looking, attended by affects so inflamed as to be barely controllable, is totally permissible—as long as it's negative affect, inflected with denunciation and hate. As long, in other words, as the locus of erotic investment in looking is the disavowal of desire. "If," as Juliet says to her parents in Shakespeare's *Romeo and Juliet*, "looking liking move" (1.3.99), the godly Protestant position replaces that "liking" with *loathing*. If looking loathing move, then look all you like.

Bartholomew Pig

The force of fancy in the Fair is even more polymorphously insidious than fascination, in that it works on all of the senses. When Dame Purecraft scolds John Littlewit for looking at the sign signifying roast pig ("Son, were you not warn'd of the vanity of the eye?" [3.2.65–66]), Littlewit points out the absurdity of this pursuit of pig that disavows it is a pursuit: "Good mother, how shall we find a pig, if we do not look about for't? Will it run off o' the spit into our mouths, think you? As in Lubberland? And cry, *wee, wee?*" (3.2.67–69). Busy, in response, makes the theological case that while looking for the pig is a sin, smelling for it is absolutely fine:

> No, but your mother, religiously wise, conceiveth it may
> offer itself, by other means to the sense, as by way of
> steam, which I think it doth, here in this place.

[Busy scents after it like a hound.]

Huh, huh—yes, it doth. And it were a sin of obstinacy, great obstinacy, high and horrible obstinacy, to decline, or resist the good titillation of the famelic sense, which is the smell. Therefore be bold—huh, huh, huh—follow the scent. Enter the tents of the unclean, for once, and satisfy your wife's frailty. (3.2.70–79)

These comical justifications actually say a great deal about the queered pathways of sense and reason through which carnival longing works in the play. Busy argues that by finding the pig by smell, the more passive sensory pleasure, he is not seeking the pig; the pig is "may offer itself" to him, even as he "scents after it like a hound." As Joseph Litvak explains, smell and smelling play an overdetermined role in histories of detecting dangerous bodies and predilections, and occupy a central place in phobic/erotic investment—of the kind that Busy displays here—not least because of the passivity with which the smeller is penetrated by smell.[59] Pointing out the queerness of the McCarthyite rhetoric of bodily "sniffing out" Jews and homosexuals, Litvak quotes Adorno and Horkheimer: "Anyone who sniffs out 'bad' smells in order to extirpate them may imitate to his heart's content the snuffling which takes its unrationalized pleasure in the smell itself. Disinfected by the civilized sniffer's absolute identification with the prohibiting agency, the forbidden impulse eludes the prohibition. If it crosses the threshold, the response is laughter. That is the schema of the anti-Semitic reaction."[60] This is also the schema of the Puritan (a cultural identity heavily associated with a phobic/erotic Hebraism) who, when called "Rabbi Busy," proclaims that he will go and "eat exceedingly" of swine's flesh in public "to profess our hate, and loathing of Judaism" (1.6.85–86). "Disinfected" by his "absolute identification with the prohibiting agency," Busy sniffs out pig in order to disapprove of it (but in order to eat it).[61] Litvak goes on to trace the queer cycle of imitation, *ressentiment,* and desire by which a phobic investment in Jewish bodies is connected to a homophobic investment in markers of gay and otherwise nonheteronormative eroticism—a dynamic that, read into this scene, reveals Busy's "unrationalized pleasure" in scenting after the pig "like

EVERYTHING THAT MOVES

a hound" to be explicitly part of a homophobic/homoerotic schema of passionate investment in threatening, potentially self-implicating, bodily appetites.

Busy's case for passive smelling amounts to an apology for yielding to those urges that feel too all-consuming to block out. The sense of smell indicates—and incites—cravings that feel more like righteous needs (like the "good titillation of the famelic sense," or hunger), than more suspect wants (discretionary things, picked out and seized upon by sight). And, crucially, cravings for things smelled are desires for which the smeller can deny any agency. Busy's protestation that his passive role makes it permissible for him to partake—that the object of his disavowed desire "may offer itself, by other means to the sense"—resonates with later discourses of closeted or identity-disavowing homoeroticism that also deny seeking.[62] His role in the Fair's libidinal economy is fueled simultaneously by pleasure and revulsion at being solicited by the vendors' "What do you lack?"

Busy's resort to the pleasures of "the famelic sense" also hails the early modern audience into a scene of pleasure. Jonson's foregrounding of smells both pleasant and offensive throughout the play makes it at least thinkable that real roast pork could have been used as a kind of olfactory prop or scenic feature at the Hope. As the "Induction on the Stage" before the play makes explicit, the Hope is "as dirty as Smithfield, and as stinking in every whit" (142).[63] The smell would then have effectively penetrated the audience's bodies—and their mental fancies—inciting an involuntary reaction of desire. Even if the smell of roast pig is not phenomenally present in the theater, the scented-after pig onstage would raise the spectral sense-memory of that craving: a desire predicated on a specific lack, a specific absence. The conflation of the Fair and the play, in name and in odor, heightens the audience's perverse enjoyment of watching Busy trying (and failing) not to enjoy it (even as some audience members would have identified with Busy's stance of anxious trepidation toward the Fair).

The roast Bartholomew pig embodies the confluence of longing and hate that a godly Puritan fairgoer feels toward the Fair. A powerful, potentially corruptive pleasure is transmitted through the sensory experience of yielding to the craving and eating it. Like gold in *The*

Alchemist, roast pig functions as the currency of desire itself—a mystical substance that is at once the ubiquitous object of desire and the fuel or stimulus to more and more consuming appetites. The pig's fantastical erotic properties are condensed and embodied in the figure of Ursula the pig-woman, who metonymically stands in for the Fair's extreme, copious carnality. Her physical body is figured as consubstantial with the entire cycle of consumption and excess at the Fair—the roast pig and ale the fairgoers take in, and the sweat and urine they excrete. "I am all fire and fat," she announces at her first entrance; "I do water the ground in knots as I go, like a great garden-pot; you may follow me by the S's I make" (2.2.49–52). The gamesters around her stall call her "Body o' the Fair," "Mother o' the bawds," and "Mother o' the pigs," imagining her body as an originary matrix giving birth to the Fair and everything in it: "Art thou alive yet, with thy litter of pigs, to grunt out another Bartholomew Fair?" (2.3.1–2). The gendered qualities of Ursula's prodigious body have been much explicated, but I see it as possessing a queerer generative function.[64] In my reading, Ursula's body exceeds sexual difference. The men hanging around her market stall compare her sex to a bog and a quagmire, an unknown quicksand, where "he that would venture for't, I assure him, might sink into her and be drowned a week ere any friend he had could find where he were." Sex with Ursula would be "like falling into a whole shire of butter," and a man would need "a team of Dutchmen should draw him out" (2.5.85–90). While this is a common enough misogynistic jibe, born from a fear of the vagina as an uncanny abyss in which a man could get lost, this line takes the image to a hyperbolic level. It is no longer a human body part, but a bizarre fairy-tale image of mythic scale and fantastical danger. There is no language of phallic penetration in the figuration of a vagina as a "shire of butter." The body's excess is not possessed or mastered in these images. It swallows men whole so that they can be rescued in homosocial fantasy feats of heroism by their loyal friends, or a brawny team of Dutchmen. In fact, these jokes reach forward in time to resonate with the fetish of macrophilia, a kink in which men fantasize about sexual contact with giantesses, which heavily features images of full-body insertion into the giantess's enormous vagina.[65]

The mechanism by which Ursula's giant body gives birth to the

Fair is not sexual reproduction at all, but something else: a generative material dissemination or diffusion. Her flesh is construed as a universal lubricant greasing the moving parts of the whole world; it is the grease used by "the coach-makers here in Smithfield to anoint wheels and axle-trees with" (2.5.73–74), and the grease that bastes and roasts the pigs. In a self-perpetuating system of desire, Ursula feeds (literally, she makes a profit) on her customers' cravings; her food and drink in turn engender in them more, and more various, cravings for other bodily pleasures. Her economy factors lack into its calculations. She tells her tapster to short her pints of beer, intentionally keeping her customers just short of satiated, so that they buy more beer, become more intoxicated, and eat more pig. The consumers then linger and keep coming back to her stall, their endlessly regenerating appetites regenerating her. Ursula's material substance sustains the Fair by being endlessly converted from energy to matter and back again, both the fuel and the product of the Fair's energies of lacking and longing.

"That a Man Should Have Such a Desire to a Thing, and Want It!"

If the group consumption of Ursula's pig that Busy orchestrates serves as foreplay, then the loathing into which he is moved by looking intensifies as he moves, full of pig, through the stalls, building to an orgiastic climax of destruction that satirizes the florid carnality of iconoclastic language. Denouncing the hobbyhorse stall as "a shop of relics!" (3.6.84–87) and the gingerbread stand as a "basket of popery,"[66] he condemns the ornamental status of the toys and sweets not just as fancy commodities but as heretical talismans or fetish objects.[67] He becomes more and more agitated over the fancies of "this wicked and most foul Fair, and fitter may it be called a foul than a Fair" (3.6.78–79). The audience might connect this repetition to the witches' incantation in *Macbeth* that "fair is foul, and foul is fair" (1.1.11).[68] Busy's paranoid assertion that fair and foul often go together (and can look a lot like one another) signals that the language of witchcraft—which, as the next chapter will explain, marshals the slippage between pleasure and disgust to generate phantasms of socially transgressive, corrupting desire—is also at home in the space of the Fair and in Busy's annihilating mode of consumption.

Overcome in his frenzy, Busy attacks the Fair, wreaking his desire on the bodies of the gingerbread men:

> BUSY: And this idolatrous grove of images, this flasket of idols, which I will pull down—
>
> *Overthrows the gingerbread.*
>
> TRASH: O my ware, my ware, God bless it!
> BUSY: In my zeal, and glory, to be thus exercised.
> (3.6.89–92)

The joke is that the Puritan's iconophobia has run away with itself. In fancying the painted dolls and gingerbread men to be spiritually threatening, he is participating in the same economy of imaginative desires bodied forth in material forms that drives the Fair, fetishism, and iconistic religious belief. Afterward, he is exhilarated by his affective expenditure: it was his "glory" to be so "exercised," to enact the destruction he desired. As the officers show up, he claims to be ready for more masochistic surrender to the destructive affects consuming him, to be ready to "thrust myself into the stocks, upon the pikes of the land" (3.6.100).

Bartholomew Cokes and Zeal-of-the-Land Busy are not as different as they at first appear. Cokes's appetites also contain a strong undercurrent of annihilation, albeit of a consuming kind. While Busy would cancel the whole Fair, Cokes finds it equally hard to bear that the things that draw his eye remain available to others. Like Busy, Cokes seeks to destroy the Fair, but by different means: by attempting to buy it up whole for himself. Leaving behind any pretense of discriminating among—or even really wanting—any specific items, Cokes buys up the toymaker Leatherhead's entire shop, and then buys the man himself, to come to his house and realize his sudden notion to stage a wedding masque. In purchasing a human being not merely for his labor but for his artistic prowess, Cokes rhapsodizes about the "fine motions" and "inventions" Leatherhead will create:

What a masque shall I furnish out for forty shillings
(twenty pounds Scotch)! And a banquet of gingerbread!
There's a stately thing! Numps! Sister! And my wedding
gloves too! (That I never thought on afore). All my wedding
gloves, gingerbread! O me! What a device will there be to
make 'em eat their fingers' ends! And delicate brooches
for the bride-men and all! And then I'll ha' this posy put
to 'em: *For the best grace,* meaning Mistress Grace, my
wedding posy. (3.4.138–45)

Cokes sounds here strikingly like a bourgeois-capitalist bride, excited for the fabulous desserts, accessories, gimmicky favors, entertainments, flowers, and witty, poetic toasts at her wedding—all of
which the self-employed artisan she has just hired will be expected
to provide. Here is where Cokes's signature appetite of infantile polymorphous perversity shades into a more material, historical form of
queerness, thereby connecting the play's economy of market desire to
the social history of gender and sexuality. Cokes's wedding commodity fetishism regenders him as a stereotypically acquisitive woman
in an economy of luxury consumption. Cokes's Jacobean counterpart in excessive bridal consumption, the upstart Gertrude in Chapman, Jonson, and Marston's *Eastward Ho!,* embodies the connection
between an emergent form of fantasmatic wedding commodity desire and the problem of capitalism. As a middle-class goldsmith's
daughter who disastrously marries a practically artificial, "new-made
knight," her fantasy of an aristocratic fairy-tale wedding highlights
the unmooring of material consumption from subjects' social status
by birth. Gertrude's aspirational gentility, constituted through the
desire for lavish material objects, fabrics, and fashions, results in
loss and degradation.[69] Cokes's wedding fantasy likewise includes
an entire meal consisting only of sweets, and a bizarrely autoerotic,
autophagic game: edible gloves with which his guests will mime *eating their own fingers* as part of the entertainment. His ecstasy over all
the ornamental touches—his wedding gloves ("that I never thought
on afore"); the "delicate brooches for the bride-men" (he notably
says nothing of the bride)—completely eclipses the marriage itself.
"Mistress Grace" in this vision is not Cokes's wife but his "wedding

posy"—an empty name that furnishes the occasion of a poem to dazzle his friends. There is nothing of heterosexual desire here. Cokes's wedding fancy—in the old sense of an imaginative vision—is implicated, through his excessive investment in luxury objects, with the emergent definition of "fancy" as a descriptor for a noneconomically productive man, and then, for a man suspiciously effeminized by his appetites: from "a man who lives off the earnings of a prostitute"[70] to "a dandy, a showy but ineffective worker or sportsman."[71]

Leatherhead is also implicated in this incipient confluence of economic and sexual pejoratives. When Cokes buys Leatherhead, he pays him only for his goods and stall rental fee (rounded slightly upward), with no additional compensation for being bought on retainer. Though Leatherhead is employed on the margins of the theater industry and as a toymaker who runs his own shop, he is apparently expected to mount the wedding masque gratis. His artistic labor will be counted as the kind of economically unproductive activity done by a fancy man. The purchase flouts the conventional structure of relations and transactions between fairgoers and artisans, even trafficking—like *The Alchemist*'s Sir Epicure Mammon in his fantasies of wealth—in the purchasing of people. Cokes's servant's horror at the transaction alludes to the next degrees of transgressive human exchange, the looming specters of slavery, prostitution, even cannibalism: "Cry you mercy! You'd be sold too, would you? What's the price on you? Jerkin and all, as you stand? Ha' you any qualities?" (3.4.97–98). Leatherhead's economic and aesthetic activity places him in a character genealogy with the stock type of the gay wedding planner from modern romantic comedy—here, an undercompensated one whose labor and taste are exploited at the pleasure of the capitalist bride. This dynamic also resonates with later forms of capitalism, making visible how thoroughly consumers are empowered over producers in a fancy-based economy. The promiscuous fancy of the Fair takes the shape of a materially deracinated form of capitalist desire, akin to the erotics underpinning the postmodern capitalist trade in service and affective labor. The comic trope of a gargantuan, childlike squire buying up artisans and singers from the Bartholomew Fair in order to assemble an ostentatious wedding masque also glances at sexually laden political satire. Cokes's masque is shaping up to be a grotesque, low-comic imitation of one Jonson's court masques, but his indiscriminate taste transforms his pretensions into camp tragi-comedy. The voracious purchasing of both artistic commodities and the artists themselves may well be a pointed comment on James's court theatricals—on the problem of an aristocrat (who is none too discriminating, and none too heterosexually interested) with a crav-ing to incorporate the creative products of a public, carnivalesque artistic marketplace (here, the Fair; for James, the commercial the-ater) into his private household. Jonson makes clear that this incor-poration enacts a certain consuming violence on the public theatrical sphere. Who will remain to sing the ballads or mount the puppet plays in the space of the Fair (or the theater) if the ballad singer and puppet maker are taken into a private retinue?

There is something almost literally masturbatory about Bar-tholomew Cokes's consumption at the Fair. He falls into a perverse and homoerotic obsession with cutpurses, in which his desire to see one is symmetrically mirrored by their desire to target him as a mark. They bait him with a ballad, "A Caveat against cutpurses," which he of course tries to buy, along with the ballad singer, to "be poet to my masque" (3.5.92). The performance stokes him into a state of childlike, narcissistic abandon. Like Zeal-of-the-Land Busy, he becomes more and more excited. He is seized with desires to touch himself and his purse, in anticipation of being touched by the cut-purse "youth." As the ballad singer sings and the cutpurse closes in, Cokes moves from clutching his purse inside his clothes to taking it out and dangling it in front of him to attract the cutpurse; the connec-tion between his purse and his genitals is easy to envision. His inter-jections of longing become more intense with each chorus: "That was a fine fellow! I would have him now" (3.5.124); and finally, summing up Cokes's entire position vis-à-vis desire, "A pox on 'em, that they will not come! That a man should have such a desire to a thing, and want it" (3.5.130–31). The cutpurse, upon him, *tickles him in the ear with a straw twice to draw his hand out of his pocket* (3.5.152). At the crucial instant, his utter inability not to satisfy a physical urge to touch himself—to rub his tickled ear—gets his purse stolen. The one thing he theoretically does not want at the Fair—getting purse-cut, which would foreclose his consumption—is the thing he compulsively solicits.

Bartholomew Cokes's and Zeal-of-the-Land Busy's erotic orientations toward the Fair are part of the same system, even though one explicitly seeks pleasure and the other explicitly disavows it. Both are founded in a negative structure of desire. The repulsive can be attractive if accessed obliquely, by a circuitous route (smelling for the pig, or singing a ballad about how you hope no cutpurses are near). Stated agendas remain unfulfilled, while repulsions can be resolved by getting and consuming—and submitting to—the repellent thing (pig eating, purse-cutting), thereby feeding the tacit attraction underneath. Cravings for specific objects can move from attraction to repulsion and back again, always circulating back through the state of lack in which fancy originates. Attraction can become repulsion as soon as it is acted on or a new object presents itself; or repulsion can spontaneously convert into attraction once the want of the object becomes acute enough.

"I Shall Not Know Which to Love Best Else"

The play's resolution brings all of its subplots together in an orgy of polymorphous queer artistic generativity at Leatherhead and Littlewit's puppet play. The puppets in this scene—a liminal category of object combining aspects of human bodies and made things—materialize the play's multifarious instantiations of fancy and lack into one aesthetic system. In operating by turns as commodities, characters in the play within a play, and love objects, the puppets demonstrate that the erotic economy of *Bartholomew Fair* is a monistic one, in which humans and nonhuman things are the same order of substance. Both can be animate, active transmitters of affect; both can be love objects; both can engage in social relations. But both can also be bought, sold, eaten, transformed, dislocated, and annihilated. Justice Overdo, whose antitheatrical lather crosses over into madness, compares the puppets to the "boys o' the Fair," whose erotic services are the occasion of lascivious suspicion. Bartholomew Cokes is consumed with liking for the array of little bodies in a basket and wants to fit them all in his mouth. Cokes predictably takes the puppets' theatrical status as surrogate thing-humans to its most erotically deviant extreme. "Handling" them in their basket, he swears, "I am in love with the actors already" (5.3.116). If the men in Ursula's stall voice a fantasy of being wholly subsumed into the gigantic sex of a supernaturally huge woman, Cokes's fussing over the puppets recalls its opposite, an erotic fetish for miniature human forms. He enjoys them narcissistically, as part-objects that can be incorporated into or accessorized with his other purchases. Believing them to be animate and to exist for his sole pleasure, he talks to them onstage as though addressing his own appendage: "My fiddle-stick does fiddle in and out too much" (5.3.180–81). Differentiating among objects of desire is so far outside of his erotic bent that he becomes agitated at the merest possibility of choosing a favorite. Cokes's joke that the puppets make better actors because one doesn't have to feed them is a nod to the material input requirements of the Fair's erotic-artistic production machine. But it can also be read as a metatheatrical comment on the play's model of subject/object relations. If a play's economy of desire does away with actors as a category—removing any role for individual motivation and leaving only a sea of consuming bodies—it solves the problem of differentiating between subjects and objects of desire by making everyone a potential object in a field of objects, afloat in a network of their own and others' roving appetites. If everyone and everything is powered by the same cycle of lack, there is always the possibility of being consumed—by one's own looking and longing, or by some organ of the Fair that hungers for bodies to buy and sell. When Leatherhead and the other vendors lament that the Fair is "pestilence dead," they mean that it lacks the bodies that bring its queer generativity to life (2.2.1).[72] Only with enough bodies can the Fair sustain the constant transmutation of longing into consumption and back to longing again—and that calculus depends on the eventuality that some consuming bodies will become objects of consumption. At the puppet play, that risk of becoming consumable is borne out, with comic flair, for the women fairgoers (including Win Littlewit), who are taken into prostitution in the act of going to the bathroom while drunk. They attend the play in disguise, dressed up as prospective objects for sale on the sexual market, their agency undone from the inside by their own incontinent bodies. The women's flirtation with commodification, like Cokes's attempt to buy up artisans and puppets, highlights that human bodies are the base material of the Fair's erotic economy.

The climax of the puppet show—which is also the climax of the play—dramatizes the fantastical output of this libidinal economy. There is puppet kissing, puppet violence, puppet battery, a puppet-ghost—and an angry revenant of flesh and blood in the person of Zeal-of-the-Land Busy, who stands up and denounces the theatrical enterprise. He engages the puppet-ghost (who takes the form of the dead Greek king Dionysius of Syracuse, roused from his grave by Damon and Pythias squabbling and assaulting Hero and Leander) in a debate over the morality of the theater. But what Busy thinks is his patriarchal, iconoclastic trump card—the stock antitheatrical outcry that "you are an abomination; for the male of you putteth on the apparel of the female, and the female of the male" (5.5.86–88)—is turned back by the puppet-ghost into a lesson about just how far this theatrical economy of desire is unmoored from sexual difference or identity. Volleying back that "It is your old stale argument against the players, but it will not hold against the puppets, for we have neither male nor female amongst us. And that thou may'st see, if thou wilt, like a malicious purblind zeal as thou art!" the puppet-ghost *"takes up his garment"* and flashes the absence of his genitals to Busy and the audience in order to prove that there is nothing there (5.5.91–94). A flashing by a puppet—by a puppet-ghost no less—could not be a purer theatrical manifestation of the queerly generative fancy bodied forth in the opening speech of *Twelfth Night,* or a more logical conclusion to *Bartholomew Fair*'s profusion of appetites proffered in response to the call, "What'd ye lack?"

This puppet-ghost flashing (a contender for my favorite moment in early modern drama) so perfectly encapsulates the mechanisms of fancy discussed in this chapter that it bears further unpacking. The idea of an absent-genital flashing by a puppet-ghost is an idiosyncratic artifact. It began life as a mental image (in Jonson's head, or in the head of someone else in the culture, who may have materially realized it to enter Jonson's eye). It is first realized in the textual form that I have reproduced here. As a theatrical performance, it has had many iterations in four hundred years, and in each of them, it has been multiply removed, at too many levels to list, from any fixed historical conditions. Just to start, there is no "real ghost of" the Greek king, and in any case the puppet is arguably costumed as the wrong Dionysius.[73] In this it resembles, to me, much of the rest of the representational universe of early modern drama. It is at once so fantastically removed, by transpositions of place and time and material order, from topical referents that it is much more about itself as form than about anything else. At the same time, in that fantastical guise, it vocalizes the ideological conflicts of the moment (or of a just-passed moment, the "old stale argument against the players").[74] As a material form, the puppet-ghost of Dionysius is also at several levels of remove from any natural or human, let alone conventionally sexual, object of desire, which is why it is so hyperbolically funny that Cokes and Busy are so obsessed with it. It is the ultimate in queer theatrical artifice.[75] As a dramatic event, the puppet's flashing of *nothing*, of not-genitals, aims literally to show that which the spectator's busy, unruly fancy is free to imagine: a "thing not present to the senses."[76] The puppet-ghost's genitals are a thing that Busy is caught out as having imagined, because they don't exist anywhere but inside his own prurient fancy. What he imagines to be a (puppet's?) sexed body is revealed to be instead a "thing not present," a wholly unnatural, aesthetic thing, a manifestation of pure form with no natural body beneath. Whatever Busy sees under the puppet-ghost's garment, the sight of it—the sight of nothing, or, even more hilariously, the sight of the puppeteer's human hand or face—is prodigious enough to perform a miracle: it converts Zeal-of-the-Land Busy to a lover of the theater. He says only, "I am confuted, the cause hath failed me" (5.5.101). The puppet and Leatherhead both beg him to "be converted, be converted!" and he assents, "Let it go on, for I am changed, and will become a beholder with you!" and sits down to watch the play (5.5.103–5). Even in its magical efficacy, the puppet-ghost flashing embodies the pointlessness of pinning too much ontological content to sexual difference. It does its unexplained something (by way of nothing) in or to Busy's psyche by means of fancy, and nothing else. The puppet-ghost flashing also signals the failure of heterosexual climax (on the part of Bartholomew Cokes) and the triumph of queer generativity, for even the end of the puppet show (and the end of the play) are not the end of festivity. The wayward Justice Overdo hospitably invites everyone to his house for dinner; Bartholomew Cokes demands that the actors (by which he means the puppets, who still hold his fancy, though in practice they cannot be delivered without Leatherhead and Littlewit) come along, to have "the rest o' the play at home" (5.6.109–10).

"His Fancy's Queen"

I now return to *Twelfth Night* to show how the production and re-production of "fancy" in its resolution can be just as anticlimactic and just as asexually generative as that of *Bartholomew Fair*'s consumption-crazed libidinal universe. In *Bartholomew Fair*, some of the most compelling objects of longing are fantasmatic and imaginative: Win's longing for pig, the wedding masque that never takes place, the puppet-ghost's sex organs. *Twelfth Night*, on the other hand, ostensibly ends with a marriage between Orsino and Viola, but in fact we see no more of their wedding than we do of Bartholomew Cokes's. And even in the resolution, the play never mentions reproduction; it projects no future offspring for any of the couples. It seems insistent in thematizing alloerotic relations, but none actually occur.

Twelfth Night's play with gender and sexuality seems to be resolved at the end, with the focus on Viola as she is being described by Orsino—but it is not exactly Viola being described. With characteristic indirection, the Duke projects himself into a future "golden time" when he and Viola will be married. The Viola onstage, though, is not Viola. She is still Cesario, he says, "for so you shall be while you are a man." "But," he tells her, "when in other habits you are seen," she will take on a different sex and a different status: "Orsino's mistress and his fancy's queen" (5.1.374–75). This last line raises real doubt as to whether Orsino will be able to corporeally apprehend that future Viola. Changed back into women's clothes, she will "be seen" as Viola by others, but she does not seem to be seen by Orsino. She will be "Orsino's mistress," not "my mistress"—Orsino refers to himself in the third person—and "his fancy's queen."

The lines efface her agency, even her presence, as they imaginatively body forth a new status for Viola. Their physical and linguistic incoherence recalls the incoherent structure and random sequence of a dream, and my final gesture will be to unpack some of their irresolvable, almost inarticulable implications for the structure of erotic desire in the play. If fancy is the intangible generative organ that conceives and holds the imaginary forms of love objects (or ideas for poems to be written), then Viola will be a mere apparition constructed inside Orsino's imagination. This model precludes any possibility of Viola's being fully embodied in her own right. Orsino would either keep her enclosed inside himself forever as an inert, unrelinquished love object, or he would have to somehow give birth to Viola, as a fancying mother. Even if some queer metaphor could be located by which this could take place, the Viola to whom Orsino would give birth would not be the embodied Viola standing before him onstage. It would be his constructed fantasy made flesh, like the racially marked child in the myth of the "mother's fancy." We would love to see Orsino's ideal form of Cesario/Viola; we wonder whether that Cesario/Viola would then possess the "little thing" that would cement their homoerotic bond—but we must recognize it would be a different being from an enfleshed, agentive Viola.

If Orsino gets his own autoerotically conjured version of Viola at the end of the play—which he arguably does here, because these lines make it so difficult for her to become differentiated—it can be taken as a piece of evidence that the play is actually "the Duke's fancy," and that Orsino is the dreamer whose wish-fulfillment structures the whole play. We can trace a narrative thread through the play that looks like something Orsino might dream into being, beginning with the manifesto on his fickle erotic desires. The push and pull of submerged (homo)erotic tension he enjoys with Cesario/Viola gives way to the boy's transformation into a juridically perfect wife, yet Orsino still stands at a remove, speaking of himself in the third person, as in the oblique proposal of marriage where Orsino reverses both his gender and Viola's: "Boy, thou hast said to me a thousand times/Thou never shouldst love woman like to me" (5.1.262–63). Alternatively, this dream may easily transmute into a nightmare. If, as in the play's first figurations of fancy, fancy is a polymorphous sea of shapes that dehierarchizes the objects of desire it receives, then it shouldn't—and arguably can't—have a queen. Viola's value and attraction to Orsino will fall "into abatement, and low price,/Even in a minute" (1.1.13–14), as swiftly as so many objects of his desire have "surfeited" before. Heterosexual marriage—especially as defined by the changes in name and status that result from entering into its economic and kinship bonds—looks surprisingly unstable from this angle. (Viola's abortive lesbian marriage to Olivia goes further in the play—all the way to the moment of sacramental solemnization—than any heterosexual union progresses.) When Viola is spoken of as "Orsino's mistress and his fancy's queen," even indirectly, she is in peril from the same ideation that was Malvolio's downfall when he murmurs "Count Malvolio" in a daydream. However hypothetical these transformations, the peril of linking one's identity to a single dominion—materially, Viola's new status as the Duke's wife and metaphorically, her queenship of his fancy—is part of the play's suspicion that reproductive heteronormativity, though inevitable, is neither natural nor safe, and that Viola is being offered a dominion that she will never be able to rule. Viola is arguably queen of nothing substantial at the end of this play—appropriately, as "nothing" fits with what Dympna Callaghan calls the "undecipherable" piling on of pudenda in the Duke's final line.[77] She has nothing but her sex, which, since it has been revealed, has arguably just fallen into "abatement and low price."

Is there no way out for Viola? The insertion of a queen here at the end of the play may undo some of the queering effected by the unpredictable, nonreproductive play of fancy. It may rehierarchize Orsino's object world, placing his wife at the top. It may (mostly) reassign to Viola a unitary female sex and feminine gender. However, even if pronouncing Viola "fancy's queen" represents an effort to those intended binarizing ends, the attempt falls as strangely null and void as a flashing by a puppet-ghost. The phrase is too bizarrely redundant. "Fancy's queen" conflates, splits, reverses, and confuses sexual roles in every possible way. It seems to turn the ostensibly heterosexual pairing of Orsino and Viola into a residually lesbian—or somehow homoerotic—pairing of two unreadable fancy queens who, even as the play ends, have in no way gotten their desires straight. Gender has not arrived at a resolution. Orsino reverses the existing master/servant power dynamic, telling Viola that "you shall from this time be/Your master's mistress" (5.1.319–20), but she has not been "seen" in her "other habits" in order to give her any identifiable bodily form in the new gender.

This ambivalent ending for *Twelfth Night* reinstates the sexes on the surface, as it must, but that does not mean that capacious, consuming fancy is resolved out of existence. In fact, as is the case when Bellario/Euphrasia remains with the prince and princess at the end of *Philaster* in the previous chapter, a major source of the resolution's pleasure is that Olivia, Viola, Sebastian, and Orsino get to remain together. The projected marriages do not seem to require them to differentiate too much among their love objects; they get to hold on to spouses, former loves, ex-suitors, and siblings in a double-crossed quadrilateral of queer incestuous love. As Laurie Shannon observes, the erotic energies between siblings, and those based on likeness, are still present among, not subordinated to, those based on sexual difference.[78] I would add to Shannon's point that reading the play through its mechanisms of generativity—fancying, promiscuous proliferation, transformation—allows us to notice other axes on which the resolution is structurally queer. It refuses any developmental telos of supersession: taking in new erotic objects does not entail releasing or demoting old ones. The household configuration of multiple interlaced conjugal and familial bonds is propagated not by any sort of sexual reproduction but by a chance materialization that looks a great deal like budding or cloning, as when Sebastian shows up, supplying his body to stimulate erotic cathexes that neither Olivia nor Orsino could have foreseen. New love objects can look like slightly different (or not at all different) imprints of the same form and shape as old ones; in fact, especially if the old love is still there too, it is almost as though they were stamped from the same mold in Orsino's capacious fancy. As the play ends, Viola's gender metamorphosis is still to be performed, and no consummation or sexual reproduction has actually taken place. In a spirit of unsated queer perversity, it is important to note (particularly at the ends of comedies, when it is the last thing anyone wants to hear) that this is not an outcome that promises or delivers erotic satisfaction of any kind, for anyone—except the audience and the readers who collectively receive these "high fantastical" shapes.

3

It Takes One to Know One

Paranoid Suspicion and the Witch Hunt

A wild thing may say wild things.
—Abigail Williams, *The Crucible* (Arthur Miller, 1953)

How is a witch made? Through the process enacted in the witch trial, a scene into which tens of thousands of people throughout Europe, mostly women, were ensnared between the late sixteenth and late seventeenth centuries. This chapter analyzes the mechanism that produces a witch—the output, so to speak, of the witch trial scene: a figure characterized by her deviant desires and sexual secrets, depraved acts, and dangerous agenda. In short, the production-through-demonization of the witch has a particularly queer shape. The affectively supercharged cycle by which this occurs is projective and attributive: it constructs queerness in another, and by the paranoid logic of implication, it reveals its own secret investments.

This chapter considers two widely publicized witch hunts in Scotland and England through their popular literature: a news pamphlet about the North Berwick witch hunt, *Newes from Scotland* (1591), and *The Witch of Edmonton* (1622), a fictionalized domestic tragedy by John Ford, Thomas Dekker, and William Rowley, based on the trial and execution of a real woman, Elizabeth Sawyer, in 1621. Plays and pamphlets about witch trials constitute a distinct genre, witch hunt literature, which follows a conventional plot trajectory of suspicion, accusation, investigation, discovery, and ultimately confession and execution.[1] I am starting from the premise that the witch hunt and witch trial process are erotic activities. They are, like sex acts, a culturally convention-bound and goal-directed set of physical and verbal procedures, collectively performed and powered by an idiosyncratic, invisible complex of investments on the part of each participant, culminating in a scripted climax the basic form of which is foreknown, though the details vary with each iteration. The witch hunt is a collective striving whose end is not a release of energy from bodies, as in a sexual consummation, but instead an impacting of built-up social energies onto the body of the accused. And as an erotic form, it is wholly perverse in that its conventional climax is a death.

Here, at its half-way point, this book moves away from a study of the multifarious queer forms and fancies of desire in comic plots, into a discussion of negative affects that take queer shapes. This chapter and the final one deal with systems of desire that refuse any presumptive association of happy or liberatory outcomes with queerness. Instead, the remainder of the book confronts queer erotic dynamics that work in and through the apparatuses of patriarchal and colonial power. In turning a queer lens on the literature of the witch hunt, I am focusing here on what happens to sexed, gendered, and classed bodies—how they're rendered monstrous, other, and inhuman, and how they're crushed in the machinery of a paranoid patriarchal order that projects its own worst content onto them. One effect of queering the witch hunt is to connect the history of what has been done to women with the history of what has been done to homosexuals and other deviant-desiring actors, illuminating deep historical consonances between the affective contours of misogyny and homophobia. Another difficult and risky move this chapter makes— but an important one at this moment of public reckoning with the pervasive realities of patriarchal sexism in every stratum of our own culture—is to work out where, how, and whether sexual violence and erotic desire should ever be considered on the same map, as part of the same affective system. My reading of witch hunt literature may complicate the claim extrapolated (and perhaps overgeneralized) from Susan Brownmiller's analysis of rape, that sexual violence is "not about desire, but about power."[2] I suspect that the two are not so easily separable, and I fear it impedes the project of understanding and resisting patriarchy to pretend that they are.

To that end, this chapter highlights the ways in which violent power dynamics *are* erotic as well as the ways in which they exploit, overlap, co-opt, and work through the erotic agendas and survival strategies of socially disempowered subjects. One of the fundamental lessons of Foucault's model of sexuality, after all, is that power and pleasures, disciplinary violence and renegade desires, are not opposite forces; rather, they are of one discursive substance, swirling and permeating through every subject's every moment, inciting and inviting. Aligning my aims with Foucault's, I want to trace, in the strange and twisted corpus of witch hunt literature, "the forms of power, the channels it takes, and the discourses it permeates [. . .] the paths that give it access to the rare or scarcely perceivable forms of desire, how it penetrates and controls everyday pleasure."[3] To that end, this chapter wrestles with the persecutory desires that are discursively enacted on and through bodies in witch hunt literature; the formal qualities of secrecy, deviance, and excess that structure the witch hunt plot; the witch hunt's fantasies; its material accoutrements; its affective, rhetorical, and physical methods; and its end: the production (and destruction) of a witch.

Witch hunt literature is an epistemologically thorny archive to read for desire. These texts are fictive, made things, yet some of the events they describe really happened, to living human bodies in the world. It is seldom clear what exact relation the dramatization of a witch hunt for popular consumption bears to the lived experiences of the players (and my aim is not to reconstruct those truths). What is apparent is that, like the colonial voyage accounts that occupy the next chapter, witch hunt pamphlets and plays are narrative and aesthetic objects that are produced out of a web of individual and communal desires (commercial, theological, nationalistic, phobic/ erotic, secret, and otherwise). It makes sense to me, then, to read both plays and prose tracts as dramatic literature—that is, to attend to how they stage affect and desire by staging embodied interaction, through dialogue, props, and the blocking of bodies in space. One of the most important contributions of queer theory has been to assert the real political import of imaginative forms, and the equally important aesthetic valences of political rhetorics and events.[4] In keeping with this tradition, I emphasize the textual figuration of affect as my object of analysis over the next two chapters, even as my texts now reach violently beyond the imagined worlds of the theater. (In previous chapters, however, the city comedies have already made this reach into real-world violence: *Bartholomew Fair* stages robbery and impressment into prostitution, and *The Roaring Girl* stages phobic, sexualized street assaults of a gender-nonconforming person.) I find in what follows that reading narrative accounts of witch trials and colonial invasions as dramatic fictions, by locating and describing (as Foucault seeks to do in his archives of discourse) their circulations of desire, violence, and identification, provides a vital methodological point of entry for reconsidering the role of eros in these much-studied sites of historical violence. And looking in particular for the complicated, perverse, and problematic circuits of *queer* affect animating them draws out new nuances in these encounters that have not been seen through other, more empirical means.

At this nexus of desire and violence, I want to be particularly precise about asking what queerness can mean in discourses of witchcraft and witch finding, what kinds of queerness are deployed in witch hunt literature and to what effect, and how queerness operates in interlocking ways with other axes of gender, class, and social status. I am calling on all of the untimely and proleptic senses of the word "queer" here, gathering up a set of associations that cluster around bodies and desires, including qualities like secret, lustful, criminal, unnatural, supernatural, duplicitous, hysterical, promiscuous, paranoid, sneaky, performative, and antisocial.

Newes from Scotland: "A Privie Marke"

Newes from Scotland locates a single woman as an origin point, a patient zero, for the North Berwick witch panics. That catalytic figure is "a maide servant called Geillis Duncane," who lived in the house of her master, David Seaton. The story begins with a moment of suspicion that carries an occult sexual valence: Geillis Duncane "used secretly to be absent and to lye foorth of her Maisters house every other night."[5] But what Geillis Duncane may be doing with her nights is fodder for suspicion of an uncannier sort: Duncane has become a healer (a role with a set of sexual and supernatural suspicions attached to it, especially for an unmarried woman), performing "manye matters most miraculous" to help the sick or infirm. Duncane's new skill is only tacitly connected to her nighttime comings and goings, in that both habits cause her employer, David Seaton, to hold "his maide in some great suspition, that she did not those things by naturall and lawfull wayes, but rather supposed it to be done by some extraordinary and unlawfull meanes" (Br). Female servants' particular vulnerability to sexual violation, sexual suspicion, and rumors of wrongdoing has been well explicated in the work of Frances Dolan and Laura Gowing.[6] Gowing writes that "in its economic position, its sexual vulnerability and its potential for sexual crime and illegitimate pregnancy, the body of the single woman (and especially the single woman in service) was barely her own," the object of constant scrutiny. "And to maintain a private body and a personal space, secure from the eyes of mistresses and neighbours, could appear positively threatening."[7] In light of this social reality, we might well ask how David Seaton knew that Geillis Duncane was "secretly absent" every other night from his house. Was she informed on, or did he go looking for her at night and find her unavailable to him? The mysteriously unelaborated fact of Duncane's night-journeying habits raises the possibility that the originary secret and crime of the North Berwick witch hunt could be illicit sex—and/or the insubordinate refusal of illicit sex—between a master and an unmarried maidservant. Could Seaton's "admiration" and "wonder" be a cover for some more private investment, his desire to use her sexually for his own purposes? We will never know; the narrative makes the causality of his "great suspition" completely inscrutable.

Out of this setup of occulted sexual suspicion grows a supposed truth-producing procedure in which Geillis Duncane is constructed as a witch. When "she gave him no answere, neverthelesse, her Maister to the intent that he might the better trye and finde out the trueth of the same, did with the helpe of others, torment her with the torture of the Pilliwinckes upon her fingers, which is a greevous torture, and binding or wrinching her head with a corde or roape, which is a most cruell torment also, yet would she not confesse any thing" (Br). A relation of suspicion—aggravated, no doubt, by Duncane's refusal to cooperate—slides seamlessly, in an instant, into torture. And this is not even public or state torture: "With the help of others" who remain unnamed, Seaton tortures Duncane himself, in a private context, before ever bringing her to court. The suspicious energy generated in Seaton has grown so strong that the affective exchange between master and servant seems to magnetically pull in "others," who make it into a scene of many-on-one physical violence, applying screws and ropes to try to wrench the "trueth" out of the invisible place where Duncane obdurately keeps it. The narrative makes no remark on Seaton's transformation from suspicious employer to vigilante witch-finder; the torture follows simply and seemingly self-evidently from his "intent" to "better trye and find out the trueth":

> Whereupon they suspecting that she had beene marked by the Divell (as commonly witches are) made dilligent search about her, and found the enemies marke to be in her fore crag or foreparte of her throate: which being found, she confessed that all her doings was done by the wicked allurements and inticements of the Divell, and that she did them by witchcraft. (Br)

With this sentence, David Seaton, whose "great suspition" is the cause of this entire undertaking, drops out of the narrative entirely, without explanation, along with whatever frustrations, passions, and prerogatives induced him to torture his servant woman in his own home. What's left is a nameless, faceless collective of citizen interrogators, moving as if automatically through the witch hunt's plot. It is "they" who first make the ghosting suspicion of witchcraft explicit, "suspecting" that the maidservant's body is "marked" in a way that a "dilligent search" of every part of it will uncover. Predictably, they find something on her neck, which is determined to be the devil's mark. As soon as this point on the surface of her skin is named as such, the pamphlet says, Duncane freely pours out the tale of her secret, "wicked" healings of her sick and infirm neighbors.[8]

Newes from Scotland quickly moves from the wayward servant girl to the other archetypal witch panic victim: an elderly country wise woman with a long history of ecclesiastical suspicion named Agnis Sampson.[9] Stiffly denying the charges against her despite the personal "persuasions" of King James and his council,[10] Sampson, like Duncane, is ritually searched for a sign of demonic relations, "a privie marke," which indicates, the pamphlet alleges, that "Witches have confessed themselues, that the Devill dooth lick them with his tung in some privy part of their bodye, before he dooth receive them to be his servants" (Biiv). The mark is regarded as evidence of an act of sex with the devil. As such, it demarcates a sexual identity, a sexual status, that must remain secret. It is only the invisibility of the devil's mark, hidden under the hair on some unmentionable part of the body, that enables the witch's silence:[11] "Generally so long as the marke is not seene to those which search them, so long the parties that hath the marke will never confesse any thing" (Biiv). *Newes from Scotland,* like many other examples of witch hunt literature, fetishizes the search for the devil's mark, dramatically drawing it out to build up to the witch's outing. Sampson will confess nothing while having all her hair shaved off and her head "thrown," or wrenched with a rope ("according to the custome of that Countrye, being a paine most greevous"), for an hour, "until the Divel's marke was found upon her privities, then she immediatelye confessed whatsoever was demaunded of her, and justifying those persons aforesaid to be notorious witches" (Aiiir). The precise violence of shaving "each parte" of an old woman's body mirrors the fetishistic function of the devil's mark, in that both body hair and the mark visually inscribe the surface of a body in terms of its sexual status (a sexually mature adult woman, or a sexually deviant witch). Almost anything could be read as a devil's mark, from a single freckle or pimple to the clitoris, a possibility here for Agnis Sampson. The clitoris is posthumously exposed as the devil's mark on the hanged body of a witch in the remarkable 1593 pamphlet, *The most strange and admirable discoverie of the three witches of Warboys.* After an old woman, Alice Samuell, is executed, the jailer and his wife find on her body "a little lumpe of flesh, in manner sticking out, as if it had beene a teate, to the length of halfe an inch." At first they intend to keep their discovery to themselves because "it was adjoyning to so secrete a place, which was not decent to be seene," but in the end they show it (and strain fluids out of it) to vindicate the assembled members of the community.[12] The truth of witchcraft produced by whatever fleshly thing is read as the devil's mark is as fantasmatic as the sodomitical sex act it is supposed to record. Moreover, *Newes from Scotland*'s account of what the devil's mark is, given here as received Scottish knowledge, does not conform exactly to either the English paradigm of a teat where the witch's familiar suckles on her body, or the Continental paradigm of a brand or scar commemorating a diabolical pact.[13] Instead, this Scottish fantasy of the mark as a trace of the secret lick of the devil's tongue is a fantasy of erotic legibility.[14] The substantial dramatic energy invested in lusting after its discovery/construction indexes a wish on the part of those in power for erotic acts—especially deviant ones, like receiving oral sex (from the devil)—to be clearly marked on the body. It is an anxious investment born of the fact that the real licks of real tongues, belonging to humans of unknown gender or social station, on various parts of bodies, do not leave any such marks.

At the climax of the witch hunt's machinations, the body of the accused becomes the body of a witch—a body defined by its seductive, antisocial, and rebellious desires—that must be abjected (expelled) from the community in death. At a social level, a witch materializes abjection in Julia Kristeva's technical sense: a part of the communal body which is thrown out—ab-jected—from the rest.[15] A vast body of scholarship exists on witch panics as this kind of abjecting, scapegoating process, describing the witch as a figure onto whom a community's anxieties are projected, where paranoia is named as mass hysteria, expurgation of an "internal other," and patriarchal violence against the repressed feminine unconscious.[16] The scholarly consensus on the causes of early modern witch persecution has undergone multiple waves of revision, in which sex and gender have moved in and out of emphasis as causal factors relative to national, religious, economic, and inhuman natural forces. One of my purposes in including a queer reading of the witch hunt in this book is to return to this scene, which has been so prolifically read through the lenses of previous critical moments, in order to place sex and the erotic closer to the center of early modern witchcraft—not as a single explanatory cause of witch panics, but as a constitutive structural feature of their enactment.

Both the content of witch panics (the desires and activities attributed to witches, the communal fears they index, and the narrative crescendo of suspicion) and the discursive forms of their production (the scenes of witch discovery, trial, and execution, and their subsequent media representations) are fundamentally powered by desire—and it shows. Though it is neither a play nor a folk ritual, the "discovery scene" in which an accused witch confesses to her crimes is a generic dramatic spectacle, with a recognizable affective economy.[17] The scene dramatizes a deviant-desiring subject who, along with an array of suspect objects, is represented and spectated upon in an erotically invested way. In other words, a specific mood of heightened communal affect is played out through a performative, legal forum (and mediatized, onstage and in print, as popular entertainment). The transactions it stages among an accused subject and her desires (to stay alive, avoid torture, receive salvation, implicate others), other subjects (interrogators, friends, family, lovers, victims), and material things (tools of witchcraft and torture) vary widely in content but retain a basic iterable plot structure. After all, according to Peter Brooks, plot itself is erotic in structure, a goal-directed, convention-bound performance, the pleasures of which derive from its rhythms of thrust and dilation.[18]

In order to get any closer to articulating the desires driving this plot, it is necessary to closely read what Kristeva calls abjection's "twisted braid of affects," which binds together suspectors, torturers, judges, and accused witches.[19] I am indebted to Lyndal Roper's work on torture and interrogation, to Lawrence Normand's and Gareth Roberts's work on witch trial records, and to Charlotte-Rose Millar's retheorization of emotion in witchcraft literature for their observations that the narratives (both official and popular) of the witch hunt should be seen as archives of a sadomasochistic, collaborative performance, "a collusive construction by examiners and examined."[20] "Collusive" is a fittingly dense word for the affect involved. It hints at a dynamic that can be inimical, even violently manipulative, but implies some mutual, possibly unspoken shared investment. "Collusion" denotes secrecy and taboo, as though the accused witch and witchfinder are cooperating in an illicit act, a forbidden relation, affectively knitted together by their need for each other in the logic of the scene. It places them in a secret, grossly unequal queer partnership, the content of which is not fully knowable even to the participants. But "collusion" also connotes an invisible betrayal, a sin of secret cooperation in which parties' loyalties do not lie where they purport to be. It is no coincidence that whispers of collusion cluster not only around secrets of a sexual kind but also around espionage and treason. Homosexuality and espionage have historically shared this suspicion, which extends from Christopher Marlowe through McCarthyism, in that both, like witchcraft, are superficially invisible practices that constitute deviant identities—secret loyalties, actually, to a shadowy, antisocial, alternative polis. And also like witchcraft (and homosexuality), collusion cannot be denied without projecting the shadow of suspicion back onto oneself. "NO COLLUSION—RIGGED WITCH HUNT!" tweets President Donald Trump at one o'clock in the morning.[21] The president vociferously protests against the investigation—and public suspicion—of his campaign's collusion with the Russian government to win the 2016 presidential election, spontaneously insisting in various formulations on television and social media: "Also, there is NO COLLUSION," "There was no Collusion (it is a Hoax)," "there was NO collusion," and, perhaps most illustrative, "Collusion is not a crime, but that doesn't matter because there was No Collusion (except by Crooked Hillary and the Democrats)!"[22] The repeated characterization of these investigations as a "witch hunt" by Trump and his supporters is also telling, despite its historical misapplication. It bespeaks how quickly the reflexive dynamic of the witch hunt lends itself to pure projection, unmoored from any truth whatsoever of what is happening, as well as how available—and desirable—it is to be claimed by those in power, in order to construe themselves as the persecuted instead.

The collusive dynamic that Roper, Normand, and Roberts observe in witch interrogations is not only a condition of historical discourse but an observable affective mode, which, along with Eve Sedgwick, I call paranoid suspicion. Paranoia is an affective mode founded in reflexive projection, in which one's suspicions about another correspond to the thing that one unconsciously suspects in oneself—fantasy suspicions about the other's desires that, inasmuch as they confirm a secret self-knowledge and compel others to confirm it as well, are discursively made true. Here what it furnishes is a witch, a figure materially, erotically, and epistemologically marked as queer by the paranoid mode of her production. The witch is queer in that she is characterized by deviant desires and practices; constructed through paranoid representations of material accessories; brought into being by an interrogation animated by projective identification and desire; climactically inscribed into witch-ness via a performative self-exposure, the confession (which fulfills the ultimate goal of paranoia, the confirmation that everyone who suspected was right); and ambiguous in meaning and status: nonexistent according to some epistemologies, criminal and/or diabolical in others, uncannily loathsome, hard to pin down precisely in language or social reality, and lacking in essence right up until the moment she or he is violently essentialized as a body being killed.

"How the World Works"

Eve Sedgwick offers an enduring account of paranoia as a recursive self- and other-implicating engine of knowledge and desire in her 1997 essay, "Paranoid Reading and Reparative Reading; or, You're So Paranoid, You Probably Think This Introduction Is About You."[23] Engaging with the theories of Melanie Klein, Paul Ricoeur, and Silvan Tomkins in order to seek alternatives to a paranoid critical practice, Sedgwick attends to the dual nature of paranoia as both an affect and an interpretive stance. As an affective mode, it is an often unpleasant state of attunement to and investment in dangerous others, whom it seems strange to call love objects. It is envious and self-conscious, defensive, and infused with persecution anxiety. But paranoia is also, as Sedgwick points out via Ricoeur, a "hermeneutic of suspicion," a mode of interpretation, typified by the critical orientation of Marx, Freud, and Nietzsche, that seeks out darker mechanisms always operating beneath the surface. It is more than just a bad feeling; it is a powerful methodology for producing knowledge, singularly focused on what is hidden versus what is shown.[24] Generating secret truths about the other, the self, and the systems that govern both is its function. In *Newes from Scotland,* for instance, David Seaton's suspicion produces what he doesn't know, but wants to know, about Geillis Duncane; what he may not want others to know about himself and Duncane; and, finally, what Duncane refuses to say about herself until a mark is found on her throat. One of my aims in examining the double-edged workings of paranoia in this archive is to bring together witchfinders and their techniques of violence, as well as the people (usually, but not always, women) who were their targets, into the ambit of a complex network of knowledge and investment that troubles simple distinctions between disciplined, licensed, and compelled desires.

Paranoia is inextricably connected with sexual secrets. As Sedgwick points out, "queer studies" (and, I would add, queer history) "in particular has had a distinctive history of intimacy with the paranoid imperative."[25] Twentieth-century gay theorist Guy Hocquenghem, whom Sedgwick cites, argues that the structure of paranoia is logically, indeed constitutively, tethered to the history of homophobia, and hence of queerness. Rewriting the received heteronormative psychoanalytic association of paranoia with homosexual neurosis, he argues that queer "persecutory paranoia" is an accurate reflection of the phobic paranoia that everywhere "seeks to persecute" queerness.[26] In Sedgwick's summation, "Paranoia is a uniquely privileged site for illuminating not homosexuality itself, as in the Freudian tradition, but rather precisely the mechanisms of homophobic and heterosexist enforcement against it. What is illuminated by an understanding of paranoia is not how homosexuality works, but how homophobia and heterosexism work—in short, if one understands these oppressions to be systemic, how the world works."[27] It is on account of this imitative reciprocity, between stigmatized and persecuted queer forms of desiring on one hand and the paranoid interpretive techniques that construct the queer as a stigmatized figure on the other that Sedgwick calls paranoia a *"reflexive* and *mimetic"* kind of desire:[28] "Simply put, paranoia tends to be contagious; more specifically, paranoia is drawn toward and tends to construct symmetrical relations, in particular, symmetrical epistemologies. [. . .] It sets a thief (and, if necessary, becomes one) to catch a thief; it mobilizes guile against suspicion, suspicion against guile; 'it takes one to know one.'"[29] Paranoid suspicion can thus be used to implicate subjects in secret knowledge (if you know, you are as well). Or it can be levied to name names—to turn an individual confession into a collective one (if I am, I know who else is as well). But it can also turn suspicion back on the accuser (if you know I am, then maybe you are too).[30] Or, as Ricoeur puts it, "Guile will be met by double guile."[31]

Reading paranoid suspicion as a queer-producing and queer-persecuting force in early modern witch hunt literature is historically and topically appropriate. Early modern witch hunts are genealogically connected to others that have deployed the same mode of erotically saturated truth production, most memorably in the twentieth-century witch hunts for communists—and crucially, inextricably, for homosexuals—staged in the House Un-American Activities Committee and the Senate hearings of Joseph McCarthy. Sedgwick's encapsulation of the paranoid/suspicious affective stance, "It takes one to know one," conjures a longer genealogy of political inquisitions based on covert knowledge of secret statuses and subversive affiliations, practiced throughout history against suspect types—both real categories of people and wholly imaginary figments of a paranoid, persecutory imagination—including gays and lesbians, spies, Jews, Muslims, former Jews or Muslims, heretics, atheists, radicals and revolutionaries, and all manner of participants who engage in illicit sex (promiscuous women, child abusers, devil worshippers). Taking note of these structural continuities across the continuum of paranoia's delusions also serves to decenter the question of the historical truth of early modern witchcraft (what the witchfinder wants to know: were they really doing anything?) in favor of exploring how persecution works.

Newes from Scotland gives us paranoia's reflexive and mimetic power fully formed. The first thing both Agnis Sampson and Geillis Duncane do when the devil's mark is found on their bodies is name names. After "a season" of torture in prison, the pamphlet narrates, Duncane "immediately" provides the names that turn an individual accusation into a regional witch panic: more than a dozen people, representing a diverse cross section of low- to upper-middle class society in Edinburgh and the surrounding towns (Br–Bv). The names are thus listed, decontextualized, erasing the affective and relational histories—with each other and with Duncane—that conditioned who was named, and whom they named in turn. The pamphlet's silence around the circumstances under which Geillis Duncane uttered or assented to these names also obscures, deliberately, the influence of the witchfinders' desires in implicating these people—the local interrogators and torturers who, since Duncane "was committed to prison," have become not only nameless but suspiciously evacuated of any grammatical presence or agency in the narrative ("she [. . .] caused them forthwith to be apprehended"). The pamphlet hints at, but does not record, the inaccessible dramatic exchange between Duncane and her interrogators in which they, together, produce one of the first ingredients of a witch hunt—a list of names—through a collusive process of suggestion, desire, and terror. We also see this name-naming apparatus in how Agnis Sampson not only produces herself as a witch, but also ratifies more fodder for the witch hunt, "justifying those persons aforesaid to be notorious witches" who must be apprehended and tortured in turn.

"The Cheefest Partes"

Sedgwick insists, along with Melanie Klein, that paranoia is a position, a flexible relational stance, rather than a diagnosis: "a position of terrible alertness to the dangers posed by the hateful and envious part-objects that one defensively projects into, carves out of, and ingests from the world around one."[32] Delving further into Klein's theory of paranoia, I find her notion of part-objects particularly useful for reading the erotics of witch hunt literature. Part-objects are unconscious, metonymic literalizations of desire that are based on single aspects of larger love objects (e.g., the "good breast" or "bad breast"). Through projection and incorporation/introjection, both good and bad part-objects "become installed, not only in the outside world but . . . also within the ego."[33] Crucially, however, the fantasized threats at the root of paranoia really do come from the dangerous objects residing within the body and psyche,[34] and, I would add, within communal bodies. The love objects of paranoid desire are not exactly other human beings, just as the erotic objects of the witch hunt's paranoia are not really specific accused individuals. They are partial, "phantastically distorted" approximations of the real things they represent.[35] Klein observes that these processes can be seen at work in adult fantasy and larger symbolic systems. There is actually the suggestion of a theory of demonology in Klein, originating

IT TAKES ONE TO KNOW ONE

in a community's or realm's internal persecutory violence against its internalized bad objects, projected outward and given culturally significant form: "In the infantile dread of magicians, witches, evil beasts, etc., we detect something of this same anxiety, but here it has already undergone projection and modification."[36] She adds, in a footnote that evokes the witch hunt's confidence in its providential righteousness, "We have an example of this in the phantastic belief in a God who would assist in the perpetration of every sort of atrocity (as lately as in the recent war) in order to destroy the enemy and his country."[37] Witchcraft literature thus voices an ancient, collective "paranoid position—understandably marked by hatred, envy, and anxiety," at the level of cultural beliefs.[38]

One of the signal features of witchcraft is its richly detailed object world. Like *The Witch of Edmonton*—and like other texts such as Thomas Potts's 1613 tract *The wonderfull discoverie of witches in the countie of Lancaster*; Heywood and Brome's 1634 tragicomedy *The Late Lancashire Witches*; and *The Wonderful discovery of the Witch-crafts of Margaret and Philippa Flower* (1619)—*Newes from Scotland* is strewn with an array of everyday things—animals, knives, body parts, food and drink, accessories, hairs, pins, ropes, and musical instruments—that are animated with uncanny properties of metonymy, attraction, and invisible entanglement.[39] Objects are endowed with supernatural effectiveness as instruments not only of witchcraft but witch finding, such as the "Pilliwinckes" used on Geillis Duncane; or the razor used on Agnis Sampson, the body hair it shaves, and the devil's mark it uncovers. Previous scholarship on witch beliefs has explained the magical cosmologies underpinning some of witches' most storied tools and techniques, and the grounding of English witch beliefs in anti-Catholic anxieties about the efficacy of performative speech acts and sacramental material rituals.[40] But reading the object world of witch hunt literature instead as a universe of Kleinian part-objects allows a more complex view of the "phantasmatic beliefs" and symbolic resonances they transmit. Furthermore, witch hunt pamphlets and plays perform their own meta-acts of interpretation, reading these uncanny powers into seemingly mundane things, thereby charging the world with supernatural properties. In other words, witchcraft literature performs a paranoid reading of the materials of everyday life. It projects a "terrible alertness" onto ordinary things and events, which become "hateful and envious part-objects" threatening the communal whole. These objects materialize the community's paranoid desires, rerouting and attaching them onto the body of the accused. Everyday accoutrements then come to signify, under the specular regime of paranoia, the suspect desires of those who possess and use them.[41]

The weird part-object-laced drama of *Newes from Scotland* unfolds with unsettling spontaneity, seemingly out of nowhere. The pamphlet has one of its younger defendants, Agnis Tompson, testify that on All Hallows' Eve, she set sail on the sea with some two hundred other witches, "each one in a Riddle or Cive;"[42] and that this supernatural horde embarked together, "with flagons of wine making merrie and drinking," to the North Berwick kirk, to commune with the devil who waited for them there.[43] It is not surprising that the moment when the pamphlet's story of the witches' doings turns truly fantastical is also the moment it hits on the political import of the North Berwick witch hunt. The storied witches' Sabbath at the North Berwick kirk is entangled with another shadowy, suspect, substitute-church ceremony taking place a year earlier, on August 20, 1589, across the North Sea: the marriage by proxy of the king, James VI, who sent one of his earls to stand in for him at the wedding, to fourteen-year-old Princess Anne of Denmark.[44] That autumn, Anne's attempts to sail to Scotland were thwarted by storms that struck her husband and shipmen as unnatural, the result of witchcraft being practiced against her in both Denmark and Scotland. After her ship was driven back once, James joined Anne and spent the winter of 1589–90 in Norway and Denmark. In 1590 James and Anne set sail together for Scotland on another storm-plagued voyage that seemed to prefigure the witches' curse from *Macbeth*, "Though his bark cannot be lost/Yet it shall be tempest-tossed" (1.3.25–26).[45]

We can never know what relation Agnis Tompson's testimony bears to public knowledge of these royal tribulations. Nor can we ever know what, if any, connection David Seaton might have perceived between Geillis Duncane's suspicious nighttime healings and the king's paranoid reading of his troubles at sea. All we know is that once Duncane names the citizens who become the North Berwick witches, suspicions of a diabolical plot against the king, his bride, and the realm are swiftly mapped onto the suspicions radiating from Seaton and Duncane, and the national momentum of the witch hunt is activated. Normand and Roberts acknowledge the devilish futility of trying to trace this story's voice up front: "Does the pamphlet reflect what the writer found in the examinations, which are probably the collusive fantasies of interrogators and interrogated? Or are these passages the invention of the writer of the pamphlet? The issue is further complicated if we suppose that [James] Carmichael [the king's minister] was present at the questioning of the accused, and also wrote the pamphlet that claims to report their answers."[46] But while the origins of *Newes from Scotland*'s singularly fabular narrative can never be definitively known, what can be analyzed are the miniature dramas it stages among actors and part-objects—twisted figurations involving the ordinary substances of domestic life, birth, and death—that make visible a multinodal network of affective investments, unrecoverable by conventional historical methods.

Agnis Tompson confesses to a plan to bewitch the king to death via a reaction between toad's venom and scrap of "foule linnen" cloth soiled by the king's bodily fluids—which only fails because her friend, a gentleman of the king's chamber, refuses to deliver the piece of linen. Another story put in Agnis Tompson's mouth tells of a charm that is at least partially efficacious:[47]

At the time when his Majestie was in Denmarke, she being accompanied with the parties before specially named, tooke a Cat and christened it, and afterward bound to each parte of that Cat, the cheefest partes of a dead man, and severall joynts of his bodie, and that in the night following the saide Cat was conveied into the midst of the sea by all these witches sayling in their riddles or Cives as is aforesaide, and so left the saide Cat right before the Towne of Lieth in Scotland: this doone, there did arise such a tempest in the Sea, as a greater hath not beene seene: which tempest was the cause of the perrishing of a Boate or vessell comming over from the towne of Brunt Iland to the towne of Lieth, wherein was sundrye Jewelles and riche giftes, which should have been presented to the now Queen of Scotland, at her Majesties comming to Lieth. (Bivv–C)

This cobbled-together fetish charm is, notably, an invention of *Newes from Scotland*'s fictional narrative voice, embellished with descriptive details not in the trials.[48] The narrative creates a chain of uncanny material objects, each of which has some power or efficacy in relation to the next, all catalyzed by witchcraft: a cat; a christening rite; a length of twine; "the cheefest partes of a dead man, and severall joynts of his bodie"; a fleet of sieves; a tempest; a foundered ship; and the "sundrye Jewelles and riche giftes" that "should have been presented" to Anne on her entry into Scotland. The paranoid imagination can run wild wondering whether the cat was cradled and baptized like a human baby—given an unknown name—in a mock sacramental ritual with overtones of bestiality.[49] The narrative is also silent as to who the "dead man" was, and what his "cheefest partes" might be.[50] The insinuation, combining necromancy with the sacrilegious use of relics in everyday life, is that the "joynts and members" are old bones obtained by robbing consecrated graves. Unlike in the case of the king's fouled linen, the salient thing about these body parts seems to be what parts they are—"the cheefest": genitals? heart? fingers?—and that they are human, rather than whose parts they were. The thing that results from all of these manipulations is a monstrous hybrid, a composite object, a blasphemously humanized cat (was the cat dead or alive?) bound up with an array of appendages, the desiccated or decaying parts of human corpses, on its body. This thing effectively wrecks a ship by raising a storm (the only act of *maleficium* in the pamphlet to cause actual destruction of property). These uncanny part-object dramas abide by a logic of metonymic substitution, where objects or fragments stand in for—and have a real effect on—a whole. Parts of a dead man are used to work magic against another man—against his "cheefest partes," keeping them from his new queen's body—and thus to harm the whole realm. The pamphlet's themes of parts, wholes, jointures, and disruptions caused by witchcraft speak to an overarching political anxiety around the joining of countries by marriage and royal succession. By keeping

James and Anne apart, the mock-baptized un-baby directly inter-rupts their royal sexual congress and reproductive futurity. The jew-els and gifts, political tokens of the queen's marriage and fertility, are displaced from their legitimating function and enlisted instead in this perverted series of witchcraft procedures, creating a threatening chain of bewitched materials linking James, Anne, their nonexistent heir, and a group of sexually and socially suspect common women (i.e., witches).

As Melanie Klein's readings of introjected part-objects remind us, persecutory fantasies lodge most powerfully in part-objects pro-duced, as the North Berwick witches are, from within bodies, within households, within realms. Paranoid fears, Klein says, are derived from "sadistic phantasies" of fashioning one's own excrement into "poisonous and destructive weapons" to persecute one's love objects: "In these phantasies [the child] turns his own faeces into things that persecute his objects; and by a kind of magic (which, in my opinion, is the basis of black magic) he pushes them secretly and by stealth into the anus and other orifices of the objects and lodges them inside their bodies."[51] Klein's model of paranoia can explain both the ma-liciously animated material objects in witchcraft narratives and the violent bodily procedures that produce witches. The "kind of magic" that Klein sees transmuting a body's solid excretions into persecutory weapons is the same paranoid interpretive magic that turns ordinary sieves, toads, traces of bodily effluvia, linen, cats, twine, and a dead man's joints into "poisonous and destructive" weapons used to dam-age the king and country. Agnis Tompson, Agnis Sampson, and the others are said to use these items to perverse ends, pushing them "se-cretly and by stealth" into the kirk, the king's bedchamber, the water of the harbor, and even the space of the witch trial, "lodging them inside" the body politic of the nation in their (mostly futile) "attacks" on the patriarchal body of the king. This is indeed "the basis of black magic": the primal paranoid fantasy underpinning beliefs about what witches are and do. It makes sense, then, according to paranoia's "re-flexive and mimetic" logic, that the apparatus of the witch hunt uses this same violent "black magic" to push the material accessories of witchcraft back into the bodies of its objects—the accused witches.

The carnivalesque gathering with the devil that ensues when

the witches arrive in their sieves at the North Berwick kirk reinforces the centrality of deviant sexuality—and not just deviant acts, but deviant pleasures—to *Newes from Scotland*'s construction of the witch. Though descriptions of witches' Sabbaths are rare in British sources (English witches were generally understood to practice *maleficium,* or material harm, in solitude or in small family groups), the Sabbath at the kirk is an idiosyncratic pastiche of gestures from English and Continental European witch beliefs. The hybridized, transnational quality of Scottish witchcraft reveals Scotland's liminal status as a site for the penetration of Continental influences into Britain, particularly in this instance northern magic from witches in Scandinavia. In *Newes from Scotland,* this paranoia clusters around the Edinburgh waterfront, which figures in the North Berwick witch panic as the setting for the witches' activities, the home and workplace of several of the accused, and the portal through which the king and queen must enter Scotland. This waterside gathering cites Continental witchcraft tropes in a perversely, even archly cheery, register. The food and drink that appear to the sieve-sailing witches is pleasurable and plentiful, unlike the rancid or loathsome food at Continental witches' Sabbaths.[52] They dance a sociable (possibly sexual) daisy-chain reel or round, rather than the involuntary, frantic bodily jerking of demonic possession. The whole scene has the atmosphere of a very outré secret midnight party, presided over by a blaspheming, sadistic yet charismatic nightlife guru. The woodcut on the pamphlet's cover evokes a rather domesticated assembly of genteel-looking witches, engaged in what look like everyday, sociable activities (cooking in a cauldron, eating, lounging, signing a register), and using an array of ordinary-looking household implements. Though the decentralized look of the gathering may be due to its being a composite of pre-existing images, these activities and tools are made sinister by their framing as the doings of the pamphlet's witches. Their maleficent effectiveness is indicated by the figures at the woodcut's margins: the ship tossed at sea on the horizon, the silhouetted devil addressing them from his tree-stump pulpit.

The devil who waits at the North Berwick kirk is not the silhouetted monster of the pamphlet's woodcut but "in the habit or likeness of a man" (Aiiiv). As a character, he is a sexualized, comic foil to

Figure 2. Woodcut illustration, *Newes from Scotland* (1592?), B4v. RB 59699, The Huntington Library, San Marino, California.

patriarchal authority; the threat he represents is as much social dis-order as supernatural damnation.[53] He has human body parts that he uses in a human manner: "Seeing that they tarried over long, he at their comming enjoyed them all to a penance, which was, that they should kisse his Buttockes, in signe of duetye to him: which being put over the Pulpit barre, everye one did as he had enjoyed them" (Aiiiv). Sexual congress with the devil, often punitive and painful, is a common marker of the diabolical pact that is often the centerpiece of Continental witches' Sabbaths.[54] And here too, the pamphlet re-ports, almost as an afterthought, the witches said the devil "would Carnallye use them, albeit to their little pleasure . . . at sundry other times" (Cv). However, the sexual sign of apostasy sworn in the kirk scene is of a very different quality from the rape of Continental accounts. The affect at play is not hellish violation but a queerer and more ambiguous one of sodomitical, scatological sadomasochism, in which the kirk and the "Pulpit barre" are just as much the objects of defilement as the witches' bodies. In this group sex act and its attendant affects of rebellion and submission, there is the potential for perverse pleasure—or at least absurd, subversive humor—in transgressive erotic relations.

From the pulpit, the devil makes "ungodly exhortations, wherein he did greatly enveighe against the King of Scotland," and specify that "the King is the greatest enemy he hath in the worlde" (Bivr). In the universe of *Newes from Scotland*'s affective politics, it becomes clear, these words are also an erotic event and a love object in and of themselves: the most gratifying thing that the king could possibly hear. James personally takes over some of the interrogations at the 1591 North Berwick witch trials, and this demonically attributed pronouncement transmits such a lasting affective load for him that he uses it in 1597 as the centerpiece of the entire system of witch beliefs in his *Daemonologie*. The king's paranoid self-styling as the central object of desire in this witch hunt calls to mind the vociferous, obviously eroticized investment of *Bartholomew Fair*'s Puritan fool, Zeal-of-the-Land Busy, in desiring while condemning the seductive Bartholomew pig. Like a queer-obsessed homophobic minister or politician of our own time, James is passionately interested in the desires of the subjects he so passionately persecutes. He delights at the news that the devil is equally interested in him as a cosmic twin, a nemesis and ur-object of desire. The king's desiring body is also foregrounded as a dramatic coparticipant with the witches, when tales of the Sabbath at the kirk visibly excite him— "these confessions made the king in a wonderful admiration" the description says. He asks for Geillis Duncane to be brought back before him to play the "reel" or dance that she is accused of playing that night as the witches danced to the kirk, on a "Jewes Trump" or harp: "Commer goe ye before, commer goe ye,/Gif ye will not goe before, commer let me" (Aiiiv). This strange little reel implies, in addition to a dance in the round, a round robin of sexual turn taking performed by the two hundred witches.[55] This song, restaged for James's viewing and listening pleasure, becomes, in addition to a piece of witchcraft evidence, a powerful transmitter of affect, which works profoundly on the most important body in the room: the king, who "in respect of the strangeness of these matters, tooke great delight to bee present at their examination" (Aii4).[56] His "great delight" is a sublimely paranoid pleasure: the pleasure of witnessing a performance that could risk inviting the devil into the space of the courtroom.[57] The song also becomes a court performance that can be understood within a future genealogy of James's predilection for court masques and witchcraft entertainments as the king of England. The insertion of a "Jewes" instrument into the gathering—and literally into the courtroom, as a theatrical prop—further augments the association, a hallmark of witch beliefs throughout Europe, between racial/national/religious otherness, sexual transgression, and demonism.[58] Geillis Duncane's harp exemplifies how familiar objects used in uncanny new ways become dramatic technologies in the witch trial discovery scene, taking on desires and investments from other places in the narrative and attaching them to the person of the witch. The collusive exchange of terror and pleasure with the king binds the accused witches and their demonized accessories as effectively as the dead man's "joynts" are bound to the cursed cat. Even more literally, according to the "symmetrical epistemology" of paranoia, the witch hunt's techniques of interrogation push, as well as press, wrench, prick, and crush, the instruments of knowledge production onto and into their bodies. (Duncane had her fingers crushed with the Pilliwinckes, remember, before she is commanded to play the harp.)

This pamphlet is a piece of political propaganda, but we can also read its narrative as a memorial reconstruction of a desperate, collaborative command performance solicited by the power apparatus in which the women are caught—a wrenching witch minstrel show. The discovery scene bears out the double bind structure of the paranoid dynamic: "Paranoia seems to require being imitated to be understood, and it, in turn, seems to understand only by imitation. Paranoia proposes both 'Anything you can do (to me) I can do worse,' and 'Anything you can do (to me) I can do first'—to myself."[59] The accused thus imitate the cravings of their inquisitors, and the inquisitors get what they crave from the accused. The king invites diabolical invasion by soliciting reenactments of witchcraft in the courtroom; and the accused in turn shape their performances of self-incrimination to his "delight" in a futile effort to save their own lives. (They do not succeed.)

Sexual secrets and secret knowledge function in *Newes from Scotland* as the linchpin of eroticized collusion between James and the accused witches. In the midst of his "great delight," the king seems to have a sudden attack of skepticism: "Item, the saide Agnis Sampson confessed before the kings Majestie sundrye thinges which were so miraculous and strange, as that his Majestie saide they were all extreame lyars" (Bivr). So the "eldest witch" performs a private exchange of secret knowledge: "Thereupon taking his Majestie a little aside, she declared unto him the verye words which passed betweene the kings Majestie and his Queene at Upslo in Norway the first night of their marriage, with their answere each to other" (Bivr). This moment is unlike anything else in *Newes from Scotland* in that the accused seeks to furnish proof of her supernatural intuition. Sampson turns the witch-producing apparatus of the trial inside out. Rather than being the object of intimate sexual probing in search of a foreknown secret about her (as when she was shaved and searched for the devil's mark), here she somehow contrives a secret of a private, sexual nature about the king, and projects it onto him, through close bodily contact, as a foreknown secret truth. Thanks to a completely impenetrable confluence of intuition, information, and investment, Sampson's secret appears to hit its affective mark: "The kinges Majestie wondered greatlye, and swore by the living God, that he believed that all the Divels in hell could not have discovered the same: acknowledging her words to be most true, and therefore gave the more credit to the rest which is before declared" (Bivr). The "credit" this adds to Sampson's foregoing confession of witchcraft under torture seems a high price to pay for the king's "wonder," and why an accused witch would do this at all seems a total mystery, until we realize that it is the particular nature of a sexual secret that provides Sampson with an opportunity to reverse the power dynamic of her interrogation and play on the king's desires. Whatever unknowable, presumably amorous words Sampson whispers, James enthusiastically assents to them, as opposed to explaining to the assembled court how they differ from what he and his fourteen-year-old bride, whom he had never met and with whom he had only French as a common language, actually had said to one another on their first night together. The palimpsest of sexual secrets layered into this exchange generates a paranoid impetus for the king to be hailed into confirming this highly suspect secret knowledge of his wedding night. James's preference for men was something of an open secret even before his marriage.[60] Here, that secret ghosts behind this one. The king's unspeakable sexual status, or the specter of sexual deviance threatening the marriage bed, is covered over and surrogated by another, urgently public intimacy in the witch trial discovery scene—the image of an elderly country wise woman and confessed witch whispering sweet nothings from his own wedding night in the eagerly receptive ear of the witchfinder king.

The Witch of Edmonton: "Our Secret Game"

Ford, Dekker, and Rowley's true-life domestic tragedy, *The Witch of Edmonton* (1621), stands out for its explicit dramatization of how another poor old woman, Elizabeth Sawyer, is made into a witch. The play's witchcraft plot is ripped from the headlines, adapted from Henry Goodcole's sensational pamphlet account of the real Elizabeth Sawyer's trial and execution at Tyburn earlier that same year.[61] But while Goodcole's pamphlet moralizes about his interrogation of Sawyer and the confession he extracts, *The Witch of Edmonton* focuses to a degree not found in any other witchcraft play on the gradual process of paranoia, harassment, and framing leading up to her arrest. It makes particularly visible the paranoid machinery by which a community constructs a woman as a witch in its midst from the materials of everyday life. A play communicates paranoid affect differently from a printed pamphlet—for one thing, the erotically suspect part-objects of witchcraft are physically present before the audience in the theater, as stage properties. For another, early modern antitheatrical suspicions cluster around the theater as a site of unnatural conjuration, with stories circulating in popular legend and antitheatrical polemic about theatrical rites conjuring real devils onstage.[62] The intimate interimplication of the uncanny objects and events onstage with conditions and events in the real world is emphatically centered in *The Witch of Edmonton,* which bills itself even in its first print edition decades later as "A known true Story, Composed into A TRAGI-COMEDY."[63]

Perversely, I locate the key to this play's construction of the witch in the substantial part of the play that seems to have nothing to do with witchcraft: the tale of Frank Thorney's bigamy, deception, and murder to preserve his inheritance. Unlike the true-to-life witch trial, Frank Thorney and the events of the bigamy plot are all fictional, concocted (chiefly, according to scholarly conjecture, by John Ford) for the purposes of the stage play.[64] There is relatively little scholarship addressing the relation between the two plots.[65] Yet this inventive and fraught domestic tragedy plot is part of the same play, intercut almost scene for scene alongside Elizabeth Sawyer's story. I argue here that the bigamy plot makes visible the affective dynamics of the witch hunt, demonstrating that something about sexual secrets—particularly secret sexual statuses—sparks or conjures suspicions of witchcraft, and vice versa. The bigamy plot also produces a queer figure—a bigamist rather than a witch—thus dramatizing a secret, nonnormative sexual identity. Reading the two plots in light of one another, then, underscores all the more vividly that the undercurrent of the witch hunt is secret sexual deviance. This requires reading the bigamy scenes with an eye to the structure of sexual secrets, and to the effects of sexual suspicion on the suspectors as well as the objects of suspicion. Without any absolute, reductive one-to-one mapping of the one onto the other, the dynamics of suspicion operating in both plots model how queerness functions as a secret. The tandem relationship between sexual secrets and witchcraft ultimately highlights the community's investments in covering over a host of other deviant and antisocial desires (including, but not limited to, master–servant rape, inheritance fraud, fornication, murder, treason, derangement, suicide, heresy, bestiality, and sodomitical sex with the devil) by projectively constructing, then executing, Elizabeth Sawyer as a witch. Sexual secrets are integral to all of my previous examples of the witch hunt's affective structure; they are manifest in *Newes from Scotland*'s content, as well as brought out by my suspicious readings. David

Seaton's suspicion of Geillis Duncane for spending nights out of the house causes us to suspect that his illicit sexual jealousy influences his interpretation. Agnis Sampson perversely proves her witch-power by producing a sexually and politically charged secret about the king, and communicating it to him in an intimate way that allows him to use her deviance as a cover for his own.

In the opening lines of the play, Frank tells his lover, the young servant girl Winnifride (whose problematic sexual status is marked on her body, as she appears "with child"), that she will be above suspicion now that they are legally married. However, Frank immediately relegates their marriage to the closet of secrecy, putting Winnifride up in another town. Winnifride objects: "Is this to have a husband?"[66] But she cannot demand more of Frank because the mark of their sexual relationship (her pregnancy) leaves her powerless to insist.[67] But for Frank and Winnifride's former employer, Sir Arthur Clarington, the marriage is a dark opportunity: unbeknownst to Frank, Sir Arthur has had a sexual relationship (of suspect consensuality) with Winnifride. When Sir Arthur upbraids Frank for debauching and ruining Winnifride (the crime he himself has previously committed), Frank protests that they are married, then asks Sir Arthur to tell Frank's father the opposite—that he is not married. Sir Arthur agrees to certify the lie, "Provided/I never was made privy to it," thereby invoking one of sexual normativity's sustaining illusions: the denial of what one hasn't seen with one's own eyes (1.1.147–50). Sir Arthur then reveals, in an aside, that his lie will be a cover for his own sexual depravity with Winnifride. He will make himself the facilitator of Frank's secret marriage because it is a more public, more visible version of the same secret crime he is committing. Lying about it, and hence keeping Winnifride sequestered in secret, creates a space for the illicit sex he apparently plans to continue having with her. Sir Arthur's exploitation of intimate scandal to extort continuing sexual favors also emphasizes, like David Seaton's persecution of Geillis Duncane, how secret sexual deviance exacerbates existing class, gender, and power inequalities. As with queer sexual secrets, those in the most stigmatized sexual positions—which overlap with positions of the least social power—have the least recourse.

As Sir Arthur's employee, Winnifride may technically be the wronged party, but outing herself as a victim could only harm her precarious marriage and social standing.

Frank Thorney's second, bigamous marriage, to the daughter of his father's creditor, is contracted so that he might save (and thus inherit) his father's lands. It looks like an unstigmatized, economically productive, socially and sexually legitimate coupling. Only the one single secret thing the audience knows about Frank—that he has already married Winnifride—transforms this normative, patriarchally endorsed match into the monstrous crime of bigamy. The secret marriage lingering in memory from the previous scene makes Frank's normally laudable response of filial obedience into an abomination. The words that fathers in early modern drama long to hear, "I humbly yield to be directed by you/In all commands" (1.2.152–53), become the setup to a sexual crime. The father even suspects the secret marriage but cannot prove it. Even confronted directly—"Speak truth and blush, thou monster./Has thou not married Winnifride, a maid/Was fellow-servant with thee?" (1.2.167–69)—Frank's refusal to confirm or deny it sends his father into a rage. Old Thorney's ranting, indignant lamentations, which echo those of his counterpart discussed in chapter 1, Sir Alex Wengrave, Sebastian's father in *The Roaring Girl,* give voice to the paranoid position regarding Frank's sexual secret. The father is subject to a "terrible alertness to the dangers" posed by the untoward sexual activities of this infuriatingly autonomous part of him—his offspring, successor, and heir—combined with a total inability to transform his suspicion into any more actionable exposure. Sedgwick observes that paranoia "places its faith in exposure," "as though to make something visible as a problem were, if not a mere hop, skip, and jump away from getting it solved, at least self-evidently a step in that direction." But then, as Sedgwick notes, just bringing a problem into speech does not bring about an end to it, or give one any purchase for redressing it.[68] Frank effectively disarms his father's ability to produce actionable knowledge of what he is: a bigamist.

Bigamist functions as a definite status in this play, one that shakes Frank's identity even as he lies to conceal it:

On every side I am distracted,
Am waded deeper into mischief
Than virtue can avoid. But on I must.
Fate leads me, I will follow. (1.2.197–200)

I have called bigamy a status rather than an act because the play
constructs it as the constitutive grounding of the character, the element in which Frank is fated to live and move. Even in a state of
shame and acute awareness of his sinfulness, he seems to feel that it
was in some sense not a choice: "In vain he flees whose destiny pur-
sues him" (1.2.236). In that respect, bigamy functions as something
more reified than an act in the play; it is something more akin to an
orientation—or even, at Frank's execution, an identity.

"Must I for That Be Made a Common Sink?"

The witch plot of *The Witch of Edmonton* mirrors the bigamy plot in
its concern with the interplay of choice and compulsion, both erotic
and social, at the moment when a subject turns from the normative
world and takes up the role of a sexually deviant, queer figure: a bigamist or a witch. When the witch of the title, Elizabeth Sawyer, first
appears (not until the second act; for the entire first act, Edmonton is
all bigamy), her opening speech is a piece of social critique objecting
to how she is seen by others:

And why on me? Why should the envious world
Throw all their scandalous malice upon me?
'Cause I am poor, deformed, and ignorant,
And like a bow buckled and bent together
By some more strong in mischiefs than myself,
Must I for that be made a common sink
For all the filth and rubbish of men's tongues
To fall and run into? (2.1.1–8)

This speech explicitly anatomizes the affective dynamics of projection
on which paranoia relies: others "throw" their "scandalous malice"

(eroticized violence and/or violent sexuality) on an old woman, attributing their own dangerous feelings of envy and persecutory fantasies to her, thus construing her as envious and malicious toward others.

Elizabeth Sawyer answers her own rhetorical question, "Why on me?" She is suspected along a number of social axes: female, poor, uneducated, and physically deformed, "like a bow buckled and bent together/By some more strong in mischiefs than myself." It is as though Sawyer's body is being cast as a persecutory bad object, bewitched and manipulated by supernatural malice into an unnatural shape. Sawyer objects to being "made a common sink/For all the filth and rubbish of men's tongues." She objects, that is, to being a receptacle for anxious projections about bodies and eroticism. But "a common sink" is an image of prodigious sexual receptivity, with which Sawyer figures her body as freakishly able to absorb the sexual aberrance of others. In what may be the most self-conscious reference in all of early modern drama to how communal desires construct the witch, Elizabeth Sawyer objects:

> Some call me witch,
> And being ignorant of myself, they go
> About to teach me how to be one. (2.1.8–10)

What is so unique about these lines is the idea that the construction of a witch goes hand in hand with the performance of the role. Charlotte-Rose Millar refreshingly recenters the allure of the diabolical in her analysis of English witchcraft pamphlets, arguing that witchcraft is a phenomenon of desire arising from affective states— and the unconscious urges they textualize—that invite the devil.[69] Indeed, the idea, presented in a stage play, that an accused witch must be taught—formed, instructed, and groomed—in how to be one invites us to go back and read the pamphlet literature (including Sawyer's interrogation by Goodcole) differently, noticing moments like Agnis Sampson's and Geillis Duncane's command performances, that record how the desires of accused witches are drawn out and used to teach the witch to collude in her own production. The people of Edmonton do this to Elizabeth Sawyer long before her arrest, insisting:

That my bad tongue—by their bad usage made so—
Forspeaks their cattle, doth bewitch their corn,
Themselves, their servants, and their babes at nurse.
This they enforce upon me, and in part
Make me to credit it. (2.1.11–15)

Here Sawyer's tongue becomes a bad part-object: her tongue is used,
badly, in others' delusions, to carry out others' sadistic impulses toward their own property, household, servants, and family members.
The role of a stereotypical English witch, engaging in material practices of *maleficium* witchcraft, is so consistently "enforced" on her
that she "in part" starts to believe it herself. In fact, it is debatable
whether at the beginning of the play Elizabeth Sawyer identifies as a
witch in any way. Practically alone among early modern witch hunt literature, *The Witch of Edmonton*'s representation of demonology starts
out skeptically and reaches at most ambivalence—a marked change
from Henry Goodcole's paranoid and credulous pamphlet. From the
first line spoken to her onstage—"Out, out upon thee, witch!"—
Sawyer's words are reflexively turned back against her ("Dost call me
witch?"/"I do, witch, I do; and worse I would, knew I a name more
hateful"), incriminating but also transforming her (2.1.17–19). After
cursing a neighbor, Old Banks, and being beaten by him, Sawyer
seems to dare to imagine that Banks was right about her:

Abuse me! Beat me! Call me hag and witch!
What is the name? Where and by what art learned?
What spells, what charms, or invocations
May the thing called Familiar be purchased? (2.1.33–36)

Her soliloquy gets more specific as to the paranoia she faces, and
what her lines and stage properties would be in the new role of witch:

I am shunned
And hated like a sickness, made a scorn
To all degrees and sexes. I have heard old beldams
Talk of familiars in the shape of mice,

Rats, ferrets, weasels and I wot not what
That have appeared and sucked, some say, their blood,
But by what means they came acquainted with them
I'm now ignorant. Would some power, good or bad,
Instruct me which way I might be revenged
Upon this churl, I'd go out of myself
[. . .] Abjure all goodness, be at hate with prayer,
And study curses, imprecations,
Blasphemous speeches, oaths, detested oaths,
Or anything that's ill, so I might work
Revenge upon this miser, this black cur
That barks and bites, and sucks the very blood
Of me and my credit. 'Tis all one
To be a witch as to be counted one. (2.1.107–26)

This crucial maxim, "'Tis all one/To be a witch as to be counted one," with which Elizabeth Sawyer comes out to herself (so to speak) as a witch, is a corollary to paranoid suspicion's queer-producing move: "It takes one to know one." Sawyer's declaration is more like, "If I am known as one, I might as well be one." But even as she imagines what she would know if she were a witch, "'tis all one" has the performative effect of making her one. One feature of "'tis all one's" queer performativity is how it plays into the community's paranoia. Rejecting any distinction between false and true accusations is a move made by suspects who do not accept that the slander against them is a bad thing (as in the conscientious refusal to deny that one is gay, HIV positive, a communist), or by suspects who desire initiation into the very thing they're accused of being, as seems to be the case for Elizabeth Sawyer. Being the object of paranoia provides her an opportunity for hyperbolic self-transformation. Reading her response forward through history, we can connect it to a tradition of queer refusal of phobic slurs by perversely embracing them—including the reclamation of the word "queer" itself. It is a queer response to projective demonization that replies, to a stream of insults, "I *wish!*," and "You want a witch? I'll show you a witch." Sawyer's longing, lusting solicitation of "some power, good or bad" that would allow her to be the thing she is counted as anyway—but to really be it, with all its attendant powers and perils—provides an alternative, queer way of imagining the desperate forms of collusion through which accused witches collude in their own production.

The little part-object produced by Sawyer's self-conjuring is the black Dog, Tom, who walks onstage and claims her as his own. Animal familiars, a hallmark of English witchcraft, are external embodiments of desire and enchanted beings of mixed or uncertain ontology.[70] Their efficacy is, like Kleinian part-object magic, a magic of feelings and desires that inheres in the interpretation of ordinary things as supernaturally animate. The Dog is an onstage embodiment of paranoia's ability to make true what it suspects: the Dog makes her a witch, but the Dog is a materialized conjuration of a wicked desire she had, which was aroused in her by the community's abuse. The Dog presumes that they already have an intimate relationship. He tells her he came to her out of love and pity to help her, and that all he wants is her soul and body, like a canine, diabolical surrogate Christ. He is both her servant and her master. He offers to run and do mischief to anyone she commands him to, but threatens "I'll tear thy body in a thousand pieces" if she refuses him an unequivocal blood pact (2.1.144). He seals her to himself by suckling blood from her arm, making her a twisted, incestuous, antigenerative, pseudo-maternal figure. One of the play's most obvious liberties with the real Elizabeth Sawyer's story from Goodcole's pamphlet narrative is changing her marital status from married to single and making the Dog her primary sexual object, a change that points up the centrality of erotic deviance in the witch hunt. The erotic bond between Elizabeth Sawyer and the Dog is extended and triangulated through the queer figure of Cuddy Banks. The son of one of Sawyer's chief persecutors, Cuddy is an infantile fool who dabbles in witchcraft and bestiality while maintaining an affect of receptive, childish innocence even as he is willingly lured into an erotic relation with the Dog as a love object and familiar. Cuddy takes the Dog as his "Ningle" (a corruption of "ingle," or homosexual boy favorite, a term with connotations of sexual service),[71] declaring his love too easily and too intensely. He later naively discloses these sexual relations to his father, protesting that he has "given [the Dog] a bone to gnaw twenty times" (4.1.253–54). The title page image of the first printed edition of the play, from 1658,

Figure 3. Title page woodcut, *The Witch of Edmonton* (1658), "A known true Story. Composed into A TRAGI-COMEDY By divers well-esteemed poets, William Rowley, Thomas Dekker, John Ford, &c." RB 111238, The Huntington Library, San Marino, California.

depicts Sawyer, the Dog, and Cuddy Banks in a triangle of mutual address, converging toward each other with speech ribbons that display their interlocking vulnerabilities and opportunisms: "Ho have I found thee cursing" (Dog), "Help help I am Drowned" (Cuddy Banks, from a pond), and "Sanctabecetur nomen tuum" (Mother Sawyer's bastardized Latin, which the historical Elizabeth Sawyer confesses in Goodcole's pamphlet was taught to her by the devil).

Cuddy Banks is witch bait. He embodies the seduction and the queering orbit of witchcraft. His lovers' quarrel with the Dog ("a pox, that morris makes me spit in thy mouth," he cries, before coming back again) confirms the sexually corrupting effects of those desires as well as the difficulty of turning away (4.1.285–86).[72] From the instant Elizabeth Sawyer becomes a witch, the audience is drawn in— as Cuddy is drawn in—to a voyeuristic fascination with her witchness and her bond with the Dog. This attraction raises the possibility that, like Cuddy, what we see as witchcraft and what we do not is a function of where our desires are invested.

"Fitted Both to One Sheath"

Bigamy is legally and socially a lie, a sin, and a crime. But in *The Witch of Edmonton*, it is also an erotic appetite, a secret status transacted through suspicion, generating hidden deviance in whatever it touches. Besides being felt as an unchosen fate, Frank's status as a bigamist seems to entail genuine erotic interest and affection for *both* his wives. When Frank is first betrothed to Susan, we initially wonder if the romantic energy of this second match is faked. But that suspicion quickly gives way to the more shocking suspicion that it is not, and that they are ardent lovers. Frank and Susan are described suggestively as a "new pair of Sheffield knives fitted both to one sheath" (2.2.41–42), a metaphor of twinning that also ominously introduces imagery of the knife, which will become a recurring figure in the play's part-object-ridden landscape, ultimately effecting a climactic nexus between the two plots. The image of two knives going into a single sheath also evokes the specter of sexual deviance: bigamy (a marriage with an extra partner in it), adultery, a bisexual/homoerotic threesome (two phalli), and doubled sexual peril.

Frank Thorney's interactions with his second wife at their secretly criminal wedding betray the distorting effects of bigamy paranoia on suspector and suspect alike. When Susan observes "strange variations" in her new husband, Frank's blithe refusal to acknowledge the discrepancy between his speech and his affect is an act of passive-aggressive violence (now known as gaslighting) that drives Susan to increasingly anxious self-abnegation.[73] Frank erratically attempts to placate Susan with praise, and even with a kind of honesty, almost telling her that he is a bigamist: "'Twas told me by a woman/Known and approved in palmistry,/I should have two wives" (2.2.118–20). Susan's craving to know the source of Frank's angst comes up against the limitations of paranoia's faith in exposure. The specific sexual deviance that is the cause of her suspicion—the state of bigamy—is so bizarre that it sounds like a lie even when spoken outright, even to someone who is already suspicious, already erotically invested, and thus primed and hungry to hear precisely this revelation. When Frank calls her the wrong name ("No, no, my Winnifride," [2.2.122]), and actually discloses that Winnifride is the girl he would choose to be a second wife, the revelation functions as further concealment thanks to Susan's normative assumption that he means a second successive wife should she die. Sedgwick makes the point that paranoia's faith in exposure means that it often loses all purchase when the truth comes to light and nothing happens, which is why counter-hegemonic paranoias are less effectual than those with social power behind them, as in the witch hunt.[74] So it follows that in this exchange, Frank's barely equivocated disclosure to Susan of what he really is has, perversely, no effectual force at all. As his wife, she is still in the disenfranchised position even though he is the criminally queer figure, the bigamist; thus her suspicions are powerless. Frank's predicament in *The Witch of Edmonton* is not played for comedy about women's sexual interchangeability or objectification. Rather, his behavior—keeping his meeting with Winnifride, guiltily kissing Susan and promising to anger her no more—provokes the suspicion that he not only has two wives, but he also feels the full measure of sexual and affective investment in both of them that a husband is supposed to bear to one wife. The monstrosity of his secret seems, at least in part, to be an erotic orientation toward a different number of love objects than the normative relational structure of marriage permits. His erotic bent queers both his marriages. If Susan's probing of Frank at their wedding echoes the schizogenic paranoia that grows out of suspecting a secret queerness in one's spouse, Winnifride's simultaneous terror of discovery and impotent, pessimistic longing to be publicly acknowledged is the aggrieved yet paranoid position of a same-sex partner whose significant other remains closeted.

"Would I Were!"

Just as Frank is about to leave one wife to run away with another, secret, pregnant wife, the two plots of *The Witch of Edmonton* come together for the first (and really only) time. The festering secret of Frank's bigamy is suddenly materialized to the audience by the same little part-object that has materialized Elizabeth Sawyer's witchcraft and rebellious sexual deviance: the Dog. The Dog's mysterious on-stage appearances with Frank Thorney, like his trysts with Cuddy Banks, embody how secret erotic deviance spreads outward—from Elizabeth Sawyer in the witch plot as from Thorney in the bigamy plot—to generate deviance in others, in a self-perpetuating feedback loop of untoward desires and illicit actions. As Frank and Susan bid a lingering farewell, the Dog inexplicably enters: "One touch from me/Soon sets the body forward" (3.3.1–3). The Dog "rubs" Frank, unseen. This rub seems to set in motion an urge to "ease all at once" (3.3.15), to annihilate the love object that is the occasion of his se-cret. "I must kill you," he announces openly to Susan (3.3.20). But, like bigamy, this is one of those secrets too horrifying to be believed even when it is said aloud. Suddenly, out of nowhere, the stage di-rections state that *He takes a knife*—indeed he seems almost sur-prised to find it (3.3.24). There is no indication of where the knife might come from; presumably it is one of the witchcraft part-objects/instruments strewn throughout the play, attached to Frank (handed to him, or placed where he will find it) by the Dog's affectionate rub. Just as the Dog declared, Frank's body is "set forward" by the touch and the knife. Menacing her with the knife, Frank calls Susan a "whore," construing her at her death as the thing that he in fact is. Mirroring the paranoid logic of the witch hunt, Frank projects his own deviant sexual state onto his legitimate wife, claiming that she is making him kill her: "You have dogged your own death" (3.3.40).

Though his murder of Susan seems to have been initially com-mitted in a fugue of eroticized witch-Dog passion ("Once past our height,/We scorn the deep'st abyss"), Thorney's agenda immediately, tellingly, turns toward secrecy (3.3.65–66). He sets about to avoid detection by "dressing" the knife in his own blood and "dressing" his body in wounds to mimic hers, wounding himself with the same uncanny knife on the "arms, thighs, hands, any place" in a performa-tive externalization of guilt that is, at the same time, a performance to conceal it (3.3.67–68). With the help of the Dog, who has presumably been onstage silently helping the murder along, Frank ties himself to a tree with ropes of mysterious origin. "How prosperous and effec-tual mischief sometimes is" (3.3.74), he muses, observing (correctly) that the projective energy of his sexual deviance, externalized in the Dog's familiar body, works to bring forth both evil deeds and the narratives blaming them on others.

The affective convergence between the bigamy plot and the witchcraft plot comes to a head in the play's juridical climax, where suspicion is fixed on the figures most available to hand. Frank's "dumb-show" of a gory attack by a stranger at first appears to work, encouraging Susan's father and his own to name two hapless young men as suspected murderers. But between the close of act 3 and the opening of act 4, Susan's murder appears to have touched off a communal flurry of witch paranoia. The citizens of Edmonton attribute a ready assortment of domestic and sexual disasters to Elizabeth Sawyer: "Our cattle fall, our wives fall, our daughters fall and maidservants fall; and we ourselves shall not be able to stand if this beast be suffered to graze amongst us" (4.1.15–18). The piece of thatch wielded by a countryman as he runs onstage yelling the long-anticipated lines, "Burn the witch, the witch, the witch, the witch!" functions as a counterpart to the demonic, Dog-implanted knife: it is a part-object fashioned not to effect witchcraft but to test for it, to draw it out. It is metonymically part of Elizabeth Sawyer, a piece of her house being taken and used against her: "They say, when 'tis burning, if she be a witch she'll come running in" (4.1.21–23). When she enters to find a piece of her roof stolen and burned, the men are exultant—in their "reflexive, mimetic" paranoid imaginary, the thatch is a flaming collective phallus that has irresistibly lured the witch, an embodiment of her deviant sexual appetite: "You hot whore, must we fetch you with fire in your tail?" (4.1.29–30). Other "proofs" offered by the townspeople similarly inscribe sexual secrets and forbidden desires onto the witch. Old Banks is compelled to perform oral sex acts on his cow: "Let me go thither or but cast mine eye at her, [. . .] I cannot choose, though it be ten times in an hour, but run to the cow and, taking up her tail, kiss, saving your worship's reverence, my cow behind" (4.1.62–66). The paranoid affective circuit of the witch panic brings such unruly bodily desires out into the center of the dramatic action. Community members are licensed to attribute what they are moved to do by their own illicit desires to Sawyer, and to her desire to make them do such things.

Sawyer attempts to call out the mechanisms of projection behind the accusation of "witch," moving from "I am none," to "Would I were! If every poor old woman be trod on thus by slaves, reviled, kicked, beaten, as I am daily, she, to be revenged, had need turn witch" (4.1.84–89). This response takes her act of resistant self-fashioning earlier in the play—"'Tis all one/To be a witch as to be counted one" (2.1.125–26)—to a more hyperbolic level of dissident witch-identification. Beyond making the point that being constructed as a witch not only *is* what it means to be a witch, but also actually inculcates the desire to be that dangerous, powerful thing, there are shades of a queer politics of reclamation in Sawyer's use of the term "witch" here. She laughs at the proclamation that she is "a secret and pernicious witch" (4.1.109) and counters, "A witch? Who is not?" (4.1.116). There is a radical fantasy of power in her point that the poor old abused women who get constructed as witches actually need the powers attributed to witches, in order to have any means of responding to the constant violence to which they are subjected.

Elizabeth Sawyer is finally undone by a pair of sexual secrets, one her own and another that she may not even know. In a diatribe against the hypocrisy of witch persecution, she rails at Sir Arthur Clarington that she never robbed a maiden of her honor. Sir Arthur takes this oblique mention of the very thing he did to Winnifride as proof that, like Agnis Sampson to King James, Sawyer has supernatural knowledge of his sex life: "By one thing she speaks/I now know she's a witch, and dare no longer/Hold conference with the fury" (4.1.159–61). In this "one thing" Sawyer speaks, the play's two plots come together. Though the text gives no indication of Sawyer's access to the secret sexual knowledge attributed to her—though Sir Arthur's guilty paranoia is at least in collusive tension with the old woman's (accurate) suspicions and intuitions about the sins of others in her community—this is enough to brand her as a witch.

The play then veers into its most graphic display of deviant eroticism. As soon as Sawyer is accused of knowing Sir Arthur's sexual secret, her own little sexual secret, the Dog, materializes to her. He suckles on her "teat" (her nipple, or the devil's teat on her arm), then stands on his hind legs to kiss and rub her. "Let's tickle," she propositions, and they presumably engage in erotic play as the Dog recounts the acts of *maleficium* he has committed (4.1.173). Elizabeth Sawyer equates him to other ornaments, pets, and transmitters of pleasure, calling him "my dainty, my little pearl!" and exclaiming that "no lady loves her hound, monkey, or parakeet, as I do thee" (4.1.175.177). This is the moment where what had heretofore been occulted intimations of bestiality, demonic sex, and *maleficium* are performed onstage for the audience's horrified pleasure. As if to confirm Sawyer's transformation into the condemned, queer figure of the witch, her black Dog disappears and returns to her white—the inverse of her own transformed status—and grave in affect. He rejects her sexual games, and he informs her that he is a harbinger of her violent public exposure and death. The Dog explains how he has brought Sawyer to the gallows by acting as object, instrument, and incitement for both her and Cuddy Banks's socially unacceptable desires.[75] Transgressive urges materialize the devil into surrogates like himself, he says: "Thy oaths,/Curses, and blasphemies pull him to thine elbow" (5.1.137–39), in the shape of "vermin" (5.1.127), or even "borrowed" bodies, such as the reanimated cadavers of suicides and strumpets (5.1.148–51). In a form conjured by desire, the Dog works by turning illicit urges into the actions of body parts: "As thy tongue slandering, bearing false witness,/Thy hand stabbing, stealing, cozening, cheating—/He's then within thee. Thou play'st, he bets upon thy part" (5.1.142–45).

The only crime of witchcraft actually staged in the play is the descent into madness of Anne Ratcliffe, whom Sawyer orders the Dog to "pinch" to the heart. "Touch her," she says to the Dog; the Dog's "touch" spurs Anne Ratcliffe to beat out her own brains, yelling, "The devil, the witch, the witch, the devil," and ranting about the man in the moon and devils grinding grain in hoppers (a metaphor for sex). This all seems to occur just offstage, as the townspeople— presumably covered in stage blood and prosthetic brains—come upon Sawyer with a newly concrete suspicion: "You have a spirit, they say, comes to you in the likeness of a dog" (4.1.234–35). Unlike his ambiguous "rubs" of Frank Thorney, the Dog's "touch" of Anne Ratcliffe is a direct transmission of witch-desire via a familiar. But for the townspeople, Elizabeth Sawyer's construction as a witch is already accomplished from what has been imputed to her by their own projective fantasies.

"What Knife?"

The play's materialized circuits of paranoid desire reach a climax in a twisted discovery scene. Frank lies creepily ensconced in his dead wife's father's house, recovering from his self-inflicted wounds while being doted on with quasi-incestuous devotion by his victim's sister, melodramatically affecting sickness and suicidal ideation as a cover for his murderous secret. Susan's sister, Katherine, presents him with a roasted chicken, a significant expenditure of labor and care; but, having forgotten a knife to cut it, she looks in Frank's coat for his pocketknife. As in the scene of Susan's murder, the ontological status and location of the knife is utterly ambiguous. *"Enter Dog, shrugging as it were for joy, and dances,"* reads the stage direction, indicating that the Dog may bring the knife into the bedchamber, stowing it where it will be found. Katherine, discovering the still-bloody knife, immediately lies about it, but Frank knows he is found out when he checks and finds the incriminating knife left in his coat pocket. In a twist on the portentous "two knives to one sheath" figure used at the bigamous wedding, the discovery of one knife conjures two apparitions: the two women Frank has wronged. The "Spirit of Susan" manifests in two places at once on both sides of the bed; at the same time, Winnifride, in the flesh and still cross-dressed as a boy, appears at its foot. At first Frank confuses the "lost creature" (4.2.69) in the room with the strangely doubled, mocking shade that menaces him.[76] He confesses Susan's murder to Winnifride, describing it as a wrongful and violent penetration: that he "dipped my sad pen [penis] in blood" (4.2.98). The sexual metaphor is extended by the discoverers, when Katherine shows Old Carter "A bloody knife in's pocket" (4.2.116).

The knife in this scene is a phallic vehicle for the sexual secret itself, and for how sexual secrets work as secret knowledge. In a thickly collusive, multiply duplicitous exchange, Frank and his suspectors switch back and forth between admitting they know about the knife and pretending not to know about it, even though all know it is there. Frank flies into a mania, crying out for "the knife, the knife, the knife!," "to cut my chicken up, my chicken" (4.2.117–18). Katherine pretends ignorance ("What knife?"). A perverse and gruesome charade ensues, in which Winnifride cuts up the roast chicken for Frank with the bloody knife that killed Susan—"A leg or a wing, sir?" (4.2.141)—while everyone pretends that nothing has been discovered. One dead bird quickly becomes a metonymic placeholder for another dead "bird" (woman), however, as Susan's wounded corpse is hauled onstage, her "one broad eye open" still staring at Frank, to "find out the murderer" (4.2.150–53). Susan's corpse is no longer a person but a thing. It is brought out, like the roof thatch, to function as a technology of knowledge production through the negative affect it incites in Frank. It throws Frank into a state of disturbance in which he can be confronted with his knife, "enameled with the heart-blood of thy hated wife" (4.2.164).

Frank is outed as a murderer by the exposure of Susan's bloody, penetrated corpse, but his outing as a bigamist requires a second exposure. In a grotesquely tragic version of what could have happened at the end of *Philaster,* suspicion falls on the cross-dressed Winnifride as Frank's servant boy and possible accomplice in the murder. Winnifride then reveals herself as "his first, only wife, his lawful wife" (4.2.178). This moment exemplifies Sedgwick's descriptions of paranoia's "extraordinary stress on the efficacy of knowledge per se—knowledge in the form of exposure," but in this sole instance in the play where paranoid exposure actually does produce truth, the truth that it produces is deviance: the crime of bigamy.[77] That the exposure of Frank's originary sexual secret occurs through the exposure of Winnifride's hidden sex highlights how bigamy functions as a queer sexual status, inhering in an improper number of "sheaths" (vaginas) for Frank's "knife." That Frank is outed as a bigamist by a cross-dressed (boy) actor's removal of "her" men's garments—over a roast chicken carved with the murder weapon, planted by a dancing devil dog—highlights that bigamy, like witchcraft, is produced through physical and affective transactions with erotically inflected material objects. But this is also the moment when the bigamist is produced as a queer figure in the phobic, disciplinary, historical sense, as an essentialized criminal type whose sexual deviance can only be remedied by his death. When Frank's homosocial page is revealed to be not only a woman but his wife, a monstrous double of the dead woman, the never-not-relational character of a queer disclosure changes the status of both partners.[78] Winnifride's only escape from certain condemnation is to pronounce Frank guilty of both murder and premeditated bigamy ("Has he done it, then?" "Yes, 'tis confessed to me" [4.2.183–84]). Turning Frank in for his crimes relegitimates Winnifride as a sexual victim rather than a sexual suspect, so when we see Frank processing to the gallows in the play's final scene, Winnifride is not in chains being hanged with him. In fact, she is the object of love and sympathy from both Frank's and Susan's fathers, who offer her comfort, pity, and assurance that "'twas not thy fault" (5.3.8).

How is it possible for Winnifride, for Sir Arthur, who is only "mildly censured" for being "the instrument that wrought all their misfortunes" (5.2.1–3), and moreover for Frank, whose scaffold scene of reconciliation and forgiveness is one of the most dilated, most thoroughly reparative execution scenes depicted in early modern literature, to be so thoroughly reincorporated into the community at the resolution of the play after such transgressive sexual offenses? The answer comes in the final moments of the scene, when the two plots of the play come together for only the second time in the twinned executions of the climax. Elizabeth Sawyer is led onstage to execution alongside Frank, to cries of "Hang her! Witch!" Old Carter exclaims, "The witch, that instrument of mischief! Did not she witch the devil into my son-in-law when he killed my poor daughter?—Do you hear, Mother Sawyer?" (5.3.21–23). This is the first time Frank's crimes, previously attributed to his own deviant desires spurred on by the Dog's ontologically ambiguous instrumental role, are pinned on Elizabeth Sawyer as something she bewitched him to do. Sawyer has become the official repository or "common sink" for all violations of social mores—those she has nothing to do with as well as those she owns—and the Dog has become her official instrument. "Cannot a poor old woman/Have your leave to die without vexation?" she answers Old Carter, who persists: "Did you not bewitch Frank to kill his wife? He could never have done't without the devil" (5.3.24–27). Sawyer does not dispute that the devil has been involved: "Who doubts it? But is every devil mine?" (5.3.28). The collective piling-on of blame onto Elizabeth Sawyer as she is on her way to die effectively makes not only the devil of bigamy but every devil hers, now that she is a witch being executed for witchcraft.

Frank Thorney's execution as a bigamist, by contrast, is ultimately more mimetic of Christ's crucifixion or the prodigal son's confession than of a witch hanging. He registers happiness that the law has foreclosed his licentiousness and disciplined his desires (5.3.76–87). However, he also disavows all love and desire for Susan, and he characterizes his patriarchally ordered marriage as a mercenary choice, utterly eliding the fact that his actual crime was his failure to choose at all (5.3.110–11). Frank's failing, which has for the entire play been construed as a sexual indulgence in too many wives at once, is resignified at the last moment as a mistaken value judgment, the vastly easier to forgive crime of marrying for money (on his father's orders). A bigamist, it turns out, can be reconstituted as a social subject in a way that a witch cannot, if the bigamist's crimes are attributed to the witch—and if bigamy is essentially erased as one of his crimes in the final reckoning.

Frank's gallows conversion to affective and romantic monogamy is further enabled by the fact that there are no longer two wronged wives present but only one, Winnifride, the sole object of his death-bound love. This would imply, in a horrifying irony, that murder plays an indirect role in purging sexual sin, allowing Frank's rehabilitation from bigamy and Winnifride's from whoredom. The discovery and resolution of Frank's bigamy would have far trickier affective consequences were Susan not "in heaven" but rather a potentially "hateful and envious" presence at the scaffold. But because the embodied marker of Frank's bigamy has been stabbed, purged, and now posthumously rejected as an object of affection or erotic love, the play can spend the last lines lingering ecstatically over Frank's repentance and his effusive blessing of everyone he has wronged, who bless him in turn, in a copious outpouring of positive affect amounting to an orgy of reparation.

By the same token, once she is saddled with the blame for Frank Thorney's bigamy, the witch's work is done, and Elizabeth Sawyer drops out of the play's resolution. She is led offstage for the last time, refusing to satisfy her audience's craving for any performative, confessional affect from her: "Have I scarce breath enough to say my prayers,/And would you force me to spend that in bawling?" (5.3.49–50). Her refusal to confess means that she is to be burned alive, but the text does not dramatize her death.[79] The disturbing outcome, at the end of a play about witchcraft and bigamy, seems to be that in order for sexual normativity to be reinstituted (as it is in Winnifride's epilogue, with her "modest hopes" of attaining "good report"), it is the supernumerary wife and the witch who must be removed, made invisible, and abjected as the embodiments of impermissible desire.

"Yet Did Hee Utterly Denie"

Newes from Scotland also elides any dramatic description of the executions of the women accused and tortured in its narrative. On the last page, we find out why: "The rest of the witches which are not yet executed, remayne in prison till farther triall, and knowledge of his majesties pleasure" (D3r). This early pamphlet, unlike *The Witch of Edmonton,* circulates as popular media before its witch hunt is brought to its grand climax: mass hangings in the heart of Edinburgh. There is, however, a single execution dramatized in gory detail: that of a male witch, allegedly named "Doctor Fian" but using the "alias John Cunningham." The erotic networks conjured in *Newes from Scotland*'s curious relation of his trial prefigure *The Witch of Edmonton,* with its pairing of a female witch and a male sexual manipulator. Like many others in the pamphlet, Fian is first accused by Geillis Duncane. For reasons we cannot know but may guess—because accused witches surely pursued their own secret agendas of retribution in naming names—he is the only accused man named at the North Berwick kirk witches' Sabbath. He is said to have acted as the Register, the scribe at the desk depicted in the woodcut in figure 2, who manages the witches' forced kissing of the devil's buttocks (C5). Reading the pamphlet's narrative of Fian's confessions and tortures in light of *The Witch of Edmonton*'s later dramatic staging of Frank Thorney's crimes and (revisionist) confession shows Doctor Fian in a new light: he is more than just a token male accused witch. Read next to Frank Thorney, Fian embodies a difficult and submerged link between sexual violence and the machinery of the witch panic: the coexistence of gender violence and sexual violation perpetrated on the bodies of accused witches, with sex and gender violence perpetrated *by* accused witches. One of the kinds of deviant desire narrated in Fian's case, producing him as an erotically dissident, criminalized figure, is rape. Unlike any of the female witches in the pamphlet, *Newes from Scotland* depicts Doctor Fian as doing harm not to the king but to other people—both adults and children—in the service of his own erotic appetites. Cases like his force the history of sexuality to confront the uneven and sometimes unknowable overlap, in paranoid sex persecutions, of what people actually did versus what they are accused of doing. These two categories are obviously not identically coextensive, but neither are they dependably separable.

The "damnable" John Cunningham/Doctor Fian wants sexual access to a young woman—or, more probably, a girl—who does not want him. He is said to bewitch a neighbor to madness "onely for being enamoured" of her, "whome he loved himselfe" (Ciir). He "used many meanes sundry times to obtain his purpose and wicked intent of the same Gentlewoman," finally turning to "conjuring, witchcraft and Sorcery" to obtain what he could not by consent (Ciiir). His clear objective is sexual coercion: rape by witchcraft. Using his power as the schoolmaster, he calls this young woman's brother, his student, to him and "demaunded if he did lye with his sister." The answer being yes, he "secretlye promised the boy to teach him without stripes, so he would obtain for him three haires of his sisters privities, at such time as he should spye best occasion for it." This is the most rapacious sort of sexual witchcraft. Like the thwarted bewitching of King James via his soiled personal linens and the toad, Fian's plot uses bits of bodily detritus, secretly obtained, to get at the victim. The relationship it intrudes on is that between a sister and a brother who are still young enough to share a bed. Fian also seduces his student to exchange the "stripes" inflicted on his back for three of his sister's pubic hairs, a substitution that initiates the boy as a sexual violator, an instrument as well as an object of violence. The boy vows to do exactly that, "taking a peece of conjured paper from his maister to lappe them in when he had gotten them." He then "practiced night-lye to obtaine his maister's purpose, especially when his sister was asleepe" (Cii4).

But in a fantastical plot twist, the children's mother is a witch herself. The mother witch already holds the schoolmaster in such sexual suspicion regarding her children that her daughter's complaint that "her Brother would not suffer her to sleepe" immediately makes her "vehemently suspect" Fian of some evil intention (Cii4). This is an amazing tossed-off revelation about the universe of *Newes from Scotland* and the North Berwick witch panic: that the Edinburgh area is so teeming with witches that their magic and interests collide. It is also an instance of the use of witchcraft to exact both sexual violence and revenge for sexual violence. Once the mother extracts Fian's plan from the boy with a beating, she decides to "meet with the Doctor in his own Arte." Taking the "conjured paper," she goes to "a young Heyfer which never had borne Calfe nor gone to the Bull," and clips off three hairs from its udder (Civr). The boy takes them to the schoolmaster, who, "thinking them indeede to bee the Maides haires, went straight and wrought his arte upon them." "But the Doctor had no sooner doone his intent to them, but presentlye the Hayfer Cow whose haires they were indeed, came into the doore of the Church wherein the Schoolemaister was," and "made towards the Schoolemaister, leaping and dauncing upon him, and following him foorth of the church and to what place so ever he went, to the great admiration of all the townes men of Saltpans, and many other who did beholde the same" (Civr).

This anecdote illuminates the structural relation between Frank Thorney's bigamy and Fian's witchcraft: their criminal machinations follow a structure of sexual secrecy that is the hallmark of both witchcraft and nonnormative sexuality. Both are middling men who will not take no for an answer, and who use nefarious means to circumvent social constraints on their sexual behavior. Both are liars and predators who take advantage of women's and children's lesser social power to satisfy their illegitimate sexual appetites. Both texts stage scenes of intimate violence committed via secret, enchanted part-objects: incestuously stolen pubic hairs and enchanted paper; a pocketknife put to sudden use as a weapon of wife murder; a quasi-gothic, epistemology-of-the-closet-laden outing involving a roast chicken; and strangely animated animals—an enamoured heifer and a mysterious telekinetic Dog, both of whom dance up to the offender and rub their bodies on him. To point out these structural parallels, as well as how both characters are produced as queer figures for their pursuit of antisocial sexual ends, does not mitigate the violence of these stories. Instead, it reminds us that the history of deviant and antisocial desires does not conform to a modern, liberal, purifying bifurcation of free and consensual perversions as distinct from violent and predatory ones.

The play and the pamphlet stage quite different fates for Frank Thorney and Doctor Fian/John Cunningham. But both plots treat the men's illicit sexual agendas within a larger web of competing desires, including women's illicit activities undertaken to counter and defend against men's sexual manipulations. When the schoolmaster Fian finds himself humiliated by being made the love object of a cow, the narrative of *Newes from Scotland* shifts suddenly into a register of revenge farce. As in *The Witch of Edmonton,* a witch appears at the scene of gendered violence. But far from being sacrificed or incriminated to apprehend a male predator, as Elizabeth Sawyer is, this mother-witch is the discoverer of the crime. She agentively targets Fian with her magic, besting him "at his own Arte," to punish him for his predation of her daughter (and son). By turning the love object of the spell from a woman to a cow, she makes Fian's erotic appetites, as well as his diabolism, the target of public suspicion and ridicule, getting him "secretlye nominated for a notable Cunjurer." She uses not only cow's hairs but the lecherous schoolmaster himself as instruments of her desire for revenge.

But this tale of attempted rape and maternal vengeance is produced and/or sworn to by Fian under multiple waves of heinous torture, which is where *Newes from Scotland*'s resolution links Fian's problematic mode of suspect male sexuality to paranoia's intractable problem of knowledge production. Why Fian meets such an exceptionally violent fate may be in part that he causes somewhat of a gender crisis by being implicated at the witches' Sabbath, or that he is more obdurate under torture than the rest and thus produces more gruesome results. I argue, however, that the self-serving sexual character of his witchcraft, combined with his refusal to play out the penitence narrative as Frank Thorney does, creates a new, masculine facet of the witch as an antisocial queer figure. Further, the persecutory paranoia this figure arouses is brought out in the narrative's prurient description of what happens to his body. Though at first, like Agnis Sampson, he refuses, and only confesses after "the rest of the witches" discover two "charmed Pinnes" stuck into his tongue (Ciir), Fian appears penitent after recounting all of his diabolical seduction attempts, performatively renouncing the devil. But then, the next night, he steals the key to the prison door and escapes. Upon being swiftly reapprehended and taken before James himself, "nonwithstanding that his owne confession appeareth remaining in recorde under his owne hande writing," "yet did hee utterly denie the same" (Diir). Fian's retraction throws the physical, affective, and epistemological workings of the witch hunt into overdrive. James hypothesizes that he has made a new pact with the devil and received a new mark, which is searched for but never found, because the logic of the witch hunt can furnish no other explanation for his "stubborne willfullnesse" in refusing to agree again with his previously sworn narrative (Diir). The torture reserved for the re-unrepentant seducer is hyperbolic, beyond protocol, "a most strange torment": his fingernails are "riven and pulled off," and needles thrust in. He continues so long in the boots that, the pamphlet says, "his legges were crusht and beaten together as small as might be, and the bones and flesh so brused, that the blood and marrow spouted forth in great abundance, whereby they were made unserviceable for ever" (Diiv). Yet no confession is driven out: "Notwithstanding al these greevous and cruell torments hee would not confesse anie thing, so deeply had the Devill entered into his heart, that hee utterly denied all that which he had before avouched, and would saie nothing thereunto but this, that what hee had done and sayde before, was onely done and sayde for feare of paynes which he had endured" (Diiv).

The interpretive mechanism of the witch hunt reads Fian's retraction as a total mystery: neither the tale of illicit love magic that Fian furnished for the court before he escaped from prison, nor its truth status, nor what was being done to his body as he narrated it, are in any way put in question. The machinery that the witchfinders (and the state, embodied in James) have enchanted with their paranoid investment and belief in its efficacy is mysteriously refusing to work. It is possible, though, to read this as a scene that pits not only the pincers, needles, and boots but also the materiality of human flesh against the account that a person is willing to give of himself—what he desired, what he did, and why. His ultimate recalcitrance, his refusal to repent even upon being tortured to death, may be seen as a more extreme, more defiant variant of Elizabeth Sawyer's passive-aggressive affect on being labeled a witch, "'Tis all one,/To be a witch as to be counted one." It is rare in early modern English crime literature for anyone to attribute the pain of torture as causing a false confession (a silence that to me indicates an unspoken anxiety around the issue). Fian's refusal, in the last instance, to satisfy the witch hunt's desire to produce a confession out of him—he is burned alive "for example sake, to remayne a terrour to all others hereafter," without ever providing one—causes such a narrative outpouring of baffled rage precisely because it shows the production of the truth of witchcraft to be driven not by logic but by desire, and its success or failure to depend as much on temperament, interpersonal affective dynamics, and trauma as on virtue or truth.

The Witch of Edmonton, conversely, disciplines bigamy with godly purgation. The resolution stages Frank's crime as a grave fall followed by a smoldering secret, which twists his behavior—and by paranoia's contagious logic of implication, that of everyone around him—until he is found out in a paroxysm of horrific exposure and somber juridical retribution. But then, as Frank prays for forgiveness at his execution, it is apparent that his redemption is possible only through the wholesale scapegoating of Elizabeth Sawyer (including for Frank's crimes) and her exclusion from the scaffold scene, as well as Susan's erasure (by which the play colludes with Frank's murderous impulse to eliminate her). Reparation for a bigamist, in short, requires the redoubled abjection of a witch (and, suspiciously, a wife). An alternative reading becomes visible, though, by juxtaposing the play's bigamy plot with Newes from Scotland's lecherous schoolmaster. As a bigamist, Frank Thorney insists on options that are normatively foreclosed to him, attempting to have it both ways. He wants to marry whom he likes (and to have however many partners he likes) while maintaining his property and respectability. As the counterpart to the titular witch, the bigamist of Edmonton emerges as an overreaching sexual outlaw of another kind, one who refuses to choose between sexual fulfillment and social status, and who refuses the enforced equation of marriage and monogamy, thereby resignifying marriage to his own ends so profoundly that he must hang for it. This reading of Frank Thorney's antisocial sexual selfishness places his bigamy within a genealogy of secret rebellion specifically clustered around sexuality. The bigamist becomes the missing link in a chain of erotic suspicion that stretches from witch panic to gay panic, revealing the resonances between the paranoid affective machinery of the witch hunt and that of homophobia.

4
Lost Worlds, Lost Selves

Queer Colonial Melancholia

The queer side of colonial desire is less about possession than about its failures, and less concerned with first contacts than with the ambivalent afterlives and melancholic echoes of colonial encounters. Thus this final chapter begins with a leave-taking: the protracted departure, in 1558, of Jean de Léry's mission to the French Huguenot outpost in Brazil. Léry's *Histoire d'un voyage faict en la terre du Brésil* (not published until 1578, more than twenty years after the voyage) is a novelistic account of how his twenty-two-year-old self, along with fifteen or sixteen other young Calvinist clergymen, undertook—and aborted—the first Protestant mission to the Americas. The text recounts a drama of disidentifications and exiles: the ministers' drastic falling-out with the governor of the "France antarctique" colony, Nicolas Durand de Villegagnon, whom Léry accuses of backsliding into Catholicism; their expulsion from the tiny island fort; their two months' sojourn on the mainland of Brazil (where the city of Rio de Janeiro now sprawls) among the Tupinamba people; their harrowing return voyage; and the turbulent years of religious war in France between the voyage and the *Histoire*'s publication.

"If It Had Not Been"

On the January 4, 1558, not quite a year after arriving in Brazil, Jean de Léry and his fellow ministers secured permission to board a ship bound for France in the Bay of Guanabara and weighed anchor:

Not, however, without great fear and apprehension: in view of the hardships we had endured going over, if it had not been for the ill turn done us by Villegagnon, several of us, who had not only found over there the means of serving God as we wished, but had also tasted the goodness and fertility of the country, might well have stayed on instead of returning to France, where the difficulties were then—and are still—incomparably greater, with respect to both religion and to things concerning this life.[1]

Léry loads down the act of setting sail with negative affects like an intangible cargo: apprehension, regret, and wistful desire for what might have been. His insistence that they were forced to leave overlays constraint on constraint: *if only* things had been otherwise in the colony, *if* Villegagnon had not been *even* more cruel than they could endure, *even* by comparison to the hardships of the voyage, *even* in comparison to the state of things in France, *then* they "might well have stayed on." But things were not, as it happened, otherwise, and so they did not stay. At this moment, when their mission is irretrievably aborted, the narrative loops into backward-looking digressions pondering the lost, hypothetical futures foreclosed by not remaining in the colony (which would fall to the Portuguese within two years).[2] This negative conditional phrasing is used throughout the *Histoire d'un voyage* to signal a mood of passive regret over what never could have been, because the conditions of its possibility were themselves impossible.

These would-be colonizers' impossible longings—for things to have been otherwise; for transformation into something they could never be; for possession of something they will never have; for another role to play besides the one in which they have been cast by the material finitudes of history—constitute a mode of desire that I call queer colonial melancholia. It is bodied forth in the text and images of Jean de Léry's *Histoire d'un voyage,* as well as in two texts from the doomed English venture on Roanoke Island: Thomas Harriot's 1588 promotional pamphlet, *A Briefe and True Report of the New Found Land of Virginia,* and John White's 1590 coda to it, "The True Pictures and Fashions of the People in That Part of America Now Called Virginia." Both the French Calvinist text about Brazil and the Elizabethan Anglican one about Virginia are shot through with anxieties of inferiority toward the colonial prowess of Catholic Portugal and Spain. They are powered by thwarted desires for lost and impossible futures. The force of their longing generates fantastical affective models of relation between Europeans and Native Americans, which exceed the logics of linear historical time and biological or sexual reproduction. These unnatural fantasies are queer in that they violate norms of whom and what the would-be colonizer is supposed to identify with, and what he is supposed to desire.

For example, during their sojourn on the mainland, Jean de Léry and the band of unarmed clergymen wander unmoored from the social structures of the French colony. Vulnerable and implicated in unorthodox relationships not only with the Tupinamba people but with the French Catholic (Norman) sailors, some of whom live with the Tupinamba, the ministers occupy a queer position as exiled not-quite-colonizers. The foundational identity categories of nationality, tribe, and religion have failed to hold, and those displacements still bear on Léry as he writes his account years later. Having "tasted the goodness" of the country, an experience Léry consistently figures as one of sensory receptivity, some "several" of the ministers had "found," in extreme dislocation, an unexpected consonance between the alien land of Brazil and a possible desired self. But it is an impossible desire to sustain, and the "means of serving God as we wished" becomes for Léry one of the lost American love objects left behind on the shore of Brazil.

Thomas Harriot and John White, by contrast, most likely first encountered the Algonkian people of Virginia on the first English expedition to Roanoke Island in 1584. They played leading roles as documentarians of the second, disastrous voyage led by Richard Grenville in 1585. The men of that company had to be rescued and transported back to England by Francis Drake on his return voyage from the Caribbean. Harriot published a quarto edition of his *Report* to promote the colony to prospective settlers in 1588—too late to accomplish its purpose—after a third expedition, led by John White, unexpectedly landed again on Roanoke after a near mutiny at sea.

Unlike the two previous expeditions, this 1587 voyage was intended to be a permanent settler colony. White returned quickly to England to attempt to deliver supplies to the colony. But due to political complications, including the Spanish Armada, three years passed before he could do so. The 1590 re-publication, in a splendid folio edition, of Harriot's *Briefe and True Report,* along with engravings by Dutch publisher Theodor de Bry of John White's "True Pictures," was dedicated to Raleigh as the patron of the Virginia venture, in hopes of raising money and support for a relief voyage. But it was again too late for the book to do any good.[3] By the time the edition appeared, White had already embarked on the long-delayed relief voyage. There was no colony to relieve, however. White arrived to find the Roanoke settlement razed and all the settlers gone. Among those lost were White's daughter and his infant granddaughter, Virginia Dare, whose birth was lauded—and whose disappearance was mourned and mythologized—as the first baby of English descent born on the North American continent. The 1590 folio thus embodies several kinds of belated, wishful, and impossible colonial ambitions between its covers. It contains material from two writers and artists, collected on two successive, failed ventures, and published at a third moment, by a third party with his own agenda, in a futile attempt to materialize a convoluted network of already-impossible national and familial desires.

"That Bizarre Figure of Desire"

By using the term "colonial desire" to refer to the historical force animating these voyage accounts, I am deliberately characterizing both colonial venturing and colonial writing as erotically driven processes, structured by a dynamic of lack, pursuit, and loss. Voyage writing is a fictive and fantastical genre that shares its historical lineage, as well as its dilated quest-and-return plot structure, with romance.[4] It comes into being as a recognizable genre through its deployment of preexisting allegorical tropes of European fantasy.[5] Undercurrents of loss and alienation are written into its material conditions. Long-distance voyaging enacts a double displacement: through the time-warping incarceration of the journey; into the presence of a civilization far different from the traveler's own; and then back, into a defamiliarized home country, in which the voyager is irreversibly altered. The encounter with the other is always dramatized as negotiation of identification and difference, attraction and repulsion.

Tales of long-distance travel, thoroughly dependent on presenting an erotics of strangeness for readers' pleasure, permeate early modern popular culture, beginning with Richard Hakluyt's famous anthologies: *Divers Voyages Touching the Discoverie of America and the Ilands Adjacent unto the Same, Made First of All by Our Englishmen and Afterwards by the Frenchmen and Britons: With Two Mappes Annexed Hereunto* (1582); and *The Principall Navigations, Voiages, and Discoveries of the English Nation: Made by Sea or Over Land to the Most Remote and Farthest Distant Quarters of the Earth at Any Time within the Compasse of These 1500 Years* (1589, 1598–1600), every edition of which included Thomas Harriot's *Briefe and True Report*.[6] Jean de Léry's, Thomas Harriot's, and John White's accounts were widely translated, collected, and circulated in print.[7] Indeed, both works became volumes in Dutch engraver and publisher Theodor de Bry's thirteen-volume series Les Grands Voyages, or America, published in lavish editions throughout Europe in the 1590s and 1600s in the interest of promoting specifically Protestant colonial ambitions. But exoticized figures of the non-European people represented in these narratives also abound in theater, masques, and public processions, far beyond the readerships of specific accounts. These include the entry of Henri II into Rouen in 1550, which included a mock village of Brazilian Indians, and Jonson's *Masque of Blackness* (1605)—only one of many performances in the Jacobean court to portray racialized others.[8] From the wondrous objects and creatures from Hakluyt described in Shakespeare's *Othello* (1603) and *Antony and Cleopatra* (1607), to the peregrinations of identity in later works such as John Fletcher's *The Island Princess* (1621) and *The Sea Voyage* (1622), colonial desire is consumed in a variety of genres in which fiction and nonfiction, politics and pleasure overlap and double back on one another.[9]

These narratives stage bodies, objects, and encounters, through the proscenium-like frame of the *Report* or *Histoire,* for the reader's delectation. The bodies and things, organic and artificial, that populate the colonial encounter scene function as contact points between the imaginary theater of the European's desire and the physical reality of the non-European community that the European viewer can see but not understand. European objects too are newly animated in alien settings, magnetizing unexpected affects of identification, wonder, and loss. People and places become objectified. Frantz Fanon characterizes the position of the racialized colonial other as "an object among other objects," and Roland Greene calls early modern Brazil "an object as well as a place of objects," which attract, hold, and transmit erotic feeling.[10] These are objects in a psychoanalytic sense—the active subjects of object relations. The texts are objects as well, efficacious things circulated to promote and engender colonial desire. They invite a European audience into an identification with the colonizer protagonist, what he sees, and what he represents. Like the pamphleteers and playwrights of the English and Scottish witch hunts discussed in the previous chapter, Jean de Léry, Thomas Harriot, and John White are mediatizing lived events. They are also a kind of go-between, mediating an affective exchange with their European readers. Their success depends on the affective states—sympathy, ambition, awe, horror—that they incite in the reader. They aim—literally, in the case of Harriot's *Briefe and True Report,* published to urge readers to become colonial settlers—to bring the reader into the encounter scene.

This literature is, for good reason, usually read with a focus on the functions of wonder, strangeness, and radical difference.[11] A dominant strain of colonial theory that might be called "straight" appears when canonical texts—Columbus's correspondence and logbooks; Cortés's *Cartas de relación*; Spenser's 1596 pamphlet *A View of the Present State of Ireland*—are read for their erotics of difference and possession. Colonial desire in these texts is triumphalist, appropriating and reproductive. It relies on representations of native ignorance to authorize the conquest of the Americas, and on representations of native sexual monstrosity to eroticize it.[12] Scholars in recent decades have generated a rich body of criticism on the complicated work of difference in these texts, attending to the force of European fantasy in shaping their descriptions of other peoples, in order to expose European ideologies of race, nation, gender, and religion.[13]

But I want to expand the affective scope of colonial desire here, from the (fruitful and inexhaustible) project of explicating representations of difference to the no less complicated dynamics of identification, which have attracted less attention.

Colonial writing, with its allegorizing and ethnographic modes of inscription, is not only an object of study in this chapter. It is also a methodological metaobject, in that the dialectical interplay between identification and alterity that governs European colonial discourse also governs the following:

1. The whole history of heteronormativity and anti-homophobic resistance to it, from the sexology of same-sex desires, to the old Freudian line construing homosexuality as an excess of narcissism,[14] to modern intraqueer conflicts over the politics of personal identities and gendered styles.

2. The ongoing methodological conversation in early modern sexuality studies in which this book intervenes, about the competing values of describing transhistorical continuities of desire versus emphasizing the contingencies of sexual regimes in specific times and places. In fact, the crisis of similitude and difference at the heart of colonial description metaphorically recapitulates the question of how modern readers should approach representations of desire in any text: as subjectively recognizable, or as inaccessibly different—or some other way.

3. Readers' attitudes toward texts. As Louise Fradenburg and Carla Freccero have incisively pointed out, the overarching valence of this third dialectic in scholarly reading has tended toward the valuation of difference (mature, rigorous, informed, suspicious, empirically substantiated, politically enlightened) and the denigration of certain pleasures of sameness (naive, narcissistic, universalizing, aestheticizing, reactionary). But, they caution, "the practice of queer theory has taught us that neither alterity nor

similarity is an inevitable conceptual guarantor of oppositional political force, that the construction of desirous identifications can be potentially destabilizing as well as totalizing."[15] Eve Sedgwick critiques the same assumed political certainties about the work of difference in her call for a "reparative" reading practice grounded in dynamics of identification and need between text and reader, as an antidote to a "paranoid" practice that holds the readerly self apart by suspecting and diagnosing the text, "disavowing its own affective motive and force."[16]

What follows can be understood as an experiment against the liberal faith—enforced by New Historicism's anthropological stance toward the past and by other forms of empiricism envy (about which I say more in the conclusion)—that more and better temporally and materially specific anatomizations of ideological and historical difference will have liberatory consequences. Instead, proliferating accounts of alterity can neutralize the political energies of the present, by placing faith in the exposure of harmful structural conditions. As is made horrifyingly clear every day at the political moment in which I write, knowledge and exposure do not bring about any certain redress, especially when spectacular terror is part of the point of state violence.[17] Other methods, other critical affects, and other angles of approach are sorely needed.

My approach to the structure of colonial desire in this chapter is informed by Frantz Fanon's analysis of the psychosexual effects of racial subjugation in *Black Skin, White Masks*. Fanon describes the colonial relation as a perverse two-way dynamic of identification and difference in which both the Black colonized subject and the white colonizer are affected, from their disparate positions of power, by a "double narcissism": a deep investment in being regarded by the other, as well as unconscious longings to be, or to be like, the other.[18] In the violent erotic complex that warps all relations in the colonial sphere, forces of envy, desire, and identification coexist with, and indeed are expressed through, violent enmity. Homi Bhabha describes the white colonist's inability to abide not being loved: "The frustrated wish 'I want him to love me,' turns into its opposite 'I hate him' and thence through projection and the exclusion of the first person, 'He hates me.'"[19] This is the originary narcissism of colonial identification: a falling in love with the image of the self as a god or conqueror, as the colonist longs to be seen in the eyes of the conquered people, followed by the transmutation of that narcissistic wish into ideations of persecution. It echoes King James VI's paranoid delight at being named as the devil's greatest enemy in the world at the North Berwick witch trials. For Fanon, because colonialism makes explicit the impossibility of any objective history, the colonial condition is expressed through psychic and affective registers—dreams, alienation, projective identifications and defenses—the paradoxical motions of "that bizarre figure of desire, which splits along the axis on which it turns."[20] It is also lived through fiction, through the assemblage of representations—including the texts I am reading here—that bear upon and construct colonial subjects. For Bhabha, "it is through image and fantasy—those orders that figure transgressively on the borders of history and the unconscious," that Fanon uncovers the erotic structure of colonialism.[21] Following Fanon's insistence on the primacy of fantasy, as well as the queer critical imperative to dismantle poses of unmarked objectivity, I aim here to bring the colonizer's psyche, voice, and gaze, in all their ambivalence, under the scope of a queer analysis. I want to look not only at the objects of the colonizers' gaze but also at their acts of looking.[22] I take it as axiomatic that however strenuously colonists' ethnographic descriptions insist on their own facticity, they are loaded with passionate investment. Furthermore, all of their intricate descriptions—as well as their puzzles, secrets, visions, and regrets—are reconstructions of encounters that were already heavily shot through with fantasy.[23]

My aim here is to explicate a queer undercurrent of melancholic, overwrought, and overidentificatory affect running through the genre of early modern colonial writing. This is actually a vital element of the form and shape of early modern colonial desire, full stop, that has largely gone unremarked.[24] It is not my aim to compile a taxonomy of queer examples as opposed to others that are straight. Rather, I offer these supersaturated texts as a framework for recognizing queer melancholia in other contexts, wherever there are

unexpected eruptions of negative affect, unresolved longings for impossible metamorphoses, weirdly persistent imagined affinities, protracted repetitions of renunciation, and time-bending, uncannily generative modes of relation. Ultimately, I use these melancholic colonizers
as an uncomfortable mirror in which to scrutinize our own methods
of reading across historical difference, comparing their investments
in their bygone love objects to our equally fantasmatic relations with
the early modern texts that bear our scholarly fascination and love.

In articulating a queer form of colonial desire, I am in no way
redeeming the Europeans who set out on these voyages of invasion,
no matter that they failed. Simultaneously with the melancholic affects I draw out of them, these accounts record an explicit litany of
murder, disease, enslavement, and theft, usually by the writers' more
militarized voyage mates. The Tupinamba and Algonkian civiliza-
tions they attempt to register in such complex ways were permanently,
genocidally damaged by the fact that these French and English men
made these voyages. The Brazil and Roanoke texts are two works
of propaganda, with nationalist and Protestant colonial agendas—
although narrative and representation have a way of escaping their
agendas, spilling into the vastly more complicated realms of pleasure, ambivalence, identification, and desire. This is especially so
under the shared condition of failure in the circumstances of both
texts' production. Both works are published belatedly, after the fact
of the voyages they chronicle; both are intensely invested in tacit
agendas that they aim—and largely fail—to accomplish. But even
though these particular colonial ventures failed, many others came
after them. Much more damage was done, and continues to be done
in the present, to the indigenous peoples from whom Europeans stole
the Americas. What I am making visible by describing a particular
queer affective mode within this larger complex of violent conquest
is how queerness can exist alongside that violence, tied up as part of
it. I want to confront what it says about queerness, what becomes of
queerness, once we realize that texts of procolonial Protestant propaganda are saturated with queer affect. In negotiating the ambivalent
politics of queerness in the history of imperialism, I enter here into
a conversation about colonial sexuality taking place across periods
and areas of study, including the work of scholars such as Elizabeth

Povinelli, Mark Rifkin, and Peter Singal.[25] These thinkers are centrally concerned with the role of sex and desire, including queerness, in colonial relations; with the history of how heterosexuality has been imposed in colonial spaces; and with asking what theoretical energies we might draw from any given set of representations to think other times, other places, and other possible futures. Like the affects of the witch hunt unpacked in the previous chapter, queer colonial melancholia is a structurally queer affective mode that is part of, not opposed to, the apparatuses of power and violence. The European colonizer's projective, identificatory, and homoerotic fantasies are constitutive of both colonial queerness and colonial exploitation.[26] Acknowledging this must complicate queer politics, removing any certainty of counterhegemonic subversiveness from the registers we call queer. This idea, which Mark Rifkin further explores in indigenous American contexts, is also indebted to the work of Jasbir Puar, whose concept of homonationalism explodes the assumption that queer expression is necessarily opposed to or apart from state violence, pointing out how queerness is deployed toward imperialist ends. Puar and Rifkin insist, in different ways, on the inextricability of queerness from European constructions of race—both of whiteness and of racialized others—in colonial projects.[27] The discursive aims of Jean de Léry's, Thomas Harriot's, and John White's texts are more ulterior and convoluted than any simple agenda of colonial inscription. The models of time and relation they construct are nonlinear, nonheterosexual, and utterly fantastical. But the reality we are left to contend with is that no necessary or foreknown politics attaches to queerness, either in the early modern period or today. The melancholic moments of failure and loss in what follows are part of the larger colonial story of conquest, extraction, slavery, conversion, and, eventually, genocide and settler colonialism. Failure does not undo the larger story; it is part of it. Queerness does not necessarily contradict or repair historical violence; here, it is part of it.

Melancholia's Queer Plot

Jean de Léry's departure from Brazil is a dilated retelling, more than twenty years after the fact, of a moment of colonial renunciation that remains laden with unresolved regret. Harriot's *A Briefe and True Report of the New Found Land of Virginia* is a text brought into being to deny—and by its denial to ward off—what virtually everyone who ever read the 1590 edition already knew to be the case: the colony fails. For Léry, the pivotal moment of dispossession is behind him in memory, while in the Virginia text the inevitable loss whispers from the near future, despite the narrative's not yet knowing it has already happened. The colonial projects these texts recount are over, aborted, or suspended in uncertainty. The American encounters they narrate are cut off, foreclosed by the return voyage. The desires they voice, then, are for love objects that are no longer present. In Freud's "Mourning and Melancholia" (1917), melancholia is a response to loss in the form of painful, protracted identification with the lost love object, which, rather than running its course, endures excessively in time and intensity.[28] Melancholia is the problem of not being able to stop loving an object that is no longer there. Mourning, or normal, nonpathological grief, follows a linear model of time, divided into discrete temporal periods in a unidirectional progression. In mourning, it is clear what happened in the past (what was lost), what one feels in the present, and how the process of detachment will unfold toward the end of the work of mourning: an ego in a normative state of being "free and uninhibited again."[29] Mourning is thus a plot, with an expected narrative trajectory and end. Its key features are its conventionality and its finitude: "We rely on its being overcome after a certain lapse of time, and we look upon any interference with it as useless or even harmful."[30] Melancholia, however, flagrantly refuses this plot. It refuses the directionality, the timeline, and the telos of mourning; it is not "overcome after a certain lapse of time." Melancholia has a queer temporality: it goes on for too long; it refuses to progress. Its objects are improper *because* they are gone. Melancholia persists in its erotic investment in pastness, defying mourning's goal of an "uninhibited" and "free" ego. It turns in on itself, negating itself in identification with the love object, which is always figured as a regression, a reversal of the heteronormative telos of Freud's sexual difference plot.[31]

Melancholia is thus a structurally queer erotic mode, connected to queer history by its hidden and unspeakable love objects, its overly identificatory orientation, its excessive affective style, and its deviant, too-long duration. It provides a language for drawing out the queer qualities of thwarted colonial desire—specifically, the transtemporal reach of its impossible identifications.[32] Thinking about the temporality of melancholia makes it easy to see its queer shape, its nostalgic (literally, the persistent pain of homesickness) and anachronistic orientation, in the shape of the voyager's longing for his lost love objects.[33] Queer subjects have been called melancholic—also immature, arrested, infantile—for the forms of refusal that Heather Love and Jack Halberstam embrace: refusals of forward motion; of prescriptive plots of "growing out of" or "getting over" interdicted attractions; and of the ultimate normative telos of alloerotic, heterosexual object choice.[34] Queerness also shares with melancholia—and narcissism—its excess of identification and its investment in sameness, in contrast to a normative plot of ideal differentiation.[35] Yet another of melancholia's queer excesses is its affect of volubility verging on mania: "insistent communicativeness which finds satisfaction in self-exposure."[36] Melancholia is expressed in intricately spiraling performances of abasement. It transmogrifies feeling low into high performance art. Colonial melancholia thus inheres in both the conditions of the Brazil and Virginia texts' production (failure, loss, disjunction) and the stylistic features of the writing itself (recursive, nonlinear narrative arcs, repetition, negation, disavowal, hyperbole). In comparing the two works, two distinct orientations of melancholia emerge, both of which voice the affective aftershocks of their respective encounters by bending time and space: longing for lost pasts, in the loss of the Native American others as problematic but gripping love objects, and longing for lost futures, in the lost fantasy of an American self.

The shape of colonial desire in the *Histoire d'un voyage* is insistently focused on the past, the narrative voice shot through with affects of nostalgia, reversal, and belatedness—what I would call an example of melancholic writing. Léry's persistent longing for the Tupinamba Indian others is troubled by questions of identity and difference; of what to admire and what to condemn; of whom to want to be like—and, impossibly, to be with—in Brazil. His backward-looking tone inverts gendered agency. Forever insisting that he had *no choice,*

Léry uses languages of passivity, compulsion, even penetration, construing himself and his fellow ministers as helplessly—and not altogether unhappily—submissive to the other players in the colonial scene. In contrast to the past-obsessed and passive erotics of *Histoire d'un voyage,* Harriot's and White's Roanoke text projects its longings into an imagined future, which it attempts conjure into being. "Melancholia" may seem more apt a term for the French memoir than for the Englishmen's wishful report. But loss, especially in the colonial sphere, is not limited to the past. Unspeakable identifications can stretch across long stretches of time in both directions. In fact, one of Freud's first moves in "Mourning and Melancholia" is to expand what is considered a loss to include indirect, ideational, even delusional attachments: losses "of a more ideal kind," where "the object has not perhaps actually died, but has been lost as an object of love," which we see here in the loss of a potential colonial future.[37] Reading the often bizarre evocations of impossible futures in the *Briefe and True Report* alongside Jean de Léry's backward gaze illuminates a new, queer form of future melancholia, bodied forth in fantasies that confound any natural or heterosexual timeline. The language in which Harriot's text figures these desires bears scrutinizing in its uneasy relation to John White's "True Pictures," in that Harriot's projective, identificatory future visions are voiced as a fantasy (or as multiple different fantasies) of annihilation. The *Report* deals in tropes of iterated, successive destruction and transformation, which I see as a cancellation of heterosexuality through annihilation, doing end runs around sexual reproduction and linear time.

Almost every line of Jean de Léry's *Histoire d'un voyage* is saturated with queer affective excess, including but not limited to regret, tears, dithering, catty one-upmanship, mockery (of self and others), untoward obsessions with the bodies and practices of Tupinamba men, overidentification, impotence, passivity, loss, ravishment, and submission. Léry's encyclopedic descriptions detailing the Tupinamba's clothes, weaponry, music making, food, law, religion, social customs, and language have canonized the *Histoire d'un voyage* as an ancestral ur-text of ethnography; indeed, Claude Lévi-Strauss famously carries with him "that breviary of the anthropologist, Jean de Léry" as he enters Brazil.[38] Its overwrought comparisons of Brazilian ritual cannibalism to the beliefs of Catholics, who want to "eat the flesh of Jesus Christ" (to "chew and swallow it raw")[39] are part of the history of Protestantism and French nation formation.[40] The famously ambivalent quality of its moral judgments about Native American versus European customs and values has had a notable afterlife of radical political and philosophical influence. Léry is credited as the major source for Montaigne's "Des cannibales" and as the co-originator of the cultural relativist idea that native peoples were no more inherently savage than the French.[41] "I think there is nothing barbarous and savage in that nation," writes Montaigne of Brazil, "from what I have been told, except that each man calls barbarism whatever is not his own practice." He says this on the authority of an unnamed friend (Jean de Léry) whom "I had with me for a long time."[42] There is a strong case to be made that this early, revolutionary relativism—or at least openness to suspending the rigid condemnations of Christian Europe to frame moral comparisons differently—fits within a tradition of protogay radical thought, questioning social norms and revaluing the practices of denigrated others. Carla Freccero has persuasively read Jean de Léry's ambiguous gender and liminal ethnic, national, and religious positions vis-à-vis the Tupinamba and the other French inhabitants of the colony as belonging to a queer history.[43] All of these agendas are constituted, I think, through the queer affective load that infuses Léry's bereft, melancholic tone.

Jean de Léry's backward longing undermines, even reverses, the romance and travel narrative's conventional telos of homecoming, with its recuperation of proper identities:

> So that saying goodbye here to America, I confess for myself that although I have always loved my country and do even now, still, seeing the little—next to none at all— of fidelity that is left here, and, what is worse, the disloyalties of people toward each other—in short, since our whole situation is Italianized, and consists only in dissimulation and words without effect—I often regret that I am not among the savages, in whom (as I have amply

shown in this narrative) I have known more frankness than in many over here, who, for their condemnation, bear the title of "Christian."[44]

His "regret that I am not among the savages" persists into the time of his writing, pervading the years in between. It carries a touch of slightly forbidden, involuntary feeling; it returns "often," and unbidden, to trouble his sense of who he is and whom he loves. It must be "confessed" to the reader that something he came to "know" in the "savages" has compounded his disidentification from Frenchness with a persistent affinity for their surpassing *rondeur,* a suggestively embodied word for frankness or fullness.[45] Whereas the native people in their greater *rondeur* are capacious—like Orsino's similarly figured fancy in chapter 2—full, round, receptive, able to hold the nostalgic desire Léry loads into them, his fellow Frenchmen are empty and degenerate, unable to hold any signification at all *(paroles sans effect).* Léry's lingering knowledge (*j'ay cogneu,* the same verb used to mean "knowing" in the carnal sense) of this life-changing *rondeur* between men, across racial and religious lines, has rerouted his affective circuits of identification and alterity. In other words, he wants what he cannot have, he wants it too much, and he wants it because he feels (though no one else agrees) that it is *like* him, and he like it. This a longing for an impossible metamorphosis in order to inhabit identities and relationalities that are always already foreclosed. It has something in common with tropes of religious conversion—a major locus of early modern anxiety about the allure of non-Christian spaces—but Léry's Calvinist sojourn is, significantly, not the story of a *renegado* or apostate. What about those who may have longed to make that break but did not, or could not? The transformation wrought in Jean de Léry is occult and unrealized, lacking the performative marker of the *renegado*'s conversion. There is no conventional narrative for mourning one's nonconversion, and no conventional archive for those feelings. They place Jean de Léry in a genealogy of subjects who would have been other than they are, who would have lived and loved otherwise, given the chance in another place and another time.

Léry regrets something he did—leave America—which it was inevitable that he would do. To point out the resonance of this regret with the history of shame-ridden gay desires, we can call Léry's love for Brazil the "love that dared not speak its name" until after there remained no possibility of its consummation.[46] Like Freud's melancholic, who can only articulate "I loved him" after the fact, Léry writes years later that he would have loved to have stayed. He compulsively repeats his regret, but it is belated and futile; it comes upon him after he is powerless to reverse it. Jean de Léry cannot mourn the Tupinamba as one mourns the death of a more conventional love, because he never possessed them. Therefore, he desires (impossibly) to retain them through writing. Writing for Léry performs a function akin to imaginative fancy, projecting the force of imagination out into the world in an attempt to furnish forth objects of desire "not present to the senses." In one of the text's signal moments of melancholic memory, he claims, "During that year or so when I lived in that country, I took such care in observing all of them, great and small, that even now it seems to me that I have them before my eyes, and I will forever have the idea and image of them in my mind."[47] Other readers, particularly Freccero, have drawn attention to the spectral quality of the native people's "quasi-material" presence in this image, and to the way they haunt Léry as figures of history, memory, and violence.[48] Léry attributes this haunting to the intensity of his "curiousness" in looking at them. His attempt to materialize these traces is powered by a still unspent remainder of that pleasure felt in their presence. This is also a deeply identificatory image of incorporation. The field on which these spectral "ideas and images" manifest is inside of Léry, at the crux of his body and mind: *"devant mes yeux"* and *"dans mon entendement"* ("in front of my eyes" and "in my understanding").[49] The melancholic desirer wants to consume his others. His ego "wants to incorporate this object into itself," Freud writes, "and, in accordance with the oral or cannibalistic phase of libidinal development in which it is, it wants to do so by devouring it."[50] Léry keeps the Tupinamba men inside him, part of him, by incorporating their bodies into his writing. As Judith Butler puts it, "What remains unspeakably absent inhabits the psychic voice of the one who remains."[51]

In the same breath, though, Léry insists on his inability to communicate these visions: "But their gestures and expressions are so completely different from ours, that it is difficult, I confess, to represent them well by writing or by pictures. To have the pleasure of it, then, you will have to go see and visit them in their own country."[52] These protestations—as to how *malaisé* (difficult, awkward) it is to represent the Tupinamba, how not easy *(mal à l'aise)* even to the point of sickening *(malaise)*—partake in a particular mode of queer histrionics, a self-deprecating disavowal of description marked by insistence on how impossible something is to describe, or how one *can't possibly* put words to, or even endure, the feelings it incites. This performative inarticulacy is immediately belied by copious outpourings of affective expression.[53] So it is here; the difficulty of conjuring the Tupinamba does anything but deter Léry. Far from abandoning his reader (whom he bitchily ventriloquizes throughout as spoiled, whiny, and averse to the hardships of travel), he fills twenty-two chapters with exhaustive detail, including a "colloquy" of the Tupinamba language. His devotion to the task is obsessive, compulsive, unstinting. Léry's queer aesthetic investments are obvious. He loves the technologies of colonial inscription—drawing and description—for their own sake. Conversely, he uses his godly religious mission—indeed, he uses its failure—instrumentally, to place himself on the mainland, closer to the Tupinamba.

The text is all too aware that in the encounter with the Tupinamba, as in melancholia, there remains something unarticulable, "something else besides," that conventional versions of the plot (of providential travel, of colonial conquest, of mourning) do not contain. That "something else besides" is Jean de Léry's thwarted transformation into a Tupinamba self, and the ghostly torque it exerts on his narrative voice. In Freud's words, "In mourning it is the world which has become poor and empty; in melancholia it is the ego itself."[54] Melancholic desire clusters around an unspeakable crux, its objects "withdrawn from consciousness."[55] Even if the subject is aware of the loss, Freud writes, it might be that his love for that other had some content that he could not consciously articulate.[56] He might know "*whom* he has lost, but not *what* he has lost in him."[57] It is *what* Jean de Léry has lost in Brazil—that unknown and unspeakable kernel of secret love and meaning—that persists; for not only were these objects not possessed, they did not leave, either. Léry did.

"I Left Some of My Belongings Behind Me"

Histoire d'un voyage is a document of loss. It is also, materially, a document on which loss is performed again and again. The preface recounts the roundabout circumstances of its publication, a story of iterated loss. One manuscript was confiscated by censors from a friend at the city gates of Lyon, "so utterly lost that in spite of all my efforts, I could not recover it."[58] A second text is literally consumed by intra-French sectarian violence when he has to leave all his books and take refuge in Sancerre. Léry laments how his scribal copies "kept slipping out of my hands."[59] Ultimately, it is the first copy, which Léry had thought to be irretrievably lost, that is returned to him in 1576 by a friend who tracks it down. In 1578, when Léry at last publishes the *Histoire*—he is forced to, he says, in order to refute what he sees as the abominable lies represented in André Thevet's *Cosmographie universelle,* to which he takes strenuous exception in his preface—it is cut off from the events it narrates by decades of religious conflict, including the St. Bartholomew's Day massacre in 1572 and the siege of Sancerre in 1572–73.[60] By the time of its publication, it is a posttraumatic text. Its memories of the Native Americans are riven by the intervening undoing, in the famine, cannibalism, and atrocity evident in the Wars of Religion, of the boundary demarcating the unthinkable in France. Permeated by loss, it has a propensity to get lost itself. Loss is its repetition-compulsion.[61]

The narrative itself recounts the ministers' fateful departure from Brazil as a series of wrenching and absurd calamities. Their much negotiated for and long-awaited ship no sooner sets sail than it is blown back by the wind. Then, not far off from shore, the ship is found to be worm eaten and leaking, already so full of water that the men can feel it sinking. When it is revealed that there is not enough food aboard for the voyage, the ship's master offers a boat for anyone who wants to return to the colony to wait (perhaps forever) for another ship from France—or build a new one. Six of the purportedly inseparable ministers, including Léry (probably already wracked by regret), decide to return. They quickly put their belongings into the proffered boat. But then, as the six returning men take leave of the rest,

> one of them, full of regret at my departure and impelled by a particular feeling of friendship, put out his hand as I was in the boat, and said, "I beg you to stay with us; for even if we cannot get to France, still there is more hope of safety on the coast of Peru, or on some island, than in returning to Villegagnon, who as you very well know will never leave you at peace over here."[62]

The overflowing of the other minister's "regret" and Léry's investment in their "particular" friendship effect a grand romantic gesture: Léry climbs back into the ship at the last possible instant. Léry is torn by the twinned forces of melancholia—attachment to love objects and the inexorable movement of time—at the point where they cross purposes, through the touch of a "particular" friend's hand stretched across the space between a ship and a boat on the sea. After more than a year away from France, six months previously at sea, and two months of living on the mainland among the Tupinamba while waiting for this ship to arrive, in this instant, Jean de Léry is out of time. He is caught, between his attachments to the Tupinamba on the shore and to this "particular" friend, in a perverse, nonlinear temporality where time seems to vary its speed. Months of stasis and immobility suddenly run out, sweeping him along—on the strength of his love for another man—into the homeward telos of the voyage narrative. But besides his never-to-be-rejoined ideational love objects, Léry loses some material objects as well: "I left some of my belongings behind me in the boat."[63] Thus a remnant of Jean de Léry is transported back to the shore to remain in Brazil forever, absent from him but closer to the Tupinamba. Like the repeatedly lost manuscripts, the left-behind belongings indicate an expulsive drive to leave behind remnants and traces of himself in the places where he has been.

But he takes a remnant of Brazil with him too: his "memoirs, most of them written with brazilwood ink, and in America itself."[64] Fashioned out of the very substance of the land of Brazil, this ur-text stands in for the parts of himself Léry leaves behind, and furnishes the germ of his melancholic memoir. Identification is lodged not just in the memoirs' content but in the thing itself—or, more accurately, in how the writing functions as a thing. From its first instantiation as notes and drawings written with brazilwood ink, the writing materializes, over and over, the absent presence of Brazil. Its production and reproduction is an always failed melancholic transformation in which the writer strives to become, if only prosthetically, through his text, what he has lost. If Montaigne can be said to melancholically incorporate a cannibal into his *Essais* as an identificatory figure for a lost ideal of nature,[65] then Jean de Léry incorporates the land of Brazil into *Histoire d'un voyage*.

The transportation of Native American people back across the ocean in the aftermath of the French colony is not a metaphor, however. The colonists at the fort purchase dozens of enslaved captives of the Margajas tribe (whom they regard as enemies) after they are defeated in battle by the Tupinamba (with whom they are allies). Jean de Léry himself buys a woman and her little boy of less than two years old for three francs, allegedly rescuing them from being cannibalized in the Tupinamba victory ritual. He laments, "I had thought to keep the little boy for myself" (for what reasons we can never know), but Governor Villegagnon, that insatiable consumer of human flesh, seizes him "for himself." In addition to the manuscript of his memoirs and his belongings in the boat, Jean de Léry loses *a small child,* and he cannot even comprehend the child's mother's rage at this. He recounts a conversation (through what medium or translated sign system is unclear) in which he tells the mother he intends to bring her little boy back to France with him. She replies, in one of the only moments in the entire work to ventriloquize an indigenous woman's speech, that she had hoped her son would escape, rejoin his people, and someday avenge them, but that she would rather her son remain and "be eaten by the Tupinamba than go off so far from her." Léry's attribution of this response to the "deeply rooted vengeance in that nation's heart," rather than a mother's abhorrence at being informed her son will be sold across the sea, shows the limits of Jean de Léry's identification with native subjects. He identifies only with the men, and only in terms of their homosocial/homoerotic customs, bodies, and virtues. The Margajas mother's defiant speech has no effect. Villegagnon keeps her son, and Léry matter-of-factly reports that the Frenchmen "chose ten young boys whom we sent to France in the returning ships, to Henry II."[66]

"Their Voices Are Still in My Ears"

Jean de Léry's ecstatic experience at a Tupinamba religious ceremony, in chapter 16, "What May Be Called Religion among the Savages," is called the climactic moment of desire in the *Histoire d'un voyage*. It is the closest Léry comes to describing himself as undergoing an erotic experience. He memorializes it in one of the book's many detailed drawings of Tupinamba men's naked bodies, rendering "a dancer and a *maraca*-player" dressed in their ceremonial ornaments: ankle decorations, feathered headpieces and tailpieces, and the feathered, rattling maracas. This plate also depicts two small animals, a parrot and a monkey, as exotic familiars, accessories and conduits to the men's enchantments. The maracas are also animate conduits for ineffable forces, Léry says, "So that (as they said) the spirit might thereafter speak through these rattles, to dedicate them to this use they made them sound incessantly." In a typical iconoclastic simile, he compares them to "the bell-ringers that accompany those impostors who, exploiting the credulity of our simple folk over here, carry from place to place the reliquaries of Saint Anthony or Saint Bernard, and other such instruments of idolatry."[67] All this language of "impostors" (and of "errors," and "charlatans" in the chapter heading) is belied, however, by the beauty and attention with which these ceremonial instruments, and the movements and sounds of the men's bodies in the ceremony, are rendered.

The religious ceremony is an unattainable, forbidden object. Léry and his two companions are warned not to watch and are strictly ordered to listen to the ceremony from the women's house. They therefore access the experience from a queerly gendered position, surrounded by two hundred women. The ceremony begins with "a very low murmur, like the muttering of someone reciting his hours."[68] The physical phenomenon of possession that follows, with the participants howling, leaping violently, making their breasts shake, foaming at the mouth, and fainting, "frightens" Léry.[69] What looks demonic,

Figure 4. Tupinamba men dressed for their religious ceremony, with feathered adornments and maracas, from Jean de Léry, *Histoire d'un voyage faict en la terre du Bresil* (Geneva: Pour Antoine Chuppin, 1580), 246. Courtesy of the John Carter Brown Library at Brown University.

however, immediately turns into an experience of the sublime. The song changes into "a harmony so marvelous" that his fear morphs into an irresistible desire to come closer. Despite warnings from the women and an interpreter,

> I drew near the place where I heard the chanting; the houses of the savages are very long and of a roundish shape (like the trellises of gardens over here). Since they are covered with grasses right down to the ground, in order to see as well as I might wish, I made with my hands a little opening in the covering. I beckoned to the two Frenchmen who were watching me; emboldened by my example, they drew near without any hindrance or difficulty, and we all three entered the house.[70]

Over the next two hours, Léry's voyeuristic desire to consume the spectacle morphs into total surrender and submission as he receives the song at a bodily, sensual level:

> At the beginning of the witches' Sabbath, when I was in the women's house, I had been somewhat afraid; now I received in recompense such joy, hearing the measured harmonies of such a multitude, and especially in the cadence and refrain of the song, when at every verse all of them would let their voices trail, saying *Heu, heu-aure, heura, heuraure, heura, heura, oueh*—I stood there transported with delight [*tout ravi*]. Whenever I remember it, my heart trembles, and it seems their voices are still in my ears. When they decided to finish, each of them struck his right foot against the earth more vehemently than before, and spat in front of him; then all of them with one voice uttered hoarsely two or three times the words *He, hua, hua, hua*, and then ceased.[71]

Carla Freccero articulates Léry's ravishment as "masochistic surrender"; Leo Bersani would call it "self-shattering" jouissance, the radical erotic identification with the other such that the boundaries of self are obliterated.[72] This self-shattering orgasm is, in Bersani's death-driven framework, a perverse act of resistance, the obliteration of difference in an experience of masculine ritual climax shared with "five or six hundred" dancing men in unison. This "ravishment" is a sensory, ecstatic marker of Léry's cross-culturally transgressive, homoerotic, and identificatory transformation. It is figured as an affective overcoming and a penetration ("whenever I remember it, my heart trembles, and it seems their voices are still in my ears"), using a language of erotic submission and receptivity that reverses colonial tropes of domination and mastery. Moreover, this ravishment also reverses colonial tropes of possession and projective futurity. The erotic opens up a space outside of Léry's Protestant divine/demonic dichotomy, a sensual distillation of time itself in which his "masochistic surrender" can persist. The voices of the men penetrate him and stay inside of him as melancholic fragments, haunting him for the rest of his life. He does not possess the Tupinamba men, or any part of Brazil. They possess him.

"Manie Strange Sightes"

Thomas Harriot's *A Briefe and True Report of the New Found Land of Virginia* and John White's illustrated appendix to it, "The True Pictures and Fashions of the People in That Part of America Now Called Virginia," also figure the time-bending reach of queer colonial melancholia—but into the future. Harriot's descriptions of the Algonkian people's reactions to and feelings about English bodies and things, and White's drawings of Algonkian (and ancient British) bodies and customs both stage a convoluted set of affective relations weaving across cultural difference and historical epochs. If Jean de Léry's lost Tupinamba are revenants of the past in the present, then the bodies and material objects in Harriot and White instead signal the uncanny absent presence of an unsettled future.

The queer colonial fantasies of and around the Roanoke texts have everything to do with the fact that the colony disappears. For one thing, it makes the *Report*'s surreal projections of futurity visible *as* fantasies that did not come to be. Further, the Roanoke text's queer appeal to a lost colonial future is avidly taken up, over the ensuing four centuries, into the racial mythology of the white American settler state. In fact, it becomes the foundational story—with Harriot and White's *Report* its central relic—of a constitutively American form of white racial melancholia, articulated through the persistent cultural myth of the "lost colony." Indeed, I suggest we read *A Briefe and True Report* retrospectively, back through the fact of the Roanoke colony's historically uncanny failure—which is, after all, how it was read by virtually everyone who read the 1590 edition. We can then see what Goldberg calls Harriot's "fantasmatically projective" writing as a queerly futuristic—even speculative—form of melancholic longing.[73] Rather than the loss of a past that can never be regained, it encodes the unmournable loss of a future that all its technologies of inscription are powerless to bring about.

Most of Thomas Harriot's fairly brief—though not notably true—report, which dates from the first English expedition to Roanoke in 1584, and which is meant to entice prospective English settlers to come to Virginia, is a nakedly aspirational description of goods and products yet to come. Jonathan Goldberg calls the tract "less a catalogue of what *is* there as what may be there once English agricultural habits are transported"[74]—once, in Harriot's words, the land is "planted and husbanded as they ought."[75] Goldberg reads this as an attempt to inscribe onto the American land what Lee Edelman has called "reproductive futurity," the heteronormative and whitenormative mandate that delimits what the political future is allowed to mean.[76] But what I see Harriot trying to speak into being does not happen through sexual reproduction, or even through human bodies. The fantasies of fertility in Harriot's catalog are about plant life and something that looks like mineral "life." Iron, copper, silver, and pearls are curiously vital substances in Harriot's listing of the fantasy fruits of the land, slipped in alongside civet cats, otter furs, sweet gums from trees, and the oud Harriot includes because it grows in the Azores, "which is the same climate."[77] Their vitality and the preternatural ease with which they will supposedly be "found"—Harriot repeats this word like an incantation—recalls the famous image from *The Travels of Sir John Mandeville* of precious gems growing spontaneously from the dew on rocks on a far-flung coast of Ethiopia, free for the gathering up without any labor of cultivation.

Even as he surveys the fortifications of their towns and estimates the army they could muster, Harriot's narrative is obsessed with communicating (or imagining?) the Algonkians' feelings about the English. He hopes that they "shoulde desire our friendships and love, and have the greater respect for pleasing and obeying us."[78] But he isn't *sure*. This comes through whenever he attempts to render indigenous people's desire and affect—for instance, in the short portion at the end of the *Report* called "Of Such Other Thinges as Is Be Hoofull for Those Which Shall Plant and Inhabit to Know Of; With a Description of the Nature and Manners of the People of the Countrey"—the only section to describe any actual relations with local people. Harriot is passionately invested in how the Algonkian people see him and the English items he has brought into their space. At several moments, he *détournes* his scientific technologies and his religious equipment into machines for generating cross-cultural pleasure. The godly mathematician and natural scientist tells us that in every town he visited in Virginia, he tried to "make declaration of the contents of the Bible" to the residents, as he saw fit. But despite his best efforts, his forays into evangelism would habitually get a bit out of hand: "Although I told them the book materially & of it self was not of any such virtue (as I thought they did conceive), but only the doctrine therein contained; yet would many be glad to touch it, to embrace it, to kisse it, to hold it to their breasts and heades—and stroke over all their bodie with it."[79] Over Harriot's protestations, his Algonkian interlocutors seemed to find great virtue in "the book materially & of it self." This can of course be read, like several passages in Léry ridiculing a Tupinamba man "in his full Papal splendor,"[80] or comparing the sound of Tupinamba maracas to the bell ringers in saints' processions, as a mapping of the Protestant voyager's anti-Catholic iconoclasm onto the New World, equating the Americans' rituals with those of another suspect other whose form is already familiar. However, this is also a vivid image of all-consuming bodily enjoyment of a material thing. The Algonkians do not perform ceremonial gestures with the Bible; rather, they gratify their senses with it, "embracing it," "kissing it," and becoming amorous with it in a style that is certainly not organized around any normative type of eroticism, genital or otherwise. The book functions as an instrument of pleasure, or a toy. Then, as they "stroke all over their body with it," it becomes a supplement to a scene of polymorphously perverse, full-body group eroticism. Harriot's investment in what his Algonkian interlocutors make of him and his book ends up bringing about a surprising eruption of affect between them (who really loves the Bible more?). This moment also reverses the familiar colonial trope in which the European interloper's wonder at strange things is at the center.

Harriot has an explanation, however. He insists that they are holding the book against their breasts and their heads "to show their hungry desire of that knowledge which was spoken of."[81] In the few pages devoted to "the nature and manners of the people," he states that the main point he wants to get across about the "naturall inhabitants" (as he calls the Algonkian), is that they *are not to be feared—* *—but that* they *shall have cause* both *to feare* and *love us, that shall inhabit with them.*"[82] But if this is an affective prescription for settler colonialism, it leaves something out. It states that the natives will feel both fear and love, and that the prospective English settlers are not to feel fear. Left unsaid, however, is whether the English are, or aren't, supposed to feel love for the American people they "shall inhabit with" (or any instruction, really, as to what feelings they are to feel about the people of this "New Found Land"). This unexplained asymmetry, this missing instruction to love or not to love, signals an unacknowledged affective load bearing on Harriot's stance toward his American informants. Its traces can be seen where the pleasures of identification and desire break through the story the text tells about itself. The reading practice that can probe these cracks and crevices derives from Eve Sedgwick's enduring articulations of what "queer" means in her essay "Queer and Now": "What if instead there were a practice of valuing the ways in which meanings and institutions can be at loose ends with one another? What if the richest junctures weren't the ones where *everything means the same thing*?"[83] In the unbridgeable disjunction between the distinct desires and pleasures (unknowable to us) that the Algonkians are expressing with and on Harriot's book, and Harriot's own account of what they feel and what they want, we see hints of queer, speculative, melancholic affect— like wishful identification, forbidden fear, or unspeakable love. It is legible in the junctures where "meanings and institutions are at loose ends with one another," where colonial rhetoric fails to completely control the meanings it attempts to inscribe onto another culture. There are many such failures in Harriot's *Report*, like his failure to account for the erotic and sensory meanings of the book.

There are other moments of imaginative bodily empathy between Harriot and his Algonkian others, moments that reverse the poles of identification and difference, or where bodies and things exceed the narratives into which they are being inscribed. Harriot carries to Virginia an array of beautiful and intriguing scientific tools. His narrative describes these instruments as though they are the Englishmen's wondrous bodily appendages: "Most thinges they sawe *with us*, as Mathematicall instruments, sea compasses, the vertue of the loadstone in drawing yron, a perspective glasse whereby was shewed manie strange sightes, burning glasses, wildefire woorkes, gunnes, bookes, writing and reading, spring clocks that seeme to goe of themselves, and manie other thinges that we had."[84] One received interpretation of this scene would say the tools are used to "dazzle" the indigenous people with Western power and knowledge.[85] But that is not entirely what is going on here. The instruments are not functioning as technologies, but as things of wonder and ornamental allure, which attract indigenous desire and conduct it back to the Englishmen. These things facilitate a two-way circulation of interlocking pleasures, in which the Englishman enjoys looking at the Algonkians enjoying looking at his instruments, which he also enjoys. The imputation of divine, not human, art to the tools reenchants them and reverses, if only briefly, the teleological time of scientific progress. In the Native Americans' eyes, familiar technologies, like "the vertue of the loadstone in drawing yron," regain some of their magical and alchemical valence. A "perspective glasse" shows not the world around it but "manie strange sightes," and incendiary tools like "burning glasses" and "wildefire woorkes" become wondrous explosions.

I am assuming that, as Jonathan Goldberg has suggested, "what is recorded as if spoken by the natives may well be in part a European fantasy." Harriot's extensive ventriloquizations of the natives must therefore, like a witchcraft confession, amount to a "hybrid text" of "complicities, accommodations, projections, mistranslations."[86] However, given that multivocality, Harriot's projection of his desire for friendship and love onto his Algonkian interlocutors is both utterly constitutive of the violent narcissistic projection that Homi Bhabha describes, with how quickly the colonizer's wish, "I want him to love me," transmutes into "I hate him," then into "He hates me,"[87] and at the same time a queer, melancholic desire. This is not only due to the intensity of Harriot's investment in other men. The desires in the *Report* belong to the history of queer affect in that they are routed through erotically enchanted material objects. The fantasy body that Harriot constructs for himself and the Englishmen in the eyes of the other is a dazzling metamorphosis, a potent, disassemble-able machine body of brass, glass, and iron that seems to "go of itself," arrayed with fire and "strange sights"; it is a body that would be irresistible as an object to identify with and desire.

By any normative standards, the Algonkians are using the scientific instruments and the even more erotically laden book (a Bible!) "wrong" in multiple ways. Yet they are enjoying them on their own terms, making and transmitting pleasures that reach us, four centuries later, and despite what the colonial narrator says about them. These improvised pleasures, as well as their public yet secret character, recall the acts of queer identification performed by the proto-queer readers that Sedgwick theorizes in "Queer and Now." Sedgwick remembers that as a child, "the ability to attach intently to a few cultural objects, objects of high or popular culture or both, objects whose meaning seemed mysterious, excessive, or oblique in relation to the codes most readily available to us, became a prime resource for survival."[88] Such objects unaccountably capture, focus, and facilitate the desires of those who feel an attraction to them, who need and use them in ways that others do not. Though the social and cultural stakes are completely different, in the Algonkians' hands, scientific instruments and the Bible become objects of communal pleasure and affiliation—a wonderfully literal iteration of "objects whose meaning seemed mysterious, excessive, or oblique in relation to the codes most readily available to us."[89]

The mystery, of course, is mutual. I am not simply comparing the Virginian Algonkians, investing their conquerors' tools with in-effable, lost meanings, to imperiled queer children (though Harriot represents them as both polymorphously infantile and erotically sus-pect). It is Thomas Harriot, actually, who is acting the role of Sedg-wick's queer child, investing this site where (as Sedgwick puts it) "the meanings didn't line up tidily with each other" with "excessive and oblique" meanings that focus his excess of "fascination and love."[90] Harriot makes a performative effort to impose the codes "most read-ily available" to *him*, claiming the instruments made many of the natives say that "if they knew not the trueth of god and religion al-ready, it was rather to be had from us, whom God so specially loved, then from a people that were so simple, as they had found themselves to be in comparison of us."[91] This is not only a fantasy of Native Americans admitting their inferiority (although it is that).[92] It is also a fantasy of perfectly knowing how one is seen by the other. These scenes of fetishistic embodied pleasure enact a different directional erotics of colonial encounter: the gazing and the wonder flow back-ward, from the Native Americans to the English. The Algonkians do not appear to be in any way altered—Christianized or scientifi-cally enlightened—by Harriot's normative readings of their gestures. Rather, Harriot is instead hailed into an Algonkian erotic economy of wonder and sensory delight by their uses of his objects. Whatever we cannot know of the Algonkians' beliefs, we register their "hungrie desire," which is obviously not delimited by "that knowledge which was spoken of."

"Invisible Bullets"

One thing Harriot imagines the Algonkians to imagine, or desires them to desire, is a system of spectral, supernaturally potent bodies for the English colonists—bodies that are projected into queer, apoc-alyptic future relations of love and violence. This vision is by far the best known passage in the *Report*—indeed, so well known that it is almost transgressively passé to return to it "once more, with feeling": the story of the spectral violence that the Algonkian people theo-rize being committed against them. This bizarre anecdote purports to archive the Algonkian people's hypotheses about the unexplained disease that follows the Englishmen around, killing them in enormous numbers:

> There was no town where we had any subtile device practised against us, we leaving it unpunished or not revenged (because wee sought by all means possible to win them by gentlenesse) but that within a few dayes after our departure from everie such towne , the people began to die very fast, and many in short space. [. . .]
>
> This marvelous accident in all the countrie wrought so strange opinions of us, that some people could not tel whether to think us gods or men, and the rather because that all the space of their sickness , there was no man of ours knowne to die, or that was specially sicke : they noted also that we had no women amongst us, neither that we did care for any of theirs.[93]

Harriot follows this with series of mystical, violent, and decidedly unheterosexual theories he imagines the Algonkians to hold as to what order of beings the Englishmen are, and how they can inflict remote and delayed death.

First, the Englishmen are construed as undead ancestors. "Some were of the opinion that wee were not borne of women, and therefore not mortall, but that wee were men of an old generation many yeeres past then risen againe to immortalitie,"[94] like revenant zombies, Christ, or the sleeping kings of European national mythologies. A second theory imagines the English as harbingers of a mystified future, a ghostly advance party: "Some would likewise seem to prophesy that there were more of our generation yet to come, to kill theirs and take their places, as some thought the purpose was by that which was already done."[95] These men yet to come, though, are imagined to be the Englishmen's invisible lovers and servants, and they are imagined to be already there, moving spectrally among the more conventionally visible-bodied people, or doing the Englishmen's deadly bidding from the future: "Those that were immediatly to come after us they imagined to be in the aire, yet invisible & without bodies, & that they by our intreaty & for the love of us did make the people to die in that sort as they did by shooting invisible bullets into them."[96] Others, Harriot reports, think the Englishmen may kill "without weapons," or "that we shot them ourselves out of our pieces from the place where we dwelt, and killed the people in any such towne that had offended us as we listed, how farre distant from us soever it was"[97]

These ventriloquized images have been read in numerous ways, including Stephen Greenblatt's influential reading of the "invisible bullets" as an "eerily prescient" prefiguration of modern germ theory.[98] Jonathan Goldberg, however, objects to the post hoc ratification of the telos of European conquest that is enacted when modern critics read this vision as a kind of Algonkian precognition of their own genocide, a move he calls a "making-acceptable of the Algonkians as our ancestors, as those who testify to their own disappearance and replacement by us."[99] Goldberg underscores how a teleological model of historical time shores up colonialist fantasies, in which European acts of domination and genocide are construed as natural or inevitable. Goldberg cautions us instead to sit with the "multiple and conflicting openings toward a future that Harriot's text cannot control," insisting on the "irreducibility of this trope to a singular historical trajectory."[100] It is crucial to keep in mind that these visions, whatever communications he thinks he has had with Algonkian people, are Thomas Harriot's—that the text "may offer a version of Western horror even as it asks the natives to articulate it."[101]

I want to focus on the European fantasies, as well as the Algonkian nightmares, that are bodied forth in these hyperpotent specters of futurity. What I see in this series of visions is not "ontological confusion,"[102] but the text's staging of a succession of ontologically specific, diachronic, uncannily generative relations between the Englishmen and the Algonkians—that is to say, a set of queer spectral genealogies that posit alternatives to both sexual reproduction and linear time. The visions Harriot posits are structurally queer in that they cast the Englishmen as ancestors or descendants, in cyclical, reversed, and nonlineal kinship relations to the Algonkians. They are temporally queer in that they traffic in visitations from the past and future, and sex and violence that can travel across time. And they are also, in no small part, sexually queer. Having noted of the first

Roanoke expedition "that we had no women amongst us, neither that we did care for any of theirs," the Algonkians see the English as a sodomitical, gender-undifferentiated race of men who reproduce with one another. There is surely literal homoerotic content to what the Algonkians "note" about the Englishmen, although it remains totally uninterrogated by Harriot (as well as by most scholarship on early modern colonial narratives). The all-male colonial venture—a space of homosocial incarceration, like all sea voyages, with the added dis-location of landing in a completely alien world—is a certain site of actual sex between men, in many and varied probable configurations. While we cannot recover further meanings besides the deep, deep strangeness that the Algonkian people impute to the first Roanoke party's homosociality, it spurs them, as Harriot has it, to imagine new, quasi-human bodies, sexualities, and ontological statuses for the English voyagers. Both the Englishmen's potent lethality and their invulnerability to the sickness are connected to a fantasy of their unnatural, untimely, womanless generation; they are "not borne of women, and therefore not mortall."

This language about men who are not born of women, and the question of what their uncanny generation enables them to do, will not stay buried in Harriot's report. It is famously reanimated onstage—through a chain of circulation, reading, diffusion, and cita-tion that we can never recover—in Shakespeare's *Macbeth* (c. 1606), in the witches' slippery prophecy that "none of woman born/Shall harm Macbeth" (4.1.79–80). Macduff, who was "from his mother's womb/Untimely ripped" (5.7.45–46), disproves Macbeth's assump-tion that he is invincible, and calls into question the link between "of woman born" and the category of the human. Macduff derives his special lethality to Macbeth from the same liminal, questionably human phenomenon as the Englishmen in Harriot's fantasy: unnatu-ral birth. The Englishmen's immunity to the strange death visited on the Algonkians, however, transmutes in *Macbeth* into a special vul-nerability for Macbeth only to Macduff, who is seemingly fated to kill him. The witches' prophecies sit pointedly alongside Harriot's Al-gonkian predictions as a foretelling of a "history that will be," in that the ontological status of the witches and their statements—whether they are describing foreordained events, or spurring Macbeth's actions through suggestion and desire, or neither, or something else—is a central and undecidable question raised by the play. One facet of Harriot's vision that is illuminated by reading it retrospectively, in light of its revenant echoes in *Macbeth,* is that the ontological statuses and consequences of the events Harriot describes—along with the status of the interpretations he attributes/concocts about them— are anything but decided. In a way that is easier to see because it is a play, and not an ostensibly "True Report," *Macbeth* speaks directly to the "the multiple and conflicting openings toward a future that Harriot's text cannot control."[103] All save the last four hundred years of that future is, of course, still the future, and still undecided. Nikolas Rose theorizes his historiography of biopolitics (an often uncanny narrative of annihilation and generation involving invisible forces and liminal forms of life) as a history that would "not so much seek to destabilize the present by pointing to its contingency, but to destabilize the future by recognizing its openness," thereby "demonstrating that no single future is written in our present": "It is important to recognize that we do not stand at some unprecedented moment in the unfolding of a single history. Rather, we live in the middle of multiple histories. As with our own present, our future will emerge from the intersection of a number of contingent pathways that, as they intertwine, might create something new."[104]

Though in light of the play's ending the witches' prophecy (like Harriot's) takes on a perverse retroactive truth effect, the scene in which it is told to Macbeth—act 4, scene 1, on the heath—presents a complex phantasmagorical tableau that (like Harriot's text) enacts not only multiple and contingent histories but also multiple intertwinings of identification, desire, and kinship across time. I see the four apparitions shown to Macbeth by the witches on the heath (the "Armed Head," the "Bloody Child," the "Child Crowned, with a tree in his hand" and finally, "eight Kings and Banquo, last with a glass in his hand") as another queer genealogy founded on spectral, unnatural historiography and asexual reproduction, to place alongside Harriot's Algonkian nightmare theories. Even as Banquo is conjured as the father of a line of kings, supposedly the play's ultimate image of reproductive futurity, each iteration does not replace the last but rather appears alongside it, looking exactly like it, so that the apparition is not a model of diachronic royal succession but of a compressed, phantasmatic temporality where kings seem to infinitely multiply themselves (with a glass that shows "many more" iterations—like Harriot's "manie strange sightes") in a way that looks more like asexual splitting or budding than Oedipal succession or sexual reproduction. In my view, *Macbeth*'s apparitions have more resonance with the mechanism of queer colonial melancholia driving Harriot's *Report* than anything found in more topical early modern plays of colonial encounter or sea voyaging (such as Shakespeare's *The Tempest*, which is mainly invested on the side of reproductive futurity).

It is no accident that the undecidedness of history and futurity in both of these texts is cracked open by their twinned evocations of an uncanny outside to the telos of natural reproduction and birth. Both patrilineal sovereignty and settler colonialism are dependent on reproduction, and both are existentially threatened by the infinite ways it can fail or go awry. Reading *Macbeth*'s portentous and ontologically unreliable specters alongside Harriot's convoluted, queer ancestor visions makes more visible the extent to which colonial anxiety is tied up in the problem of reproduction. Moreover, a queer historical practice of reading texts in light of their afterlives reveals that both texts are haunted by an absence or failure of reproductivity—a lost child. Just as the possible indeterminate or dead child to whom Lady Macbeth has "given suck" is the substrate for *Macbeth*'s proliferation of spectral and bloody children, the lost white baby, Virginia Dare, has haunted the reception and afterlife of the Roanoke text since its first publication, becoming the locus for centuries' worth of accumulation of racialized colonial melancholia. Indeed, Harriot's account of Roanoke—with its womanless, out-of-time killers, its canceled reproductive agenda, the lost colony it was supposed to save, and the spectral child suspended in memory, whose absence seems to drive the whole delusional, bloody undertaking—can be read as a kind of alternate, Bizarro World *Macbeth*. Macbeth's untimely, usurping ambition, Macduff's not-of-woman-born potency, and the witches' maleficent destruction are all wrapped up in the English colonists' failed and fruitless colonial violence. The pamphlet's vi-

sions of space-time-bending congress and spectral, queer kinship relations are placed in the mouths of the Algonkian people, who appear
as cryptic, oracular others, rather than spoken by witches. Yet it is
the Englishmen who appear to the Algonkians as supernatural, non-
gender-differentiated beings (as Banquo says of the witches, "You
should be women/And yet your beards forbid me to interpret/That
you are so" [1.3.46–48]) whose instruments show "manie strange
sightes." And the Algonkians are also endowed with qualities of the
tragic king's vulnerability to an uncanny foe not "borne of women,"
as it is their futurity that is being "wrenched with an unlineal hand"
(3.1.63) away from them.

The strangeness in these visions brought out by juxtaposition
with *Macbeth* can be used to counter the prophetic critical gloss it has
taken on in the settler–colonial present. To that end, I want to offer
a new, antiteleological reading of the second vision, the fantasy of a
coming race of men "in the aire" who are from the future yet already
invisibly present, men "come to kill them and take their places."
This fantasy bespeaks a queer model of descent and a queer drive
toward annihilation, not reproduction. Though the men of air seem as
uncannily automated as zombies, this is not precisely an "Algonkian
'Night of the Living Dead,'" as Greenblatt dubs it.[105] The men of air
are not back from the dead; they are not yet alive. Like a phalanx of
sprites or ghostly familiars, they seem erotically enslaved to the present Englishmen, whose telepathic "intreaty" to kill they obey "for
love of us." But what has conjured them into this moment from their
own time? What call did they hear? What bonds of identificatory love
between men, stretching across history, were they hailed by, binding
them to those who came before? They can *almost* be read as queer
descendants called back by historical love and debt to defend their
gay ancestors, except that instead of antiretroviral drugs and tales of
liberation, they bring the plague. They are queer descendants, but on
the side of genocide.

The Algonkian "phisitions" read a corroborating material explanation in a strange sign they observe in the victims' bodies: "that
the strings of blood that they sucked out of the sicke bodies, were
the strings wherewithal the invisible bullets were tied and cast."
These invisible bullets on "strings of blood" invite comparison to

Cupid's invisible heart-arrows, or to the invisible powers of alteration possessed by an analogous bodily fluid: semen. Shot for the love of other men, in this instance they cause death rather than generation. The English are not the Algonkians' ancestors here, but they may not be in any way their descendants—or anyone's ancestors—either. The "more of our generation yet to come" may be asexually or homosexually generated, as these first English explorers seem to be. In one possible future hinted at in this prophecy, the replacement of one generation with another will be enacted not by heterosexual sex but by homoerotic murder, a queer fantasy (in the style of Leo Bersani or Lee Edelman—or Patricia Highsmith) of an end to heteroreproductive futurism itself.[106] If we read it literally, homoerotic annihilation and replacement will replace reproduction and descent as the new relation between generations. Such a queer mechanism of iteration would mirror the paradox of melancholia's nonheterosexual directionality: its death-driven, self-destroying affects, its incorporation of the lost other, and the eerily self-perpetuating duration of its negativity. This next-order model of polymorphous proliferation—in which the very mechanism of reproduction is constantly remaking itself—also echoes postmodern narratives of capitalism and biopolitics, including posthuman models of artificial life. Read in this queer light, the cryptic fantasies of invisible destruction that Harriot records are not teleological predictions but rather unpredictable manifestations of a complicated melancholic vision, predicated on identification as well as difference, on annihilation as well as reproduction, on loss and impossible futurity, and on unnatural mechanisms of generation and twisted models of historical time.

"In Times Past as Sauvage"

When John White's 1590 appendix to Theodor de Bry's Folio edition of *A Briefe and True Report,* titled "True Pictures and Fashions of the People in That Part of America Now Called Virginia," is mentioned in criticism, it tends to be framed as a set of illustrations corresponding to Harriot's *Report,* which adds visual interest and novelty but makes no substantive claims of its own. Read on its own terms, however, it quickly becomes apparent that White's images and descriptions constitute a distinct, visual account of fantasmatic relations between the English and the Algonkians, which differs from Harriot's in subtle but significant ways. The complex multitemporal, multimedia life of White's images makes the "True Pictures" a key site of the 1590 folio's construction of colonial fantasies wrought from homosocial currents of desire. Traces of the complex network of power relations that brought the 1590 edition into being are visible on the title page and in the dedication, which feature obsequies in the voice of the engraver and publisher, Theodor de Bry, to Raleigh, whose lauded status as the volume's honorary patron effaces the three years John White unsuccessfully petitioned him for a relief voyage. De Bry's address "To the gentle Reader" at the beginning of the "True Pictures" reveals that it was "Maister Richard Hakluyt of Oxford Minister of God's Word" who, out of his own history with Harriot's account and their shared affection for White's images, "first Incouraged me to publish the Worke."[107] De Bry credits White's actual "Pictures" as being produced by way of Raleigh again (twice) and by himself: "Diligentlye collected and draowne by IHon White who was sent thiter speciallye and for the same purpose by the said Sir Walter Ralegh the year abovesaid 1585. and also the year 1588. now cutt in copper and first published by Theodore de Bry att his wone chardges."[108] This appendix thus condenses years of accumulated transactions of affection, money, texts, and images between men. As a made thing, it is a manifestation of the multilayered economies of service, instrumentality, debt, knowledge, pleasure, and capital around the colonial enterprise. These networks of desire are not only homosocial, but melancholic; by the time of its publication, it is a record of what has already been lost.

John White was on all of the Roanoke voyages, and led the last, aspirationally reproductive venture; he left to seek relief for the colony soon after landing. His drawings date from the second, 1585 Grenville expedition, for which he was the recording artist. They existed first as watercolors and drawings made from life in North America—over seventy of them, made during the year White spent in privation with the other men of the Grenville party before being picked up and returned to England by Francis Drake in 1586. The exhaustive attention to detail evident in the watercolors is a trace of the dilated, uncertain temporality of waiting, with no way to know if or when relief was coming, amid a society that is utterly alien, and that White had no idea whether he would ever leave. They embody, first of all, White's attempt to see something new—an intricate and prosperous urban and agricultural civilization to which he did not, and never could, belong, but in which he is inescapably implicated by virtue of his bodily presence and his recording gaze. White's surviving watercolors also evince an attempt to put the new and specific people and things of Virginia into conversation with other contemporary colonial representations of difference. He copied several images and poses from the work of two fellow failed Protestant colonizers: Jacques Le Moyne in Florida in the 1560s, and Jean de Léry.[109]

The main body of the 1590 "True Pictures" maps a deliberate, encyclopedic set of American subjects, objects, and relations in twenty-one richly detailed portraits and descriptions of the people of Roanoke Island and of the cities of Secota, Pomeiooc, and Dasemonquepeuc on the mainland, including their dress, hunting techniques, foodways, and religious ceremonies. De Bry's presentation of White's work features men and women equally, with detailed information about their locality, age, and social station. These images are shot through with a curious mix of identification and alterity that undercuts many of Harriot's stated claims about Virginia and its people. In contrast to the techniques for seeing and rendering bodily and cultural difference that John White developed on Roanoke, the figures in the 1590 folio edition have undergone a shift toward identification, inviting a European readership to see the familiar in their classical, humanist visual vocabulary. Theodor de Bry bears much of the credit for the identificatory erotics of these bodies. He altered White's watercolors, moving the Algonkian figures into classical poses with Mannerist musculature, and Europeanizing their faces and bodily habitus.[110] But De Bry's classicized naked bodies are overlayered in each plate with White's intricate representations of bodily fashions and cultural objects, among the most detailed of the entire colonial period, and meticulous written descriptions of what each plate shows. A "weroan or great Lorde of Virginia" is shown in a warrior's pose with his bow and arrow; the caption details the exact architecture of the hairstyles, jewelry, feathers, face paint, and body paint of the "Princes of Virginia," including their aesthetic choices

Figure 5. "A weroan or great Lorde of Virginia. III," in "The True Pictures and Fashions of the People in that Parte of America Now Called Virginia . . . ," appendix to *A Briefe and True Report of the New Found Land of Virginia* (Frankfurt: J. Wechel for T. De Bry, 1590), A. RB 18531, The Huntington Library, San Marino, California.

within the parameters of custom: "They hange at their eares ether thickepearles, or somwhatels, as the clawe of some great birde, as cometh in to their fansye."[111] Subsequent plates give similar attention to the meanings of a priest's hare-skin cloak, and of a "plate of copper hanging from a string" worn as a necklace "in token of authorityе, and honor" on the body of "a chieff Lorde of Roanoac."[112] The undeniable foreign civility of these socially ranked, gendered, and materially productive Algonkian bodies exposes Harriot's insistence on Virginia's emptiness as a delusional colonial fiction.

The "True Pictures" also subtly refuses to fix the Algonkians in a static, archaic past, by including material traces of the present in which Europeans and Native Americans have already begun to change and affect each other. "A chieff Ladye of Pomeiooc" holds one arm through a skein of beads folded about her neck and carries "a gourde full of some kind of pleasant liquor." Her child, a girl of "7 or 8 yeares olde," has her girdle "drawen under neath" between

Figure 6. "A cheiff Ladye of Pomeiooc. VIII," in "The True Pictures and Fashions of the People in that Parte of America Now Called Virginia . . . ," appendix to *A Briefe and True Report of the New Found Land of Virginia* (Frankfurt: J. Wechel for T. De Bry, 1590), A5. RB 18531, The Huntington Library, San Marino, California.

her legs "to cover their priviliers withall." De Bry gives the child a generic American rattle, not shown in White's original drawing, but in the other hand she holds a European baby doll.[113] This is the single object in the "True Pictures" that brings the time of European colonial invasion into collision with the quotidian indigenous temporality flowing through the Algonkian scenes.[114] The doll in the little girl's hand indexes the material and affective contacts that have already taken place: "They are greatlye Deligted with puppetts, and babes which wear brought oute of England."[115] But it also hints at how those exchanges touch the Algonkian world these plates aspire to archive, invisibly but inexorably altering the relations of the *weroans* to his bow and arrow, the men to their boats, the women to their cooking pots and food (some of which they are now giving to the English, who are unable to feed themselves), and their god, "The Idol Kiwasa," to his worshippers.[116]

But then, at the end of White's "True Pictures" in the 1590

Report, there is a curious coda—unlisted in the table of contents—
that presents "Some Picture of the Pictes which in the olde tyme did
habite one part of the great Bretainne." De Bry claims that he included these pictures, found "in an oolld English Cronicle," at John
White's behest, "for to showe how that the Inhabitants of the great
Bretannie have bin in times past as sauvage as those of Virginia."[117]
This move points to the past in order to prove the telos of colonial
development—to turn Virginia into England. However, in overlay-
ering a temporal difference onto a cultural one, it also disintegrates
essential notions of English identity or fixed, eternal racial difference. It recasts "straight" temporality as something more occult: an
uncanny coexistence, within a fractured and non-self-identical present, of two different temporalities warped or bridged together in a
visual colonial encounter. The addition of the Picts transforms the
colonial dyad into a three-way circuit of transtemporal connection,
opening up new relational possibilities outside of linear, heteronormative history. It places the Englishmen into a nonpatrilineal, queer
genealogy with their mythic pasts and their colonial others. After all,
the connection between the vanished Picts and the present Englishmen is a roundabout, twisting, imagined one (the root of "queer,"
-twerkw, yielding the Latin *torquere*, "to twist").[118] It is forged by a
series of intra-European conquests in late antiquity and the early
Middle Ages, and in early modern England's colonial ambitions toward Celtic peoples, just as the connection between Shakespeare's
audience and the quasi-mythical history behind *Macbeth* is one of
transhistorical identification with, and colonial appropriation of, the
"unlineal" Scottish royal genealogy through Banquo, the ancestor of
James VI and I.

John White's Picts project a dream of futurity onto America,
enabling the colonizing Englishmen to imagine themselves as men
from the future race "yet to come" that the Native Americans ostensibly expect. But they also project the Englishmen's mythical past—an
inherently foreign past, tied up in twisting and contested narratives
about where barbarism was located and who the ancestors of the English even were—onto America's present.[119] The Algonkians thus
become like some sort of ancestors of the Englishmen, uncannily
translated through history to meet their spectrally begotten queer

children in the space out of time of America. The voyage to America could equally be imagined as a voyage back in time or a voyage to the future, complicating a simple primitivist or futurist trajectory either way. If the Picts evoke a past where the "inhabitants of the great Bretannie" "have been in times past *as* sauvage," then they open up possibilities for oblique identifications between the present Virginians and the only contingently less savage present inhabitants of Great Britain. This strange continuity is triangulated through the aestheticized coexistence of alterity and identification communicated in the engravings of the Picts' bodies. The Pictish man's naked body is intricately painted, his ceremonial rings, chains, and weapons anatomized in the caption just as those of the Algonkians are. But most strikingly, his pose with his spear echoes the classical posture of the *weroance* with his bow and arrow. Both figures are presented in settings of war, the *weroance* in front of a raging battle and the Pict with the severed heads of his enemies, thus highlighting that the fantasmatic continuities being forged here are immanently dependent on the violence of conquest.

Such hinted-at counterhistories and possible futures can be glimpsed by reading through and around the engravings' illusory claim "to showe" any kind of ethnographic or historical truth. The model of history posited by the Picts connects ancestors and descendants (adding fictive linkages and confusing who plays which role) in relations that exceed the time of a natural human life, and across suprahistorical time spans that negate any attempt to inscribe patrilineal descent. Nor does it seem to have any basis in the heterosexual dyad, or in intercourse. It is a fantasy kinship relation forged between present, deterritorialized Englishmen and a queer array of lost past and future selves. Like Harriot's ventriloquized apocalyptic visions, the Picts insinuate radical alternatives to the telos of reproductive futurity, enacting many possible, irreducible identifications and affinities across time.

Afterlife: The History that Will Not Be

As the whole of this book has endeavored to show, any act of reading a text is always saturated by the currents of history flowing between

Figure 7. "The truue picture of one Picte I," in "The True Pictures and Fashions of the People in that Parte of America Now Called Virginia . . . ," appendix to *A Briefe and True Report of the New Found Land of Virginia* (Frankfurt: J. Wechel for T. De Bry, 1590), E2. RB 18531, The Huntington Library, San Marino, California.

its production and our present. The Roanoke text's web of affects is inextricable from the larger web binding it and its readers—all of its readers—into the violent history of European colonialism. Consequently, any attempt to reckon with the melancholic desires archived in Harriot's and White's text must reckon with its narrative afterlives. John White returned to Roanoke in 1590 to find the settlement razed to the ground and the word "Croatoan" carved on a post. Harsh weather forced the Englishmen to give up the search, and they returned, bereft, to England—and into the ensuing epoch of colonial melancholia for, and mythologization of, the "lost colony."[120] This event has immediate effects on the reception of the *Report*. By the time anyone read De Bry's 1590 book, the real, mortal English settlers—whom White's mythical Picts are raised up out of an "oolld English Cronicle" to mobilize the money and political will to rescue—had already joined their fictive ancestors in the lost, apocryphal time of legend. A 1593 letter to Richard Hakluyt, the last trace of John White in the archive, continues in a register of failed Protestant colonial anxiety that is immediately recognizable from Jean de Léry: impotence, frustration, regret, and longing. It wearily recounts a litany of obstacles—never enough time, never enough money, promises made and broken by Raleigh and the merchants who owned the ships. Sentence after sentence follows in this mode of nested negation: "Neverthelesse that order was not observed, neither was the bond taken according to the intention aforesaid," and so on.[121] White echoes Jean de Léry's "if it had not been": "Which evils and unfortunate events (as wel to their owne losse as to the hinderance of the planters in Virginia) had not chanced, if the order set downe by Sir Walter Ralegh had bene observed, or if my dayly and continuall petitions for performance of the same might have taken any place."[122] He ends the letter with an admission of defeat and insufficiency: "And wanting my wishes, I leave off from prosecuting that whereunto I would to God my wealth were answerable to my will."[123] There is no amount of wealth, though, that could bend space-time so as to grant John White his wish, which is merely, impossibly, for *everything to have gone another way.*

Through the circulation of Harriot's and White's text in the wake of the colony's disappearance, the English mood of colonial anxiety takes a sudden melancholic turn before England has even a toehold on the American continent. Once Jamestown and Plymouth are established, however, this colonial melancholia is directly transmitted to the new colonies—and to the ensuing settler state, the United States of America—as an acutely mythologized, racialized nostalgia for the "lost colony." The afterlife of Harriot's and White's *Report* in American culture provides a vexed and frightening study in how the history of a text's reception can, over time, fundamentally alter its meanings. It is a dramatic example of the power of transhistorical readerly identification to magnetize and amplify affects in a text that cannot be known in advance. The English colonial melancholia encoded in this text has been kept alive, continually reanimated, through a reading practice that is itself melancholic: that of the white nationalist racial imaginary. One of the things we urgently need to know at the current political moment is how queer analysis can shed light on the formation and workings of racism. To that end, I now delve into the afterlives of the Roanoke story in order to acknowledge and account for the historical connections between queer colonial melancholia and the white racial melancholia embedded in the American myth of the lost colony.

Rumors of the disappeared settlers' fates continued to circulate through the subsequent English settlements. They become ghosts whose absent presence haunts Jamestown in the form of ever-shifting stories about their death and/or survival.[124] Stories of a place to the south of Jamestown where there were "houses walled as ours" and men "cloathed like me" tantalize Captain John Smith when he arrives in 1607.[125] One source for these fragments is Smith's storied conversation with Wahunsonacock, the Algonkian ruler of more than thirty nations under the Powhatan chiefdom, who famously held Smith captive in 1607. A 1608 map from the expedition Smith mounted to search for it notes the area—the two place-names that keep recurring are the Tuscarora villages of Ocanahonan and Pakerakanick, on what today are called the Roanoke and Neuse rivers—where rumors locate the men clothed like Englishmen: "Here remayneth 4 men clothed that came from Roonock to Ocanahowan."[126] But Smith's men seem not to have come any closer than hearsay.

These fragmentary traces of the settlers' survival coexist with the news, transmitted thirdhand through delayed and disparate channels, that Wahunsonacock also told of massacring the settlers from Roanoke after they had been living with and as Chesapeake people for years. This may have occurred as late as 1607, seventeen years after they fled Roanoke. The same place-names to the south were recorded in 1609, with the rumor that there were "foure of the englishe alive" who had escaped there after Wahunsonacock's late attack, but "you shall never recover them."[127] Many years later in England, the prolific anthologizer, Samuel Purchas, discloses that John Smith recounted to him how the great chief described being present at the murder of the white settlers.[128] A subsequent secretary of Jamestown, veteran colonizer William Strachey, learned from Wahunsonacock's emissary, Machumps, that the English "men women and childrene" of Roanoke for "twenty and od yeares had peaceably lyved intermixt with those salvages," until Wahunsonacock decided, via a prophecy, that the Chesapeake represented a threat to his empire, and so put to the sword the entire tribe, its *weroance,* and everyone living under its protection.[129] In Strachey's narrative, Machumps cites the same two villages where "the people have howses built with stone walles, and one story above another," and "breed up tame turkeis about their howses."[130] These artifacts of material life—clothes, houses, turkeys—are supposed to be the telltale signs of Englishness. In a desperate inversion of John White's meticulously comparatist descriptions of Algonkian clothes and houses, these unseen, imagined artifacts are compared with the crudest, most sweeping similies (houses "walled as ours," men "clothed like me") in an attempt to make man-made materials stand in for the bodies of English people.

One of the ways in which this narrative acquires some of its force of historical melancholia is in the warping of geographical distance by time and technology. None of the villages to the south named in the rumors are far from Jamestown today—only one to two hundred miles. But from the perspective of the Jamestown colonists' extremely limited local knowledge and mobility, they are as inaccessible as if on another planet. Again and again, from native informants who, as Michael Leroy Oberg notes, have their own various political motives, the colonists hear of the Roanoke survivors, somewhere out

LOST WORLDS, LOST SELVES

there in the interior of the continent of which they have only the barest grasp; but they are completely unable to reach them.[131] These anecdotes of impotence become central to white settler melancholia by being repeated again and again as industrial technologies accelerate and compress the space-time of travel.

Another Jamestown colonist, George Percy, in 1607 saw a boy of about ten with "a head of hair of a perfect yellow, and a reasonable white skin" on a river expedition in Powhatan territory, but he was unable to follow up—an anecdote that inaugurates the explicit discourse of *whiteness* as a thing that was lost with the colony, and may be found again.[132] Percy's glimpsed and lost boy also inaugurates the practice—which continues into the present day—of reading the bodies of Native American people in the area for signs of European descent. Phenotypical traces of white ancestry—embodied, biological remnants of the lost colony—have been sought in, attributed to, and claimed by modern native tribes, most notably the storied recurrence of gray, blue, or green eyes noted among the Hatteras Indians (constructed since the eighteenth century as the descendants of the Outer Banks Croatoan people) and the North Carolina Tuscarora.[133] Descent from the Roanoke English has also been posited by and about other modern native tribes of North Carolina, including the Lumbee and the Coree or Cohari people, and deployed to political ends of both native sovereignty and white nationalist nostalgia.[134] In recent times, the allure of genetic science has led to a concerted search for traces of this specific "lost" Englishness in the DNA of present Americans of white, Native American, and African ancestry.[135]

Strachey also records that in another place, a copper-mining town called Ritanoe, seven English survivors, "fower men, two boyes, and one yonge mayde," remain, beating copper for another *weroance*.[136] This reference to a "mayde" has fueled centuries of racialized fantasy about the survival of the much heralded first English baby, Virginia Dare—a story that signals the gathering nostalgia around whiteness and the problem of reproduction in settler colonialism. From the start, Virginia Dare fits into a preexisting chain of allegorical meanings in the colonial romance, where the American continent is figured as both Virginia's namesake, the bygone Virgin Queen, Elizabeth, and a pure and resistant, exoticized indigenous female body.[137] The lost white female child offers an irresistible way for white settlers to extend this virgin/Virginia/America imagery into the future, transposing it into a distinctly white feminine birthright that is "lost," and that thus must be aspirationally fought for and reattained. This mythology of Virginia Dare is cultivated over the nineteenth century in sentimental literature (mostly written by women) deploying all the conventional tropes of romance. Starting with a fictional treatment in 1840 by Cornelia L. Tuthill, this genre imagines her as a beautiful maiden who sanctifies the primeval Virginia woods (and converts natives to Christianity) with her pure white Englishness, and has star-crossed (chaste) love affairs with worthy native suitors.[138] One of the recurring Elizabethan tropes in this lore casts Virginia Dare as the elusive and immortal "white doe" of Englishness.[139] The white doe myth circulates at least from 1888, when it appears in a fanciful travel article in the *New York Times,* framed in the style of Mary Shelley's *Frankenstein* as a tale spun by a garrulous captain on an uncannily protracted sea voyage.[140] It enters mass circulation as a faux Native American epic poem titled "The White Doe, or The Fate of Virginia Dare, an Indian Legend," written in 1901 by Sallie Southall Cotten. In Cotten's poem, a chaste and genteel Virginia Dare, living among friendly Algonkians as a half-assimilated (yet thoroughly white) princess, is transformed into an enchanted white deer by a curse from a native sorcerer whose advances she rejects. In an exoticized American twist on the triangulated love-lies-a-bleeding romance trope recognizable from Beaumont and Fletcher's *Philaster,* the deer is shot while drinking from a stream by two men at the same instant. One of the men is her true love, whose enchanted arrow will break the curse, and the other is a striving young warrior. Virginia Dare becomes a maid again at the moment of her death, and a new vine of sweet red grapes (North Carolina scuppernongs) springs up where her blood has spilled.[141] The claim to the land that Cotten's poem posits through sacrificial white womanhood is materially continuous with the projected planting enterprises that Thomas Harriot imagines in his *Report*: Cotten was a bourgeois booster of both women's rights and the wine industry, and "The White Doe," with its agricultural origin myth, was written to market Virginia Dare–brand scuppernong wine to women.[142]

The story becomes more fantastical over a proliferation of re-tellings, in print, on television, and, copiously, in the virtual space of the Internet. These retellings posit the "mystery" of the lost colony as a foundational uncanny tale, installing a kernel of the supernatural, weird, or unexplained at the origin of the English colonization of North America.[143] Part of the allure of the uncanny version of the Roanoke story, with its combination of overwrought mystery (No one knows!) and fantastical speculation (Alien abduction? A massive royal conspiracy?) is that it elides the unforgiving reality: a group of people out of place, completely unable to provide for themselves, died of exposure or starvation, or were killed, or joined another society. Interjecting an element of the mysterious into the story is a tactic to explain this spectacular colonial failure as a glitch in an otherwise righteous and feasible agenda rather than confronting its essential folly.[144] Beginning the story of a white Protestant presence on this continent with a founding uncanny mystery also lends it the patina of myth, throwing events of the late 1580s back into mythological time, or drawing the time of ancient wonders forward into the early modern and modern eras.[145] A vast body of speculative literature and film in recent decades (including fiction by Philip José Farmer, Harlan Ellison, Michael Scott, and Neil Gaiman, and television by Stephen King and Ryan Murphy, most recently an entire season of *American Horror Story*) imagines what became of Virginia Dare and the colonists, spinning out fantastical plots involving alien planets, time travel, spirit realms, immortality, vengeful gods and demons, vampirism, and human sacrifice.[146] The lost girl-child has become a homegrown archetype who can be used to construct darker fantasy versions of American history, as part of the long tradition of engaging with the haunting echoes of colonial violence through speculative and gothic fiction.

What bears further interrogation when tracing the queer affective posterity of the Roanoke story is the dependence of so many of the melancholic offspring it has spawned on fantastical models of descent. This is not incidental. Michael Harkin, in one of the few scholarly interrogations of the Roanoke myth, notes how the telling and retelling of the lost colony narrative bends time and space to endow the white settler colony with legitimacy.[147] But the myth bends, and indeed queers, sex and reproduction as well, endlessly inventing asexually and mystically generative futures for Virginia Dare. As Harkin points out, the uncomfortable paradox of the Roanoke myth for white nationalists is that the melancholically longed-for white survival depends, inescapably, on interracial sex and reproduction. In any scenario in which Virginia Dare's life or reproductive futurity may have continued, it was with and in a community of indigenous people. Subsequent white romanticizing narratives like Sallie Southall Cotten's have then devised spiritual genealogies connecting Virginia Dare to later Native Americans, to cover over their discomfort with interracial sex as the prerequisite for descent.[148] Yet Michael Leroy Oberg makes the point that any possible survival of the English from Roanoke, among the Chesapeake or Tuscarora or any other nation, could only have taken place through full adoption, a formal ritualized process for the making of kin in which people take on new identities, clans, and lineages—an alternative system to what Mark Rifkin calls white "settler sexuality," with its heteronormativizing biological definition of kinship.[149] Thus, ghosting all of these fantasies is the trace of a real historical practice of nonbiological, nonpatrilineal kin making, on which all of the imaginary, white-authored narratives unknowingly depend, even as they ignore it.

Along with Harkin, I reject efforts to "strip myth away" from this story, as if that were possible.[150] The writing of history, as Hayden White and others have shown, is a performative process of myth making and narrative production. So too, as this book has demonstrated, is the act of reading. The supreme irony of the Roanoke myth lies in the contrast between reality and how it gets interpreted: that the successful indigenous defeat and/or absorption of a precarious settlement of incompetent white invaders has been mythologized as proof of the rightness, even foreordination, of an English settler state. This entire meaning-making complex is predicated on a desperate white settler wish: that the disappearance of the Roanoke colony has to mean something. The meanings made for it, then, have been conditioned by white nationalist ideology. Despite the longevity of their tale, the Roanoke settlers were by no means the only group of people lost in the longer story of this particular stretch of Atlantic coastline. The ship of Sir Francis Drake that rescued Ralph Lane and his men from the Grenville voyage in 1586 had on board *several hundred* people—both enslaved and free, including indigenous people from South America, African people from the Guinea Coast, people of African descent from Cape Verde and Hispaniola (Santo Domingo), and some number of Turks and Moors[151]—people from almost every continent, in other words. All but one hundred of these people were evidently left on Roanoke when Drake departed with Lane's men, and their fate has merited none of the romantic mythologizing that has attended the disappearance of the white settlers. Their possible survival through adoption by native peoples of the area is another lost chapter in the story of North American race, irrecoverable except through a different kind of speculative melancholia, in which they introduce a foundational element of *créolité* on the continent, at a moment before the triumph of English racial schema.[152] The storied lost colony was not even the only lost *white* colony. The fifteen English men that Richard Grenville left behind on Roanoke in a doomed attempt to hold the fort when he returned to find that Lane's colony had departed with Drake also disappeared without a trace.[153]

When we start counting Native American people among the lost, the company expands to include the peoples known as the Roanoke Indians, the Hatteras Indians, and the Chesapeake. All those lost to the "invisible bullets" of epidemics must have seemed uncannily spirited away en masse by their mysterious assailants. Individual native people experienced other dramatic losses and displacements. The fabled Algonkian interlocutors Manteo and Wanchese were lost to their people and their country, first when they were taken to England by the Amadas and Barlowe expedition in 1584 and brought to reside in Raleigh's house, and further lost—loss compounded upon loss—when they traveled again to Roanoke as agents, guides, and translators for the English, their fates ultimately diverging as Wanchese returned to his people to oppose the English while Manteo appears to have shared the fate of the disappeared white settlers. Another Algonkian man who was taken back to England and named Raleigh by Richard Grenville died of illness in Devonshire.[154] Just as Jean de Léry cannot directly mourn the impossibility of remaining with the Tupinamba, none of these losses can be directly mourned in the racial and sexual imaginary of the American settler state, because to mourn them would entail acknowledging them, and to acknowledge them would require accepting the ragged, blood-soaked, perverse multiplicity of colonialism—and of race. It is only the reproductive lost colony, the one with the white baby girl, that gets installed as the melancholic object, precisely for the fantasies it incites.

The undercurrent of white racial nostalgia running through the romanticized Virginia Dare lore morphs into an uglier form in the late twentieth century. In 1999, an English-born journalist, himself an immigrant to the United States, founded the VDARE Foundation, under the sign of the white doe, as a media outlet and activist organization devoted to construing (nonwhite) immigration as an existential threat to American and Western culture, and promulgating eugenics-based alarms about racial degeneration.[155] The name of Virginia Dare functions in this context as a rallying point for the belief that white Anglo-Saxon and Celtic people have a natural entitlement to the continent of North America (a claim ironically staked through a baby who was immediately lost). White supremacist political movements are broadly attracted to this period of history, which they invest in through the ideology of "the Renaissance," not least because it marks the start of European colonial invasions in the Americas and Africa. One currently ascendant white supremacist group, Identity Evropa, uses Renaissance art, specifically Michelangelo's *David,* on its posters and in its messaging (following in a long tradition of fascist deployments of classical European art) as shorthand for an imagined moment of generalized European triumph.[156] Such white nationalist positions have gained new visibility in the current political moment in the United States, activating and giving voice to the feelings of white dispossession and white aggrievement that fueled the rise of Donald Trump. (Trump's slogan, "Make America Great Again," explicitly evokes an idea of American Renaissance—which is also the name of a white supremacist organization.)[157] Activists who unabashedly appeal to white nationalism, including Steve Bannon (until 2018) and Stephen Miller (currently as I write this), have been elevated to advisory positions in the Trump administration, crafting policies— such as the 2017 travel ban on citizens of Muslim countries, and the policy of separating children from their families (including those legally seeking asylum) at the Mexican border—that seek to restrict the opportunities, benefits, and protections of American life to white people, tacitly defining real or rightful Americans as those of European descent. Meanwhile, the VDARE Foundation and its promoters are a regular presence at conservative political conventions, inveighing against the contaminating influence of "foreign" immigration and selling their publications, fevered screeds that embody the blatantly desire-fueled concatenation of evidence and fantasy, fact and myth that marks both early modern colonial writing and the political rhetoric of Trumpism.[158]

The deployment of the myth of the lost colony to white nationalist political ends, specifically through the figure of the lost white female child, is a part of the erotic legacy of the Roanoke venture that cannot be ignored. The same libidinal currents that fuel Thomas Harriot's text and John White's drawings continue to animate its afterlives. There is an affective through line here that extends from Jean de Léry's and Thomas Harriot's florid descriptive fantasies; to White's queer Picts, resurrected from an ancient chronicle; to John Smith's and George Percy's and James Strachey's thwarted chasing after traces of Englishness in the wilderness. It then extends from the Renaissance to our own time, through Sallie Southall Cotten's sacrificial white doe; to Virginia Dare imagined as the immortal time-traveling witch of science fiction; to the VDARE Foundation's installation of John White's lost granddaughter as the rightful white Eve of the North American continent. The affect that knits these figures together is colonial melancholia, the unmournable loss of something one could never have had in the first place, because what one has lost is not the thing in its own right, but the ideational part of oneself represented in the thing.[159] To be explicit, it is the unmournable, still-disavowed loss of the fantasy that white Europeans are the rightful and natural inhabitants of North America. In the white nationalist imaginary, the refutation of this fantasy cannot be assimilated, only transmuted into various fantastical forms. That this is a queer form of colonial desire does not mean that its political consequences are subversive or liberatory. Queer desires can be violent, appropriating, annihilating, racist, fascist; and violent desires can be queer.

What I have endeavored to show by tracing these stories is how queer colonial melancholia is structured by—and implicated with—racial melancholia.

Ann Anlin Cheng describes the constitutive melancholia at the heart of race as a mechanism of neither transparent identification nor alterity, because these are not pure or opposite poles, but rather one of dissimulation: "What if colonial desire itself is melancholic, and longs clandestinely to mime the 'foreigner' inside? What if we recast the failure of mimicry (in Bhabha's terms), as instead an allowance for dissimulation? And what if dissimulation—the other that is me—provides the very structure of identification?"[160] Both Harriot's ventriloquized theories of murderous future air-lovers and the yearning genealogical image-magic retroactively performed by John White's drawings of the Picts can be read as artifacts of dissimulation. They betray clandestine identifications that work in both directions, for a displaced subject that is both itself and other to itself. Jean de Léry, too, imagines a self from another time, neither straightforwardly American nor European, neither past nor future, but combining elements of both. Dissimulation holds back and encrypts the dangerous and powerful secret parts of the self; as such, it is intimately implicated with queer desire, with shameful feelings that are at once disavowed and assiduously cultivated. In fact, these same affective currents of impossible identification and unspeakable love, as traced by Cheng, Bhabha, Fanon, Sharon Patricia Holland, Siobhan Somerville, and others, have been the shaping conditions for the inextricably entwined historical development of race and sexuality.[161]

Judith Butler's account of melancholia resonates with the colonial longings I have unpacked and sets up the final point I want to make: that the overwrought affective outpourings of renunciation, loss, obsession, projection, and delusion that I have spent the foregoing pages describing as queer in affect, as queer moods and modes of expression, are intrinsically, at every level—structurally, psychically, topically, and historically—part of the omnipresent, polymorphous discursive regime of sexuality. The melancholias at the heart of whiteness, heterosexuality, and binary gender work by an interrelated mechanism. To recall Eve Sedgwick's observation about paranoia and homophobia, this is just "how the world works."[162] To posit a corollary to Sedgwick's and Guy Hocquenghem's point that gays have been construed as paranoid because paranoia is how homophobia works: queers are not uniquely melancholy; melancholia is the structure by which sexual identity is violently formed. We live in "a culture of gender melancholy," Butler says, "in which masculinity and femininity emerge as the traces of an ungrieved and un-grievable love."[163] When a prohibition—say, against a same-sex love object—is ritualized and repeated throughout the culture, identity in that culture is then formed in response to the unmournable, unspeakable loss of that interdicted love object. Yet not only the object but also the loss itself—any trace of grief or mourning or acknowledgment of ever having loved—must also be disavowed. What we call heterosexuality comes into being through these incorporated disavowals, and gender is then "formed and consolidated through identifications that are composed in part of disavowed grief."[164] This grief is not only for the unmournable loss of the same-gendered love object, though; it is also for the unmournable loss of the other-gendered self. "If one is a girl to the extent that one does not want a girl," then becoming a girl not only entails, as Butler notes, giving up the girl as love object; it also means giving up the ideation of oneself as a boy—a boy being, of course, the kind of creature who could want, and have, a girl.[165] This is what I see in Léry's, Harriot's, and White's registers of colonial writing: longing for impossible transformation into something they can never be, in order to have something they can never have.

Butler makes the point that this impossible wanting need not be for another human being: "The 'other' may be an ideal, a country, a concept of liberty" that haunts the conscience as an internalized ideality.[166] "An other or an ideal may be 'lost' by being rendered unspeakable," she says, "impossible to declare," but it is guaranteed to escape, somehow, in affect, "emerging in the indirection of complaint and the heightened judgments of conscience."[167] I think of Jean de Léry's complaints and "heightened judgments of conscience" about the relative savagery of his own countrymen versus the inhabitants of Brazil—complaints that founded, through his bond of friendship with Montaigne, an incipient future discourse insisting on native peoples' humanity in, even because of, their difference. The gory fantasias and identificatory ravishments recorded by these three would-be colonists are indelibly about violence, about the historical and psychic processes by which so many people, things, possessions, lands, loves, and affiliations were, and are, forcibly lost. But they are also invitations, which I want to heed, to reconsider the very meanings of identification, alterity, and interpretation. Like the gaze of Richard Brome's delusional pseudotraveler Peregrine in *The Antipodes,* the gazes of these melancholic voyagers offer themselves as lenses for gazing at the larger concern of this book: the problem of reading. The European invaders' narratives reveal more about them than about the Americans they describe—as, I contend, our critical approaches to early modern texts, as readers in the present (for what else could we be?), do about us. But these documents of failure also contain new imaginings of how time and generation and descent might work, in light of the new dimensions of desire and death engendered by colonial contact. In other words, they perform a kind of queer theory, rethinking relationality and pleasure and empathy in a world fractured and turned upside down.

Conclusion

The Persistence of Fancy

I don't think that anyone reads anything with more than the most cursory utilitarian attention, let alone closely ponders any text as an aesthetic object, without loving it ("love" in this instance encompassing a full range of intense and irrational responses to texts, including the distinct pleasures of the "hate read"). It is surprising (though perhaps it should not be) how embarrassing, how threatening, it feels to make such an assertion, in an academic and political climate arguably even more constrained and hostile than that in which Eve Sedgwick wrote "Paranoid Reading and Reparative Reading: or, You're So Paranoid, You Probably Think This Introduction Is about You" (the Introduction to the collection *Novel Gazing: Queer Readings in Fiction*, in 1997). Sedgwick's essay intervenes on behalf of responses of readerly love and readerly need against a critical climate in which readerly suspicion, trained on anticipating and exposing systemic and historical violence, had come to seem "entirely coextensive with critical theoretical inquiry, rather than being viewed as one kind of cognitive/affective theoretical practice among other, alternative kinds."[1]

One of the things that has happened since 1997, which bears on the affective and methodological constraints felt by those of us who read and write and teach in the humanities, is the wholesale disinvestment and top-down imposition of austerity conditions in American colleges and universities (private and public) in the wake of the 2008 financial crisis. A set of decisions made over the past decade by state governments and university administrators have so profoundly restructured the conditions of teaching and learning as to amount to a politically self-inflicted version of what Naomi Klein calls "disaster capitalism"—that is, taking advantage of an adverse event to gut preexisting institutions and replace them with a new, radically privatized order that serves the interests of capital, rendering all labor precarious and making it difficult to impossible for those institutions to function as checks on capitalism's stratifying force.[2] The political denigration and destruction of spaces for full, nuanced, creative thinking and reading was underway long before 2008, of course; Sedgwick pled eloquently for such spaces her entire life.[3] But at this dark moment, when it can feel impossible to see any queer, circuitous route around, athwart, or beside paranoid reading's foregone conclusion that "things are bad and getting worse,"[4] the overarching affect in academia (including but not limited to the occupants of the *three quarters* of all instructional positions that are fixed term or part time, often paid by the course with no benefits or job security) is one of anxiety.[5]

In literary and cultural studies, these conditions have real methodological consequences. The rising demand (in higher education systems worldwide) to quantify and justify the market utility of our teaching and scholarship imposes the language, and the value system, of the science and technology sectors across the whole enterprise of higher learning. In the humanities, this means that instructors and scholars competing for increasingly scarce resources are incentivized to narrate what we do in terms of concrete solutions to practical problems, useful invention, and the production of verifiable new knowledge. These austerity-driven pressures dovetail in an unfortunate way with the best impulses of Marxist/materialist, feminist, and historicist scholarship to uncover and expose, via a hermeneutic of suspicion, the lived material and discursive conditions of specific places, times, and cultural contexts. One of the urgently needed things that can be reliably produced, and used to satisfy the proliferating institutional metrics of value and relevance, is concrete knowledge about how terrible things have been and how terrible things are.

Thus the habits of paranoid reading that Sedgwick described have morphed over the past two decades into what I call an anxiety of empiricism, a privileging of materialist and historicist narratives, with their causal explanations and deterministic shifts.[6] This is still a paranoid reading practice, one that attaches prestige to "exposing and problematizing" the hidden, violent structures conditioning the production of texts, cultural objects, and historical subjects, and to assessing how language voices (resists, or perpetuates) the ideological constraints of its moment.[7] But there is an additional kind of preemptive, anticipatory pain avoidance layered in to the current anxiety of empiricism in the humanities: a terrible alertness to the real, material, institutional, and professional dangers of being seen as "merely" literary—as being motivated, I think definitionally, by a dynamic of love (complex and ambivalent love, to be sure) and the seeking of pleasure, both as an end in itself and as an intrinsic element of knowledge production, in relation to texts. We are looking at a different version of the problem Sedgwick articulated in 1997: "The vocabulary for articulating any reader's reparative motive toward a text or a culture has long been so sappy, aestheticizing, defensive, anti-intellectual, or reactionary that it's no wonder few critics are willing to describe their acquaintances with such motives."[8]

It doesn't have to be this way. One of my reasons for writing this book has been to recenter the affective relations between readers and texts, not only to the discussion of where and how to define queerness, but also to how we theorize reading at all, particularly reading across historical distance and other vectors of difference. I want to revivify reading—its purposes and uses—at a moment when rearticulations of what the humanities can do are urgently needed. In this climate of political revanchism, both in the United States under the Trump administration and worldwide, the achievements of inclusion and citizenship wrought by a so-called modern, liberal era (from higher education for nonelites to reproductive and sexual autonomy) are revealed to be extremely fragile and under reversal. At this moment, my call to restore attention to love, identification, and other affective wounds and burdens in our teaching and scholarship is a call to turn *toward,* not away from, the complex politics and histories of interpretation. As Sedgwick says, it is not the case that reparative reading practices will yield a sunnier account of the brutal realities of the present: "In a world full of loss, pain, and oppression, both epistemologies are likely to be based on deep pessimism—the reparative motive of seeking pleasure, after all, arrives, by Klein's account, only with the achievement of a depressive position. But what each looks for—which is again to say, the motive each has *for looking*—is bound to differ widely. Of the two, however, it is only paranoid knowledge that has so thorough a practice of disavowing its affective motive and force, and masquerading as the very stuff of truth."[9] This disavowal is one of the reasons that I do not believe paranoid reading alone is doing, or will continue to do, the jobs—historical, political, or institutional—we have set for it.

Instead, we need a full reconsideration of the functions of critical love and desire, both in how we read and how we model techniques of reading. Sedgwick's radical claim is that in relation to literary and cultural texts, we are as Melanie Klein's infants, ingesting and incorporating fragments of others' psyches into ourselves. In reading, as in object relations more broadly, the reparative position is a hard-won achievement, that the infant or adult "only sometimes, and often only briefly, succeeds in inhabiting: this is the position from which it is possible in turn to use one's own resources to assemble or 'repair' the murderous part-objects into something like a whole—though not, and may I emphasize this, *not necessarily like any preexisting whole.* Once assembled to one's own specifications, the more satisfying object is available both to be identified with and to offer one nourishment and comfort in turn. Among Klein's names for the reparative process is love."[10] My aim in this book has been to reassemble the texts I have treated thus into new objects, *not necessarily like any preexisting whole,* in order to ask what new forms of nourishment they might have to offer, not only to me, but to others.

People use literature, particularly the literature of the Renaissance, in myriad ways. We perform it, teach it, identify with it, share it, marvel at its strangeness, and love it with a variety of messy, complicated, and not always logical passions. We analyze its form and style; and we read it as a record of material conditions, ideas, social structures, artistic practices, and sexualities, in all of the ways that sexualities leave traces. The histories we tell about sexuality— much like the colonial voyage histories and reports treated in the last chapter—contain an ambivalent mix of empiricism and fantasy, desire and loss, identification and alienation. They bear tacit affective loads about their own strategies of representation and interpretive frameworks, investing too much, reversing ends and means, and betraying pleasures and priorities that run athwart of their stated imperatives of knowledge production and political intervention. And, often, they are shot through with moments of queer recognition that confound the supposed conditions of historical and cultural difference. I submit that it is part of what Bruno Latour calls the delusion of a "modern critical stance," a fantasy of purification, to imagine that the writers of any history or theorizers of any literature (especially those of sexuality) today are entirely more objective, more enlightened, freer of biases and blindnesses, less powered by not-always-flattering desires and motives, than Jean de Léry, Thomas Harriot, or John White.[11] Nor should we hold the conditions of knowledge production in academia today separate from the projects of colonial conquest in which those writers were engaged; they're not. Describing the queerness in a culture without such a category is no less dense an object, no less temporally and epistemologically convoluted an undertaking than early modern projects of representation and description—and, at a fundamental level, just as impossible. That there can be no definitive, morally rehabilitating solution is not a reason to abandon the problem.

The method I have offered here is one possible approach. The previous chapters represent an attempt to use the artifacts of the past—texts that archive a complicated load of desires for transformation, instrumentality, lack, alterity, annihilation, and other objects less amenable to being put into words—to hone an affectively invested, reparative reading practice that can make visible new eruptions of erotic energy, mediated through word and image, in a text. But this particular book's project is by no means the only one to which this method can lend itself. My approach retheorizes the relationship between the past and the present, history and literary studies, readers and texts, desire and scholarship. It asks (and offers some answers toward) what *else,* besides mining and narrating the past, literature and literary criticism can contribute to the study of how the world works. How else can we use them? What else can they *do*? What can the desires we uncover in past archives do; what do they mean for readers, critics, teachers, artists, and activists in the present? To me, any rethinking of what literature is and does must take place through attending to the play of affect in literary form. *The Shapes of Fancy* is at its heart an inquiry into the complex systems of desire of which literature and reading are made. Valerie Traub has been eloquently teaching us for years that sex in any period or archive—very much including notions of what has been legible as "sex" to people in their own time and culture—has always been constructed by acts of reading.[12] Desire is obviously a matter for, and a practice of, interpretation. But what I have endeavored to explore here is the other side of the intrinsic link between reading and desiring: the idea that reading itself is a practice of desire.

We must make the case for the centrality of love and desire to the teaching, reading, and criticism of literature; and we must make it without apology, if we want to revitalize and sustain humanistic inquiry in colleges and universities. I think it is a grave mistake, born out of the paranoid defensive posture in which both literature and gender and sexuality studies departments find themselves at this moment of institutional and political threat, to think that empirical learning about past and present structural problems will furnish all of what our students need from texts and cultural objects—or that such a program of paranoid knowledge production will attract students, draw them in, or outfit them as thinkers, dreamers, and citizens with the energy to make the world they will need. "The monopolistic program of paranoid knowing," Sedgwick objects, "systematically disallows any explicit recourse to reparative motives, no sooner to be articulated than subject to methodical uprooting. Reparative motives, once they become explicit, are inadmissible within paranoid theory both because they are about pleasure ('merely aesthetic') and because they are frankly ameliorative ('merely reformist'). What makes pleasure and amelioration so 'mere'?"[13] I hear this as a call to reclaim some of the ground we are at risk of ceding in the humanities. There is *nothing mere* about pleasure and amelioration; they are two of the survival and world-making techniques that literature, and literature classrooms, are best equipped to offer.

University students today are brutally, intimately acquainted with structural violence: student loan debt; sexual assault; pathetically inadequate and expensive health care, including mental health care, for themselves and their family members; addiction; disenfranchisement; exploitative low-wage labor; the crushing contraction of their economic horizons in this upwardly redistributive economy; and the void where the state social safety net should be. I think of my public university students when Sedgwick rails against what makes pleasure and amelioration so "mere": "Only the exclusiveness of paranoia's faith in demystifying exposure: only its cruel and contemptuous assumption that the one thing lacking for global revolution, explosion of gender roles, or whatever, is people's (that is, *other* people's) having the painful effects of their oppression, poverty, or deludedness sufficiently exacerbated to make the pain conscious (as if otherwise it wouldn't have been) and intolerable (as if intolerable situations were famous for generating excellent solutions)."[14] My students are quite conscious of the pain they and their loved ones endure under capitalism and patriarchy. Without the tools to access pleasure in literary and aesthetic forms—to dismantle and ingest and worry about and feel heartbreak over texts; to love them with a demanding, depressive, reparative love—they are being systematically denied their full humanity. They will miss half of how the psyche creates a livable world, for it's only from the depressive position that one can extend resources to others in relations of ethics and care. And we as scholars and teachers will miss the chance to give what we uniquely can give them: the painstaking, rewarding practices that are the wellspring of human beings' capacity to imagine it could be otherwise. "Hope, often a fracturing, even a traumatic thing to experience, is among the energies by which the reparatively positioned reader tries to organize the fragments and part-objects she encounters or creates," says Sedgwick. "Because she has room to realize that the future may be different from the present, it is also possible for her to entertain such profoundly painful, profoundly relieving, ethically crucial possibilities as that the past, in turn, could have happened differently from the way it actually did."[15] I exist in a fairly constant state of rage, so badly do I want this for my students, even as institutional austerity-driven policies make it ever harder for them to access it, or for us to offer it.

Rita Felski's manifesto *The Uses of Literature* is helpful here in its insistence that making the case for the text as an object of desire *is* a theoretical undertaking, for "theory simply is the process of reflecting on the underlying frameworks, principles, and assumptions that shape our individual acts of interpretation."[16] In the pedagogy and reading practices that I am advocating for, readerly desire is not apart from this process of reflection; it is one among many kinds of meaning available to be theorized. Felski, in her recent work, including *The Uses of Literature* and *The Limits of Critique,* takes up and joins in Eve Sedgwick's project, begun in the 1990s, of thinking about alternatives to symptomatic reading practices that know in advance what they will uncover, arguing that criticism needs to be alert in a more capacious way to the needs and uses readers bring to literature.[17] (Even the words "criticism" and "critical reading" assume a totalizing hermeneutic of suspicion—and we don't have other words.) The questions that matter to students and nonspecialists—to the vast majority of readers—Felski says, and I agree, are the questions we can no longer afford to sidestep by holding up the production of historical knowledge *or* political critique as self-evidently sufficient goals, the questions that reveal the mysterious, always personal, and always political affective encounter between text and reader: "Why has this work been chosen for interpretation? How does it speak to me now? What is its value in the present?" And "What of its ability to traverse temporal boundaries, and to generate new and unanticipated resonances, including those that cannot be predicted by its original circumstances?"[18]

Some of the questions I have probed to these ends are about reception. Why have the erotic dynamics of this particular literary canon proven so irresistible as an object of speculation, identification, and interpretation across so many changing sexual regimes and material contexts? Why does the Renaissance persist, in popular cultural fantasy and academic inquiry, as a site of investment in the history of sex, love, and desire? There are many, important materialist answers to these questions, having to do with Shakespeare, Englishness, empire, class, and capital. But there is also something else—something that innumerable readers, past and present, have felt pulling them back, something recalcitrant and excessive that continues to resonate, weirdly and strongly, in all of the different contexts of reception it has found. *"The literary,"* Wai Chee Dimock ventures, "might refer to that which resonates for readers past, present, and future."[19] But—and this is the central mystery of the text in history—the "that which resonates" is not a kernel of meaning but "a relation, a form of engagement," substantively, constitutively in flux even as it keeps resonating, like a human being who somehow remains the same person even though most of their cells have died and regenerated. "For since readers past, present, and future are not the same reader, a text can remain literary only by not being the same text. It endures by being read differently."[20] One of the ways I would phrase an answer to this mystery is that "literature" is a space of affective experimentation, a chance to enter into the pleasures and problems of identification and other weighty affects. To be in spaces where texts and reading, sex and desire are discussed requires a particularly intense kind of attention and affective labor. But there is an urgent need for it, and that need, like sexuality, isn't going anywhere. Unapologetically centering erotic desire, the "subject of universal interest" that often consumes students no matter what or how anyone is teaching them, is a winning pedagogical and critical strategy because it is *honest* about how both reading and the world work. The exciting task before us, then, is to channel the force of readerly desires and investments—our own and others'—to assemble, out of this world's flawed, inviting, unstable textual objects, the most nuanced, plentitudinous, resourceful, resonant histories—and futures—imaginable.

Such radical ambitions, I believe, are only realized by paying deep attention to very small details. Several years ago, there was a blizzard in New York City a few days before Christmas that half shut down the city. With holiday flights canceled and out-of-town visitors unexpectedly stranded sleeping on our floors, my little extended family of friends went walking in Riverside Park. On our way home, the snow was drifted up inches thick, pristine, in the ledges and recessed corners of the marble colonnades on the old apartment buildings of the Upper West Side. Passing one facade where drifted snow piled around the base of a column right at eye level, I took off my glove and gently shoved my four fingers, horizontally and only up to the knuckle, into the light diamond-white unpacked powder, so that four perfect little holes were left in the snowdrift. Then I looked a few feet over, and saw that someone else, unknown to me, had pressed their fingers into the snow in the exact same, careful way. I had stuck my fingers in the snow like that before, on reflection; it was something I did occasionally (I do it still in honor of this memory). But it was an urge that, until that moment, I had not conceived of *as* a predilection, as an urge that could be consummated, or not, and then described as a thing some people want to do. Suddenly, here, in the last place I would go looking for shared desire—in a spot that would seem utterly inconsequential to expressions of desire—I was surprised with evidence, anonymous and ephemeral, that one other person alive on that street on that day shared my predilection, making it visible to me as a desire for the first time. If I had passed by hours later, the wind would already have blown the evidence away. Such surprising resonances, unexpectedly connecting one moment in time to another, revealing things that no one, perhaps, was looking for until they are made visible by an act of queer grace, are what I have tried to capture in this book.

Acknowledgments

This book, like all life, comes into being via a thick web of energies, cares, and desires. The process of finishing it has brought home to me how fully we are nodes in networks of relation that condition who survives and who thrives, and how deeply beholden we are to others in every way, at every level. First thanks must go to Jean Howard, Julie Crawford, and Alan Stewart, all of Columbia University, for the painstaking work of shepherding this project, and me, through the rough formative stages. Mario DiGangi and Kim F. Hall offered revolutionary feedback.

It would never have been a book at all, however, without the interest, enthusiasm, and vote of confidence of Douglas Armato at the University of Minnesota Press. My debts to him and to everyone else who worked on the book are profound. I am deeply grateful to Kathryn Schwarz, Karl Steel, and Holly Dugan for their incredibly charitable and rigorous reviews, which helped to give the project its final shape. Samuel Wylie at the Huntington Library and Ian Graham at the John Carter Brown Library were extremely helpful with images, and Doug Easton prepared the index.

I owe tremendous gratitude to my teachers, every one of whose ethical and methodological insights are visible in these pages: Ian Baucom, Sarah Beckwith, Tom Ferraro, Maureen Quilligan, Jan Radway, Tom Robisheaux, Marc Schachter, and Laurie Shannon at Duke University; Wes Williams at Oxford; and Jenny Davidson, Erik Gray, Molly Murray, and Elizabeth Povinelli at Columbia. I was supported during my time at Columbia by the Andrew W. Mellon Graduate Fellowship in Humanistic Studies, and by the Harry S. Truman Scholarship, which in 2001 generously and convictingly defined my proposed career path as a professor of English literature and gender and sexuality studies as public service, a designation I strive to uphold.

In navigating the early years of an academic career, I have been privileged to benefit from the mentorship and advice—and the sterling scholarly and collegial examples—of Jeffrey Jerome Cohen, Carolyn Dinshaw, Elizabeth Freeman, Stephen Guy-Bray, and Jeffrey Masten. My life as a scholar has been vitally enriched and molded by my friendships with a merry band of colleagues in my field. Beloved Shakes-queers, some of whom I have been having this conversation with for a decade now, include Jim Bromley, Simone Chess, Drew Daniel, Will Fisher, Ari Friedlander, John Garrison, Anna Klosowska, Vin Nardizzi, David Orvis, Ryan Singh Paul, Nicholas Radel, Melissa Sanchez, John Staines, Goran Stanivukovic, and Will Stockton. I also thank my brilliant, kind, and generous early modernist friends Patricia Akhimie, Liza Blake, Urvashi Chakravarty, Adhaar Desai, Jean Feerick, Katherine Gillen, Miles Parks Grier, Wendy Beth Hyman, Miriam Jacobson, Shannon E. Kelley, Justin Kolb, Steve Mentz, Tripthi Pillai, Katie Vomero Santos, Emily Shortslef, and Julian Yates.

For invaluable feedback on sections of this project as it took shape, I am grateful to Carla Mazzio, Valerie Wayne, and Cynthia Wu. I benefited greatly from workshopping portions of it at Columbia University's Early Modern Colloquium, at the University at Buffalo Humanities Institute's New Faculty Seminar series, and in the works-in-progress talks of Buffalo's early modern and queer studies research workshops.

At the University at Buffalo (SUNY), I am deeply grateful to all of my colleagues in the new Department of Global Gender and Sexuality Studies for the life-changing work we are doing together. The mentorship of Carine Mardorossian, Marla Segol, and especially Gwynn Thomas makes my career possible in a very real way. We have all been held afloat by the support, knowledge, and labor of Karen Cleary, Karen Reinard, and Caitlynn Strong.

At Buffalo, I am extremely fortunate to be represented by the Union of University Professionals. I thank them for the NYS/UUP Dr. Nuala McGann Drescher Affirmative Action/Diversity Leave, which they granted me in order to complete this book. I am grateful for the University at Buffalo's support of this book's publication through the Julian Park Fund of the College of Arts and Sciences and through the Toward an Open Monograph Ecosystem (TOME) initiative. I am sustained by the support and intellectual community of wonderful colleagues at Buffalo, most of all Barbara and Jim Bono, Carrie Bramen, David Castillo, Keith Griffler, Graham Hammill, Jim Holstun, Jonathan D. Katz, Arabella Lyon, Carla Mazzio, Stephen Miller, Carl Nightingale, Elizabeth Otto, Randy Schiff, and Ewa Ziarek. And I could not live without the solidarity and mutual aid, past and present, of Dave and Katie Alff, Stephanie Clare, Lindsay Brandon Hunter, Theresa McCarthy, Alyssa Mt. Pleasant, Dalia Muller, Theresa Runstedler, Paige Sarlin, LaKisha Simmons, Camilo Trumper, Jasmina Tumbas, Jang Wook-Huh, and Cindy Wu. Sarah Kolberg's labor has made many things possible. My students, particularly Seth Arico, Anne Marie Butler, and Julien Fischer, are an inspiration, and it is an honor to work with them. I have also been awed and energized by Ana Grujić, Adrienne Hill, and the other brilliant grassroots queer historians of the Buffalo–Niagara LGBTQ History Project, for their revolutionary embodied historiography, and their cultivation of a living, speaking, dancing archive of queer desires resonating through space and time on the streets of Buffalo.

For opening their homes and providing shelter and hospitality for conference-going, research, and writing, I am grateful to Casey Black and Sarah Irvin, Pearl Brilmeyer, Helen Estabrook, Aileen Gien, Peter Hughes and Britt Welter-Nolan, Amber Musser, Tim Portice, Peter Tsapatsaris, Anna Rubbo, Santiago Taussig-Moore and the whole Taussig-Rubbo family, my oldest best friend Devon Wesley-Whelan, and—though this book will absolutely not sell as many copies as the book he wrote while crashing at my house—Graham Moore.

For their love and solidarity I thank Barbara Andersen, Veronica Davidov, and Anjuli Raza Kolb. For the friendships in which we grew up together, I thank Alexis Blane, Juliet Pulliam, Desi Waters, and Katy Wischow. For my intellectual formation and my very survival, in graduate school and still, I thank Alice Boone, Jen Buckley, Musa Gurnis, Adam Hooks, John Kuhn, and Atticus Zavaletta. And for being my family, my sustenance, I am unspeakably grateful to Jessica Barnett-Moseley, Anya Bernstein, Michael Boucai, Nick Day, Armando Mastrogiovanni, Brian Moseley, Yuki Numata Resnick, Kyle Resnick, Leeore Schnairsohn, and Mateo Taussig-Rubbo.

Abigail Joseph is my collaborator in this project on much more than the pages where she's cited—my co-creator of a home, a life, and a universe of ideas, aesthetics, and values that made me the person who could write this book.

I am humbled by the love of Peggy Brockman Varnado, Carey and Sharon Varnado, Paul Varnado, Scott Varnado, Lauren Worsek, Charly du Bois, and the scruffy and faithful Darla. Above all, it is my enormous privilege to share this life's adventures, burdens, and overwhelming joys with Tony O'Rourke.

The long and not uncomplicated effort to conceive, gestate, and birth this book overlapped substantially in time with another long and fraught generative effort, miraculously resulting in the birth of Ardis Marie. She came into the world a desiring machine, and this book is dedicated to her. May she ever invent new shapes of fancy and new ways of being alive.

Notes

Introduction

1 John Aubrey, *Brief Lives*, ed. Andrew Clark, 2 vols. (Oxford: Clarendon Press, 1898), 1:95–96, quoted in Jeffrey Masten, *Textual Intercourse: Collaboration, Authorship, and Sexualities in Renaissance Drama* (Cambridge: Cambridge University Press, 1997), 61.

2 Francis Beaumont and John Fletcher, *Philaster, or Love Lies a-Bleeding*, Arden Early Modern Drama edition, ed. Suzanne Gossett (London: Methuen Drama, 2009), 1.2.140.

3 Eve Kosofsky Sedgwick, "Foreword: T Times," in *Tendencies* (Durham, N.C.: Duke University Press, 1993), xii.

4 On the reanimation of "queer" as a reclaimed slur with the potential to affect and animate things and events in the world, setting matter in motion in new ways, see Mel Y. Chen, *Animacies: Biopolitics, Racial Mattering, and Queer Affect* (Durham, N.C.: Duke University Press, 2012), chapter 2, "Queer Animation," 57–88.

5 See Valerie Traub, *The Renaissance of Lesbianism in Early Modern England* (Cambridge: Cambridge University Press, 2002); Mario DiGangi, *The Homoerotics of Early Modern Drama* (Cambridge: Cambridge University Press, 1997); Bruce R. Smith, *Homosexual Desire in Shakespeare's England: A Cultural Poetics* (Chicago: University of Chicago Press, 1994); the essays in *Queering the Renaissance*, ed. Jonathan Goldberg (Durham, N.C.: Duke University Press, 1993); and, foundationally, Alan Bray, *Homosexuality in Renaissance England* (London: Gay Men's Press), 1982.

6 On homosocial relations within the structures of patriarchy, see Julie Crawford, "The Place of the Cousin in *As You Like It*," *Shakespeare Quarterly* 69, no. 2 (2018): 101–27, and "All's Well That Ends Well: Or Is Marriage Always Already Heterosexual?," in *Shakesqueer: A Queer Companion to the Complete Works of Shakespeare*, ed. Madhavi Menon (Durham, N.C.: Duke University Press, 2011), 39–47. On erotic

power dynamics, see Melissa Sanchez, *Erotic Subjects: The Sexuality of Politics in Early Modern English Literature* (Oxford: Oxford University Press, 2011); and Alan Bray, "Homosexuality and the Signs of Male Friendship in Elizabethan England," *History Workshop* 29 (1990): 1–19.

7   James M. Bromley, *Intimacy and Sexuality in the Age of Shakespeare* (Cambridge: Cambridge University Press, 2012); and Jonathan Goldberg, *Sodometries: Renaissance Texts, Modern Sexualities* (Stanford, Calif.: Stanford University Press, 1992). The foundational work navigating this tension between "normal" and "deviant" early modern sexualities is Bray, *Homosexuality.*

8   Carla Freccero, "Queer Times," in "After Sex? On Writing since Queer Theory," ed. Janet Halley and Andrew Parker, special issue, *South Atlantic Quarterly* 106, no. 3 (2007): 485.

9   David Halperin, *How to do the History of Homosexuality* (Chicago: University of Chicago Press, 2002), and *One Hundred Years of Homosexuality* (New York: Routledge, 1990); Goldberg, *Sodometries*; and Bray, *Homosexuality.*

10   Eve Kosofsky Sedgwick, introduction to *Touching Feeling: Affect, Pedagogy, Performativity* (Durham, N.C.: Duke University Press, 2003), 10.

11   Adam Philips, *Unforbidden Pleasures* (New York: Farrar, Straus and Giroux, 2015).

12   This claim is indebted to the work of Shoshana Felman and Peter Brooks in developing a formally attuned psychoanalytic criticism. See Peter Brooks, *Reading for the Plot: Design and Intention in Narrative* (Cambridge, Mass.: Harvard University Press, 1982); and Shoshana Felman, ed., *Literature and Psychoanalysis: The Question of Reading: Otherwise* (Baltimore, Md.: Johns Hopkins University Press, 1977). However, their archive skews toward the Victorian-to-modern period and toward the novel. Among the smaller number of early modern works using psychoanalytic terms to analyze language and form, to which this book is indebted, are: Madhavi Menon, *Wanton Words: Rhetoric and Sexuality in English Renaissance Drama* (Toronto: University of Toronto Press, 2004); Graham L. Hammill, *Sexuality and Form: Caravaggio, Marlowe, and Bacon* (Chicago: University of Chicago Press, 2000); and Valerie Traub, *Desire and Anxiety: Circulations of Sexuality in Shakespearean Drama* (London: Routledge, 1992).

13   Peter Brooks, "Narrative Desire," *Style* 18, no. 3 (1984): 312–27.

14   I explore this question in depth in a previous essay. See Christine Varnado, "'Invisible Sex!': What Looks Like the Act in Early Modern Drama?," in *Sex before Sex: Figuring the Act in Early Modern England,* ed. James M. Bromley and Will Stockton (Minneapolis: University of Minnesota Press, 2013), 25–52.

15   Gilles Deleuze and Félix Guattari, *A Thousand Plateaus: Capitalism*

and *Schizophrenia,* trans. Brian Massumi (Minneapolis: University of Minnesota Press, 1987); Teresa Brennan, *The Transmission of Affect* (Ithaca, N.Y.: Cornell University Press, 2004); on models of embodiment in Deleuze, Guattari, and Spinoza, see Brian Massumi, *Parables for the Virtual: Movement, Affect, Sensation* (Durham, N.C.: Duke University Press, 2002).

16 Sedgwick, *Touching Feeling,* and *Shame and Its Sisters: A Silvan Tomkins Reader,* ed. Eve Kosofsky Sedgwick and Adam Frank (Durham, N.C.: Duke University Press, 1995). Heather Love, *Feeling Backward: Loss and the Politics of Queer History* (Cambridge, Mass.: Harvard University Press, 2007); Lauren Berlant, "Starved" and Ann Cvetkovich, "Public Feelings," in Halley and Parker, "After Sex?," 433–44 and 459–68; and Ann Cvetkovich, *An Archive of Feelings: Trauma, Sexuality and Lesbian Public Cultures* (Durham, N.C.: Duke University Press, 2003).

17 Gail Kern Paster, *Humoring the Body: Emotions and the Shakespearean Stage* (Chicago: Chicago University Press, 2004). See also Lesel Dawson, *Lovesickness and Gender in Early Modern English Literature* (Oxford: Oxford University Press, 2008); the essays in Gail Kern Paster, Katherine Rowe, and Mary Floyd-Wilson, eds., *Reading the Early Modern Passions: Essays in the Cultural History of Emotion* (Philadelphia: University of Pennsylvania Press, 2004); and Katharine Eisaman Maus, *Inwardness and Theater in the English Renaissance* (Chicago: University of Chicago Press, 1995).

18 A variety of other approaches now being pursued at the nexus of affect studies and early modern literature are represented in Amanda Bailey and Mario DiGangi, eds., *Affect Theory and Early Modern Texts: Politics, Ecologies, Form* (New York: Palgrave, 2017).

19 In addition to Bray, *Homosexuality*; Goldberg, *Sodometries*; and Smith, *Homosexual Desire,* see also Gregory W. Bredbeck, *Sodomy and Interpretation: Marlowe to Milton* (Ithaca, N.Y.: Cornell University Press, 1991).

20 Valerie Traub, "Friendship's Loss: Alan Bray's Making of History," in *Thinking Sex with the Early Moderns* (Philadelphia: University of Pennsylvania Press, 2016), 37–56, 154.

21 On the contrary, this book is deeply indebted to the wealth of recent queer early modern scholarship on the social significance (or insignificance) of erotic acts, particularly Will Fisher, "The Erotics of Chin-Chucking in Seventeenth-Century England," in Bromley and Stockton, *Sex before Sex,* 141–69; Bromley, *Intimacy*; Mario DiGangi, *Sexual Types: Embodiment, Agency, and Dramatic Character from Shakespeare to Shirley* (Philadelphia: University of Pennsylvania Press, 2011); and Daniel Juan Gil, *Before Intimacy: Asocial Sexuality in Early Modern England* (Minneapolis: University of Minnesota Press, 2005).

22 Eve Kosofsky Sedgwick, "Introduction: Axiomatic," in *Epistemology of the Closet* (Berkeley: University of California Press, 1990), 48.

23 Chen, *Animacies,* 2. The posthuman or ontological turn is represented in premodern literary studies by the work of Jeffrey Jerome Cohen, Eileen Joy, Stephen Mentz, Vin Nardizzi, and Julian Yates, among others. See the essays in Jeffrey Jerome Cohen's edited collection *Animal, Vegetable, Mineral: Ethics and Objects* (Washington, D.C.: Oliphaunt Books, 2012).

24 Chen, *Animacies*; Karen Barad, "Nature's Queer Performativity," *Qui Parle: Critical Humanities and Social Sciences* 19, no. 2 (2011): 121–58; and Jane Bennett, *Vibrant Matter: A Political Ecology of Things* (Durham, N.C.: Duke University Press, 2010).

25 Much of the extant work on early modern material culture investigates the historical meanings of objects as they bear on subjects and practices in the period, often with a focus on contemporary religious, economic, and social suspicions about the efficacies of made things. Will Fisher details material objects' construction of sexuality and gender in *Materializing Gender in Early Modern English Literature and Culture* (Cambridge: Cambridge University Press, 2006). See also Ann Rosalind Jones and Peter Stallybrass, *Renaissance Clothing and the Materials of Memory* (Cambridge: Cambridge University Press, 2000).

26 One important ancestor text is the anonymous 1990 pamphlet, published by Queer Nation and handed out on the street at the New York City Pride March, "Queers Read This (I Hate Straights)." The pamphlet's legacy was recently explored in Ramzi Fawaz and Shanté Paradigm Smalls, eds., "Queers Read This! LGBTQ Literature Now," special issue, *GLQ* 24, no. 2–3 (2018).

27 Deleuze and Guattari, *A Thousand Plateaus,* 10.

28 Sedgwick, *Epistemology,* 25.

29 Sedgwick, *Epistemology,* 11.

30 Maggie Nelson, *The Argonauts* (Minneapolis: Graywolf Press, 2015), 62.

31 Nelson, *Argonauts,* 62.

32 Sedgwick, *Epistemology,* 24.

33 Sedgwick, *Epistemology,* 22.

34 Sedgwick, *Epistemology,* 22.

35 Sedgwick, *Epistemology,* 23.

36 Sedgwick, *Epistemology,* 24.

37 See Christopher Pye, *The Vanishing: Shakespeare, the Subject, and Early Modern Culture* (Durham, N.C.: Duke University Press, 2000); Carla Mazzio and Douglas Trevor, eds., *Historicism, Psychoanalysis, and Early Modern Culture* (New York: Routledge, 2000); and Maus, *Inwardness and Theater.*

38 A major origin point of this anxiety is Stephen Greenblatt's "Psycho-

analysis and Renaissance Culture," in *Literary Theory/Renaissance Texts,* ed. Patricia Parker and David Quint (Baltimore, Md.: Johns Hopkins University Press, 1986), 210–24.

39 The question of what, if anything, is outside of "sex" is probed deeply in Halley and Parker's introduction to "After Sex?," 421–32. This point is particularly well made in the assertion by Joseph Litvak, "Glad to Be Unhappy," 526, that queer theory "lodges the 'nonsexual' firmly within the 'sexual.'"

40 Elizabeth Freeman, "Still After," in Halley and Parker, "After Sex?," 499.

41 This received narrative can be traced to Freud's particularly enduring explication of *Hamlet* in *The Interpretation of Dreams,* trans. James Strachey (New York: Basic Books, 1955).

42 Jonathan Dollimore, *Sexual Dissidence: Augustine to Wilde, Freud to Foucault* (Oxford: Clarendon Press, 1991), 179.

43 Nelson, *Argonauts,* 62. See also Philips, *Unforbidden Pleasures*; and Eve Kosofsky Sedgwick, "Melanie Klein and the Difference Affect Makes," in Halley and Parker, "After Sex?," 625–44.

44 Sedgwick, "Melanie Klein," 629.

45 Meira Likierman, *Melanie Klein: Her Work in Context* (London: Continuum, 2002), 55, quoted in Sedgwick, "Melanie Klein," 628.

46 Sedgwick, "Melanie Klein," 629.

47 Sedgwick, "Melanie Klein," 629.

48 Wai Chee Dimock, "A Theory of Resonance," *PMLA* 12, no. 5 (1997): 1061.

49 Dimock, "Theory of Resonance," 1060–61.

50 Sedgwick, *Epistemology,* 23.

51 See Varnado, "Invisible Sex!," 29.

52 One of my most influential methodological touchstones in attempting such a fantasmatic, queer historiography is Carla Freccero, *Queer/Early/Modern* (Durham, N.C.: Duke University Press, 2006).

53 Citations from *The Antipodes* are from the Globe Quartos edition, ed. David Scott Kastan and Richard Proudfoot (London: Nick Hern Books, 2000), hereafter cited by act, scene, and line number in the text.

54 Dimock, "Theory of Resonance," 1060–65.

55 See the MLA "Forum: Conference Debates" panel featuring Robert Caserio, Tim Dean, Lee Edelman, Jack Halberstam, and José Esteban Muñoz and entitled "The Antisocial Thesis in Queer Theory," *PMLA* 121, no. 3 (2006): 819–28. See also Lee Edelman, *No Future: Queer Theory and the Death Drive* (Durham, N.C.: Duke University Press, 2004); and Leo Bersani, *Homos* (Cambridge, Mass.: Harvard University Press, 1995), and "Is the Rectum a Grave?" *October* 43 (1987): 197–222.

56 Ann Cvetkovich, *Depression: A Public Feeling* (Durham, N.C.: Duke

University Press, 2012); Jack Halberstam, *The Queer Art of Failure* (Durham, N.C.: Duke University Press, 2011); Lauren Berlant, *Cruel Optimism* (Durham, N.C.: Duke University Press, 2011), and "Starved"; and Love, *Feeling Backward.*

57 José Esteban Muñoz, *Cruising Utopia: The Then and There of Queer Futurity* (New York: New York University Press, 2009), 1.

58 Carolyn Dinshaw, *Getting Medieval: Sexualities and Communities, Pre- and Postmodern* (Durham, N.C.: Duke University Press, 1999), 1.

59 Dinshaw, *Getting Medieval,* 11–12.

60 Sedgwick, *Epistemology,* 156.

61 Wolfgang Iser, *The Act of Reading: A Theory of Aesthetic Response* (Baltimore, Md.: Johns Hopkins University Press, 1980), 166-167.

62 Roland Barthes, *S/Z,* trans. Richard Miller (New York: Hill and Wang, 1974), 10.

63 Julia Kristeva, "Word, Dialogue, and Novel," in *The Kristeva Reader,* ed. Toril Moi (New York: Columbia University Press, 1986), 37; see also Barthes, *S/Z,* 20.

64 Barthes, *S/Z,* 16.

65 Eve Kosofsky Sedgwick, "Paranoid Reading and Reparative Reading; or, You're So Paranoid, You Probably Think This Introduction Is About You," in *Novel Gazing: Queer Readings in Fiction* (Durham, N.C.: Duke University Press, 1997), 2–3.

66 Sedgwick, "Paranoid Reading," 27–28.

67 Heidi Brayman traces the uneven and incomplete representation of reading as a supposedly solitary activity, which was nevertheless still communal in practice, in *Reading Material in Early Modern England: Print, Gender, and Literacy* (Cambridge: Cambridge University Press, 2005). See also Pamela Allen Brown, *Better a Shrew than a Sheep* (Ithaca, N.Y.: Cornell University Press, 2003); and Adam Fox, *Oral and Literature Culture in England, 1500–1700* (Oxford: Oxford University Press, 2000).

68 William Shakespeare, *Twelfth Night, or What You Will,* 1.1.1. All Shakespeare citations are by act, scene, and line number from *The Norton Shakespeare,* 3rd ed., ed. Stephen Greenblatt, Walter Cohen, Jean E. Howard, Katharine Eisaman Maus, Gordon McMullan, and Suzanne Gossett (New York: Norton, 2015), hereafter cited parenthetically in the text.

69 Stuart Hall, "Notes on Deconstructing the Popular," in *Cultural Theory and Popular Culture: A Reader,* ed. John Storey (Harlow, U.K.: Pearson/Prentice Hall, 1998), 442–53.

70 Iser, *Act of Reading,* 169-70.

71 Shoshana Felman, "Turning the Screw of Interpretation," in Felman, *Literature and Psychoanalysis,* 126.

72 The inherent collectivity of early modern theatrical process is empha-

sized in some important recent work on theater history, notably the essays collected in Henry Turner, ed., *Early Modern Theatricality* (Oxford: Oxford University Press, 2014); and Holger Schott Syme, *Theatre and Testimony in Shakespeare's England: A Culture of Mediation* (Cambridge: Cambridge University Press, 2012).

73 Keir Elam, *The Semiotics of Theatre and Drama* (London: Metheuen, 1980), 93.

74 Elam, *Semiotics*, 94.

75 Elam, *Semiotics*, 95.

76 Greenblatt elaborates on his methodological debt to Geertz in "The Touch of the Real," in "The Fate of 'Culture': Geertz and Beyond," special issue, *Representations* 59 (1997): 14–29.

77 Johannes Fabian, *Time and the Other: How Anthropology Makes Its Object* (New York: Columbia University Press, 2002).

78 Louise Fradenburg and Carla Freccero coined the influential axis of oscillation between identification and alterity in "Introduction: Caxton, Foucault, and the Pleasures of History," in *Premodern Sexualities* (New York: Routledge, 1996), particularly xv–xx. This tension is further elaborated in Jonathan Goldberg's and Madhavi Menon's methodological intervention in "Queering History," *PMLA* 120, no. 5 (2005): 1608–17.

79 In recent contributions, scholars have taken a wide range of theoretical positions on this question: radical anti-identitarian universalism (Madhavi Menon, Lee Edelman); a recuperation of historicism and how to do history (Valerie Traub); new theorizations of knowledge production (Valerie Traub, Jeffrey Masten, Carla Freccero, Heather Love); a turn from straightforwardly sexual subjects to ecological and biological matters (Carolyn Dinshaw, Stephen Guy-Bray, Vin Nardizzi); and several new investigations of sexuality (Melissa Sanchez, James Bromley, Will Stockton, Will Fisher), which take as their objects of analysis various aspects of embodiment, pleasure, gender, and relationality. For an excellent summary and analysis of the theoretical claims and conflicts shaping this debate, see Ari Friedlander, "Desiring History and Historicizing Desire," *Journal for Early Modern Cultural Studies* 16, no. 2 (2016): 1–20.

80 This is the formulation Bruno Latour uses to describe the inextricable identity of these two processes of knowledge production in *We Have Never Been Modern*, trans. Catherine Porter (Cambridge, Mass.: Harvard University Press, 1993), 5.

81 The turn toward studies of temporality in queer theory is subjected to a thoughtful exchange among Carolyn Dinshaw, Lee Edelman, Roderick A. Ferguson, Carla Freccero, Elizabeth Freeman, Jack Halberstam, Annemarie Jagose, Christopher Nealon, and Nguyen Tan Hoang, in "Theorizing Queer Temporalities: A Roundtable Discussion," in

"Queer Temporalities," ed. Elizabeth Freeman, special issue, *GLQ* 13, no. 2–3 (2007): 177–95.

82 This idea is suggested in Fradenburg and Freccero, "Introduction: Caxton, Foucault, and the Pleasures of History," xx. See also Freccero, *Queer/Early/Modern*; and Dinshaw, *Getting Medieval.*

83 See Jacques Derrida, *Specters of Marx: The State of the Debt, the Work of Mourning, and the New International,* trans. Peggy Kamuf (New York: Routledge, 1994), 29.

84 Derrida, *Specters of Marx,* 18.

85 Jack Halberstam, *In a Queer Time and Place: Transgender Bodies, Subcultural Lives* (New York: New York University Press, 2005); Love, *Feeling Backward.*

86 William Faulkner, *Requiem for a Nun* (1951; reprint, New York: Vintage Books, 2011), 69.

87 Sedgwick, *Epistemology,* 46–47.

88 Latour, *We Have Never Been Modern,* 72–75.

89 Elizabeth Freeman, *Time Binds: Queer Temporalities, Queer Histories* (Durham, N.C.: Duke University Press, 2010).

90 Jonathan Goldberg, "After Thoughts," in Halley and Parker, "After Sex?," 503. This idea is picked up in other criticism, including Goldberg and Menon, "Queering History," in which they call for recovering same-sex eroticisms of the past to illuminate "the non-self-identical nonpresent" rather than reifying present or past identities (1609). See also Freccero, "Queer Times," 486–89, and *Queer/Early/Modern,* 69–72.

91 Sedgwick, *Epistemology,* 45.

92 Sedgwick, *Epistemology,* 52, breaks down the myriad ways in which homoerotic feelings, language, and acts of the past are adjudicated "completely meaningless" under a heteronormative reading practice: either because it was everywhere, because there was no language for it, because it was so forbidden, or because there were no prohibitions against it.

93 Dimock, "Theory of Resonance," 1061.

94 Dimock, "Theory of Resonance," 1061.

95 Latour, *We Have Never Been Modern,* 3.

96 See Varnado, "Invisible Sex!," 47.

97 Sedgwick, *Epistemology,* 8.

98 The still-definitive work on the structure and referents of the play's satire is itself an artifact from the intervening "thick modernity" of the twentieth century: Joe Lee Davis, "Richard Brome's Neglected Contribution to Comic Theory," *Studies in Philology* 40, no. 4 (1943): 520–28.

99 See Musa Gurnis, *Mixed Faith and Shared Feeling: Theater in Post-Reformation London* (Philadelphia: University of Pennsylvania Press, 2018).

100 Sedgwick, "Paranoid Reading," 22.
101 Valerie Rohy, "Ahistorical," in *GLQ: A Journal of Lesbian and Gay Studies* 12, no. 1 (2006): 71.
102 Though he would not use the term "queer," Ira Clark's reading of *The Antipodes* in *Professional Playwrights: Massinger, Ford, Shirley, and Brome* (Lexington: University Press of Kentucky, 1992) has informed my analysis of the disunified, shifting, and unresolved political and dramatic structure of the play.
103 Valerie Traub, "The Joys of Martha Joyless: Queer Pedagogy and the (Early Modern) Production of Sexual Knowledge," in *Thinking Sex with the Early Moderns* (Philadelphia: University of Pennsylvania Press, 2015), 103–24.
104 Sedgwick, "Paranoid Reading," 8.
105 See Laura Gowing, *Common Bodies: Women, Touch, and Power in Seventeenth-Century England* (New Haven, Conn.: Yale University Press, 2003).
106 Traub, "Joys of Martha Joyless," 109.
107 As I explain in more detail in chapter 1, Mary Frith (or Moll) and Bellario (or Euphrasia) are more accurately described as genderqueer or on the transmasculine spectrum than as cross-dressed women; their masculine yet androgynous gender performance does not line up with their ostensibly female sex, and unlike the female heroines who temporarily disguise themselves as boys in *Twelfth Night* or *As You Like It*, their genital anatomy is actually unknown or confused in the play, even from the audience's perspective.
108 Bersani, in "Is the Rectum a Grave?," elaborates on the solipsistic nature of both subjectivity and sexuality in his queer and deconstructive reading of psychoanalytic theories of sexual development, specifically in his deprivileging of the partner relation and his reclamation of primal, antirelational narcissism.
109 Dimock, "Theory of Resonance," 1060–61.
110 I am thinking here of Lauren Berlant and Michael Warner, "What Does Queer Theory Teach Us about X?," *PMLA* 10 (1995): 343–49; and Eve Kosofsky Sedgwick, "Queer and Now," in *Tendencies* (Durham, N.C.: Duke University Press, 1993), 1–20.
111 A related intervention, dedicated to complicating the usually assumed opposition between queer and normativity by renewing the historical specificity and nuance of normalization, is undertaken in Robyn Wiegman and Elizabeth Wilson, eds., "Queer Theory without Antinormativity," special issue, *differences* 26, no. 1 (2015).
112 See André Gide, *Oscar Wilde*, trans. Bernard Frechtman (London: William Kimber, 1951), on his encounter with the "marvellous youth" he calls "Mohammed" in Algiers, for only one example (280–85, quoted in Dollimore, *Sexual Dissidence*, 5–6).

113 Halberstam, *In a Queer Time and Place*, 157–58.

114 Sedgwick, *Epistemology*, 91–97 (on *Billy Budd*), and 242–46 (on Mc-Carthyism and the outing of homophobes).

115 Jasbir Puar, *Terrorist Assemblages: Homonationalism in Queer Times* (Durham, N.C.: Duke University Press, 2007).

116 See Frantz Fanon, *Black Skin, White Masks*, trans. Charles Lam Markmann (New York: Grove Press, 1991); and Homi Bhabha, *The Location of Culture* (New York: Routledge, 1994).

1. Getting Used, and Liking It

1 As befits an argument about the work of Beaumont and Fletcher, I am indebted to a collaborator, Abigail Joseph, who in 2006 pointed out Bellario's function as a technology for the communication of affect.

2 "There was a wonderfull consimility of phansey between [Francis Beaumont] and Mr. John Fletcher, which caused the dearnesse of friendship between them. . . . They lived together on the Banke side, not far from the Play-house, both batchelors; lay together—from Sir John Hales, etc.; had one wench in the house between them, which they did so admire; the same cloathes and cloake, &c., betweene them." Aubrey, *Brief Lives*, 1:95–96, in Masten, *Textual Intercourse*, 61. On identification, friendship, and homoeroticism in Beaumont and Fletcher's collaboration (and in early modern literary collaboration as a whole), see Masten, *Textual Intercourse*, esp. chaps. 1 and 2. See also Masten, "My Two Dads: Collaboration and the Reproduction of Beaumont and Fletcher," in Goldberg, *Queering the Renaissance*, 280–309; and Masten, "Beaumont and/or Fletcher: Collaboration and the Interpretation of Renaissance Drama," *ELH* 59 (1992): 337–56.

3 Aubrey, *Brief Lives*, 1:96, in Masten, *Textual Intercourse*, 61.

4 There are a few exceptions; three affectively motivated readings of the play, which nonetheless examine feeling in the service of their respective historical arguments, are: Jeffrey Masten, "Editing Boys: The Performance of Genders in Print," in *From Performance to Print in Shakespeare's England*, ed. Peter Holland and Stephen Orgel (New York: Palgrave, 2007), 113–34; Denise Whalen, "Anxiously Emergent Lesbian Erotics," in *Constructions of Female Homoeroticism in Early Modern Drama* (New York: Palgrave Macmillan, 2005), 83–85—although I disagree with Whalen's conclusion that the "frail waif" or "retiring virgin" is the operative homoerotic type for Bellario; and Jo E. Miller, "'And All This Passion for a Boy?' Cross-dressing and the Sexual Economy of Beaumont and Fletcher's *Philaster*," in *English Literary Renaissance* 27, no. 1 (1997): 129–50—although I disagree with Miller's readings of Arethusa and Bellario as devoid of erotic desires.

5 Beaumont and Fletcher, *Philaster,* 1.2.108–9. All citations from *Philaster* are hereafter cited by act, scene, and line number in the text.

6 William Shakespeare, *Hamlet,* 4.5.170–71. All subsequent citations from Shakespeare are from Greenblatt et al., *Norton Shakespeare,* 3rd ed., and are hereafter cited parenthetically in the text.

7 More on the homoerotic affect and desire of weeping shepherd boys— specifically the delectable shepherd boys of Richard Barnfield—can be found in Kenneth Borris and George Klawitter, eds., *The Affectionate Shepherd: Celebrating Richard Barnfield* (Selinsgrove, Pa.: Susquehanna University Press, 2001), especially the contributions of Raymond-Jean Frontain, "'An Affectionate Shepheard Sicke for Love': Barnfield's Homoerotic Appropriation of the Song of Solomon," 99–116; Julie W. Yen, "'If It Be Sinne to Love a Sweet-Fac'd Boy': Rereading Homoerotic Desire in Barnfield's Ganymede Poems," 130–48; and Mario DiGangi, "'My Plentie Makes Me Poore': Linguistic and Erotic Failure in 'The Affectionate Shepheard,'" 149–73.

8 "Of the nature of an instrument (material or subservient); serving as an instrument or means; contributing to the accomplishment of a purpose or result." *Oxford English Dictionary Online* (hereafter *OED Online*), http://oed.com/, s.v. "instrumental, *a.* and *n.,*" A. *adj.,* 1.a.

9 "Serving well for the purpose; serviceable, useful; effective, efficient." *OED Online,* "instrumental, *a.* and *n.,*" A. *adj.,* 1.c.

10 The sense of the word in meaning 1.a., "a means to an end," takes on a connotation of more causal force when construed with *to* or *in,* or rarely *of* or *for,* followed by the noun form of a verb. Whereas the purely adjectival form means "secondary," this adverbial usage posits an instrumental agent as an essential catalyst for action. These connotations of specificity and indispensability are also present in the "Old Physiological" meaning, "Having a special vital function; that is a bodily organ; organic." *OED Online,* "instrumental, *a.* and *n.,*" A. *adj.,* 1.b. and 4.

11 Masten, "Editing Boys," 126.

12 Mario DiGangi describes a "homoerotics of mastery" within the power structure of service (and within comic plots of mastery and humiliation), arguing that discourses of service are used to signify "disorderly" homoerotic practices that cannot be represented onstage; these sodomitical dynamics, which can be manipulated by masters or servants, both inhere within and threaten the master/servant power differential. See DiGangi, *Homoerotics of Early Modern Drama,* 64–66.

13 Susan Sontag, "Notes on Camp," in *Camp: Queer Aesthetics and the Performing Subject—A Reader,* ed. Fabio Cleto (Ann Arbor: University of Michigan Press, 1999), #23, 59.

14 Sedgwick, "Paranoid Reading," 28.

15 Sontag, "Notes on Camp" #11, 56.

16 Eugene M. Waith, *The Pattern of Tragicomedy in Beaumont and Fletcher* (New Haven, Conn.: Yale University Press, 1952), 9–10.

17 Sontag, "Notes on Camp" #10, 56.

18 In comparing Bellario to Hylas and Adonis, Megra cites two ancient and pervasive queer myths of the androgynously, omnisexually alluring young man.

19 See Eve Kosofsky Sedgwick, *Between Men: English Literature and Male Homosocial Desire* (New York: Columbia University Press, 1985).

20 The instability of this three-way relational dynamic is dependent on, though not synonymous with, the literal indeterminacy of the play's signifiers around the term "boy" that Masten describes in "Editing Boys."

21 These hyperbolic exchanges of love, pain, self-abnegation, and deferred violence constitute a tragicomic camp version of the early modern trial discovery scene, wherein the court attempts to extract invisible, interior truth from the accused by means of interrogation and threatened violence. See Elizabeth Hanson, *Discovering the Subject in Renaissance England* (Cambridge: Cambridge University Press, 1998).

22 *Philaster* dramatizes many of the same anxieties that Maus documents in *Inwardness and Theater*—worries about the potential for deception created by the phenomenon of interiority—transposed into the melodramatic register of tragicomedy.

23 My comparison of *Epicoene*'s social satire to *Philaster*'s tragicomic celebration of desire for the androgyne makes some of the same observations as Phyllis Rackin's reading of *Epicoene* in contrast to the fantastical world of Lyly's *Gallathea* in her canonical essay "Androgyny, Mimesis, and the Marriage of the Boy Heroine on the English Renaissance Stage," *PMLA* 102, no. 1 (1987): 29–41.

24 Stephen Orgel also unpacks the subversive erotic punch of the transvestite figure, particularly in his observation that it owes its allure to the convention of gender disguises being regarded as convincing enough to fool a sexual partner, in *Impersonations: The Performance of Gender in Shakespeare's England* (Cambridge: Cambridge University Press, 1996), particularly chap. 2, "The Performance of Desire." Masten, "Editing Boys," 123, alludes to *Philaster*'s homosexual brinksmanship in declining to show Bellario/Euphrasia first in women's clothing and pushing the gender reveal to the very end.

25 Citations from *The Roaring Girl* are from Thomas Middleton and Thomas Dekker, *The Roaring Girl*, New Mermaids edition, ed. Elizabeth Cook (London: A&C Black, 1997), 1.1.97–100, and are hereafter cited parenthetically in the text by act, scene, and line number.

26 See Ann Rosalind Jones and Peter Stallybrass, "Transvestism and the 'Body Beneath': Speculating on the Boy Actor," in *Renaissance Clothing*; Marjorie Garber, *Vested Interests* (New York: Routledge, 1997);

Jean Howard, *The Stage and Social Struggle in Early Modern England* (London: Routledge, 1994); Stephen Orgel, "Nobody's Perfect, or Why Did the English Stage Take Boys for Women?," *South Atlantic Quarterly* 88, no. 1 (1989): 7–29; and Stephen Greenblatt, "Fiction and Friction," in *Shakespearean Negotiations: The Circulation of Social Energy in the Renaissance* (Berkeley: University of California Press, 1988), 66–93. My argument is particularly indebted to these canonical works' attention to the surprising cathexes that can erupt between desiring subjects and their objects, both people and material things; and to their illumination of how fully cross-dressing comedy depends on audiences' libidinal investments in gender illusion.

27 Fisher, *Materializing Gender.*

28 On Moll's masculine embodiment as an early modern example of queer gender on the transmasculine spectrum, see Simone Chess's reading of *The Roaring Girl* in her "Introduction: Passing Relations," in *Male-to-Female Crossdressing in Early Modern English Literature* (New York: Routledge, 2016), esp. 16–19.

29 See Masten, "Editing Boys," on the textual undecidedness of Bellario/Euphrasia's sex at the level of speech prefixes.

30 Sawyer K. Kemp, "'In That Dimension Grossly Clad': Transgender Rhetoric and Shakespeare," *Shakespeare Studies* 47 (2019): 120–26.

31 Traub, *Renaissance of Lesbianism,* 230.

32 Traub, *Renaissance of Lesbianism,* 436n106.

33 Jack Halberstam, *Female Masculinity,* Twentieth Anniversary Edition (Durham, N.C.: Duke University Press, 2018), 53.

34 Sedgwick, *Epistemology,* 45.

35 Traub, *Renaissance of Lesbianism,* 32. More recently, however, Traub, in "The New Unhistoricism in Queer Studies," *PMLA* 128, no. 1 (2013): 35, argues for more diachronic methods of historical knowledge production using "a queer historicism dedicated to showing how categories, however mythic, phantasmatic, and incoherent, came to be."

36 See the forthcoming essays in *Early Modern Trans Studies,* ed. Simone Chess, Colby Gordon, and Will Fisher, special issue, *Journal for Early Modern Cultural Studies* 19, no. 4 (2019).

37 The definitive treatment of the historical evidence for Moll Frith's performance is P. A. Mulholland's "The Date of *The Roaring Girl,*" *Review of English Studies* 109 (1977): 18–31. Two other sources that provide helpful context on Mary Frith as an historical figure are: Natasha Korda, "The Case of Moll Frith: Women's Work and the All-Male Stage," in *Women Players in England, 1500–1600: Beyond the All-Male Stage* (Burlington, Vt.: Ashgate, 2005), 71–88; and Bryan Reynolds and Janna Segal, "The Reckoning of Moll Cutpurse: A Transversal

Enterprise," in *Rogues and Early Modern English Culture,* ed. Craig Dionne and Steve Mentz (Ann Arbor: University of Michigan Press, 2006), 62–97.

38 Dinshaw, *Getting Medieval,* 12.

39 *Hic Mulier. Or, The Man-Woman: Being a Medicine to cure the Coltish Disease of the Staggers in the Masculine-Feminines of our Times* (London, 1620).

40 See Jean Howard, "Sex and Social Conflict: *The Roaring Girl,*" in *Erotic Politics: Desire on the Renaissance Stage,* ed. Susan Zimmerman (New York: Routledge, 1992), 132–47; Stephen Orgel, "The Subtexts of *The Roaring Girl,*" in Zimmerman, *Erotic Politics,* 12–26; Marjorie Garber, "The Logic of the Transvestite: *The Roaring Girl,*" in *Staging the Renaissance: Reinterpretations of Elizabethan and Jacobean Drama,* ed. David Scott Kastan and Peter Stallybrass (New York: Routledge, 1991), 221–34; and Mary Beth Rose, "Women in Men's Clothing: Apparel and Social Stability in *The Roaring Girl,*" *English Literary Renaissance* 14 (1984): 367–91.

41 James M. Bromley, "'Quilted with Mighty Words to Lean Purpose': Clothing and Queer Style in *The Roaring Girl,*" *Renaissance Drama* 43, no. 2 (2015): 143–72.

42 Colby W. Gordon, "A Woman's Prick: Trans Technogenesis in Sonnet 20," in *Shakespeare and Sex,* ed. Jennifer Drouin (London: Bloomsbury Arden Shakespeare, forthcoming).

43 The endemic violence visited on twentieth-century butch women by straight men, specifically police, is proof of the challenge female masculinity poses to a patriarchal order that regards its expression as a usurpation of natural maleness. See Leslie Feinberg, *Stone Butch Blues,* Twentieth Anniversary Author Edition (2014), https://www.lesliefein berg.net/; and Madeline Davis and Elizabeth Lapovsky Kennedy, *Boots of Leather, Slippers of Gold: The History of a Lesbian Community* (New York: Routledge, 1993).

44 Another critic using a queer reading of *The Roaring Girl* to analyze what the transvestite does—in this case, what the transvestite body does to the interplay of knowledge and ignorance—is Ryan Singh Paul, "The Power of Ignorance and *The Roaring Girl,*" *English Literary Renaissance* 43 (2013): 514–40.

45 Sedgwick, *Epistemology,* 80.

46 Sedgwick, *Epistemology,* 79.

47 Sedgwick, *Epistemology,* 79.

48 Sedgwick, *Epistemology,* 80–81. This must hold particularly true under "the literal patriarchism that makes coming out to *parents* the best emotional analogy to Esther's self-disclosure to her *husband*" (King Ahasuerus in the Book of Esther, the story on which Sedgwick builds her

case for the distinctive dynamics that set gay coming out apart from other kinds of disclosure) (82).

49 Sedgwick, *Epistemology*, 81.

50 For a comprehensive account of the gay resonances attached to women's tailors, and a useful argument for the validity of tracing gay sexual stereotypes in the Renaissance, see Simon Shepherd, "What's So Funny about Ladies' Tailors? A Survey of Some Male (Homo)sexual Types in the Renaissance," *Textual Practice* 6, no. 1 (1992): 17–30. Shepherd does, however, mistake one crucial fact about *The Roaring Girl*: judging by the clothing Moll's tailor makes for her and for Mary, he is not a ladies' tailor but a men's tailor (21). The same kind of ribald, homoerotic insinuation is operative around men's tailors in other early modern plays as well—cf. Ben Jonson's *Every Man Out of His Humor* (1599). I am also indebted to Aaron Santesso's helpful précis of sexual discourse around tailors extending back to the early modern period in "William Hogarth and the Tradition of Sexual Scissors," *SEL Studies in English Literature 1500–1900* 39, no. 3 (1999): 499–521.

51 Bromley, "Quilted with Mighty Words," 158–60.

52 This is Maggie Nelson's phrasing of the scope of Sedgwick's intervention in the proliferation of erotic desire; *Argonauts*, 62.

53 "An opening or slit in a garment which enables the wearer to put it on or which gives access to a pocket; *spec.* (now *hist.*) an opening in a woman's skirt or underskirt, esp. as offering a man the opportunity for sexual activity; (hence, in extended use) the vagina." *OED Online,* s.v. "placket, *n.*," I. 2.

54 Though the exact origins of these words are unknown, it is not unlikely that "pimp" derives from the Middle French word *pimper,* "to adorn, attire (a person, oneself) (1578)." *OED Online,* s.v. "pimp, *n.*," Etym.

55 See Varnado, "Invisible Sex!," 38–42.

56 Sedgwick, *Epistemology*, 81.

57 A cyborg, or cybernetic organism, is a hybrid of natural and artificial components. See Donna Haraway, "A Cyborg Manifesto: Science, Technology, and Socialist-Feminism in the Late Twentieth Century," in *Simians, Cyborgs and Women: The Reinvention of Nature* (New York: Routledge, 1991), 149–81.

58 Thomas Nashe's 1592 poem, "The Choise of Valentines," exemplifies these associations: a dildo takes the place of a man's fatigued, dysfunctional penis to satisfy his female lover's voracious, receptive desire. Traub discusses how the dildo in Nashe's poem (and the poem itself, which embodies the "choice" and substitution of the artificial tool) functions anxiously, and literally, in the manner of the Freudian fetish, unintentionally confirming the substitutability of the penis. Traub,

Renaissance of Lesbianism, 98. But I suggest we consider Moll as a dildo in a less paranoid light—as a materialization of a "lost object of desire" (196) which never was: the ideal, universally functional imaginary phallus, which can be found on a body of any sex.

59 Two readings of the play that treat the mask and dress as signs of political containment are: Valerie Forman, "Marked Angels: Counterfeits, Commodities, and *The Roaring Girl*," *Renaissance Quarterly* 54, no. 4, part 2 (2001): 1531–60; and Jane Batson, "Rehabilitating Moll's Subversion," in *SEL Studies in English Literature 1500–1900* 37, no. 2 (1997): 317–35.

60 Michel de Montaigne, *The Journal of Montaigne's Travels in Italy by Way of Switzerland and Germany* (1903), in *The Literature of Lesbianism: A Historical Anthology from Ariosto to Stonewall*, ed. Terry Castle (New York: Columbia University Press, 2003), 80.

61 "Avec son contentement, à ce qu'on dit." Michel de Montaigne, *Journal de voyage en italie* (Paris: Gallimard, 1983), 1118 (my translation).

62 "Et fut pendue pour des inventions illicites à suppléer au defaut de son sexe." Montaigne, *Journal de voyage*, 1118 (my translation).

63 "Elle avoit esté condamnée à estre pendue: ce qu'elle disoit aymer mieux souffrir que de se remettre en estat de fille." Montaigne, *Journal de voyage*, 1118 (my translation).

64 Greenblatt, "Fiction and Friction," 66–67, 79–80. See also Lorraine Daston and Katharine Park, "The Hermaphrodite and the Orders of Nature: Sexual Ambiguity in Early Modern France," in Fradenburg and Freccero, *Premodern Sexualities*, 117–36.

65 Thomas Laqueur, *Making Sex: Body and Gender from the Greeks to Freud* (Cambridge, Mass.: Harvard University Press, 1990), 8.

66 Traub, *Renaissance of Lesbianism*, 193–94; see also Traub, "The (In)significance of 'Lesbian' Desire in Early Modern England," in Zimmerman, *Erotic Politics*, 150–67.

67 Traub, *Renaissance of Lesbianism*, 193.

68 Greenblatt, "Fiction and Friction," 67. I am indebted for this critique, and for the call to move beyond the literal, legalistic interpretation, to Richard L. Regosin's treatment of this story in *Montaigne's Unruly Brood: Textual Engendering and the Challenge to Paternal Authority* (Berkeley: University of California Press, 1996), 191–93.

69 Masten, "Editing Boys," 121; also Nicholas Radel, "Fletcherian Tragicomedy, Cross-dressing, and the Constriction of Homoerotic Desire in Early Modern England," *Renaissance Drama* 26 (1995): 53–82.

70 Masten, "Editing Boys," 122, acknowledges the possibility of female–female eros in the play's resolution.

71 Masten, "Editing Boys," 122–27, details the differences in character labeling and gender dynamics among the printed editions of the play.

2. Everything That Moves

1   William Shakespeare, *Twelfth Night, or What You Will*, 1.1.1–8. All
    subsequent citations from Shakespeare are from Greenblatt et al., *Nor-
    ton Shakespeare*, 3rd ed., and are hereafter cited parenthetically in the
    text.

2   René Girard, "O, What a Deal of Scorn Looks Beautiful: Self-Love in
    Twelfth Night," and "'Tis Not So Sweet Now as It Was Before: Orsino
    and Olivia in *Twelfth Night*," in *A Theatre of Envy: William Shakespeare*,
    2nd ed. (Oxford: Oxford University Press, 2000), 106–11, 112–20.

3   See Crawford, "*All's Well That Ends Well*"; Julie Crawford, "The Ho-
    moerotics of Shakespeare's Elizabethan Comedies," in *A Companion to
    Shakespeare's Works, Volume 3: The Comedies*, ed. Richard Dutton and
    Jean E. Howard (Malden, Mass.: Blackwell, 2003), 137–58; Dympna
    Callaghan, "'And All Is Semblative a Woman's Part': Body Politics
    and *Twelfth Night*," in *Shakespeare without Women: Representing Gen-
    der and Race on the Renaissance Stage* (New York: Routledge, 2000),
    26–48; Laurie Shannon, "Nature's Bias: Renaissance Homonormativity
    and Elizabethan Comic Likeness," *Modern Philology* 98, no. 2 (2000):
    183–210; and Jean Howard, "Crossdressing, the Theatre, and Gender
    Struggle in Early Modern England," *Shakespeare Quarterly* 39, no. 4
    (1988): 418–40.

4   See Joseph Pequigney, "The Two Antonios and Same-Sex Love in
    Twelfth Night and *The Merchant of Venice*," *English Literary Renais-
    sance* 22 (1992): 201–21; Lisa Jardine, "Twins and Travesties: Gender,
    Dependency, and Sexual Availability in *Twelfth Night*," in Zimmerman,
    Erotic Politics, 27–38; Jardine, *Still Harping on Daughters: Women
    and Drama in the Age of Shakespeare* (New York: Columbia Univer-
    sity Press, 1989); and Janet Adelman, "Male Bonding in Shakespeare's
    Comedies," in *Shakespeare's "Rough Magic": Essays in Honor of C. L.
    Barber*, ed. Peter Erickson and Coppelia Kahn (Newark: University of
    Delaware Press, 1985), 73–103.

5   Bruce R. Smith thinks through some related implications of Orsino's
    "fancy" in his contribution, "'His Fancy's Queen': Sensing Sexual
    Strangeness in Twelfth Night," in *Twelfth Night: New Critical Essays*,
    ed. James Schiffer (London: Routledge, 2011), 65–80. We agree about
    the queer play of fancy as a converse to nature; I go a step further to
    posit fancy as an engine of queer generation, connected to an historical
    genealogy of degraded desires.

6   "A mental apprehension of an object of perception; the faculty by which
    this is performed." *OED Online*, "fantasy, phantasy, *n.*," 1.a.

7   "Fancy, *n.* and *adj.*," A. *n.* 4.a., first quoted 1581, *OED Online*.

8   "Fancy, *n.* and *adj.*," A. *n.* 8.b., first quoted 1559, *OED Online*.

9   "Fancy, *v.*," 8., first quoted 1545, *OED Online*.

10   The word's appeal to poets attempting to write the unrequited, non-reproductive desire of Petrarchan love in English is not surprising; it was commonly used to refer to the imaginative flights of the lover in poetry both about and in the style of Petrarch in English for the next two centuries—including Mary Darby Robinson's "Petrarch to Laura" (1791) and Hartley Coleridge's sonnets (1833). For example, George Frederick Nott's nineteenth-century translation of Petrarch's Sonnet 69, "To Laura in Life," has "Yet haply fancy my fond sense betray'd," for "Non so se vero, o falso mi parea" (literally, "I don't know whether [it is] true or false, it appeared to me"). See *The Sonnets, Triumphs, and Other Poems of Petrarch, Now First Completely Translated into English Verse by Various Hands,* ed. Thomas Campbell (London: George Bell and Sons, 1879).

11   Sanchez, *Erotic Subjects,* 3–10, 239–44.

12   "Fancy, *n.* and *adj.*," A. *n.* 4.a., first quoted 1581, *OED Online.*

13   "Fancy, *n.* and *adj.*," A. *n.* 2., first quoted 1609, *OED Online.*

14   "Fancy, *n.* and *adj.*," A. *n.* 3., first quoted 1597, *OED Online.*

15   "Fancy, *n.* and *adj.*," A. *n.* 5.a., first quoted 1665, *OED Online.*

16   "Fancy, *n.* and *adj.*," A. *n.* 5.b., first quoted 1577, *OED Online.*

17   "Fancy, *n.* and *adj.*," A. *n.* 4.a., first quoted 1581, *OED Online.*

18   The "mother's fancy," detailed by Montaigne (among others), was a popular explanation for how a woman's erotic fantasy about another man—an image in her mind's eye—could impress her unborn child with the appearance of someone other than its "natural" or legitimate father. Florio's 1603 translation of Montaigne's *Essais* famously reads: "So it is, that by experience wee see women to transferre divers markes of their fantasies, unto children they beare in their wombes: witnes she that brought forth a blacke-a-more." Michel de Montaigne, "20. On the Force of Imagination," in *Essays: Book 1,* trans. John Florio, Renascence Editions E-text, http://www.luminarium.org/renascence-editions/montaigne/1xx.htm. This belief is thoroughly historicized by Marie-Hélène Huet in "Part 1: The Mother's Fancy," in *Monstrous Imagination* (Cambridge, Mass.: Harvard University Press, 1993), 11–123.

19   Traub, *Renaissance of Lesbianism,* 69. The queerness of the category of "virgin" is also documented by Theodora A. Jankowski, *Pure Resistance: Queer Virginity in Early Modern English Drama* (Philadelphia: University of Pennsylvania Press, 2000); and Mary Bly, *Queer Virgins and Virgin Queans on the Early Modern English Stage* (Oxford: Oxford University Press, 2000).

20   Alicia Andrzejewski, "'For Her Sake': Queer Pregnancy in *A Midsummer Night's Dream,*" *Shakespeare Studies* 47 (2019): 105-11.

21   Sigmund Freud, "2. Infantile Sexuality," trans. James Strachey, in *Three Essays on the Theory of Sexuality* (New York: Basic Books, 2000), 57.

22   Sigmund Freud, "Introductory Lectures on Psycho-analysis" (1917), in *The Standard Edition of the Complete Psychological Works of Sigmund Freud,* trans. James Strachey (London: Hogarth Press and the Institute of Psycho-analysis, 1953–74), 15: 209.

23   Shannon, "Nature's Bias," 208.

24   Aubrey, *Brief Lives,* 1:95–96, in Masten, *Textual Intercourse,* 61.

25   Sigmund Freud, "On Narcissism: An Introduction" (1914), trans. James Strachey, in *The Freud Reader,* ed. Peter Gay (New York: Norton, 1989), 546.

26   Jacques Derrida, *Of Grammatology,* trans. Gayatri Chakravorty Spivak, Fortieth Anniversary Edition (Baltimore, Md.: Johns Hopkins University Press, 2016), 168.

27   Jami Ake, "Glimpsing a Lesbian Poetics in *Twelfth Night,*" *SEL Studies in English Literature 1500–1900* 43, no. 2 (2003): 375–94; Jankowski, *Pure Resistance*; and Traub, *Desire and Anxiety.*

28   Olivia's degree of awareness and the intensity of her homoerotic investment could be a directorial or acting choice in production.

29   Shannon, "Nature's Bias," 209–10, reviews the applicability of a language of "swerving."

30   The tailor was hanged for using "inventions illicites," "illicit inventions to supply the defect of her sex," in 1580 in Vitry-le-François: "Elle fut pendue pour des inventions illicites à suppléer au defaut de son sexe," Montaigne, *Journal de voyage,* 1118 (my translation).

31   Stallybrass, "Transvestism and the 'Body Beneath,'" 207–19.

32   Ben Brantley, "How Mark Rylance Became Olivia Onstage," *New York Times,* August 15, 2016, https://www.nytimes.com/.

33   This is true in the central cross-dressed/homoerotic bonds as well; cf. all Viola's exchanges with Olivia.

34   "Fancy, *n.* and *adj.*," A. *n.* 5.c., first quoted c. 1652, *OED Online.*

35   Sedgwick, *Epistemology,* 23.

36   "Fancy, *n.* and *adj.*," C.1.c., *OED Online.*

37   "Fancy, *n.* and *adj.*," B., *adj.* 5.; and "fancy man, *n.*," 1., *OED Online.*

38   "Fancy, *n.* and *adj.*," C.2., "fancy-woman, *n.*," first quoted 1819, *OED Online.*

39   "Fancy man, *n.*," 3., first quoted 1811, *OED Online.*

40   "Fancy, *n.* and *adj.*," C.2., "fancy Dan, *n.*," first quoted 1943, *OED Online.*

41   Freccero, "Queer Times," 485.

42   "Fancy, *n.* and *adj.*," A. *n.* 6., 7., 8., *OED Online.*

43   "Fancy, *n.* and *adj.*," B. *adj.*, 1.a., first quoted 1753, *OED Online.*

44   "Fancy, *n.* and *adj.*," B. *adj.*, 1.a. and 2.a, *OED Online.*

45   "Fancy, *n.* and *adj.*," A. *n.*, 11., first quoted 1712, *OED Online.*

46   The music video of Rufus Wainwright's song "Rules and Regulations" from *Release the Stars* (Geffen Records, 2007) cites the gay heritage of

boxing, which still adheres to the Marquess of Queensberry Rules, originally written by John Douglas, ninth marquess of Queensberry—Lord Alfred "Bosie" Douglas's father and Oscar Wilde's libel adversary. RufusWainwrightVEVO, "Rufus Wainwright—Rules and Regulations," YouTube, November 22, 2009, https://www.youtube.com/.

47 "Fancy, *n.* and *adj.*," A. *n.*, 13., and B. *adj.*, 1.c., *OED Online.*

48 See Jonathan Goldberg's essay grappling with the illusion of history's teleological decidedness in the scene of colonial violence, "The History That Will Be," in Fradenburg and Freccero, *Premodern Sexualities,* 1–21.

49 Sigmund Freud, "Fetishism" (1927), in *Standard Edition,* 21:147–58.

50 Fisher, *Materializing Gender; Marxist Shakespeares,* ed. Jean Howard and Scott Shershow (New York: Routledge, 2001); Jones and Stallybrass, *Renaissance Clothing;* Lisa Jardine, *Worldly Goods: A New History of the Renaissance* (London: Norton, 1996); and Kim F. Hall, *Things of Darkness: Economies of Race and Gender in Early Modern England* (Ithaca, N.Y.: Cornell University Press, 1995).

51 Elena Levy-Navarro makes use of an analytic connected to queer theory in her brilliant "fat studies" reading of the play, "Weigh Me as a Friend: Jonson's Multiple Constructions of the Fat Body," in *The Culture of Obesity in Early and Late Modernity: Body Image in Shakespeare, Jonson, Middleton, and Skelton* (New York: Palgrave Macmillan, 2008), 147–92. In theorizing the need for a "fat history," which, much like queer history, recovers the subjugated bodies and pleasures of a different time and critiques the assumptions of a progressivist, modernizing telos for the category of "fat," Levy-Navarro treats the fat bodies of Ursula the pig-woman and Bartholomew Cokes as sites of bodily resistance and revolt against the "civilizing" bourgeois norms of aesthetics, embodiment, consumption, and behavior that are operative at the Fair.

52 All citations from Jonson's works, hereafter cited parenthetically in the text, are from Ben Jonson, *The Alchemist and Other Plays,* Oxford English Drama series, ed. Gordon Campbell (Oxford: Oxford University Press, 1995), 1.5.129.

53 Like the desire to be made erotically instrumental that is the focus of chapter 1, this acute, all-consuming longing frequently has at its beginnings some kind of device or ruse, such as Philaster's question, "How shall we devise/To hold intelligence?" Beaumont and Fletcher, *Philaster,* 1.2.108–9. The constitutive element of artifice in both structures of erotic investment is key to what makes them queer: what started out as performative or artificed desire often gradually becomes—and is revealed to have already been—real attraction.

54 See Gowing, *Common Bodies,* for more on the complicated interplay of bodily surveillance, power, truth production, and social fiction involved in pregnancy detection.

55 The processes I am describing in early modern drama are the product of mental artifice in a way that Deleuze and Guattari's thoroughly materialist account of desire is not; but Deleuze and Guattari also conceive of materially produced and materially productive desire as a queerly, asexually generative, self-replicating force. See Gilles Deleuze and Félix Guattari, *Anti-Oedipus: Capitalism and Schizophrenia,* trans. Robert Hurley and Helen Lane (Minneapolis: University of Minnesota Press, 1985).

56 Jonson's satire of "Puritan" Protestant behavior here plays on the interpenetration of some social control sects' habits of religious discipline and the popular discourse about them, which stereotyped their prohibitions against pleasure and appetite. See Christopher Durston and Jacqueline Eales, "Introduction: The Puritan Ethos, 1560–1700," and Patrick Collinson, "Elizabethan and Jacobean Puritanism as Forms of Popular Religious Culture," in *The Culture of English Puritanism, 1560–1700,* ed. Christopher Durston and Jacqueline Eales (Basingstoke, U.K.: Palgrave Macmillan, 1996).

57 Thomas Adams, *A Commentary, or Exposition vpon the Diuine Second Epistle Generall, Written by the Blessed Apostle St. Peter* (London, 1633), 424.

58 My notion of the imaginative fancy is rooted in the early modern period's nonhumoral, Neoplatonist model of how erotic affects enter into the body/mind. The model Ficino articulates in *De Amore* is based on Ibn Sina (Avicenna)'s idea of materialized "mental faculties": images drawn from matter that travel into the "ventricles" of the brain. This alternate genealogy is treated in Dawson's *Lovesickness and Gender,* 21–26. See also Sibylle Baumbach, *Literature and Fascination* (Basingstoke, U.K.: Palgrave Macmillan, 2015).

59 Litvak, "Glad to Be Unhappy," 523–31.

60 Max Horkheimer and Theodor W. Adorno, *Dialectic of Enlightenment: Philosophical Fragments,* trans. Edmund Jephcott, ed. Gunzelin Schmid Noerr (Stanford, Calif.: Stanford University Press, 2002), 151–52, quoted in Litvak, "Glad to Be Unhappy," 525.

61 For more on the interplay between Puritans' Hebraism and anti-Semitism, including an analysis of *Bartholomew Fair,* see Nicholas McDowell, "The Stigmatizing of Puritans as Jews in Jacobean England: Ben Jonson, Francis Bacon, and the *Book of Sports* Controversy," *Renaissance Studies* 19, no. 3 (2005): 348–63.

62 Compare to a satirical faux opinion piece by "Bruce Heffernan," "Why Do All These Homosexuals Keep Sucking My Cock?," *Onion,* October 28, 1998, https://www.theonion.com/.

63 Jonathan Gil Harris asks similar questions about the historical phenomenology of smell and the audience's experience of the stink of gunpowder on the Shakespearean stage, with reference to the stink mentioned

in *Bartholomew Fair*, in "The Smell of Macbeth," *Shakespeare Quarterly* 58, no. 4 (2007): 465–86.

64 See Levy-Navarro, "Weigh Me as a Friend"; Kathleen Rowe, "Pig Ladies, Big Ladies, and Ladies with Big Mouths: Feminism and the Carnivalesque," in *The Unruly Woman: Gender and the Genres of Laughter* (Austin: University of Texas Press, 1995), 25–49; and Gail Kern Paster, "Leaky Vessels: The Incontinent Women of City Comedy," *Renaissance Drama* 18 (1987): 43–65. Grace Tiffany, in contrast, characterizes Ursula's body as queerly, monstrously desexed and powerfully "mannish" in a Falstaffian mode, in *Erotic Beasts and Social Monsters: Shakespeare, Jonson, and Comic Androgyny* (Cranbury, N.J.: Associated University Presses, 1995), esp. 105–69.

65 This predilection or fetish receives one of its only cultural studies treatments in the chapter on "Macrophiles: Giantess Fans" in Katharine Gates, *Deviant Desires: Incredibly Strange Sex* (New York: Juno Books, 1999). See also Valerie Billing's groundbreaking work on the erotics of size, "The Queer Language of Size in *Love's Labour's Lost*," in *Queer Shakespeare: Desire and Sexuality*, ed. Goran Stanivukovic (London: Bloomsbury Arden Shakespeare, 2017), 107–22.

66 The gingerbread people are made in the image of Saint Bartholomew for the Fair; hence, they are also wafers endowed with some human attributes, recalling the Catholic Eucharist. Jonson, *The Alchemist and Other Plays*, 510n68.

67 All of the toys in hobbyhorse-maker Leatherhead's stall are in some sense ceremonial objects, if children's play is considered to be ceremonial. Early evangelical Protestants generally did not, as a rule, formally make or buy toys for children. See Bruce C. Daniels, *Puritans at Play: Leisure and Recreation in Colonial New England* (New York: St. Martin's Press, 1995), esp. 186–89, on Puritans' opposition to childhood play as potentially corrupting.

68 Busy also makes witch-producing insinuations about Ursula the pig-woman's "having the marks upon her of the three enemies of man . . . the devil." Jonson, *Bartholomew Fair*, 3.6.32–34.

69 See George Chapman, Ben Jonson, and John Marston, *Eastward Ho*, ed. R. W. Van Fossen (Manchester: Manchester University Press, 1979), 1.2.

70 "Fancy man, *n.*," 3., first quoted 1811, *OED Online.*

71 "Fancy, *n.* and *adj.*," C.2., "fancy Dan, *n.*," first quoted 1943, *OED Online.*

72 Though outbreaks of plague often did disrupt the Bartholomew Fair, this line is also haunted from the future by the specter of the AIDS epidemic, which showed what it looks like when a pestilence depopulates an entire culture of artistic production.

73 Jonson, *The Alchemist and Other Plays*, 514n336.

74 On the puppet-ghost-flashing as an encapsulation of a related problem at the heart of early modern culture—the problem of interpretation, of how to read texts and objects—see Nicole Sheriko, "Ben Jonson's Puppet Theater and Modeling Interpretive Practice," *SEL Studies in English Literature 1500–1900* 59, no. 2 (2019): 281–304.

75 Laura Levine sees the puppet's absence of a sex as emblematic of the radical gender artifice at the heart of the theater that is the focus of antitheatrical hysteria. See Levine, "The 'Nothing' under the Puppet's Costume: Jonson's Suppression of Marlowe in *Bartholomew Fair*," in *Men in Women's Clothing: Anti-theatricality and Effeminization, 1579–1642* (Cambridge: Cambridge University Press, 1994), 89–107.

76 "Fancy, *n.* and *adj.*," A. *n.* 4.a., first quoted 1581, *OED Online*.

77 Callaghan, "And All Is Semblative," 37, calls this phrase "genitally un-decipherable" in respect of the multiple words associated with female genitalia juxtaposed in this triply proprietary grouping—presumably, Orsino has a "fancy," and Viola will be "queen" of it?

78 Shannon, "Nature's Bias," 208, calls the pair of couples at the resolution "an expanded group of siblings based on the axis of the twins."

3. It Takes One to Know One

1 Some of the most widely circulated examples of English witch hunt pamphlets include: *The most strange and admirable discoverie of the three witches of Warboys arraigned, convicted, and executed at the last assises at Huntington* (London, 1593); *The araignement & burning of Margaret Ferne-seede for the murther of her late husband Anthony Ferne-seede* (London, 1608); Thomas Potts, *The wonderfull discoverie of witches in the countie of Lancaster, With the arraignement and triall of nineteene notorious witches* (London, 1613), the trial that is the source for Thomas Heywood and Richard Brome's 1634 tragicomedy *The Late Lancashire Witches*; *The Wonderful discovery of the Witchcrafts of Margaret and Philippa Flower, daughters of Joan Flower neere BeverCastle: executed at Lincolne, March 11th 1618* (London, 1619); and the trial pamphlet that is the source for *The Witch of Edmonton* (1622), Henry Goodcole's *The wonderfull discoverie of Elizabeth Sawyer a witch late of Edmonton, her conviction and condemnation and death. Together with the relation of the Divels accesse to her, and their conference together* (London, 1621).

2 Susan Brownmiller, *Against Our Will: Women, Men, and Rape* (New York: Simon & Schuster, 1975).

3 Michel Foucault, *The History of Sexuality, Volume 1: An Introduction*, trans. Robert Hurley (New York: Pantheon Books, 1978), 11.

4 I am thinking here of D. A. Miller's work on the queer meanings of Jane

Austen and Alfred Hitchcock; see Miller's *Jane Austen, or The Secret of Style* (Princeton, N.J.: Princeton University Press, 2003), and "Anal Rope," *Representations* 32 (1990): 114–33; as well as Sedgwick's literary treatments of the AIDS quilt, Supreme Court decisions, and culture war rhetorics in *Tendencies* and *Epistemology.*

5 *Newes from Scotland, declaring the damnable life and death of Doctor Fian a notable sorcerer, who was burned at Edenbrough in Ianuary last. 1591. Which doctor was regester to the diuell that sundry times preached at North Barrick Kirke, to a number of notorious witches. With the true examination of the saide doctor and witches, as they vttered them in the presence of the Scottish king. Discouering how they pretended to bewitch and drowne his Maiestie in the sea comming from Denmarke, with such other wonderfull matters as the like hath not been heard of at any time. Published according to the Scottish coppie* (London, [1592?]), BOD 8o Douce F 210, Aivv, hereafter cited parenthetically in text by signature and leaf number.

6 See Gowing, *Common Bodies,* as well as Laura Gowing, *Domestic Dangers: Women, Words, and Sex in Early Modern London* (Oxford: Oxford University Press, 1999); and Frances Dolan, *Dangerous Familiars: Representations of Domestic Crime in England, 1550–1700* (Ithaca, N.Y.: Cornell University Press, 1994).

7 Gowing, *Common Bodies,* 73.

8 One of the important connections to be made between the history of witchcraft and the histories of medicine and state violence toward poor people is this recurring narrative strand: the criminalization of women for providing health care on a lay, community basis. See Barbara Ehrenreich and Deirdre English, *Witches, Midwives, and Nurses: A History of Women Healers* (New York: Feminist Press at CUNY, 1973).

9 Document 20, "The Trial of Agnes Sampson, 27 January 1591," items 1–12, 19, in *Witchcraft in Early Modern Scotland: James VI's Demonology and the North Berwick Witches,* ed. Lawrence Normand and Gareth Roberts (Exeter: University of Exeter Press, 2000). All subsequent citations from early modern legal documents are from this book, identified by document number, name, and item number. Sampson's accusation concentrates on her long-standing practice of midwifery and folk medicine for clients from a wide range of social stations. Presented with ill clients who came to her to ask if they would live or not, she correctly told, many times, how long it would be before they were well again, and whether they would die of their current illnesses.

10 *Newes from Scotland*'s emphasis on James's personal involvement in the trials reflects authorship by someone close to James, a collaborator in fashioning his public persona. Though the pamphlet was speculatively attributed to James himself in nineteenth-century scholarship, modern research suggests that James Carmichael, the minister of Haddington

who was in charge of some of the trials, may have written the original source text for the pamphlet. Normand and Roberts, *Witchcraft*, 8. See Robert Pitcairn, *Ancient Criminal Trials in Scotland, Compiled from the Original Records and Manuscripts, with Historical Illustrations* (Edinburgh: Bannatyne Club, 1833); and George Lincoln Burr's edition of *Translations and Reprints from the Original Sources of European History*, "The Witch Persecutions," vol. 3, no. 4 (Philadelphia: University of Pennsylvania History Department, 1897).

11 The idea that the witch's silence was attributable to demonic assistance, potentially through charms hidden on her body, dates from the *Malleus Maleficarum* (1487) by Heinrich Kramer, though the devil's mark is a later belief that postdates medieval witchcraft theory. See Dyan Elliott, "The Physiology of Rapture and Female Spirituality," in *Medieval Theology and the Natural Body*, ed. Peter Biller, Alastair J. Minnis, and Eammon Duffy (Suffolk, U.K.: York Medieval Press, 1997), 173n142. See also S. W. McDonald, "The Devil's Mark and the Witch-Prickers of Scotland," *Journal of the Royal Society of Medicine* 90, no. 9 (1997): 507–11.

12 *The most strange and admirable discouerie of the three witches of Warboys arraigned, conuicted, and executed at the last assises at Huntington, for the bewitching of the fiue daughters of Robert Throckmorton esquire, and diuers other persons, with sundrie diuellish and grieuous torments: and also for the witching to death of the Lady Crumwell, the like hath not been heard of in this age* (London, 1593), O3v–O4r.

13 Deborah Willis, "Magic and Witchcraft," in *A Companion to Renaissance Drama*, ed. Arthur F. Kinney (Oxford: Blackwell, 2002), 138–39.

14 Levine, *Men in Women's Clothing*, 120–33, reads the mark discovered on Sampson as the central sign that belies the antirepresentational belief system of Protestant antitheatrical discourse. The investment in finding it, she says, reveals a deeply repressed paranoid anxiety that material signs can indeed have transformative efficacies, which she connects explicitly to the antitheatrical anxiety that sexual difference, gender, and desire could be altered by material accessories.

15 Julia Kristeva, *Powers of Horror: An Essay on Abjection*, trans. Leon S. Roudiez (New York: Columbia University Press, 1982), 1.

16 Influential work on the systemic conditions of gender, communal psychology, and the witch hunt includes: Lyndal Roper, *Witch Craze: Terror and Fantasy in Baroque Germany* (New Haven, Conn.: Yale University Press, 2004), and *Oedipus and the Devil: Witchcraft, Sexuality, and Religion in Early Modern Europe* (London: Routledge, 1994); Diane Purkiss, *The Witch in History: Early Modern and Twentieth-Century Representations* (New York: Routledge, 1996); Deborah Willis, *Malevolent Nurture: Witch-Hunting and Maternal Power in Early Modern England* (Ithaca, N.Y.: Cornell University Press, 1995); and Carol F. Karlsen,

The Devil in the Shape of a Woman: Witchcraft in Colonial New England (London: Norton, 1987).

17 Influential studies of the epistemology of "discovery" and the "discovery scene," arguing for its constitutive significance to early modern ideas of interiority, truth, and subjectivity, have been presented by Christopher Pye, "Froth in the Mirror: Demonism, Sexuality, and the Early Modern Subject," in *Vanishing*, 38–49; and Maus, *Inwardness and Theater*, 44–46.

18 Brooks, *Reading for the Plot*, 37, 102–4.

19 Kristeva, *Powers of Horror*, 1. I appreciate Kristeva's figurative description of the state of being beset by abjection as a "twisted braid of affects" rather than a clean-cut or unitary mechanism.

20 Normand and Roberts, *Witchcraft*, 209. See also Charlotte-Rose Millar, *Witchcraft, the Devil, and Emotions in Early Modern England* (London: Routledge, 2017); and Roper, *Oedipus and the Devil*, 204–8.

21 Donald Trump (@realDonaldTrump), "NO COLLUSION—RIGGED WITCH HUNT!," Twitter, August 23, 2018, 1:10 a.m.

22 Donald Trump (@realDonaldTrump), "Collusion is not a crime, but that doesn't matter because there was No Collusion (except by Crooked Hillary and the Democrats)!," Twitter, July 31, 2018, 7:59 a.m.

23 Sedgwick, "Paranoid Reading," 1–37.

24 Paul Ricoeur, *Freud and Philosophy: An Essay on Interpretation* (1965), trans. Denis Savage (New Haven, Conn.: Yale University Press, 1970), 33–34, quoted in Sedgwick, "Paranoid Reading," 4–5.

25 Sedgwick, "Paranoid Reading," 6.

26 Guy Hocquenghem, *Homosexual Desire*, trans. Daniella Dangoor (Durham, N.C.: Duke University Press, 1993), 56.

27 Sedgwick, "Paranoid Reading," 6.

28 Sedgwick, "Paranoid Reading," 9.

29 Sedgwick, "Paranoid Reading," 6.

30 Dinshaw, in *Getting Medieval*, 55–99, also uses this phrase to illustrate the paranoid and projective desires animating the complex of shifting, reflexive accusations around Lollardy, murder, simony, sodomy, and leprosy in late medieval England.

31 Ricoeur, *Freud and Philosophy*, 34.

32 Sedgwick, "Paranoid Reading," 8.

33 Melanie Klein, "A Contribution to the Psychogenesis of Manic-Depressive States" (1935), in *Love, Guilt, and Reparation and Other Works, 1921–1945* (New York: Free Press, 1975), 262.

34 "Since the dread of internalized objects is by no means extinguished with their projection, the ego marshals against the persecutors inside the body the same forces as it employs against those in the outside world. These anxiety-contents and defence-mechanisms form the basis

of paranoia." Klein, "Contribution to the Psychogenesis of Manic-Depressive States," 262.

35 Klein, "Contribution to the Psychogenesis of Manic-Depressive States," 262.

36 Klein, "Contribution to the Psychogenesis of Manic-Depressive States," 263.

37 Melanie Klein, "Personification in the Play of Children" (1929), in *Love, Guilt, and Reparation*, 203n1.

38 Sedgwick, "Paranoid Reading," 8.

39 "Entanglement" is a technical term in quantum mechanics for particles that are ontologically related such that, regardless of their distance from one another over space or through time, they can instantly coordinate their properties with one another. The information that entangled particles disperse and share through their mysterious communication network is by its nature secret and invisible as long as it's held among entangled particles. Once observed, the particles are no longer in a state of entanglement. Rivka Galchen, "Dream Machine: The Mind-Expanding World of Quantum Computing," *New Yorker*, May 2, 2011, 34–43.

40 See Stuart Clark, *Thinking with Demons: The Idea of Witchcraft in Early Modern Europe* (Oxford: Oxford University Press, 1999), particularly chap. 12, "The Magical Power of Signs."

41 Suspicion around domestic material objects is famously on display as a queer-constructing and queer-persecuting force in the trials of Oscar Wilde, where the fabrics of drapes, the stains on bedsheets, the lines of furniture, and the dishes ordered on restaurant bills are marshaled as evidence of Wilde's "gross indecency" with other men. See *The Trials of Oscar Wilde*, ed. H. Montgomery Hyde (London: The Stationery Office, 2001); and Abigail Joseph, *Exquisite Materials: Episodes in the Queer History of Victorian Style* (Newark: University of Delaware Press, 2019).

42 Normand and Roberts, *Witchcraft*, document 23, "The Trial of Euphame MacCalzean, 9–15 June 1591," items 25 and 26.

43 The image of witches sailing in sieves on the sea (like uncanny seafarers, which some of the accused are by occupation) to attend demonic business is thought to originate in *Newes from Scotland*, because it does not appear in Jean Bodin, Reginald Scot, or any earlier sources on witchcraft. It is the putative source for the witches' declaration that they will sail in sieves to do harm to the sailor's wife in *Macbeth*. For a detailed analysis of *Newes from Scotland*'s afterlives as source material for Shakespeare's and Jonson's Jacobean drama, see Edward H. Thompson, "*Macbeth*, King James, and the Witches," paper presented at "Lancashire Witches: Law, Literature and 17th Century Women," December 1993, University of Lancaster. http://faculty.umb.edu/gary_

zabel/Courses/Phil%20281b/Philosophy%20of%20Magic/Arcana/
Witchcraft%20and%20Grimoires/macbeth.htm.

44 Normand and Roberts, *Witchcraft*, 20.

45 Normand and Roberts, *Witchcraft*, 21.

46 Normand and Roberts, *Witchcraft*, 303.

47 This is where accused women become truly fungible in *Newes from Scotland*, their identities shifting from criminal suspects individually subjected to examination and torture into a conglomerate of interchangeable witches acting in concert. The pamphlet attributes this confession to "Agnis Tompson," but the cat christening comes from the record of Sampson's trial. Normand and Roberts, *Witchcraft*, document 20, "The Trial of Agnes Sampson, 27 January 1591," item 40.

48 The trial records (including the indictment where sieve sailing originates) mention throwing a dog overboard and conjuring cats: "Ye and they took the sea, Robert Grierson being your admiral and masterman, passed over the sea in riddles to a ship where ye entered with the devil your master therein, where after ye had eaten and drunken, ye cast over a black dog that skipped under the ship, and thereby ye hewing the devil your master therein, who drowned the ship by tumbling, whereby the queen was put back by storm. (26) Item, indicted for consulting with the said Annie Sampson, Robert Grierson and divers other witches for the treasonable staying of the queen's homecoming by storm and wind, and raising of storm to that effect, or else to have drowned her Majesty and her company by conjuring of cats and casting of them in the sea at Leith and the back of Robert Grierson's house. *To stay the queen's homecoming.*" Normand and Roberts, *Witchcraft*, document 23, "The Trial of Euphame MacCalzean, 9–15 June 1591," items 25 and 26. The elder witch, Agnis or Agnes ("Annie") Sampson, also confesses to baptizing a cat in the chimney hearth of a house. Normand and Roberts, *Witchcraft*, document 20, "The Trial of Agnes Sampson, 27 January 1591," item 40.

49 It is possible that the cat may have been christened James, Anne, or some other reference to the royal targets of the storm. Or it may have been given a diabolical moniker out of folk tradition, like Tom (the name by which the devil dog in *The Witch of Edmonton* introduces himself)—or somehow christened, in a fully perverted version of the sacrament, with no name at all.

50 Their possible provenance is hinted at in the trial dittay of Agnes Sampson (who is after all a longtime healer and midwife) when she is accused of "taking off the pain and sickness" of women in childbirth (including Euphame MacCalzean, the other witch accused of cat conjuring) by "putting of moulds or powder, made of men's joints and members in Newton kirk, under Euphame MacCalzean's bed ten days before her birth." Normand and Roberts, *Witchcraft*, document 20, items 42–43.

51 Melanie Klein, "A Contribution to the Theory of Intellectual Inhibition" (1931), in *Love, Guilt, and Reparation,* 238.

52 Robin Briggs, *Witches and Neighbors: The Social and Cultural Context of European Witchcraft* (New York: Viking, 1996), 40–49.

53 Normand and Roberts, *Witchcraft,* 215, read the North Berwick gathering as a sort of populist political carnival or rally, "an astonishingly democratic meeting presided over by a devil who can be criticised [. . .] We may even see this moment as an image of political argument and challenge [. . .] The devil berated in North Berwick kirk for late delivery of an image is not the super-subtle and supremely powerful enemy of God of the demonologists. He is, at least in part, the devil of popular belief, ballads and stories, of many proverbs and popular woodcuts, who has close, chatty relationships with clowns in early modern drama."

54 Briggs, *Witches and Neighbors,* 25. Briggs also explains the early modern identification of the devil with a sadistic father figure in Continental witch beliefs, and the respective Catholic and Protestant psychologies around the devil's role in the seduction of witches (385).

55 The lore of the witches' Sabbath frequently includes music and dancing; this is presumably some form of a popular folk song, but its antiphonal leader-and-chorus structure and the repetitive, linked dance it implies give it additional associations with archaic communal ritual life such as morris dancing and the maypole.

56 The pamphlet narrative identifies at an emotional level with the king here, indicating the author's possible presence with James in the courtroom to witness his "delight," and/or an investment in aligning the voice of the pamphlet as closely as possible with James's emotive political persona, in order to imprint the king's personal pleasure on this particular construction of witchcraft for circulation in both Scotland and England.

57 James imagines the realm to be secretly teeming with witches who are constantly fashioning technologies through which to harm him. In the chains of simulacra James imagines, people (such as himself) are roasted via their wax images, using representation and likeness to create a material conduit from the devil, through the witch, to the victim: "To some witches the Devil teaches how to make Pictures of waxe or clay. That by the rosting thereof, the persones that they beare the name of, may be continuallie melted or dryed awaie by continuall sicknesse." James VI, *Daemonologie, in forme of a Dialogue* (Edinburgh: Robert Waldgrave, 1597; fascimile ed., Amsterdam: Theatrum Orbis Terrarum, 1969), 44.

58 The Jew's harp also underlines the historical and thematic links between the Continental idea of the witches' Sabbath (popularly called a synagogue) and long-standing communal paranoia around the ritual

practices of heretics and Jews, including cannibalism, blood libel, and sexual orgies. See Martine Ostorero, "The Concept of the Witches' Sabbath in the Alpine Region (1430–1440): Text and Context," in *Witchcraft Mythologies and Persecutions,* ed. Gábor Klaniczay and Éva Pócs (Budapest: Central European University Press, 2008), 20–23.

59 Sedgwick, "Paranoid Reading," 10.

60 See Alan Stewart, *The Cradle King: The Life of James VI and I, the First Monarch of a United Great Britain* (London: Chatto and Windus, 2003), 100–140. English agent Thomas Fowler reported before the wedding that Anne bore the king a great deal of "affection which his Majestie is apt in no way to requite." Quoted in Ethel Carleton Williams, *Anne of Denmark* (London: Longman, 1970), 14–15.

61 Goodcole, *Wonderfull discoverie.*

62 William Prynne, for example, alleges that at an Elizabethan performance of Marlowe's *Doctor Faustus* (c. 1592), the actors and audience were amazed at "the visible apparition of the Devill on the stage." Prynne, *Histrio-mastix, the players scourge, or actors tragedie . . .* (London, 1633). E. K. Chambers locates performances of *Doctor Faustus* as a common site for such urban legends, which formed a "curious mythos" registering audiences' anxieties and appetites around witchcraft onstage. Chambers, *The Elizabethan Stage* (Oxford: Clarendon, 1923), 3:423–24.

63 The first and only printed edition of the play dates from thirty-seven years into its popularity: William Rowley, Thomas Dekker, and John Ford, *The Witch of Edmonton: A known true Story. Composed into A Tragi-Comedy By divers well-esteemed Poets, William Rowley, Thomas Dekker, John Ford, &c. Acted by the Princes Servants, often at the Cock-Pit in Drury-Lane, once at Court with singular Applause. Never printed till now* (London, 1658).

64 Peter Corbin and Douglas Sedge, introduction to *The Witch of Edmonton,* by William Rowley, Thomas Dekker, and John Ford, Revels Student edition, ed. Corbin and Sedge (Manchester: Manchester University Press, 1999), 6.

65 Anthony Dawson and Viviana Comensoli have offered structural and historicist accounts in which the bigamy plot highlights the pressures on women and the threat of social marginality. See Dawson, "Witchcraft/Bigamy: Cultural Conflict in *The Witch of Edmonton,*" in *Renaissance Drama* 20 (1989): 77–99; and Comensoli, "Witchcraft and Domestic Tragedy in *The Witch of Edmonton,*" in *The Politics of Gender in Early Europe,* ed. Jean R. Brink, Allison P. Coudert, and Maryanne C. Horowitz (Kirksville, Mo.: Sixteenth Century Journal Publishers, 1989), 43–59. David Atkinson's position is that the plots enact complementary dramas of antisocial hubris and moral reckoning. Atkinson,

"The Two Plots of *The Witch of Edmonton*," *Notes and Queries* 31, no. 2 (1984): 229–30. Other scholars have pointed to both plots' concern with the efficacy and truth status of language and oaths. Todd Butler reads the legal problem of bigamy alongside Goodcole's affirmations of the truth of witchcraft in the pamphlet in "Swearing Justice in Henry Goodcole and *The Witch of Edmonton*," *SEL Studies in English Literature 1500–1900* 50, no. 1 (2010): 127–45; Elyssa Y. Cheng reads Elizabeth Sawyer and Susan as victims of an overarching social pathology resulting from private/patriarchal land ownership in "Marginalizing Women: Forced Marriage, Witchcraft Accusations, and the Social Machinery of Private Landownership in *The Witch of Edmonton*," *Concentric: Literary and Cultural Studies* 36, no. 1 (2010): 119–34; and Cindy L. Vitto reads the twinned performative rituals of marriage and witch initiation in a destabilized Reformation context in "Mismatched Words and Deeds: Rituals in *The Witch of Edmonton*," in *Ceremony and Text in the Renaissance*, ed. Douglas F. Rutledge (Newark: University of Delaware Press, 1996), 167–79.

66 Rowley, Dekker, and Ford, *Witch of Edmonton*, 1.1.44. All subsequent citations in the text are from the Revels Student edition and are cited parenthetically in text by act, scene, and line number.

67 The portentous mood of secrecy, stigma, and fear around Winnifride's bridal pregnancy in *The Witch of Edmonton* may reflect a changing disciplinary norm in which church courts attempted to crack down on premarital fornication and bridal pregnancy (which was extremely common) after about 1600, in an effort to insist that only church marriage made sexual relations licit. This push for official condemnation (which was especially intense in areas of economic scarcity) contends against a preexisting and coexisting social norm in which premarital sex and bridal pregnancy were relatively widespread and accepted as long as marriage took place before the birth; see Martin Ingraham, *Church Courts, Sex, and Marriage in England, 1570–1640* (Cambridge: Cambridge University Press, 1987), 219–37.

68 Sedgwick, "Paranoid Reading," 17.

69 See Millar, *Witchcraft*.

70 Millar, *Witchcraft*, 101–7.

71 "Ingle" has connotations of service that are interesting in that they bear out the witch/familiar dynamic—which is itself a reversal of the larger cosmic order enacted by the familiar's seducing the witch into the devil's service. In this relation, Dog appears to take the submissive sexual role, although he obviously wields control over Cuddy; see DiGangi, *Homoerotics of Early Modern Drama*, 64–67.

72 "Spit in thy mouth" refers to a gesture of affection that was believed to please dogs. Rowley, Dekker, and Ford, *Witch of Edmonton*, 107n286.

It is also an explicit sexual metaphor, along with "given him a bone to gnaw twenty times," both of which allude to oral sex between the Dog and Cuddy Banks.

73 The term for this particular gendered form of manipulation originates with the film *Gaslight* (dir. George Cukor, 1944), based on the 1938 play by Patrick Hamilton, *Gas Light*. As in *The Witch of Edmonton*, a husband convinces his wife she is going mad in order to conceal his past criminal acts—by dimming the lights and denying to her that they are dimming.

74 Sedgwick, "Paranoid Reading," 19.

75 Cuddy Banks's scenes with Dog (thought to be chiefly Rowley's work) are the only place where any details of the play's demonology are presented. See Corbin and Douglas Sedge, introduction to Rowley, Dekker, and Ford, *Witch of Edmonton*, 6.

76 The ontological status of the "Spirit of Susan" is as ambiguous as the Dog's placement of the murder weapon; if not a ghost, it could be construed as the uncanny materialization of Frank's guilty imagination, or as a demonic apparition in Susan's shape, sent out by the Dog to torment him.

77 Sedgwick, "Paranoid Reading," 17.

78 Sedgwick, *Epistemology*, 81.

79 A February 8, 2011, production directed by Jesse Berger for the Red Bull Theater in New York City included a silent, stylized tableau of Elizabeth Sawyer burning alive alongside Winnifride's recitation of her epilogue, with the two women lit by twin spotlights on an otherwise pitch-black stage, providing a convicting reminder of the cost at which Winnifride's redemption is bought.

4. Lost Worlds, Lost Selves

1 Jean de Léry, *History of a Voyage to the Land of Brazil*, trans. Janet Whatley (Berkeley: University of California Press, 1990), 197. All subsequent citations of Léry's text are from Janet Whatley's authoritative translation, based on the 1580 edition. I also refer to the first printed edition, *Histoire d'un voyage faict en la terre du Bresil autrement dite Amerique/le tout recueilli sur les lieux par Jean de Léry* (Geneva, 1578), as well as a modern French edition also based on the 1580 text, *Histoire d'un voyage faict en la terre du Brésil*, 2nd ed., ed. Frank Lestringant (Paris: Librarie Générale Française, 1994).

2 Janet Whatley, introduction to Léry, *History of a Voyage*, xxi.

3 Paul Hulton, "Introduction to the Dover Edition" of Thomas Harriot's *A Briefe and True Report of the New Found Land of Virginia: The Complete 1590 Theodor De Bry Edition*, ed. Paul Hulton (Frankfurt: J. Wechel for T. De Bry, 1590; fascimile ed., New York: Dover, 1972), vii–ix.

4　For more on the history of generic cross-currents between colonial travel narratives and romance, see Donald Kimball Smith, *The Cartographic Imagination: Re-writing the World in Marlowe, Spenser, Raleigh, and Marvell* (Burlington, Vt.: Ashgate, 2008); Karen Newman, *Cultural Capitals: Early Modern London and Paris* (Princeton, N.J.: Princeton University Press, 2007), especially chap. 6, "Armchair Travel"; and Joan Pong Linton, *The Romance of the New World: Gender and the Literary Formations of English Colonialism* (Cambridge: Cambridge University Press, 1998).

5　See Shankar Raman, "Back to the Future: Forging History in Luís de Camões's Os Lusíadas," in *Travel Knowledges: European "Discoveries" in the Early Modern Period,* ed. Ivo Kamps and Jyotsna Singh (London: Palgrave, 2001), 134; Thomas Scanlan, *Colonial Writing and the New World, 1583–1671: Allegories of Desire* (Cambridge: Cambridge University Press, 1999), 3–4; and Jacques Lezra, *Unspeakable Subjects: The Genealogy of the Event in Early Modern Europe* (Stanford, Calif.: Stanford University Press, 1997), 40–41.

6　Hulton, "Introduction to the Dover Edition," xiv.

7　The 1590 folio edition of Harriot's report with White's "True Pictures" was the inaugural volume of De Bry's America series. Léry's *Histoire d'un voyage* was enormously successful as well, enjoying reprintings in 1580, 1585, 1594, 1599–1600, and 1611 after the initial publication in 1578. Translated into Latin and German, it becomes part of De Bry's third volume of the America series in 1592. Léry's text is also anthologized in English, as "Extracts out of the Historie of John Lerius a Frenchman, Who Lived in Brasill with Mons. Villagagnon, Ann. 1557, and 58," in the 1625 edition of Samuel Purchas's compendium of travel writing, *Hakluytus posthumus, or Purchas his Pilgrimes* (first published in 1613). See Janet Whatley, "Editions and Reception of Léry," in Léry, *History of a Voyage*, 220–21, as well as the book's bibliography, 258–59.

8　On the entrance of Henri II, see Michael Wintroub, *A Savage Mirror: Power, Identity, and Knowledge in Early Modern France* (Stanford, Calif.: Stanford University Press, 2006). On the uses of blackness in the Jacobean court, see Hall, *Things of Darkness,* 127–40.

9　Virginia Mason Vaughan addresses the stage as a site for representing racial difference in "Enter Three Turks and a Moor: Signifying the 'Other' in Early Modern English Drama," in *Speaking Pictures: The Visual/Verbal Nexus of Dramatic Performance* (Teaneck, N.J.: Fairleigh Dickinson University Press, 2010), 119–40. Nabil Matar refines the historical connections between early modern Britain's "triangular" relationships with Muslims from the Levant and North Africa and Native Americans in Virginia in *Turks, Moors, and Englishmen in the Age of Discovery* (New York: Columbia University Press, 1999).

10 Fanon, *Black Skin, White Masks*, 89; Roland Greene, *Unrequited Conquests: Love and Empire in the Colonial Americas* (Chicago: University of Chicago Press, 1999), 81.

11 Major examples include Stephen Greenblatt, *Marvelous Possessions: The Wonder of the New World* (Oxford: Oxford University Press, 1991); Michel de Certeau, *The Writing of History*, trans. Tom Conley (New York: Columbia University Press, 1988); and Tzvetan Todorov, *The Conquest of America: The Question of the Other*, trans. Richard Howard (New York: Harper & Row, 1984).

12 An explication of the "straight" reading of colonial desire can be found in Greenblatt's treatment of the writings of Columbus and Cortés in chap. 3, "Marvelous Possessions," and chap. 5, "The Go-Between," of *Marvelous Possessions*. On racialized colonial desire, see Hall, *Things of Darkness*, 25–43.

13 See Hall, *Things of Darkness*, especially chap. 1, "A World of Difference: Travel Narratives and the Inscription of Culture"; Louis Montrose, "The Work of Gender and Sexuality in the Elizabethan Discourse of Discovery," in *Discourses of Sexuality from Aristotle to AIDS*, ed. Donna C. Stanton (Ann Arbor: University of Michigan Press, 1992), 138–94; and Mary Louise Pratt, *Imperial Eyes: Travel Writing and Transculturation* (New York: Routledge, 1992).

14 Other scholars of psychoanalysis have traced how Freud's revisions of his ideas on narcissism and sexual inversion "subordinate[d] both to the teleology of procreative heterosexuality," so that "inversion becomes not a separate dynamic of cathexis with its own authority, but a misplaying of the singularly authorized heterosexual cathexis." Gregory W. Bredbeck, "Narcissus in the Wilde: Textual Cathexis and the Historical Origins of Queer Camp," in *The Politics and Poetics of Camp*, ed. Moe Meyer (New York: Routledge, 1994), 62–63. See also 59–64 on Freud's subtle heteronormativizing of his account of sexual maturation.

15 Fradenburg and Freccero, "Introduction: Caxton, Foucault, and the Pleasures of History," xix.

16 Sedgwick, "Paranoid Reading," 16–17.

17 Sedgwick, "Paranoid Reading," 17–19.

18 See Fanon, *Black Skin, White Masks*, xiv; also chap. 7, "The Black Man and Recognition."

19 Homi Bhabha, *The Location of Culture* (New York: Routledge, 1994), 100. Bhabha is analyzing nineteenth-century colonial administrative processes of civil address and legal inscription, but the cycle of craven investment in the other's gaze that he describes can be seen long before the advent of those regimes.

20 Bhabha, *Location of Culture*, 63.

21 Bhabha, *Location of Culture*, 61.

22 This also serves to make explicit the limitations of this study to a focus

on European desires. There is important work being done that seeks to recover the perspectives of American people looking at the European invaders. See Beatríz Pastor, "Silence and Writing: The History of the Conquest," trans. Jason Wood, in *1492/1992: Re/discovering Colonial Writing*, ed. René Jara and Nicolas Spadaccini (Minneapolis: University of Minnesota Press, 1996). Pastor takes up the project of "rewriting" the history of the conquest, which requires "retracing the lost steps, listening to other voices that could have related the history of a discovery rooted in dreams and lies" (147).

23 "The form [of the event's] appearing—the morphology of the culture or of the moment—'precedes' the event, which comes to form always and already in the shape of a sign, an event that 'means something.'" Lezra, *Unspeakable Subjects*, 40–41.

24 Of the critics who have written on same-sex, gay, or queer erotics in the colonial sphere, only Freccero, in the last chapter of *Queer/Early/Modern*, a methodological intervention titled "Queer Spectrality," has articulated a similar valence of melancholic desire in colonial writing. Freccero advocates for a queer historiography of being haunted by the past, which she distinguishes from melancholia's "entombment"—although her model of queer, transtemporal historical affect resonates with the past- and future-oriented melancholias I am describing.

25 See Mark Rifkin, *When Did Indians Become Straight? Kinship, the History of Sexuality, and Native Sovereignty* (Oxford: Oxford University Press), 2011; Elizabeth A. Povinelli, *The Empire of Love: Toward a Theory of Intimacy, Genealogy, and Carnality* (Durham, N.C.: Duke University Press, 2008); and Peter Sigal, *Infamous Desire: Male Homosexuality in Colonial Latin America* (Chicago: University of Chicago Press, 2003).

26 The coexistence of forms of queer identification and desire with violent exploitation in colonial sexuality has been clarified for me by Rifkin's work, particularly *When Did Indians Become Straight?*, and by Canadian First Nations (Cree) artist Kent Monkman's Old Masters–style paintings, which render fantasy histories of graphic colonial homoeroticism and violence (https://www.kentmonkman.com/). See Rifkin, *When Did Indians Become Straight?*, 26–30, for an incisive critique of the ways in which queer theory has been implicated in settler colonial imperatives through binary and white-normative conceptions of kinship, family, individuality, citizenship, and the nation-state.

27 Rifkin, *When Did Indians Become Straight?*; Puar, *Terrorist Assemblages*.

28 Sigmund Freud, "Mourning and Melancholia" (1917), in *Standard Edition*, 14:243–58.

29 Freud, "Mourning and Melancholia," 245.

30 Freud, "Mourning and Melancholia," 244.

31 Freud, "Mourning and Melancholia," 249, categorizes identification as

the surrogation of the desire for difference, "a substitute for the erotic cathexis." But some attachments—or some subjects, it seems—were always suspiciously narcissistic in their object-choices: when "the object-choice has been effected on a narcissistic basis," the melancholic's object-love has some essential susceptibility to "regress into narcissism" at the first "obstacle." However, this regression is also a return, back to "a preliminary stage of object-choice . . . the first way— and one that is expressed in an ambivalent fashion—in which the ego picks out an object." Freud, "On Narcissism," 554, defines narcissism as the "original" erotic condition, which is sustained and intensified in "perverts and homosexuals" and at "the maturing of the female sexual organs," and which only normal, Oedipal, heterosexual men completely banish.

32   Other critics have used the idea of melancholia to discuss the aftermath of colonial violence, notably Paul Gilroy, *Postcolonial Melancholia* (New York: Columbia University Press, 2005); Ranjana Khanna, *Dark Continents: Psychoanalysis and Colonialism* (Durham, N.C.: Duke University Press, 2003); and Anne Anlin Cheng, *The Melancholy of Race: Psychoanalysis, Assimilation, and Hidden Grief* (Oxford: Oxford University Press, 2001).

33   "Nostalgia, *n.*," 1. and 2.a., *OED Online*.

34   Halberstam, *Queer Art of Failure* and *In a Queer Time and Place*; Love, *Feeling Backward*.

35   Michael Warner treats the history of often reductive associations in psychoanalytic thought between homosexuality and narcissistic overidentification in "Homo-Narcissism; or, Heterosexuality," in *Engendering Men*, ed. Joseph A. Boone and Michael Cadden (New York: Routledge, 1990), 190–206. Earl Jackson Jr. offers a critique in *Strategies of Deviance: Studies in Gay Male Representation* (Bloomington: University of Indiana Press, 1995) of psychoanalytic theory's construction of a gay subject. However, Jackson also seeks to rehabilitate one nuance of Freud's notion of narcissism: "a range of identificatory operations . . . a potentially compelling descriptive model of the dynamic interchanges constituting psychosocial subject formation (and the economic fluctuations of external or internal libidinal investments)." Jackson, *Strategies of Deviance*, 21–26.

36   Freud, "Mourning and Melancholia," 247.

37   Freud, "Mourning and Melancholia," 245.

38   Claude Lévi-Strauss, *Tristes Tropiques* (1955), trans. John Russell (New York: Atheneum, 1972), 85.

39   Léry, *History of a Voyage*, 41; "ils la vouloyent mascher et avaler toute crue," *Histoire d'un voyage* (1994), 177.

40   Sara Castro-Klarén, "Parallaxes: Cannibalism and Self-Embodiment; or, The Calvinist Reading of Tupi A-Theology," in *Thinking the Limits*

of the Body, ed. Jeffrey Jerome Cohen and Gail Weiss (Albany: SUNY Press, 2003), 101–28. See also the canonical work of Frank Lestringant, particularly *Le huguenot et le sauvage: L'Amerique et la controverse coloniale, en France, au temps des Guerres de Religion (1555–1589)* (Paris: Aux Amateurs des Livres, 1990) and "Calvinistes et cannibales: Les écrits protestants sur le Brésil français (1555–1560)," *Bulletin de la société de l'histoire du protestantisme français* 126 (1980): 19–26.

41 Whatley, "Editions and Reception of Léry," 221; Carla Freccero, "Heteroerotic Homoeroticism: Jean de Léry and the 'New World' Man," in *The Rhetoric of the Other: Lesbian and Gay Strategies of Resistance in French and Francophone Contexts,* ed. Martine Antle and Dominique Fisher (New Orleans, La.: University of the South Press, 2002), 101–14.

42 Michel de Montaigne, "Of Cannibals" (c. 1580), in *The Complete Essays of Montaigne,* trans. Donald M. Frame (Stanford, Calif.: Stanford University Press, 1957), book 1, chap. 13, 150–52.

43 Freccero, *Queer/Early/Modern,* 69–104; "Heteroerotic Homoeroticism"; and "Cannibalism, Homophobia, Women: Montaigne's 'Des cannibales' and 'De l'amitié,'" in *Women, "Race," and Writing in the Early Modern Period,* ed. Margo Hendricks and Patricia Parker (New York: Routledge, 1994), 73–84.

44 Léry, *History of a Voyage,* 198.

45 "Ausquels . . . j'ay cogneu plus de rondeur qu'en plusieurs de par-deça, lesquels à leur condamnation, portent titre de Chrestiens." Léry, *Histoire d'un voyage* (1994), 508.

46 The iconic trope of queer desire I cite here, "I *am* the Love that dare not speak its name," is the last line of a poem, "Two Loves," by Lord Alfred (Bosie) Douglas, the perpetually absconding object of Oscar Wilde's melancholic desire, which appeared in the sole issue of the sexually transgressive and queer-affiliated Oxford undergraduate literary journal *The Chameleon* 1, no. 1 (1894): 28. Quoted in Sedgwick, *Epistemology,* 74.

47 Léry, *History of a Voyage,* 67.

48 Freccero, *Queer/Early/Modern,* 95.

49 "Je les voye tousjours devant mes yeux, j'en auray à jamais l'idée et l'image en mon entendement." Léry, *Histoire d'un voyage* (1994), 233–34.

50 Freud, "Mourning and Melancholia," 249–50.

51 Judith Butler, *The Psychic Life of Power: Theories in Subjection* (Stanford, Calif.: Stanford University Press, 1997), 196.

52 Léry, *History of a Voyage,* 67; "je confesse qu'il est malaisé de les bien representer, ni par escrit, ni mesme par peinture," *Histoire d'un voyage* (1994), 234.

53 This particular register of histrionic disavowal of the possibility of description coupled with florid description has been explicated as a

specifically camp sensibility by Abigail Joseph. See Joseph, "'Excesses of Every Kind': Dress and Drag around 1870," in *Crossings in Text and Textile*, ed. Katherine Joslin and Daneen Wardrop (Durham: University of New Hampshire Press, 2015), 13.

54 Freud, "Mourning and Melancholia," 245.

55 Freud, "Mourning and Melancholia," 245.

56 "One feels justified in maintaining the belief that a loss of this kind has occurred, but one cannot see clearly what it is that has been lost, and it is all the more reasonable to suppose that the patient cannot consciously perceive what he has lost either." Freud, "Mourning and Melancholia," 245.

57 Freud, "Mourning and Melancholia," 245.

58 Léry, "Préface," *History of a Voyage*, xlv.

59 Léry, "Préface," xlvi.

60 Freccero, *Queer/Early/Modern*, 87, characterizes these events of re-ligiously motivated torture and mass murder as modern or protomod-ern traumas that do shattering, haunting violence to the narratives of French nationhood.

61 Freud characterizes repetition-compulsion as an unconsciously self-destructive neurotic response to a trauma, especially a trauma like the ministers' sojourn in Brazil, in which the subject is passive and power-less. Sigmund Freud, "Beyond the Pleasure Principle" (1920), in *Standard Edition*, 18:1–64.

62 Léry, *History of a Voyage*, 199.

63 Léry, *History of a Voyage*, 200.

64 Léry, "Préface," xlv.

65 Freccero, "Cannibalism, Homophobia, Women," 78.

66 Léry, *History of a Voyage*, 121.

67 Léry, *History of a Voyage*, 142.

68 Léry, *History of a Voyage*, 141.

69 I am intrigued by Léry's belated insertion into his narrative of a parallel between his memory of the ceremony and a witches' Sabbath. Léry even adds a passage from Jean Bodin's witch-crazed treatise, *De la démono-manie des sorciers* (1578), to the 1585 edition of *Histoire d'un voyage*, concluding that Bodin best describes what he witnessed twenty years before. Greenblatt, *Marvelous Possessions*, 15–19, is perceptive when he describes how thoroughly literal and material—not metaphorical—negative affects are for Jean de Léry; he experiences suffering, pain, and torment as part of the same erotic mechanism as wonder and pleasure.

70 Léry, *History of a Voyage*, 141–42.

71 Léry, *History of a Voyage*, 144.

72 Freccero, *Queer/Early/Modern*, 99; Bersani, *Homos*, 101.

73 Goldberg, "History That Will Be," 16.

74 Goldberg, "History That Will Be," 15.

75 Harriot, *Briefe and True Report*, 9. Citations to this text are hereafter cited in the footnotes according to the text's 1590 folio page numbering.
76 Edelman, *No Future*, 1–32.
77 Harriot, *Briefe and True Report*, 11.
78 Harriot, *Briefe and True Report*, 25.
79 Harriot, *Briefe and True Report*, 27.
80 Léry, *History of a Voyage*, 64.
81 Harriot, *Briefe and True Report*, 27.
82 Harriot, *Briefe and True Report*, 24.
83 Sedgwick, "Queer and Now," 6.
84 Harriot, *Briefe and True Report*, 27.
85 Goldberg, "History That Will Be," 18, reads Harriot as attempting to "dazzle" the natives with writing and to endow writing with magic-making power by including it on this list.
86 Goldberg, "History That Will Be," 15.
87 Bhabha, *Location of Culture*, 100.
88 Sedgwick, "Queer and Now," 3.
89 Sedgwick, "Queer and Now," 3.
90 Sedgwick, "Queer and Now," 3.
91 Harriot, *Briefe and True Report*, 27.
92 This fantasy appears periodically in the voyage-history genre, including George Best's 1570s accounts of Martin Frobisher's voyages to Baffin Island. It appears as a claim that Native Americans communicate—in words or by gestures—a self-consciousness of their relative cognitive simplicity compared to the invaders, as well as an inability to grasp the abstract principles that animate European technology and scientific thought. See Greenblatt, *Marvelous Possessions*, 114–16.
93 Harriot, *Briefe and True Report*, 29.
94 Harriot, *Briefe and True Report*, 29.
95 Harriot, *Briefe and True Report*, 29.
96 Harriot, *Briefe and True Report*, 29.
97 Harriot, *Briefe and True Report*, 29.
98 Greenblatt, "Invisible Bullets," in *Shakespearean Negotiations*, 35–36.
99 Goldberg, "History That Will Be," 15.
100 Goldberg, "History That Will Be," 16.
101 Goldberg, "History That Will Be," 16.
102 Goldberg, "History That Will Be," 16.
103 Goldberg, "History That Will Be," 15.
104 Nikolas Rose, *The Politics of Life Itself: Biomedicine, Power, and Subjectivity in the Twenty-First Century* (Princeton, N.J.: Princeton Univeristy Press, 2007), 4–5.
105 Stephen Greenblatt, "Invisible Bullets: Renaissance Authority and Its Subversion," *Glyph* 8 (1981): 50, quoted in Goldberg, "History That Will Be," 16.

106 Edelman, *No Future*; Bersani, "Is the Rectum a Grave?"; Patricia Highsmith, *The Talented Mr. Ripley* (1955).

107 Theodor De Bry, "To the gentle Reader"; "The True Pictures and Fashions of the People in that Parte of America Now Called Virginia . . . ," in Harriot, *Briefe and True Report*, [41].

108 "True Pictures," [36].

109 The definitive modern edition of John White's Roanoke watercolors is *The American Drawings of John White*, ed. Paul Hulton and David Beers Quinn, 2 vols. (Chapel Hill: University of North Carolina Press, 1964).

110 Hulton, "Introduction to the Dover Edition," xi.

111 John White, "A weroan or great Lorde of Virginia. III"; "True Pictures," A. Further citations from "True Pictures" will be cited in notes under John White's name and the "True Pictures" page signature.

112 White, "True Pictures," A5.

113 White, "True Pictures," A6.

114 See Mark Rifkin, *Beyond Settler Time: Temporal Sovereignty and Indigenous Self-Determination* (Durham, N.C.: Duke University Press, 2017), for an intervention into how native peoples have been situated in time—both by primitivist relegation to the past and by the liberal settler state's erasure of indigenous temporalities via inclusion in the modern present.

115 White, "True Pictures," A6.

116 White, "True Pictures," D2.

117 White, "True Pictures," E.

118 Sedgwick, "Foreword: T Times," xii.

119 See Sam Smiles, "John White and British Antiquity: Savage Origins in the Context of Tudor Historiography," in *European Visions: American Voices*, ed. Kim Sloan (London: Trustees of the British Museum, 2009), 106–12.

120 The Roanoke story has inspired hundreds of books of varying degrees of historicity and imaginative speculation. I have relied on the work of David Beers Quinn, whose numerous publications on English colonialism include *Set Fair for Roanoke: Voyages and Colonies, 1584–1606* (Chapel Hill: University of North Carolina Press, 1985); see also James Horn, *A Kingdom Strange: The Brief and Tragic History of the Lost Colony of Roanoke* (New York: Basic Books, 2010); and Lee Miller, *Roanoke: Solving the Mystery of the Lost Colony* (New York: Arcade, 2000).

121 John White to Richard Hakluyt, letter, February 4, 1593, in *The Roanoke Voyages, 1584–90: Documents to Illustrate the English Voyages to North America under the Patent Granted to Walter Raleigh in 1584*, ed. David Beers Quinn (New York: Dover Publications, 1991), 2:714.

122 White to Hakluyt, letter, 2:715.

123 White to Hakluyt, letter, 2:715.

124 The multiple narratives about the lost settlers are contextualized within the political history of the indigenous nations in the area in Michael Leroy Oberg's masterful historical study, *The Head in Edward Nugent's Hand: Roanoke's Forgotten Indians* (Philadelphia: University of Pennsylvania Press, 2007).

125 John Smith, *A True Relation of Such Occurrences and Accidents of Noate as Hath Hapned in Virginia, 1608,* in *The Complete Works of Captain John Smith, 1580–1631,* ed. Philip L. Barbour (Chapel Hill: University of North Carolina Press, 1986), 48, 54.

126 This map, known as the Carta Zúñiga because it was leaked to Spain by an ambassador, is reproduced in William P. Cumming's *The Southeast in Early Maps,* 3rd ed., revised and enlarged by Louis De Vorsey Jr. (Chapel Hill: University of North Carolina Press, 1998), map 21.

127 "Instructions Orders and Constitutions to Sir Thomas Gates Knight Governor of Virginia," May 1609, printed in *The Records of the Virginia Company of London,* ed. Susan M. Kingsbury (Washington, D.C.: Government Printing Office, 1906–35), 3:17.

128 This comment appears in editions of Purchas, *Hakluytus posthumus, or Purchas his Pilgrimes,* beginning in 1624–25, both as a marginal footnote to Smith's account and in an editorial tract Purchas appends to the reports he includes from the Virginia colonies. See *Hakluytus posthumus* (London, 1625), vol. 4, book 9 ("English Plantations, Discoveries, Acts, and Occurents, in Virginia and Summer Ilands, Since the Yeere 1606. Till 1624"), chap. 4 ("The proceedings of the English Colonie in Virginia"), 1728; and chap. 20 ("Virginia's Verger"), 1813.

129 William Strachey, *The Historie of Travaile into Virginia Britannia* (London: Hakluyt Society, 1849), 85–86, 101.

130 Strachey, *Historie of Travaile,* 26.

131 Oberg, *Head in Edward Nugent's Hand,* 127–39, reads the Jamestown colonists' search for Roanoke survivors in the context of the contested political terrain of the Powhatan empire. Effectively, the Englishmen went where their native hosts, guides, protectors, and enslavers wanted them to go, and were told what served the native leaders' purposes.

132 George Percy, *A Discourse of the Plantation of the Southerne Colonie in Virginia,* printed in *A Library of American Literature from the Earliest Settlement to the Present Time: Early Colonial Literature, 1607–1675,* ed. Edmund Clarence Stedman and Ellen Mackay Hutchinson (New York: Webster, 1889), 1:33.

133 Oberg, *Head in Edward Nugent's Hand,* 130–31, recounts the Christian racial uplift fantasies around the Hatteras people's supposed European descent recorded by colonial surveyor John Lawson in the early eighteenth century. On the isolation of the North Carolina Tuscarora from the rest of the Tuscarora nation, traces of the Roanoke settlers in Tuscarora oral history and phenotypes, and the role of light eyes in Tuscarora

conflicts with white settlers, see Arwin D. Smallwood, *Bertie County: An Eastern North Carolina History* (Charleston, S.C.: Arcadia Publishing, 2002), 28–29, 44–45.

134   See Malinda Maynor Lowery, *Lumbee Indians in the Jim Crow South: Race, Identity, and the Making of a Nation* (Chapel Hill: University of North Carolina Press, 2010).

135   This genetic-nostalgia imperative is exemplified by such popular genealogy efforts as the Lost Colony DNA Project (http://www.lost-colony .com/DNAproj.html), organized by the Lost Colony Center for Science and Research, a lay historical and genealogical society in North Carolina. The racial fetishism around DNA, particularly as it is used to reconstruct the histories of indigenous people in the Americas, is unpacked by Kim TallBear, *Native American DNA: Tribal Belonging and the False Promise of Genetic Science* (Minneapolis: University of Minnesota Press, 2013).

136   Strachey, *Historie of Travaile*, 26.

137   Michael Harkin, "Performing Paradox: Narrativity and the Lost Colony of Roanoke," in *Myth and Memory: Stories of Indigenous–European Contact*, ed. John Sutton Lutz (Vancouver: University of British Columbia Press, 2007), 104.

138   For a thorough history of the Roanoke narrative's romanticization in and as literature confirming the providential rightness of white Manifest Destiny in America, see Robert D. Arner, "The Romance of Roanoke: Virginia Dare and the Lost Colony in American Literature," *Southern Literary Journal* 10, no. 2 (1978): 5–45.

139   Harkin, "Performing Paradox," 110–15

140   "Sad Fate of the White Doe. Deadly Work of the Silver Bullet. The Captain Becomes Reminiscent on a Trip which Seems to Have Neither Start Nor Finish," *New York Times*, April 22, 1888.

141   Sallie Southall Cotten, *The White Doe, or The Fate of Virginia Dare—An Indian Legend* (Philadelphia, Pa.: Lippincott, 1901).

142   Arner, "Romance of Roanoke," 26.

143   Entries about the Roanoke colony are included in many encyclopedias of the paranormal and unexplained, including Time-Life Books's Mysteries of the Unknown series. It is listed in compendia of ghost-haunted places on the earth and is featured in several television documentaries investigating famous unsolved mysteries.

144   Michael Wallis makes this point about the sensationalistic and moralizing media narratives surrounding the Donner party, which characterized the survivors' cannibalism as an outbreak of exceptional, diabolical, inhuman monstrosity in order to downplay the challenge their ordeal posed to the entire westward expansion project. Wallis, *The Best Land under Heaven: The Donner Party in the Age of Manifest Destiny* (New York: Norton, 2017).

145   The American Protestant origin myth that draws mystical biblical time into the settler colonial present even more explicitly is the founding myth of Mormonism: the story of Joseph Smith being given the golden tablets containing the Book of Mormon by the angel Moroni, which takes place in Palmyra, New York, in the early nineteenth century, and which can in some ways be considered a sequel and a companion tale to the story of the lost colony.

146   *American Horror Story: Roanoke,* season 6, created by Ryan Murphy and Brad Falchuk, 2016; Michael Scott, *The Secrets of the Immortal Nicholas Flamel* (series, 2007–12); Neil Gaiman, *Marvel 1602* (2003); *Storm of the Century,* created by Stephen King, 1999; Harlan Ellison, "Croatoan" (1975); Philip José Farmer, *Dare* (1965).

147   Harkin, "Performing Paradox," 103–17.

148   Harkin, "Performing Paradox," 115.

149   Oberg, *Head in Edward Nugent's Hand,* 136. Rifkin theorizes indigenous adoption as a land-based, political practice, in opposition to white settler sexuality's imposition of the heterosexual nuclear family. Rifkin, *When Did Indians Become Straight?,* 31, 50–52.

150   Harkin, "Performing Paradox," 103–4.

151   Quinn, *Set Fair for Roanoke,* 132–34.

152   See Scott L. Malcomson, *One Drop of Blood: The American Misadventure of Race* (New York: Farrar, Straus and Giroux, 2000).

153   Quinn, *Set Fair for Roanoke,* 153.

154   See Alden T. Vaughan, *Transatlantic Encounters: American Indians in Britain, 1500–1776* (Cambridge: Cambridge University Press, 2006), 26–27.

155   The Southern Poverty Law Center (https://www.splcenter.org/) lists VDARE as a white nationalist extremist group.

156   Ben Davis, "The New White Nationalism's Sloppy Use of Art History, Decoded," *Artnet News,* March 7, 2017, https://news.artnet.com/.

157   "American Renaissance," Southern Poverty Law Center, https://www.splcenter.org/.

158   Documentation of VDARE's presence at the 2017 Conservative Political Action Conference is provided by journalist Osita Nwanevu in "The True Face of Trump Conservativism Can Be Seen in CPAC's Swag Center," Slate, February 25, 2017, https://slate.com/.

159   In Freud's "Mourning and Melancholia," 245, the subject may know "*whom* he has lost, but not *what* he has lost in him."

160   Cheng, *Melancholy of Race,* 126.

161   Cheng, *Melancholy of Race*; Bhabha, *Location of Culture*; Fanon, *Black Skin, White Masks*; Sharon Patricia Holland, *The Erotic Life of Racism* (Durham, N.C.: Duke University Press, 2012); and Siobhan Somerville, *Queering the Color Line: Race and the Invention of Homosexuality in American Culture* (Durham, N.C.: Duke University Press, 2000).

162 Sedgwick, "Paranoid Reading," 6.

163 Judith Butler, "Melancholy Gender-Refused Identification," *Psychoanalytic Dialogues* 5, no. 2 (1995), 172.

164 Butler, "Melancholy Gender," 171.

165 In Butler, "Melancholy Gender," 169, the analogy is actually: "If one is a girl to the extent that one does not want a girl, then wanting a girl will bring being a girl into question; within this matrix, homosexual desire thus panics gender."

166 Butler, *Psychic Life of Power,* 196.

167 Butler, *Psychic Life of Power,* 196.

Conclusion

1 Sedgwick, "Paranoid Reading," 6.

2 Naomi Klein, *The Shock Doctrine: The Rise of Disaster Capitalism* (New York: Picador, 2008).

3 In addition to Sedgwick, "Paranoid Reading," see the section titled "Thought as Privilege" in "Queer and Now," 18–20.

4 Sedgwick, "Paranoid Reading," 20.

5 "Data Snapshot: Contingent Faculty in U.S. Higher Ed," AAUP: American Association of University Professors, October 11, 2018, https://www.aaup.org/.

6 Sedgwick, "Paranoid Reading," 4–5.

7 Sedgwick, "Paranoid Reading," 18.

8 Sedgwick, "Paranoid Reading," 35.

9 Sedgwick, "Paranoid Reading," 16–17.

10 Sedgwick, "Paranoid Reading," 8.

11 Latour, *We Have Never Been Modern,* 5–10.

12 Most recently Traub, *Thinking Sex with the Early Moderns.*

13 Sedgwick, "Paranoid Reading," 22.

14 Sedgwick, "Paranoid Reading," 22.

15 Sedgwick, "Paranoid Reading," 25.

16 Rita Felski, *The Uses of Literature* (Oxford: Blackwell, 2008), 2.

17 Rita Felski, *The Limits of Critique* (Chicago: University of Chicago Press, 2015).

18 Felski, *Uses of Literature,* 10–11.

19 Dimock, "Theory of Resonance," 1064.

20 Dimock, "Theory of Resonance," 1064.

Index

INDEX

garments, 72, 114; masculine, 86, 93; phallic, 89

Gaslight (film), 302n73

Geertz, Clifford, 27

gender, 3, 12, 26, 58, 94, 116, 119, 145, 150, 154, 173, 205, 262; binary, 72, 254; performance of, 84

gender reveal, 59, 69–70, 91

genderqueer, 41, 75, 86, 95, 279n107

genealogy, 231, 254; queer, 48, 116, 241

generation, 33, 109; asexual, 32, 43, 105–6, 233–34, 236; sexual, 106–7, 108

genitals, 8, 13, 39, 81, 100, 119, 140, 141, 164; eroticism and, 14

genocide, 209, 231, 235

Girard, René, 103

God, 161, 229, 299n53

Goldberg, Jonathan, 30, 224, 227–28, 231, 278n90, 290n48

Goodcole, Henry, 171, 176, 179–80, 301n65

Gordon, Colby, 76

Gowing, Laura, 151

Greenblatt, Stephen, 27, 94, 95, 231, 235, 277n76, 304n12

Greene, Roland, 203

Grenville, Richard, 201, 237, 251

Guattari, Félix, 6, 10, 126, 291n55

Guy-Bray, Stephen, 277n79

Hakluyt, Richard, 203, 237, 244

Halberstam, Jack, 19, 28, 73, 211, 277n81

Halperin, David, 29

Hamlet (Shakespeare), 275n41

Harkin, Michael, 249, 250

Harriot, Thomas, 47, 48, 201, 202, 203, 204, 209, 212, 223, 224, 226, 228–29, 231–33, 234, 237, 239, 244–45, 248, 253, 254, 255, 261

Harris, Jonathan Gil, 291n63

Henry II, 203, 220

heteroeroticism, 42, 114, 115

heteronormativity, 5, 28, 30–31, 92, 93, 116, 205

heterosexuality, 18, 20, 66, 71, 84, 92, 96, 97, 104, 115, 120, 209, 212, 242, 254, 255

Heywood, Thomas, 293n1

Hic Mulier. Or, The Man-Woman, 75, 81

Highsmith, Patricia, 236

Histoire d'un voyage faict en la terre du Brésil (Léry), 47, 199, 200, 203, 211, 212, 217, 219, 220

historicism, 19, 27, 31, 258, 277n79, 283n35

historiography, 16, 20, 30–31, 205, 250

history, 17, 64, 74, 148, 234, 249, 256, 259

History of Sexuality, Part I (Foucault), 14

Hoang, Ngyuen Tan, 277n81

Hocquenghem, Guy, 158, 255

Holland, Sharon Patricia, 254

homonationalism, 45, 209

homophobia, 30–31, 45, 91, 130, 131, 148, 158, 168, 254, 255, 280n114; patriarchy and, 78–80; witch hunts and, 197

homosexuality, 29, 30, 46, 117, 130, 156, 236, 306n31, 306n35; paranoia and, 158

homosociality, 12, 66, 95, 100, 219, 232

Horkheimer, Max, 130

House Un-American Activities Committee, 46, 159

Ibn Sina (Avicenna), 291n58
identification, 33, 47, 150, 204, 208, 214, 219, 238, 242, 245, 256, 260; alterity and, 27, 205, 214, 238, 254; colonial, 205, 207, 209, 219; desire and, 26, 206; erotic, 222; foreclosed/impossible, 210–11, 254; rea-derly, 21, 48. *See also* alterity; difference
identity, 8, 74, 144, 201, 214, 255; erotic, 47, 80, 81; gender, 29, 52; markers, 11–12; queer, 7, 42, 305n26; sexual, 29, 30, 52, 100, 111, 140, 153, 172
Identity Evropa, 252
ideology, 5, 6, 33, 105, 141, 206
"Idol Kiwasa, The," 240
instrumentality, 12, 52–53, 77, 220, 261; erotic, 66, 70, 88, 89, 99, 100
interpretation, 12, 14, 16, 17, 48–49, 256, 264
intertextuality, 21, 22, 24, 25
inversion, 17, 28, 33, 35, 40, 246, 304n14
Inwardness and Theater (Maus), 282n22
Iser, Wolfgang, 21, 24
Island Princess, The (Fletcher), 203

Jackson, Earl, Jr., 306n35
Jagose, Annemarie, 277n81
James VI (James I), 45, 153, 162, 165, 168, 185, 192, 195–96, 241; court theatricals and, 137; witches and, 170–71
Jamestown, 244, 245, 246

Jauss, Hans, 25
Jew of Malta, The (Marlowe), 124
Jews, 130, 159, 300n58
Jonson, Ben, 1, 34, 42, 68, 101, 124, 125, 135, 140, 290n52; court masques of, 137
Joseph, Abigail, 280n1
Joy, Eileen, 274n23

Kemp, Sawyer K., 34, 72
kinship, 35, 81, 144, 231, 233, 242, 250, 305n26; queer, 109, 235
Klein, Melanie, 46, 157, 165, 259–60; demonology and, 160–61
Klein, Naomi, 257–58
Kristeva, Julia, 21, 154, 155, 296n19

Lane, Ralph, 250, 251
Laqueur, Thomas, 94
Late Lancashire Witches, The (Brome), 161
Latour, Bruno, 27, 30, 31, 81, 261, 277n80
Le Moyne, Jacques, 238
Leatherhead, Lantern, 121, 123, 127, 128, 134, 136, 137, 139, 142
Léry, Jean de, 48, 199–200, 204, 209, 212–20, 225, 238, 244, 251, 253, 254, 255, 261; Brazil and, 44, 47, 219; desire and, 222; dispossession and, 210; Tupinamba and, 211, 212, 220, 223
Letoy, 32, 33, 34, 35, 38
Lévi-Strauss, Claude, 212
Levine, Laura, 293n75, 295n14
Levy-Navarro, Elena, 290n51

past: artifacts of, 15, 16, 20, 261; future and, 15, 231, 241; queerness of, 28, 29, 30, 34. *See also* future; present

Paster, Gail Kern, 7

Pastor, Beatríz, 305n22

patriarchy, 39, 74, 78, 91, 148, 271n6

pedagogy, 37, 44, 264, 265

penis, 84, 85, 89, 94, 96, 114, 285n58

Percy, George, 253

Peregrine, 17–18, 20, 22, 25, 27, 33, 36, 38, 39, 40, 42, 47, 86–87, 256; desire and, 22–23, 26, 37, 48

performance, 6, 58, 77; collaborative, 155; command, 169, 170; gender, 58, 68, 70, 76, 91; theatrical, 24–25

persecution, 10, 46, 154, 157, 159, 173, 175, 185, 192, 207

Petrarch, 106, 288n10

phallus, 85, 184, 286n59

Philaster, 41, 51; Arethusa and, 54, 57, 59, 61, 62, 63, 65, 69, 71, 96, 97–98; Bellario and, 54, 55, 56, 61, 62, 63, 66–67, 68, 83, 95–96, 97–98

Philaster, or Love Lies a-Bleeding (Beaumont and Fletcher), 2, 41, 51, 52, 53, 84, 86, 93, 94, 145; ending of, 95, 96, 100, 188

Philips, Adam, 5

Picts, 48, 241, 242, 253, 254

Pilliwinckes, 151, 161, 169

pleasure, 33, 59, 89, 108, 208, 225–26, 229, 256, 262

politics, 33, 44, 49, 125, 137, 253, 258, 259, 261; queer, 20, 35, 185, 209

polymorphous perversity, 12, 13–14, 109, 110, 113, 115, 126, 135

Povinelli, Elizabeth, 208–9

power, 37, 75, 81, 149, 173, 185, 237; knowledge and, 227; violence and, 209

Powhatan empire, 245, 246, 247, 311n131

present, 16, 17, 22, 30, 73–74, 75. *See also* future; past

Prester John, 23

progress: heteronormative model of, 104; narratives of, 27–28, 32; reversal/refusal of, 210, 227

prostitution, 117, 118, 120, 136, 150

Protestantism, 48, 127, 213, 249

psychoanalytic theory, 12, 13, 15, 16

Puar, Jasbir, 45, 209

puppet-ghost flashing, 140, 141, 142, 144

Purchas, Samuel, 246, 303n7, 311n128

Purecraft, Dame, 121, 127, 129

Puritans, 17, 120, 128, 130, 131

queer, 3–5, 8, 13, 29, 35, 52, 60, 86, 93, 98, 100, 105, 116, 138, 145, 168, 178, 179, 182, 188, 213, 235, 253, 254, 255; aesthetics/style, 63, 216; category/expansion of, 2–3, 9–11, 41; political stakes of, 19, 45, 208–9; reading practice, 16, 20–21, 104, 154, 207, 226; structural/systemic/qualitative forms of, 9, 17, 26, 39, 105, 107, 117, 231; term, 2, 20, 44, 274n26, 279n102. *See also* camp

"Queer and Now" (Sedgwick), 226, 228

queer figures, 46–47, 92, 148, 175, 194

Queer Nation, 274n25

queer theory, 2, 9–10, 19, 27, 34, 36, 149, 158, 256; early modern literature and, 17, 21, 49, 205–6

Quinn, David Beers, 310n120

race, 44, 119, 204, 245, 247, 254

racism, 45, 245, 253. *See also* nationalism: white

Rackin, Phyllis, 282n23

Raleigh, Walter, 202, 237, 244, 251

reading, 16, 21, 23–24, 262, 276n67; early modern practices of, 22–23, 202–3; paranoid, 46, 258, 259, 260; reparative, 22, 259, 260, 262–63; theater and, 24–25

relations: affective, 74, 241, 259; colonial, 206–7; queer modes of, 20, 41, 52–53, 70, 86, 100, 201

Release the Stars (Wainwright), 289n46

religion, 5, 119, 127, 134, 169, 200–201, 204, 217, 220–23

Renaissance, 5, 15, 29, 94, 260, 264; white supremacist uses of, 252

Renaissance of Lesbianism in Early Modern England, The (Traub), 73

renunciation, 102–3, 208, 211, 254

reparative position, 22, 260, 263. *See also* depressive position; reading: reparative

representation, 24, 33, 260–61

reproduction, 106, 108, 109, 121, 165, 173, 234, 236, 259; of desire, 43, 104, 126; sexual, 105,
111–12, 118, 128, 145, 201, 224, 231

Ricoeur, Paul, 157, 159

Rifkin, Mark, 209, 250, 313n149

Roanoke, 44, 47, 201, 202, 208, 212, 223, 224, 234, 237, 238, 251, 253; fate of, 245, 246, 247, 249; homosociality of, 232; myth of, 248, 249, 250; story, 244, 245, 310n120, 312n138

Roaring Girl, The (Middleton and Dekker), 41, 51, 52, 53, 54, 58, 70–71, 73, 74, 86, 89, 91, 93, 94, 96, 99, 150, 174

Roaring Girle, or Moll-Cut-Purse, The (Middleton and Dekker), frontispiece of, 90 (fig.)

Roberts, Gareth, 155, 156, 163

Rohy, Valerie, 34

Romeo and Juliet (Shakespeare), 129

Roper, Lyndal, 155, 156

Rose, Nikolas, 233

Rousseau, Jean-Jacques, 113

Rowley, William, 45, 147, 171

"Rules and Regulations" (Wainwright), 289n46

Rylance, Mark, 114, 115

Sabbath, 45, 166, 168

sadism, 14, 165, 166, 177, 299n54. *See also* masochism

St. Bartholomew the Great, 119

St. Bartholomew's Day, 119, 217

Sampson, Agnis, 159, 160, 161, 165, 173, 185, 195, 294n9, 295n14, 298nn47–48, 298n50; confession of, 170; performance by, 176; torture of, 152–53

Samuell, Alice, 153

Sanchez, Melissa, 107, 277n79

Santesso, Aaron, 285n50

Sawyer, Elizabeth, 172, 180, 185, 189, 194; accusation against, 175, 190; domestic/sexual disasters and, 184; scapegoating, 190–91, 196; self-styling as witch by, 177, 178, 179; trial/execution of, 45, 147, 171, 191; woodcut of, 180 (fig.)

Scot, Reginald, 297n43

Scott, Michael, 249

Sea Voyage, The (Fletcher), 203

Seaton, David, 150–52, 157–58, 162–63, 172–73

Sebastian *(Roaring Girl)*, 70, 77, 91; Mary and, 80, 86, 88, 89, 92, 99; Moll and, 71, 82–83, 84, 85, 86, 88, 93, 99

Sebastian *(Twelfth Night)*, 104, 111–12, 113, 114

secrecy, 4, 183; sexual, 156, 170, 171, 172

Sedgwick, Eve Kosofsky, 21, 22, 33, 116, 174, 206, 226, 228, 229, 254, 255, 257, 258, 264; affect theory and, 5, 7; homophobia, analysis of, 45, 78, 79–80, 158, 280n114, 284n48; Klein and, 14–15, 46, 156, 157, 158, 159, 160, 259–60, 262, 263; queerness, definition of, 2, 10, 226; sexual identity and, 8, 11, 29, 79–80

sex, 8, 49, 100, 262, 264, 265; anatomical, 12, 57, 72, 76, 85, 94–95, 96; dyadic, 37, 38, 53–54, 59, 73, 83; group, 47, 86, 87, 88, 168, 226; heterosexual, 39, 40, 118, 236; procreative, 37, 40, 105; refusal of, 19–20,

40. *See also* acts; generation; reproduction

sexual, 10, 117; nonsexual and, 13

sexual difference, 11, 12, 13, 14, 36, 94, 100, 110, 132, 140, 141, 210

sexuality, 7, 19, 28, 176, 260, 262, 265; history of, 9, 29, 105, 116, 149

Shakespeare, William, 3, 13, 23, 28, 31, 42, 53, 58, 72, 101, 203, 232, 234, 241, 264; fancy and, 106; Globe productions of, 114; mythologized figure of, 30

Shannon, Laurie, 145

Shelley, Mary, 248

Shepherd, Simon, 285n50

Singal, Peter, 209

slavery, 136, 185, 209

Sleep No More (Punchdrunk), 34

Smith, Bruce R., 287n5

Smith, John, 245, 246, 253

Smithfield, 119, 131, 133

sodomy, 7–8, 94, 95, 296n30

Somerville, Siobhan, 254

Sontag, Susan, 63, 64

Spenser, Edmund, 204

Spinoza, Baruch, 6

Stockton, Will, 277n79

Strachey, James, 246, 253

subjectivity, 6, 14, 99; history of/scholarship on, 12; sexuality and, 279n108

submission, 62, 64–65, 107, 168, 212, 222–23, 301n71. *See also* dominance

supersession, 29, 104, 145

Susan, 181, 183–84, 187–89, 190, 301n65, 302n76

suspicion, 2, 47, 59, 65, 97, 117,

118, 138, 144, 150, 152, 155, 163, 171, 173, 174, 181, 182, 184, 185, 186, 188, 194, 197, 257, 258, 264, 297n41; paranoid, 4, 45, 46, 53, 156, 157, 158–59, 178; sexual, 10, 68, 82, 151, 172, 193, 197

TallBear, Kim, 312n135
technology, 224, 258; affective, communication, 54, 60, 70, 89; erotic, 70, 89, 91; gender, 70, 76, 89; knowledge, truth production, 152, 154, 188; scientific, 227–28; travel, 246–47
telos, 108, 145, 211, 213, 218; heterosexual, 110, 210
Tempest, The (Shakespeare), 234
temporality, 34, 234; indigenous, 310n114; nonlinear, 28, 218; queer, 27–28
Theatre of Envy, A (Girard), 103
Thevet, André, 217
Thorney, Frank, 172, 173, 181, 186, 187, 188, 192; bigamy of, 174–75, 182–83, 189, 190, 193, 196–97; execution of, 175, 190, 194, 196; witchcraft and, 195
Thousand Plateaus, A (Deleuze and Guattari), 6, 10
"three witches of Warboys, The," 153, 293n1, 295n12
time, 15, 28, 246; historical, 17, 201; of mourning, 210
Tomkins, Silvan, 7, 157
Tompson, Agnis, 162, 163, 165, 298n47
torture, 151–52, 155, 159, 160, 170, 194, 195, 196, 308n60
transformation, 143, 144, 178, 186,

261; gender, 93, 145; impossible, 48, 200, 214, 255; melancholic, 214–15, 219
transgression, 19–20, 99, 186; sexual, 116, 169, 189
transmasculinity, 73, 114, 279n107, 283n28
Trapdoor, 84–85, 89
Traub, Valerie, 8, 37, 39, 73, 74, 89, 94, 113, 262, 277n79, 285n58
Travels of Sir John Mandeville, The, 23, 224
triangulation, 42, 59, 60, 66
Troilus and Cressida (Shakespeare), 53
"True Pictures and Fashions of the People in That Part of America Now Called Virginia" (White), 200–201, 202, 212, 223, 236, 237, 238, 239, 240; illustration from, 239 (fig.), 240 (fig.), 243 (fig.)
Trump, Donald, 45, 156, 252, 259
"truue picture of one Picte I, The," 243 (fig.)
Tupinamba, 47, 199, 201, 208, 211, 212, 213, 215, 216, 218, 219, 220, 223, 225, 251; religious ceremony of, 221 (fig.)
Tuscarora, 245, 247, 250, 311n133
Twelfth Night (Shakespeare), 23, 42, 43, 54, 60, 94, 97, 98, 101, 102, 103, 104, 114, 116, 118, 124, 140, 142, 145; fancy in, 106–7, 109, 110, 113, 119, 126
"Two Loves" (Douglas), 307n46

Ursula, 132, 133, 139, 290n51, 292n68

190, 191, 195; production of, 147, 157, 176–78, 189; torture of, 151, 160, 169, 195, 297n47
witches' Sabbath, 162, 166, 167, 191, 194, 222, 299n55, 299n58
witchfinders, 152, 158, 159, 171
wonderfull discoverie of witches in the countie of Lancaster, The (Potts), 161
Wounderful discovery of the Witch-crafts of Margaret and Philippa Flower, The, 161

Yates, Julian, 274n23

CHRISTINE VARNADO is assistant professor of gender and sexuality studies at the University at Buffalo–State University of New York.

Made in the USA
Columbia, SC
24 February 2024

32232320R00185